AN ISLAMIC HERITAGE IN CHINA

MA ZHANMING

2018

NOTH AMERICAN BUSINESS PRESS

NORTH
AMERICAN BUSINESS
PRESS

Seattle, WA
Atlanta, GA
Toronto, Canada

About Modern China Series

China, as one of the oldest civilized regions in the world, has emerged as something of a "new world" because it is working to embrace its own essence and heritage and link them to viable economic strategies. In the last 25 years, China has made tremendous strides by doing so. The country and her people have every right to take pride in these accomplishments. With these successes under their belt, many Chinese leaders and intellectuals anticipate continuing growth. China's plans and strategies, furthermore, are often based upon this premise.

There is tremendous interest in the US on the Chinese economy and business environment. China has emerged as a global super power, and scholars and businessmen in the US are keenly interested in learning how this is going to continue to affect them and how they can do business with China. In response to growing interest from international and Asian scholars, North American Business Press is pleased to announce our Modern China Series (MCS) books, which is first of such series in the US and has garnered tremendous interest both in the US and around the world. With our first book reaching stores in September 2011, this initiative is aimed at developing relationships between NABP and Chinese scholars who desire to promote their academic and applied business writings to the rest of the world.

We have had overwhelming demand for the Modern China Series from both authors who would like to publish in the series and people who would like to read the books. Currently, there are ten books published in the series and, additionally, we have a couple of dozen books that we are considering for the series. The books have been viewed by tens of thousands of people from the U.S. and the rest of the world.

We have published books relating to several areas revolving around the Chinese business environment. We have a few that focus on the best practices in marketing in China; a couple relating to “best practices” in doing business in China; and a few on the outlook of the Chinese economy. The market for the Modern China Series is huge. There are tens of thousands of scholars that are keenly interested in the continued growth of the Chinese economy and the implications that will have on the business world. Even more significant are the millions of businessmen that are interested in the impact that China will continue to have on the global economy. It is difficult to pin down the exact demand for the series, but it is very large.

We have big plans for growing the Moderns China Series. This has the potential to one of the most significant economic/business series ever produced. We are very selective with the books that we will add to the collection, but we encourage any scholars who think they have unique and interesting perspectives on China to submit their books to us. From the readers’ perspective, we are committed to producing high quality books on a regular basis so that readers should expect a steady stream of insightful books to be coming out for many years to come.

This initiative is headed by Dr. Robert Tian, a renowned researcher and academic, who spearheads our efforts in partnering with foreign authors and administering day-to-day operations of this series. Dr. Tian, a Vice-President with North American Business Press and Editor of this series, spends much of his time in Beijing, Shanghai, and other Chinese cities, focusing on developing and managing our interests with authors and universities. Below is the list for the books we have published:

Enterprise Strategy: New Horizon authored by Zhang Xiuyu

Governance of Private Enterprises in Modern China authored by Zhong Qin

The Art of War and Enterprise Strategy Management by Fu Shouzhi

Marketing Issues in Modern China edited by Robert Guang Tian et al.

The Footprints of the Academician authored by Fu Zhouzhi

Marketing and Economics in Modern China (I) edited by Xiaoguang Qi et al.

Marketing and Economics in Modern China (II) edited by Wang Tianjin et al.

An Islamic Heritage in China authored by Ma Zhanming

Environmental Anthropology in Modern China authored by Wang Tianjin et al.

Can China Rule the New World? Authored by Tian Guang and Chen Gang

AN ISLAMIC HERITAGE IN CHINA

MA ZHANMING

2018

NOTH AMERICAN BUSINESS PRESS

TABLE OF CONTENTS

Preface

This study aims to introduce English readers to *Qingzhen Shiyi*, a book written by a Chinese Muslim scholar, Jin Tianzhu, during the time of the Qing Dynasty (1616-1909), in the year 1737. According to our present knowledge, this was the first book ever written by a Chinese Muslim scholar entirely composed in the Chinese language, for defending the rights of Muslims. The author clarifies the objectives and significance of the rules of *Shariah* which were practiced by Chinese Muslims in their daily life and compares them with other religions in China. Our study of the book consists of six chapters, namely, the introduction, historical background, Jin Tianzhu and his book, the translation of the edited texts, commentaries and comments on the main body of the texts and a conclusion followed by an appendix. The method adopted in this study is library research, editing the text, and translation. This is the first study of the book in the English language, through which, one will find that Muslims in China were practicing *Shariah* and keeping their own identities, which had caused doubts and suspicions from the wider society and put them in a very difficult condition. Mr. Jin, as a scholar, tried to remove these doubts and clarify the suspicions by showing the similarities between Islam and Confucianism, presenting the advantages of Islam over other main religions in some respects, and criticizing some of them, in a period of history when there was no free-speech and democracy in the modern sense. He or she also will be aware through this study that Religious or Civilizational Dialogue between Muslims and non-Muslims started in China as early as in the 18th century.

Foreword

China is a great state not only for its wide land and its large population, but also for its traditional culture, especially Confucianism. There have been many great thinkers in China such as Lao Zi, Kong Zi, Mo Zi and many others. When Muslims came to China for the first time in the early Tang Dynasty, they liked the land and the people and so preferred to stay and live there. Their posterities – like other ethnicities in China - made great contributions to varied areas of their country in different periods of its history. Today, there are more than 20 million Muslims in China living in harmony with other groups of people, and are together building their country now.

However, there are some differences between Muslims and mainstream society in terms of culture and religion and therefore, misunderstandings between Muslims and non-Muslims cannot be avoided. This is what happened in China in the eighteenth century. To eliminate the misunderstandings of other ethnic groups, Muslim scholars at the end of the Ming Dynasty and the beginning of the Qing Dynasty made great contributions in writing and dialogue including Jin Tian Zhu.

Very few academics know about Jin Tian Zhu because his work hasn't been introduced to the academia of the world. I met him for the first time through Dr. Ma Zhan Ming when I was teaching at the International Islamic Institute (ISTAC), a post graduate school of the International Islamic University (IIUM), and the school appointed me as supervisor to several PhD students, one of which was Ma Zhan Ming who had chosen Jin Tian Zhu's work "*Qingzhen Shiyi*" as the topic for his doctoral thesis.

When he used to attend my courses as a doctoral student, and during the 3 years I supervised his PhD thesis, I knew Dr. Ma Zhan Ming as a diligent and intelligent student. He is also a morally upright person who is friendly and mixes easily with fellow students and Professors. He is determined to succeed in life and I am sure with such a determination and many positive personal qualities he will be able to achieve his ambition. Ma

Zhan Ming finished his thesis on time and to a high quality that was publishable. Three years after graduating, when he sent me a copy of the thesis and asked me to write a preface for publishing, I did not hesitate to fulfil his request, not only because he was a good student as I mentioned above, but also because the thesis is valuable enough to publish in terms of quality and can be considered a very good contribution to academia not only in China, but the world. According to my knowledge, this is the first English translation of Jin Tian Zhu's *Qingzhen Shiyi* and the first study on it. I believe that Dr. Ma Zhan Ming is an asset to his community as well as his country; I wish him all the best.

Dr. Osman Bakar
Emeritus Professor Datuk
Director of Sultan Omar Ali Salahuddien Centre for Islamic Studies
University of Brunei Darussalam

March 30, 2018

Acknowlegements

My thanks go firstly to the International Islamic University Malaysia for providing Muslim youth with a good environment for both life and study, and to the International Institute of Islamic Thought and Civilization (ISTAC), particularly the dean and deputy dean for their kind guidance. I also thank the Professors for educating me, and I am grateful to all the staff for their very kind services. In addition, I would like to express my gratitude to Mr. Hai Zhengzhong who provided me with the book-manuscript; Ms. Xue Lian and her colleagues in Dalian library, China, for their serious co-operation; the staff in the department of ancient books in Beijing University library; Professor Mi Shoujiang and his student Li Rui for their kind help, and Professor Sun Zhenyu for his valuable suggestions. I am also very grateful to Sister Soraya Khairu Al-Din who made a great contribution to the modification of the English language of this study. I do not forget to thank my wife Ma Xiao Ling for her patience in caring for my children, and my daughter Ma Fei Ya for her help whenever I needed references from my house. My special thanks go to my supervisor Emeritus Professor Datuk Dr. Osman Bakar, who not only gave me remarkable guidance during my writing from the beginning to the end, but also gave me generous material support without which my work might be lacking something important. I would also like to express my gratitude to Professor Dr. Mohammed Ajmal Abdul Razak Al-Aidrus, who suggested the topic, gave me the necessary advice as well as some valuable references during my study, read my dissertation and corrected the errors contained in my first manuscript.

This book is a partial outcome from the project entitled "Generalized Argumentation Theory Research" sponsored by the

Key Research Project Base, the Humanities and Social Science Foundation, Ministry of Education, PRC (No.16JJD720017).

PART ONE:
INTRODUCTION

CHAPTER ONE:

HISTORICAL BACKGROUND

1.1 When Did Muslims Come to China?

According to historical records, contact between China and Arabia started a long time ago. In 97 C.E., a man named Ganying (甘英), was sent to the Western (i.e. Roman) Empire, and although he failed to arrive in Egypt, he returned to China with some information about Arabia. After that, the Han Dynasty (25-220 C.E.) sent envoys every year to states in central and western Asia, and relations were maintained between China and Arabia both directly and indirectly. In addition, there were also frequent contacts between China and Persia.[1] Both the land Silk Road and the Maritime Road had been in use long before the Tang Dynasty (618-907). [2]

Establishment of the Sui Dynasty (581-618) united China and brought an end to a period of internal struggle that had lasted around 300 years. However, a sudden change in society pushed the Sui from the stage of history to be replaced by the Tang dynasty. As its successor, the Tang Dynasty drew a lesson from the causes that had led to the precipitous downfall of the Sui. Therefore, it tried to make peace in society and established policies that promoted its own stability and longevity. Tang

---

[1] For more details, see Qiu Shuseng, *History of Hui Race in China*, (Yinchuan: Ningxia publishing house. 1996), vol. 1, 3; Yu Zhengui, *Chinese Past Dyncsties and Islam*, (Ningxia publishing house, 1996), 13.

[2] Most of scholars named both the Sea road and the Land road as the Silk Road. However, scholars used the term Perfume Road to refer to the Sea Road. I prefer to use this term because the perfume was the most important good that Muslims brought by the sea, which was welcomed very much by royal families, especially in the time of the Song era. See Li Xinghua, *History of Islam in China*, (China social sciences publishing house, 1998), 63.

Taizong (627-650) abolished oppressive policies which had been adopted by Sui Yangdi (605-617) and decreased taxes. As a result, production quickly returned to normal and productive forces were rapidly enhanced. The improvement of the agriculture and handcraft industries stimulated commerce. Increased wealth in society and increased consumption led to an expansion of trade, which gave rise to urban trading centers. At the same time, the Tang Dynasty opened its doors to foreigners to solicit business, promote the circulation of goods and stimulate markets.[1]On the social front, the Tang Dynasty adopted a policy which allowed minorities to practice their own customs and follow their own modes of production, as well as their own social systems and religious beliefs. This policy not only harmonized the relation between ethnic groups in the Chinese heartland, but also stabilized with the border areas. Along with the development of the economy, envoys, businessmen and students came from abroad to Changan (today's Xian) and other cities to dwell and live. They were accorded a courteous reception. By adopting such a policy, the Tang gained a high reputation in the world. As a result, music, dance, arts, medicine and calendars came from central and south Asia and spread in China, where some cities became centers of foreign cultures. The traditional culture of China was enriched and further matured. Taoism developed more than at any other time, Buddhism reached its golden age,[2] and some religions abroad were introduced to China as well. These were the historical conditions and the social environment when Islam came to China.

A history book written in biographical style, entitled Jiu Tangshu, Xuanzong Benji (旧唐书·玄宗本纪),[3] had this to say about the events of

---

[1] Yu Zhengui, *Chinese Past Dynasties and Islam*, 10-12.

[2] Although it was repelled by some people in the time of the Tang, Buddhism was supported by most of the emperors and people, and as a result, it developed and expanded significantly. One of the best examples is that many of its books were translated into the Chinese language now.

[3] It is a book of history of the Tang era which was officially compiled in the time of Houjing (936-947). Xuanzong (玄宗) is the title of one of the emperors

the second year of Yonghui (永徽, 651): "In the eighth month, the Arab country first sent its envoy for the purpose of having an audience with our emperor and paying tributes to the dynasty."[1]

Based on this report, most non-Muslim scholars believe that this year was the beginning of the first Muslims' coming to China. However, most Muslim scholars disagree. They think that Islam came to China earlier than that. Some of them argue that it was in the interregnum between the Sui and Tang dynasties (610-622); others believe it was in the fourth year of Tang Wude (武德),[2] in the year of 622; while some say it occurred in the time of Tang Zhenguan (唐贞观)[3] in general, and in the year of 628 particular.

Although we cannot deny the relevance of the mention of the Arab envoy on this issue, an official contact between China and Arabia is not necessarily proof that it was the first time that a Muslim came to the country. It was well known that Muslims in the early history of China did not come for the express purpose of spreading Islam among Chinese people, so when we talk about the first appearance of Islam in China, we mean by this time Muslims started to come and conduct certain activities, including religious practices. In this sense, we can say that it is possible that some Muslims came to China before the emigration of Prophet Muhammad to Madinah in 622 CE. It is possible because, as is well known, some Muslims in Mecca were forced to emigrate to a Christian country, Habashah (Ethiopia) to secure their lives and faith. As we noticed above, the contact between China and the Arabs started and continued from the time of the Han Dynasty. This means that the Arabs noticed the existence and importance of China before

---

of the Tang dynasty. His name is Li Longji (李隆基) and he was on the throne during the years 712-742.

[1] Fu Tongxian, *History of Islam in China*, (Yinchuan: Ningxia Publishing House, 2000).14.

[2] It is the title of Gaozu (高祖)'s reign whose name is Li Yuan (李渊), the founder of the dynasty (610-627).

[3] It is the title of Tai Zong (太宗)'s reign whose name is Li Shimin (李世民), son of Gaozu and the second emperor of Tang dynasty which was on throne during the years 627-650.

and after Islam began to spread. Therefore, it is reasonable, if we say that some Muslims came to China when the religious persecution was very severe, that they came to China by themselves, not for spreading Islam,[1] but to seek asylum. If this is accepted, it can be argued that Islam came to China between 618-626.[2] As to what some Muslim scholars say that the Prophet sent some of his companions for dawah, we disagree with them, because it is well known that the Prophet sent envoys to certain countries, but there is no narration that the envoys were sent to China.

1.2 How Did Muslims Come to China?

With regards to the way Islam came to China, Mr. Yang Huaizhong, a famous contemporary Muslim scholar in the field of Hui studies, stated, as quoted by Yu Zhengui, a Hui scholar as well: "Christianity came to China with the invasion. Buddhism came by Indian white elephants, while Islam

---

[1] Some scholars said that it is impossible for Muslims to come to China before the Holy Quran was collected and united, because, in their view, Muslims came to China for the purpose of making *da'wah* and therefore, they must have brought the whole Quran. However, we do not agree them because the Prophet Muhammad said: "Convey from me, even it is one verse." Therefore, it would not have been necessary for them to bring the whole Quran even if they came for the said purpose.

[2] Our statement is based on the following: the number of the Sahabah who immigrated to Habashah was 101, (male and female). Then, 77 of them went to Madinah at various times, and it was said that 4 of them died in Habashah. However, historians have said nothing about where the remaining 20 of them went. According to Dr. Sayyid FaÏimy, as Dr. Saizar AdÊb MajËl, five of them went to India; one of them was buried under the wall of Istanbul. There are some resources say that 4 Sahabah came to China between 618 and 626. Therefore most Chinese Muslims and some non-Muslim scholars believe that Islam reached China between the Sui and the Tang. See Dr. Saizar Adib Majeed, The role of Arabic Chinese Trade in the entry of Islam in Southeast Asia, *Journal of Arab Asian Trade*, (Taiwan: Arab Asian Trade, Issue No. 237-Sep. 1999), 122.

came by the trade ships of the Arabs."[1] , Muslims came to China by two paths: by sea and by land.[2] They came by sea mainly for trade. They started from the Persian Gulf, passed through the Indian Ocean, moved around the Malay Peninsula, and reached Canton, today Guangzhou, the main trade center of that time, a place where many merchants gathered and markets flourished. This situation lasted until the time of Tang Xuanzong (唐玄宗)[3] who forbade trade contacts. After the Turks (突厥)[4] was defeated by the Tang Dynasty, the land road opened, and merchants could come to China freely. They set out from the east coast of the Mediterranean Sea, crossed Persia, passed Central Asia, and south of Tianshan reached Chang An. "There were more than 4000 foreign families doing business inside and outside of the city; the Persian and Arabs were the richest of them. The Tang government founded a department to manage foreign trade affairs and impose customs duties."[5] In addition to political and economic associations, there had been military contact between the Tang and the Arabs. The former asked the latter to send a military force to put down a rebellion launched by An Lushan (安禄山) and Shi Siming (史思明) in 755 and suppressed it in 762. When they accomplished their mission, some solders chose to stay in China; they became one of the earliest of the Chinese Muslim community.

During the Song Dynasty (960-1279), the land road was completely blocked as it was forbidden by Xuanzong (玄宗); however, trade by sea continued and therefore, Arab and Persian men steadily came to China. The trade management system developed and became more refined and effective. The custom duty was very large, and it became the main economic mainstay

---

[1] Yu Zhengui, *Chinese Past Dynasties and Islam*, 9.

[2] See Baishou, *Brief History of Islam in China*, (Ningxia publishing house, 2000), 4-6.

[3] It is the title of Li Longji (李隆基), one of the emperors of Tang, who was on throne during the years 721-756.

[4] Fu Tongxian, *History of Islam in China*, 15. Tujue (突厥) is one of the races in Central Asia, and the origin of Uighur Muslims in Xinjiang, China.

[5] See Fu Tongxian, *History of Islam in China*, 15.

of the Song Dynasty.[1] Most Muslims in this period were guests of China, not citizens, which is why they were called "Fanke" (蕃客)[2]. There were some other sources for Muslims in China in this period, one of which was Muslim immigration from the Muslim countries of Nanyang (which refers to Malaysia, Indonesia, Singapore and Brunei) to China in groups. Most of them settled in Hainan (海南) province. The second source was the first Muslim generation, who married Chinese women. These women followed their husband's religion. The next generation was called "Tusheng Fanke" (土生蕃客).[3] The third source of Chinese Muslims was people who had lost their lands. Some of them were forced to go and seek refuge with rich people. Because Muslims were rich, many Muslim families looked after some of these poor people, who were non-Muslims, in their own homes. As a result, some of them converted to Islam.

In brief, the number of Muslims had increased by the time of the Song, and they were widely dispersed. There were many Muslims in the central plains of China, especially Kaifeng (开封) in Henan (河南) province, as well as the cities of the southeast, like Guangzhou (广州), Quanzhou (泉州), Hangzhou (杭州), Yangzhou (扬州) and Hainan (海南). Islam was a foreign religion at the time of the Tang, but it had already become localized by the Song era.

When the Mongols conquered the Muslim world, they brought back many Muslims from Arab lands, Persia and Central Asia. Among them were religious scholars, craftsmen, and skilled workers. Later, a member of the royal family converted to Islam, and his officers and soldiers followed him and became Muslims. This was another source of Chinese Muslims.

1.3 Position of Muslims in the Yuan era

The situation of Muslims in this period differed from the era of both the Tang and the Song. First, they were no longer foreigners; they had become citizens of China. Second, they were distributed all over China, yet within

---

1 See Fu Tongxian, *History of Islam in China*, 20.

2 It means foreign guest.

3 It means locally born guest.

that general distribution pattern, a closer look reveals that they tended to cluster in small groups; dwelling mainly in the cities of the southeast, but also in the countryside of the northwest and southwest. Third, their social position was high compared to the other races (except the Mongols.) The Yuan Dynasty divided its citizens into three classes: Mongol (蒙古), Semu (色目) and Han (汉). Mongols were the first class because the rulers were from among them. Semu were mainly Muslims who originated from central and western Asia. One of the important reasons why Muslims were the second class was because they played a significant role and made great contributions to the Mongol's unification of China. Twelve of the sixteen ministers in the first Yuan administration were Muslims. Since the start of the imperial examinations in the beginning of Yanyou (严祐, 1314-1321), at least ten Semu men passed the examination and become Jinshi (进士).[1] Because of this, many qualified Muslims appeared, and they made significant contributions in the policy, economy, military and culture of the dynasty.

Because of the considerable number of Muslims and their prominent position, Islam became one of the major religions in China in the Yuan era. Moreover, Islamic law had some influence on the law of the dynasty. In order to administer Muslim societies, the central government set up the department of Qadi (卡迪司), who was in charge of implementing Islamic law and reciting du‘a for the dynasty. Based on all of this, we have enough reason to say that the period of the Yuan was the golden age for Islam and Muslims in China.

1.4 Situation of Muslims in the time of the Ming

It is reported in historical books that Zhu Yuanzhang (朱元璋, 1368-1399), the founder of the Ming Dynasty, was well acquainted with Islam. He wrote a hundred Chinese characters in praise of the Prophet Muhammad (peace be upon him):

---

[1] It refers to the one who passed the palace examination which is the final stage in any sequence of civil service recruitment examinations.

乾坤初始 天籍注明 传教大圣 降生西域 授受天经 三十部册 善化众生 万圣领袖 协助天运 保庇国王 五时祈佑 默祝太平 存心真主 加惠穷民 拯救患难 洞澈幽冥 超拔灵魂 脱离罪业 仁覆天下 道贯古今 降邪归一 教名清真 穆罕谟德 至贵圣人。[1]

Meaning:

At the beginning of heaven and earth, it was stated in the divine book that a messenger of God would be sent in the western area. He would be taught a divine book in 30 volumes, based on which, he would call people to charitable deeds. The messenger is the leader of all messengers; he helps our state, saves our king and prays five times a day to beg God to give us peace. He always remembers God in his mind and asks Him on behalf of poor people to give them favors and deliver them from trials and tribulations. He knows unseen things, releases souls from purgatory and expiates the sins of the dead. His kindheartedness illuminates the entire world. His doctrine linked the ancient with the present, superseded all deviated religions and unified them into one. The name of his religion is Qingzhen. Muhammad is the noblest messenger.

After one hundred years, his grandson Wuzong (武宗, 1506-1522) did a similar composition. He wrote a poem:

一教玄玄诸教迷，其中奥妙少人知。佛是人修人是佛，
不尊真主却尊谁？[2]

Meaning:

[1] Fu Tongxian, *History of Islam in China*, 60.

[2] Fu Tongxian, *History of Islam in China*, 62.

> All religions are wrong except one. Unfortunately, very few people know its profundity. Manmade Buddha, who was a man. Nothing is worthy of worship but Allah.

However, such sentiments were considered nothing but the individual opinions of some royal members, and their attitude had no positive impact on Islam in China.[1] The reason for this is that Zhu Yuanzhang (朱元璋) overturned the Mongol dynasty and established a Han state power in the name of a racial revolution. Although the Ming Dynasty was tolerant to Muslims, respected their faith, and even built some mosques for them, its policy toward Islam was not helpful in increasing the number of Muslims and developing Islam. This can be seen in the following:

First, it adopted a policy of national assimilation which forbade Muslims from marrying amongst themselves; they were forced to marry other races.[2]

Second, in the Chinese heartland Muslims were forbidden to speak their own language, wear their own dress, and use their own names.

Third, the mosques were controlled by the government, and the power of the imams was severely limited.

---

[1] It is well known that officials of ancient Chinese governments began to kneel on the ground in front of the emperor starting from the time of Yuan era. When it was the time of Ming, Zhu Yuanzhang initiated the courtesy of kowtow which is just like *sujud* in Islamic prayer, which is the main reason that Muslims said, "When a Muslim reached to the second rank in terms of official position, he will rebel against his religion."

[2] One could say that to marry non-Muslims would increase the number of Muslims and therefore, it would be good for Islam to be spread in Chinese society. This, in my view, might be true if Muslims were the majority in the society so that they could affect non-Muslims in terms of faith and way of life. But the fact is that they were a minority and furthermore, they were demanded to give up their own language and their Muslim names and forbidden to wear their own dress. If this was the case, how could they affect non-Muslims?

Fourth, motivated by Han chauvinism, Zhu Yuanzhang (朱元璋) took reprisals against the descendants of those Muslims who had helped the Mongols to overturn the Han-ruled Song Dynasty.[1]

Based on that, we believe that the rulers of the Ming Dynasty showed tolerance toward Muslims, not because they were concerned with Islam and its development, but because they were trying to win the support of the Muslims, who had played a significant role in establishing the dynasty and made great contributions afterwards. Those Muslims who were appointed to the government knew that very well and therefore they were reluctant to manifest their Muslim identities,[2] and so did not make any great contribution to the spread of Islam in China.

1.5 Contributions of Muslim Scholars

1.5.1 Islamic Education in China

Because of the national policy of the Ming Dynasty, a lot of Muslims lost their own languages and identities, started to speak Chinese and wear Chinese clothes. Some of them even lost their faith, and most of them stopped practicing Islamic teachings. This situation led to an effort to develop Islamic education, the pioneer of that endeavor being Hu Dengzhou (胡登洲).[3]

---

[1] For more information, see Ma Mingda, *Zhu Yuanzhang's Discriminate Against Seme*, published in Journal of *Hui Studies*, (Yinchuan: Editorial department of HZYJ, 2006, no.1), 98.

[2] A good example of that is that Zhenghe (郑和), a Muslim and by whom, according to some scholars, Islam was brought to Southeast Asia. This fact was known by Chinese scholars in the late 20th century, whilst most of society still doesn't know this today. The reason for this is either that he didn't do anything significant for Islam and Muslims in China or that he couldn't do because of the political situation at the time.

[3] Muslim education started at the time of the Song era (860-1279), and Islamic education at the end of the Yuan (1346). Bai Shouyi quoted from Sir Henry Yule's *Cathay and the Way Thither* the following: "Ibn Battuta said that an

Hu Dengzhou (胡登洲) was from Xianyang (咸阳), Shanxi (陕西) province. He was born in 1522 and died in 1597. He was a very learned man, so much so that people called him Hu Taishi (胡太师), meaning: "the most senior teacher". Mr. Hu went to Mecca for Hajj. He was affected by what he saw of the Islamic environment and how much better the situation of Muslims was compared to that of China. After he came back, he started to recruit students, teaching them in his house. Later, one of his students changed the venue to the mosque. From here the foundation of Islamic education, namely Jingtangjiaoyu (经堂教育), was established. Its influence spread to many places in China where Muslims inhabited. They followed the example of Shanxi and initiated education in the mosques. By the end of the Ming and beginning of the Qing, the education program had become popular, not only in all the mosques in Shanxi, but also in Shandong (山东), Jiangzhe (江浙), Huguang (湖广), Yunnan (云南) and Guangxi (广西). The aim of Jingtangjiaoyu (经堂教育) was to prepare and train qualified men, expand Islamic culture, and ensure Islam's transmission from one generation to the next. The courses of Jingtangjiaoyu (经堂教育) included: Morphology (الصرف), Grammar (النحو), Rhetoric (البلاغة), Theology (علم الكلام), Jurisprudence (الفقه) and Sufism. Jingtangjiaoyu (经堂教育) eventually split into two schools: the Shanxi school and the Shandong school. The differences between them focused on the teaching methodology as well as the courses offered. Indeed, Jingtangjiaoyu (经堂教育), which was founded by Mr. Hu Dengzhou, trained many ulama', ensured Islam's persistence amongst the Muslims, and established a foundation for academic activities and Islamic institutions in its modern form.

Egyptian man namely Ath-man bin Anffan built a magnificent school. He supports the students." This means that Islamic education started before Hu Dengzhou. However, it is well known in China that he was the founder of the system of Islamic education. See Li Xinghua, Qin Huibin, Feng Jinyuan and Sha Qiuzhen, *History of Islam in China*, (China Social Academy Publishing House, 1998), 84; Bai Shouyi, *Collection of Essays on Nationalities and Religions*, (Ningxia Publishing House, 2001), 435.

Although Jingtangjiaoyu (经堂教育) made a very important contribution for Islam, it had obvious limitations. First, the study in mosques was full-time, so only very few people had the opportunity to learn. Most people had to learn Islam through reading books. Unfortunately, almost all available books were either in Arabic or in Persian, which people in general could not understand. Second, to continue in China, Islam had to be recognized by both the ruling class and the mainstream culture, which was Confucian. This required Muslims to communicate with them by either translating Islamic books into Chinese or writing books in the Chinese language directly to introduce Islam. As it was obvious that education in the mosque Jingtangjioayu (经堂教育) was unable to meet such demands in its contemporary conditions, there was no choice but to open another way to meet that need, and as a result, academic ulama appeared.

1.5.2 Academic Activities of Chinese Ulama

Translation of Arabic and Persian books into Chinese took place at the end of the Ming Dynasty. Its most prominent practitioners included Wang Daiyu (王岱舆), Ma Wenbin (马文柄), Liu Jielian (刘介廉) and Ma Dexin (马德新), who was the last of them. Wang Daiyu's ancestors had come from western Asia and settled in Nanjing. He was greatly respected by Zhu Yuanzhang (朱元璋), who appointed him to a position in the directorate of astronomy. Wang Daiyu was born about 1585 and received an Islamic education in his childhood. He learned Arabic and Persian and became well versed in the sciences of Islam, law and Sufism. When he came of age, Mr. Wang began to study the books of Confucianism, Taoism and Buddhism, as well as the varied schools of thoughts and their exponents from the pre-Qin (221-206 B.C.) period to the early years of the Han Dynasty (206 B.C. – 220 C.E.). Mr. Wang became a great scholar proficient not only in Islam but also in Confucianism, Taoism and Buddhism. He was well known for his many discussions and debates with non-Muslim religious men. Daiyu acquired the moniker of Zhenhuilaoren (真回老人), meaning: "the real Muslim old man". Mr. Wang left three important academic works, namely: Zhengjiaozhenquan (正教真诠), meaning: The Real Commentaries on The Real Doctrine, Qingzhendaxue (清真大学), meaning: The Islamic Great Learning,

Xizhenzhengda (希真正答), meaning: The True Answers. The first book is comprised of two volumes, each of which consist of twenty chapters. In the first volume, Mr. Wang mainly discusses the oneness of God and the religious philosophy of how to illuminate the mind and purify the heart. The second volume of the book is about Islamic regulations and rules and the customs of Muslims. The second book, Qingzhendaxue (清真大学), is an Islamic treatise of philosophical theory. It is formed of three parts: the first part is like a summary of the whole book, in which the author introduces the main contents of the book and its importance. The second part is about the oneness of God. The author uses three terms, namely Zhenyi (真一, The Real One), Shuyi (数一, The Numerical One) and Tiyi (体一,The Embodied One), to express the oneness and unity of God in Islam. The third part is a general discussion of the three "Ones". In addition to that, creation, life, death and other matters are also discussed in this part. Daiyu's Xizhen Zhengda (希真正答) is a collection of his discussions and debates with various people, as recorded by his students and compiled by one of them, Wu Liancheng (伍连城), who completed the work in 1659.

The second exemplar of translation and writing in the Chinese language was Mazhu (马注). His second name is Wenbing (马文炳) and his Arabic name is Yusuf. He was born in Baoshan, Yunnan (云南宝山) and lived from 1640 to 1711. It is said that he was a fifteenth-generation descendant of Sayed al-Ajall Shams al-Din,[1] who was appointed by a Yuan emperor as prince of Xianyang (咸阳王). Mazhu lost his father when he was very young. Although his family was very poor, he had an opportunity to go to school and became a Xiucai (秀), meaning: "skillful writer", when he was 16 years old. Two years later he got a position in "small" administration of Yongle (永乐 1403-1425).[2] His job was to write important documents. He then gave up the position and started to study Islamic books. After thirty

---

[1] He claimed that he was the 45th generation of offspring of the Prophet Muhammad (peace be upon him). See Li Xinghua, *History of Islam in China*, 567.

[2] His administration was called 'small government' because it was not recognized yet at the time by most areas of China.

years spent in study, Mazhu completed a book entitled Qingzhenzhinan (清真指南), meaning: The Guide to Islam. At that time, he was 44 years old. This book is his representative work and the distillation of his thirty years of study. It is comprised of ten volumes of one hundred thousand words. It contains an autobiography, a preface, a discussion of how to know God, predestination (القضاء والقدر), angels, the five pillars, Isra' and Mi'raj (الإسراء والمعراج), repentance (التوبة) and other topics. Mazhu tried to present his book to Kangxi (康熙), the emperor of the dynasty, but failed to do so. He was considered by the Muslims in Yunnan (云南) as the first Muslim scholar and the first person who translated an Islamic book into Chinese.

He was followed by Liuzhi (刘智), who was born in 1660 and died in 1730. His second name is Jielian (刘介廉). Mr. Liu was from Nanjing (南京). He was another exemplary scholar who translated and wrote in Chinese, and was the most comprehensive of them. Mr. Liu began studying the books of Islam, Buddhism and Taoism from a youthful age. He then travelled to many places in search of knowledge. Mr. Liu started to translate and write when he came back to Jinling (金陵).[1] In his later years. Liuzhi wrote dozens of works, including Tianfangxingli (天方性理) Islamic Theology, Tianfangdianli (天方典礼), Islamic Rules and Regulations, and Tianfangzhishengshilu (天方至圣实录), The Life of the Prophet. Liu Zhi's first book is a philosophical one. It consists of two parts: text and patterns. The text has five chapters, the first and the second of which are about the order of the universe and the functions and changes of the heavens. Chapters Three and Four discuss the microcosm of the human body. Chapter Five is about the consistency between the macrocosm and the microcosm. The included patterns were designed to help readers to understand the text. They are 60 patterns with 60 illustrations.

The second work consists of 20 sub-books. Books 1-4 are about theology, which includes the creation of the universe, the way to know God, some words of witness (al-kalimah al-tayyibah and kalimat al- shahidah), formulas in praise of God, a discussion of traditional Chinese religions, and criticisms of Taoism and Buddhism. Books 5-9 are about the five pillars of

[1] It is the title of the old name of Nanjing city.

Islam: shahadah, prayer, fasting, zakat, and hajj. In association with Hajj he discusses qurban (animal sacrifice). The author explains each of the pillars and the rules associated with them (fiqh al-ibadat). Books 10-20 are about relations between people (fiqh al- muamalat) and the way of Muslim life.[1]

The third work, as the title indicates, is about the life of Prophet Muhammad (peace be upon him). These three books of Liuzhi are his representative works, for which he gained great fame among scholars as well as the Muslim community. In addition to that, his Wugongshiyi (五功释义), Tianfanglijing (天方礼经) and Tianfangsanzijing (天方三字经) are also quite well known in the Muslim community in China. With these works Liuzhi built the system of Islamic thought in China. He also made a very important contribution to traditional Chinese philosophy.

Beside the abovementioned, there were other Muslim scholars who made remarkable contributions to Muslim scholarship in China. They include: Zhangzhong (张中, 1584-1670), Wu Zunqi (伍遵契, 1598-1698), Ma Boliang (马伯良), Mi Wanji (米万济) and others. When Liuzhi completed his Tianfangzhishengshilu (天方至圣实录), the movement of translation and writing started to slow down. However, there were still some scholars writing, one of whom was Jin Tianzhu (金天柱), the subject of this study.

No foreign culture would be recognized and accepted by the main culture of a land unless the former frames its discourse in terms familiar to the latter. Islamic culture must do the same. To let the main, i.e. Confucian, culture recognize Islamic culture, Chinese Muslim scholars chose a special road. First, they tried to find similarities between the two cultures and showed them to readers as much as they could. Second, they used Confucian terms to express Islamic concepts so that people could understand them easily. Third, they put the Confucian culture in a central position, willingly or unwillingly. Fourth, they demonstrated the correctness of Islam, and

---

[1] These mentioned books were included in *Siku Quanshu* (四库全书) which is the encyclopedia compiled in the mid-term of the time of Qianlong (1736-1796) but they were regarded as important by the government. See Li Xinghua, *History of Islam in China*, 579.

therefore the reasonableness of its co-existence and the necessity of its development in China. All these features can be found in all the previously-mentioned works of the Muslim scholars introduced above.

1.6 Cultural Differences between Muslims and non-Muslims

The traditional culture of China in its initial period had three branches, namely: Confucianism (儒家), Legalism (法家) and Mohism (墨家).[1] The second was subsumed in the first and became a part of it, and the last one eventually disappeared.[2] The main religion in China is Taoism. When it came to China, Buddhism was recognized and accepted by the Chinese people, after some initial conflict and after its incorporation of Confucian and Taoist elements. The mixing and conflicts between different religions and cultures caused the emergence of new religions and qualitative changes in the traditional culture. To a certain extent, we can say that Chanzong (禅宗), one of the branches of Buddhism in China, was the result of those conflicts and fusion with Confucianism and Taoism. It became a secular religion after it gave up some important Buddhist teachings. At the same time, Song-Ming Li Xue (宋明理学), the Confucian school of idealist philosophy of the Song and Ming dynasties, is a crystallization of those conflicts and blends with Taoism and Buddhism.

It cast away the concept of God, which had been a part of the pre-Confucian doctrine, and became atheist. Most Chinese people during the Ming and Qing dynasties were Confucian in terms of philosophy; however, they practiced doctrines of Buddhism and Taoism in their daily lives. It would have been difficult to find people who believed exclusively in Confucianism, or only in Buddhism, or only Taoism. In terms of food and drink, there was no limitation for them except for the vegetarians among

---

[1] See, Xia Zhaoyan, *General Study of Chinese Cultures*, (Haikou: The Southern publishing house, 1999), 97-104; Mou Zhongjian, and Zhang Jian, *Comprehensive History of Religions in China*, (Beijing: Social Academy Publishing House, 2000), 185-189.

[2] Mohism stands for peace and love, therefore, today, there are scholars trying to promote its doctrine because it is good for building a *Harmonised Society*.

them. Even today, they eat whatever they like, if it can be eaten. They hang up couplets (written on scrolls) when it is Chinese New Year. If someone dies, they place the body in a coffin to bury it. They do so to prevent the body from being touched by the earth. To save the body of the deceased, they put gold and silver or other valuables in the grave.

On the anniversary of the death, they burn paper money and provide food for the dead. They do not wear white clothes unless someone has died. In their view, all hairs on the human body are a bestowal from the parents and therefore, should not be cut. In terms of faith, they believe in Buddhism and worship idols for seeking good fortune. They also believe that Taoist priests can help them and answer their prayers. They ask some of them who claim to be masters of Feng Shui (风水) to find the right location for them to build their houses.[1]

The Qing Dynasty was established by the Manchus, one of the minor nationalities in China. Based on the exigencies of rule, the Qing Dynasty developed a specific policy for Muslims, which was "to regulate their political life without changing their customs". Religious life was considered a part of custom. The effect of this policy was that it gave Islam a good opportunity to develop, and Muslims could practice their own customs if they followed the rules of the dynasty and obeyed its system and law.[2] Therefore, Jingtangjiaoyu (经堂教育) took a prominent role. As a result, Muslims who had lost their identities and had been seriously diverted started to return to Islam and regain their own identities. Although they used Chinese language in their daily lives, many of them could read the Qur'an, and some of them could write in Arabic or Persian. They did not drink alcohol or eat the meat of pigs, dogs, mules or donkeys, nor the meat of domestic animals slaughtered by non-Muslims.

---

[1] See Zhan Qizhi, *Traditional Chinese culture*, (Beijing: Higher Education Publishing House, 2005), 261-265.

[2] For more information about the policy of Qing dynasty towards Muslims, see Li Ziran, *Policy of Qianlong towards Hui People*, published in *Collection of Essays on Hui Studies*, (Beijing: Nationalities Publishing House, 2005), Volume One, 141.

When they wanted to get married, they invited an Ahong (阿訇, the imam of the mosque) to be a witness and to recite specific words (called 'nikah', i.e. certain Qur'anic verses and hadiths of Prophet Muhammad). When someone died, they would wash the body (الغسل), then wrap it in a white cloth before burying it. When burying the dead body, they would not use a coffin as non-Muslims did. They would make wudu' (الوضوء) before the formal prayer (salah) and ghusl (الغُسل) after sexual intercourse. They would not welcome non-Muslims to enter mosques. They would fast for one month every year, during which they would not eat or drink during the daytime; they would pray Tarawih prayer (صلاة التراويح) at night during Ramadan; when the fasting month ended, they would wear their new clothes, go to the mosques, perform the prayer; and then they would celebrate and congratulate one another. They still used the Muslim calendar, although it had been abolished by the government.[1]

1.7 Abuses of Some Officials Against Muslims

It is very clear from our presentation that there were obvious differences between Muslims and other Chinese people in terms of sensibilities and culture. Muslims were a minority living among the non-Muslim majority; therefore, their behaviour was open to the scrutiny of the latter, which felt that Muslims should give up their own culture to be like them. A very famous scholar, Gu Yanwu (顾炎武), said in his book that "only the Huihui[2] still follow their own custom and do not want to change it." Many officials who served the Qing Dynasty were Han people of a narrow outlook who rejected any culture but their own. Some of them even tried to use official power to uproot Islamic culture. In the ninth month of the second year of Yongzheng (1724), a provincial governor named Chen Shiguan (陈世倌) submitted a written statement to a higher official in which he said, "Muslims, for example, do not respect Tian (天) and Di (地), do not offer sacrifices to gods; they set up their own king and have their own calendar; their population is very large; they help villains to hurt people. Please have

---

1 See Fu Tongxian, *History of Islam in China*, 75.

2 "Huihui" refers to Chinese Muslims.

them withdraw from their religion and destroy their mosques." In another example, in the fifth month of the eighth year of Yongzheng (1730), a surveillance commissioner named Lu Guohua (鲁国华) presented a memorandum to the emperor that "Muslims live in the heartland, they take official exams and do their business as other people do, and there is no difference between them and others.

However, they have their own calendar, according to which there is neither a lunar month of 30 days, nor an intercalary month, and one year consists of 360 days. Muslims take a certain day as the beginning of the year and congratulate one another on the occasion. In addition to that, they always wear white hats; they build mosques; we don't know which god they worship. They are citizens of the dynasty, so they should follow our calendar and wear our clothes. How are they allowed to have their own calendar and wear white hats and clothes? Doing that is against our system and regulation. Please permit us to make them follow the official calendar and the regulations on clothes. As to their mosques, they should be prohibited and abolished. If they don't stop doing that and continue to follow their calendar, they should be punished as any other heretical sect; whoever wears a white hat should be punished for violating the rules. If any local official tolerates them and tries to harbor them, he should be reprimanded according to the relevant law." [1]

1.8 The Emperor's Attitude towards Muslims

It seems that the attitude of the Qing emperor toward Muslims was positive in general, although he despised them at the beginning. This can be seen in his reply to the above statement presented by those officials. Yongzheng (雍正)[2] replied to Chenshiguan's (陈世倌) statement:

> Those Muslims are worthless; nevertheless, they came to China a long time ago. People are not influenced by their

[1] See Fu Tongxian, *History of Islam in China*, 78.

[2] It is the reigning title of Shizong (世宗) who ruled the Qing dynasty from 1723-1736.

> religion, and they are humble people. Most educated men among the Muslims seem to be following the religion against their will. The common people never converted to their religion; therefore, their population will not increase anymore. As to their mosques, they use them for nothing but worship; how then can they mislead people? I commanded you to strictly forbid things which are strange, dazzling and shocking. Buddhist monks, Taoist priests and Huihui (Muslims) came long ago, so if you want to change and abolish them without excuse, you will not only be unable to do that, but you will make the situation more disordered. How can you administer in such a way?[1]

Here we can see that what those officials wanted to do was not in accordance with the will of the emperor, who held that Muslims should be dealt with just like Buddhist monks and Taoist priests, not because he respected or liked Muslims, but because he wanted to avoid unnecessary problems.

However, later, the emperor's attitude toward Muslims became more positive; he described them as citizens of the dynasty, and considered their religion nothing but their customs handed down from their ancestors, so they should not be slandered because of it. As for Muslims who committed crimes, the emperor observed that criminals are be found in all races, including the Han. He commanded the officials to treat Muslims in the same way they did in dealing with other people. At the same time, the emperor required Muslims to be good citizens and not to commit crimes. Commenting on Lu Guohua's (鲁国华) presentation against Muslims, the emperor said:

> I checked the history of Muslims in China and I found that they have been in this country for a long time. Thus, they are our citizens because they are officially registered people,

---

[1] Fu Tongxian, *History of Islam in China*, 77.

so I treat them the same as other people. How could I leave them alone without educating? That was why I issued a decree to promote filial piety and to encourage people to be honest and tolerant with each other, and to be righteous and just. For several years I have not heard that any Muslim violated the law and committed crimes. On the contrary, I heard that there are Muslims of noble aspirations with the desire to do better. They take exams to be officials, just like other educated people. There is no lack of such people among Muslims who have become civil and military officials, like Ma Jinliang (马进良) and Ma Xiong (马雄) in the past and Ha Yuansheng (哈元升) today. There are many others who have made great contributions to the dynasty. As for their following of their own religious regulations, it is nothing but a custom left by their ancestors. That's how things are in China, it being so vast. The general mode differs from place to place; therefore, people's customs also differ. They came to China long ago, and their religion is nothing new. It was not forbidden by previous dynasties nor did they force it to be changed. Lu Guohua's presentation is harsh and bizarre. Who said that Muslims do not follow the official calendar? How can we charge them with not following the official calendar for nothing more than their recording the dates and times (of fasting and prayer) in writing? Who said that Muslims do not practice the official regulation on clothing? How can we charge them with that just because they wear their own head-coverings (turbans)? As for mosques, they are just like temples in villages in which people worship their gods that are not recorded in relevant books. Why should we make punctilious and excessive demands only against Muslims and conclude that they are committing crimes? Before, there were many officials who presented complaints against the Muslims. I blamed them for that; Lu Guohua knows that, yet he has

> raised the same subject. I don't know what his intention is. If Muslims broke laws and regulations, they should be punished accordingly; there is no clause to remit them. If they have not committed any crimes, and officials in different ranks present complaints against them only because their customs and culture are different from ours, I will punish them severely! Lu Guohua is a mediocre and in-ambitious man; we used him because there was a vacancy in Anhui province, so we appointed him temporarily. He did not do his job carefully for the benefit of the local people; instead he busied himself with a study of the customs of Muslims with an eye to changing them; moreover, he requested imposition of strict laws to forbid them, which made innocent Muslims homeless. This kind of presentation means that he either has an axe to grind against the Muslims or he wants to mislead the administration of the dynasty. Send Lu Guohua to the ministry to be examined and treated with severity.[1]

From these presentations of officials and the emperor's responses and instructions, it is obvious that Chinese society at the time of Qing seriously misunderstood Islam. As a result, Chinese Muslims were placed in very difficult situations in which mosques might have been damaged. Many Muslims were forced to give up their religion and be totally assimilated. In such a historical, social and political context, Jin Tianzhu appeared.

---

[1] See Fu Tongxian, *History of Islam in China*, 78.

CHAPTER TWO:

JIN TIAN ZHU AND HIS *Qingzhen Shiyi*

2.1 JIN TIAN ZHU's Life

2.1.1 Jin Tianzhu's Ancestors

The author's name is Jin Tianzhu (金天柱), he is also called Jin Beigao (金北高) or Mr. Beigao (北高先生). [1] Jin's ancestors came to China from Rumi, a place in Turkey,[2] at the time of the Ming dynasty. Zhu Yuanzhang (朱元璋), the founder of the dynasty, paid great attention to foreign affairs. In the fourth year of Hongwu (1372), he appointed a man named Yiblajin (Ibrahim), from Rumi, as Chief Minister of Court for State Protocol. In the fifth year of Yongle[3] (1408), to train translators and teach the languages of minorities in China as well as dwellers of neighboring countries, the Ming Dynasty established in Hanlin Academy (翰林院) an institution named Si Yi Guan (四夷馆).[4] It consisted of four branches, one of which was the institution of Huihui (Muslims). Its duty was to translate and teach. One of the lecturers in this institute was also named Yiblajin (Ibrahim), and he was

---

[1] Generally, Chinese Muslims have two names: one is a Muslim name and the other is a Chinese name. However, we haven't found anyone so far who has mentioned the author's Muslim name.

[2] Rumi is also spelled as Romi. According to Mr. Chen Zhanshan, Rumi might be originated from the term "Roman" of Eastern Roman Empire. If this is the case, then, it is in Ankara, the present capital city of Turkey. See his article, "The Achievements of Islamic Astronomy in the History of Chinese Astronomy and its Impacts on the Latter", published in *Northwest Nationalities Study*, 1998.

[3] It is the reigning title of Zhuli (1403-1425) who took power from his uncle and chose Beijing as the capital of the Dynasty.

[4] It means 'institution of foreigners'.

also from Rumi. Some scholars believe that, most probably, Jin Tianzhu is a descendant of that Yiblajin. This is reasonable because, according to relevant historical data, most lecturing posts in the institute of Huihui were hereditary, so that, when a father was too old to lecture his son would take his place. Jin Tianzhu lived in Nanjing; however, according to a letter he wrote to his senior boss, his father's grave was in Beijing. This might mean that the latter left Nanjing and went to Beijing to work in a field related to Yiblajin's. His family name "Jin" (金) is derived from the last part of the name of his ancestor. However, the hereditary system had been abolished by the time of Jin Tianzhu, so he had to take an exam to become a lecturer.

2.1.2. Jin Tianzhu's Birth, Life, Knowledge and Later Years

Despite exerting significant effort, we couldn't find any specific data for the date of birth and death of Jintianzhu. Therefore, we deduce as follows: According to some references, Liuzhi (刘智) was born around 1660 and died in 1745. In his preface, Jin referred to Liu as belonging to the older generation. Jin entered Hanlin Academy in 1727 and completed his book in 1737. Eight years later, when he was preparing to publish the book, he wrote a letter to his senior boss, in which he explained that the reason he wanted him to write the preface was to remind him after he retired to remember the days he had worked under the boss. That was in 1746. Based on this, it might be possible to venture that Jin was born around 1690 and died around 1756.

Jin Tianzhu grew up in an intellectual Muslim family. Since his childhood he had been educated in both Islamic teachings and Confucian doctrine. In the fourth year of Yongzheng (1727), Jin went to Beijing to visit his father's grave. By chance, within days of his arrival in the capital, he met the minister of Hanlin, who was admitting applicants by examination. Jin took the exam and passed. Hence, he started work as an instructor in Si Yi Guan, which was mentioned above. The name had been changed to Si Yi Guan (四译馆) which means "The Translators' Institute" during the Qing dynasty. As an instructor, his job, Jin said, was to interpret the textbooks, teach alphabets and pronunciation, explain their meanings, and to clarify customs and daily etiquette. After 10 years, in the second year of Qianlong

(1737),[1] Jin was promoted to master of translators and lecturers; at the same time, he was a lecturer in the department of Huihui of the institute.

As a lecturer, Jin had to be well versed in either Arabic or Persian or both languages. From the contents of the book, it is obvious that Jin had read not only the works of Muslim scholars such as Wang Daiyu (王岱舆) and Liuzhi (刘智), but also some Arabic and Persian books. He was well versed in Islamic theology (the science of Kalam) and Islamic law, and very familiar with the history of Islam and the life of prophets (peace be upon them). The quotations in the book show us that the author was well acquainted with the traditional culture of China in general, and The Four Books (四书) and The Five Classics (五经)[2] in particular. As well, he was not unfamiliar with Buddhism and Taoism. Furthermore, Jin had detailed knowledge of the history of China and the life of its ancient emperors. He had also made studies in the science of critical interpretation of ancient texts.

With regards to his later life, we could not find any information. About his descendants we have only two clues. First, Chen Dashao (陈大韶), author of one of the prefaces, mentioned that Jin's two sons were being trained in the same official institute, that they were accomplished masters of writing, and that they would join the imperial examination and would, hopefully, be officials after that. Secondly, a well-known Muslim scholar at the time of the Republic of China (1912-1949), namely Jin Shihe (金世和), in his preface to Wang Daiyu's *The Great Learning of Islam*, said: "The most famous Muslims scholars in Jinling (Nanjing) who were proficient in Islamic and Chinese literature, were Wang Daiyu in the time of the Ming

---

[1] Qian Long (乾隆) is the title of the reign of the Gao Zong Emperor of the Qing dynasty named Hong Li (弘历) who was on throne from 1736-1796.

[2] The titles of The Four Books (四书) are: The Great Learning (大学), The Doctrine of The Mean (中庸), The Analects of Confucius (论语) and Mencius (孟子); the titles of The Five Classics are: The Book of Songs (诗经), The Book of History (书经), The Book of Changes (易经), The Book of Rites (礼记), and The Spring and Autumn Annals (春秋). These books were the main books Chinese learners must read, and from which the questions in the government examinations came.

Dynasty, Liu Jielian and Jin Tianzhu Beigao in the time of Kangxi and Qianlong. Bei Gao is the ancestor of Shi He. He wrote the *Qingzhen Shiyi*. He is well known together with Wang and Liu up to now."[1]

2.2 The Writing of the *Qingzhen Shiyi*

2.2.1 The Reasons and Objectives for Writing *Qingzhen Shiyi*

As a Muslim intellectual, Jin Tianzhu had long intended to write a book in Chinese, yet he did not. The most important reason that caused him to start writing was the presentations of the officials who incited discussions among people and the spread of slanders about Muslim behavior. Jin thought the reason for the situation was that people were ignorant about Islam, which made them have doubts and suspicions about it. He believed that the only way to remove these doubts and suspicions was by writing. He did not forget the books written by the older generation; however, he found that, in terms of objective, those books were:

> To expound the teachings of Islam by collecting from Islamic books; in terms of contents, they are about how to know and worship God, as well as the regulations for daily life. In terms of language, they are mainly to teach Muslims. Furthermore, they are of enormous size. Who is willing to read and study them?

Moreover, they were regarded as too obtuse and profound to understand.[2] Therefore, Mr. Jin decided to write. Yet he did not start immediately because

---

[1] See, Yu Zhengui, One-volume edition of Wang Daiyu's *The Real Commentary on The True Teaching, The Great Learning and The True Answers*, (Yinchuan: Ningxia publishing house, 1988), 227.

[2] In this regard, Mr. Yang Huaizhong said in his letter to Du Weiming: "When Liu Zhi's books emerged, very few people were able to understand." See Yang Huaizhong, *Re-recognition of scholarship of Wang Daiyu and Liuzhi*, published

he was not sure if his style of writing was good enough and feared that people might despise his book. There might have been another reason that made Mr. Jin postpone his writing. It was the bad political situation at the time, which may have also caused problems for him. By the second year of Qianlong (1737), Mr. Jin's position had risen, which caused him look at the current situation more positively and consider his own abilities with more confidence. It was in those circumstances that he started writing. Having studied both Islamic knowledge and Confucian books for a long time and drawn upon his accumulated experiences, Mr. Jin completed the book within one month and then spent several months revising it. He named it *Qingzhen Shiyi* (清真释疑).

His main objective of writing this book, as he stated several times in his preface, was to remove people's suspicions, which, in his view, were not fair to Islam and Muslims. As we pointed out in the introduction, the dominant culture at that time was Neo-Confucian. Other cultures, especially foreign religions, had to be in accordance with or like the dominant culture; otherwise, there was no space accorded them to develop at all. Mr. Jin proposed that Buddhism, Taoism, Mohism and the theory of Yangzhu (炀朱)[1] were all, to varying extents, contrary to Confucian doctrine; however, people did not say anything against them. Islam, on the other hand, was in accord with the dominant culture, but they doubted it. Those suspicions, he feared, would eventually lead Islam to be banned and Muslims to be

---

in Journal of *Hui studies*, (Yinchuan: HZYJ Editorial Department, 2007, 1.), 107.

[1] He is a philosopher who lived in the Wei state during warring states period (403-221 B.C.). His philosophy of life was to benefit one's self. Mencius criticised both Yang and Mo that the former was so selfish that if you asked him to pull out a fine hair to benefit entire world, he would say no; and the latter, who stood for love of people, loved others so much that he didn't care even if all his hairs perished and his feet were tattered (ragged) because of long travel, as long as it was beneficial to others. According to Mencius, Confucianism is the doctrine of the mean (balanced doctrine). (http: zhidao.baidu.com/question/38054261.html).

assimilated. Mr. Jin wrote the book to defend Islam and Muslims by removing people's suspicions and to demonstrate that the former is harmonious with Confucianism with some minor exceptions and that, therefore, it has the right to spread in China. He also wanted to show that Muslims had been good citizens of China since their arrival during the Sui and Tang dynasties. They had served the country and made great contributions to it, whereby they had earned the right to live in China without giving up their identities. According to our present knowledge, *Qingzhen Shiyi* was the first book on Islam written for this purpose by a Chinese Muslim scholar entirely composed in the Chinese language and not a translation.[1]

2.2.2 Subject Matter, Main Sources and Method of Presentation

In this book Mr. Jin Tianzhu addresses the main religions, namely Buddhism, Taoism, and Catholicism, in addition to Islam. His discussion of Confucianism takes more pages than any religion except Islam. With regards to Confucianism, he talks about its philosophy of creation, some regulations for daily life, rites, education and so on. As for Buddhism, Mr. Jin criticizes some of its beliefs, such as the godhood of Buddha, karma and reincarnation, and some of its doctrines, such as withdrawing from society to be a monk. For Taoism, his focus is on people's belief in the priests and their worship of them to get their help. He also discusses their practice of magic. In addition to that, the philosophies of Yang Zhu (杨朱) and the Mohist school (墨翟, 476-391 B.C.) are repeatedly mentioned as examples of erroneous beliefs. At the end of his book, Mr. Jin discusses the place of Sufism in Islam.

Throughout his discussion, Mr. Jin expresses his own points of view about Confucianism and the dominant religions in his time. Confucianism in

---

[1] As for the academic works done by Chinese 'ulama before Jin Tianzhu, they are translations and compilations of Arabic and Persian Islamic books. Moreover, their objectives were to spread Islamic teachings amongst Muslims, and therefore, their main target was Muslims, and not to remove the doubts and suspicions of Chinese society, let alone touching on political issues to defend Islam and Muslims.

the author's time, as we pointed out before, had been changed and had become a new theology, named Lixue (理学). It was no longer the original Confucianism. It is obvious in his presentation that Mr. Jin distinguishes between its previous doctrine and its new theology. In this he differed from Liuzhi, who—as pointed out by Professor Tu Weiming (杜维明)[1]—accepted Lixue without any criticism. Mr. Jin affirmed the original doctrine and criticized the revised form, a stance that required considerable courage in his time. Regarding Islam, it is very clear that his belief in it was very strong and that he was very proud of being a Muslim. However, his view of Buddhism, Taoism and Catholicism is generally negative.

As Jin's target audience was mainly non-Muslim readers, especially educated people who were proud of being Confucians, his sources were the traditional Chinese books, especially those Confucian texts that were helpful to him in proving the validity of Islam and the reasonability of Muslim practices. He considered the thoughts of Chinese sages like Yao (尧), Shun (舜) Yu (禹), Ji (稷), Tang (汤), Wen (文) and Wu (武) as orthodox ideas. He also referred to books like *Lunyu* (论语), *Shijing* (诗经), *Quli* (曲礼) and *Fogubiao* (佛骨表) and quoted from them many sayings of Confucian wise men from the distant past, such as Confucius (孔子), Zisi (子思), Zilu (子路), Mencius (孟子), Zhuxi (朱熹), Su Dongpo (苏东坡), and Hanyu (韩愈), using them to present his own opinions and convince his readers that Islam was not a strange thing but a religion very similar to Confucianism. Beside Confucian books, Mr. Jin also consulted medical, literary, historical and linguistic works. He mentioned, for instance, *Bencao Gangmu* (本草纲目), written by Li Shizhen (李时珍 1518-1593) in the Ming Dynasty; he also cited poems of Dufu (杜甫) and other poets as proof or evidence; and he took information from *Gangjianyizhilu* (纲鉴易知录) about Pangushi (盘古氏) and stories of ancient emperors who took so-called miraculous cures. This shows us how wide and extensive Mr. Jin's reading was.

As for Islamic references, the author mentions only two books: Liuzhi's *Tianfang Xingli* (天方性礼) and *Tianfang Dianli* (天方典礼). When it is

---

[1] He is an American Chinese leading scholar in this field. To read his statement, see HZYJ Editorial department, *Hui Studies*, (Yinchuan: No. 1, 2007), 107.

necessary to mention Islamic literature, he says, for example: "Our prophet said such and such" or "It is stated in our book such and such".

To make the book user-friendly, the author adopted a dialogue format in which a guest asks questions, which he then answers. It consists of 16 questions and 16 answers. As to his method of presentation, he declares from the very beginning that comparison and contrast is the only way by which doubts and suspicions can be successfully removed. He is very aware that the one who wants to carry out this task must be well learned in both Islamic knowledge and Confucian culture; otherwise, he will not be able to do so. According to Mr. Jin, there is nothing to compare between Islam and Buddhism and Taoism, so he limits himself to a comparison between Islam and Confucian doctrine. His main aim in doing so was to show people the similarities between the two in most cases; however, he also takes the opportunity to demonstrate that Islam is more advanced than Confucianism. Prenatal education for instance, according to Confucianism, starts after the woman has become pregnant. This, in Mr. Jin's view, is less advanced than Islamic hygiene, which starts with a bath before sexual intercourse. It restrains the couple from illegal sexual acts and keeps their bodies clean and their hearts pure. Once a couple has had sex after a bath and the wife becomes pregnant, the baby must be either a sage or a wise man.

The most common method used by Mr. Jin to present his idea is a description, the purpose of which is to open the readers' eyes to let them judge for themselves. The author's descriptions in many parts of his book are magnificent. They could be compared with works of great masters in the field of literature, and this might be the reason why Ma Tingfu said that he "interprets Islamic profound books by using words of Han (韩), Liu (柳), Ou (欧) and Su (苏)".

To help his readers, discriminate between the right and the wrong, Mr. Jin uses a critical methodology to point out flaws in Confucianism, Buddhism, Taoism and Catholicism. It took plenty of courage for him to do so in that period of history. His criticisms of Confucianism focus on its new theology, which held that there is no God. He also criticized it for its lack of guidance on food and drink, allowing people to consume whatever they want. When a person dies, the body was placed in a coffin. Rich people bury things like gold, silver, pearls and jewels along with the deceased. Mr. Jin criticizes all these practices. With regards to God, for example, he quotes a poem and its interpretation by Confucian thinkers to demonstrate that ancient Confucianists believed in God. He says: "If you claim that there is no god, then both the ancient poem and Zhuxi's interpretation are wrong, aren't they?" Regarding diet, he quotes Confucius' words, then he said: "People respect Confucius very much, but how many of them follow his words and do not eat what he did not eat?" As to coffins and burying commodities with the dead, he points out that the former leads poor people to be exposed in the wilds while the latter entices thieves to steal buried valuables.

His argument against Catholicism concentrates on the nature of Jesus. According to Catholics, Jesus is God, who created everything. Jin Tianzhu raises three issues for debate; first, Catholics call Mary "Shengmu" (圣母), which means "the mother of the sage". If Jesus is God, they should call his mother the mother of God, not the mother of the sage. Secondly, if he is God and he created everything, then he must have created Mary. How then could a created woman give birth to the Creator? Third, Catholics believe that Jesus, who is God, came down to persuade people to believe in him and do charitable deeds. This, according to Mr. Jin, is quite fantastic. God can create everything; He is able to send wind and thunder to warn mankind; does He have to come down to the earth by being born? He concludes that Jesus is not God himself but one of his messengers.

Jin Tianzhu criticizes Buddhism and Taoism extensively and shows them no mercy. Buddhists worship Buddha as people do with God. Buddhism teaches belief in reincarnation, requires its followers to conduct fasting and ceremonies to save the dead from punishment, and encourages people to leave society to be monks. Jin Tianzhu analyzes and criticizes all of this in detail. As for Taoism, his criticism focuses on its priests and their so-called magic arts. He frames his criticism in terms of the Muslim belief in the existence of angels who manage the universe in absolute obedience to God's will. They will not do anything against His will, so those priests have no chance to call on angels to do anything for them. Because of this, when floodwater comes to a certain place, they can't do anything to stop the disaster. Some of them claim that they can divine for people their past and future; however, it is, in Jin's sight, nothing but a dirty trick. According to him, the true priests, who really can touch a stone and turn it into gold, do not meet human society anymore.

In addition to the three methods mentioned above, the author also uses the method of analogy. For example, when discussing the direction of God, he compares God with the life of man. There is no specific direction for life in the body of man; likewise, there is no specific location for God in the universe. When explaining why Muslims trim their beards, he says: "For every kind of thing, there is an emperor and subjects." He continues that, unless the positions of both the emperor and his subjects are properly arranged and settled, society would be disordered. He compares the mouth to the emperor and the beard to his subjects. "The mouth has the right when a man eats; how can subjects obstruct when the emperor eats?"

A distinctive feature of Mr. Jin's presentation is that he coins examples drawn from people's common experience so that they can easily understand. He takes examples from the administration of China, lives of emperors in varied periods of history and the daily life of common people. To avoid lengthening the discussion, we will not go into further detail.

2.2.3 Editions of *Qingzhen Shiyi*

After completing the book, Jin Tianzhu did not immediately publish it; instead, he laid it aside for several years. Later, when some educated Muslims saw the book, they were greatly impressed and wanted to raise funds to publish it. Mr. Jin's mind was somewhat aroused by the proposal, however, he did not pursue it. He wanted to submit his book to the senior minister and ask him to write a preface. He wrote a letter to the minister for that purpose, declaring that he would publish the book, even if the minister did not consent to his request. It was the nineteenth year that Mr. Jin had worked in the Institute. As we have mentioned before, he had started there in the fourth year of Yongzheng (雍正). His nineteenth year was the tenth or the eleventh year of Qianlong. Based on that, we can conclude that the first edition of the book was printed in 1746-1747.

There is an edition in Beijing University without any information on the title page except the title of the book. It lacks the author's name and a publishing date, but it is registered in the computer as the edition of the tenth year of Qianlong, which would make it the first edition of the book. The text of the edition consists of prefaces by Chen Dashao, Ma Tingfu and the author, followed by the main body of the text. 161 characters are missing. A person named Zhuoya (卓雅) inked them in on the 17th day of the third month in the twelfth year of Tongzhi [1](同治 1874). He says: "This edition is very nice, which is why I filled in [the missing parts]." Nontheless, the edition is still incomplete; the last character is "客", which means that there are some things left out.[2] Zhuoya also mentions that a letter and a postscript were lost, but he did not replace them because they were too long and not important. I was told by the librarian that they considered this edition to be from the tenth year of Qianlong based on Ma Tingfu's preface, which was written in that year. I think it is possible that it is the first edition, not based on the preface of Ma Tingfu, but on the postscript[3] mentioned above, which may have been the words written by the senior minister in response to Mr. Jin's request. If our inference is tenable, then this is the first edition of the book. Even if it is not the first, it must be earlier than other editions that we know of to date.

The earliest edition of *Qingzhen Shiyi* (清真释疑) that we have seen so far is the one published in the thirty-third year of Qianlong (1769). On the title page of this edition, the following information is given: reprinted in the thirty-third year of Qianlong (in top margin), by Mai Changfa (买长发), Zhaoxiang (兆祥氏) together with Wang Yongan (王永安), Wannianshi (万年氏), both from Zhongzhou (中州, on the right side of the page). *Qingzhen Shiyi* (清真释疑 in the middle), saved in Changlezhai (常乐斋, left side). There are five seals on the page, the first of which is the date the manuscript

---

1 It is the title of Mu Zong (穆宗) emperor's reign who was on throne from 1862-1875.

2 "客" means the guest, this means that the question of guest and the answer of the author is lost.

3 I mean by the term "postscript" something like a forward or preface.

was added to the collection of the S.M.R. LIBRARY, i.e. the Library of the South Manzhou Railway Organization. The date was May 23, 1930.[1] The second is the title of the organization in Chinese characters without a date. The third is for a person named Gong Zeshou (恭则寿), from whom, I think, the Japanese collected the manuscript. The fourth one consists of words inscribed by Qianlong for Yuan Guozuo (袁国祚), which we will discuss shortly. The fifth is not clear enough to read. On the front cover, only the title of the book and "Ying Xianshi" (瀛仙氏), the name of a person, are written. The main body of the text comes in the following order: the preface and the poem by Hu Huiyuan, both handwritten, the preface of Chen Dashao from the third year of Qianlong, the preface of Ma Tingfu from the tenth year of Qianlong, and the author's preface from the third year of Qianlong, then the letter written by the author to the senior minister in the tenth year of Qianlong. The text comes next and ends with the character "客". This means that the edition is also incomplete.

The authors of *The History of Islam in China* believe that it is almost impossible for *Qingzhen Shiyi* to have been published before Qi Cheng Tang (启承堂) reprinted it sometime between the fortieth to the forty-fourth year of Qianlong (1776-1779).[2] Based on the Hai Furun (海富润) incident, to be discussed later, Mr. Hai Zhengzhong concluded that the latest date the book could have been published was 1781. The information we have acquired, especially from the edition published in the thirty-third year of Qianlong, demonstrates that they are mistaken in this claim.

The next edition is the one published in the second year of Guangxu[3] (1876). The book was published at least twice in this year by the same publisher. The first printing was based on the edition stored in Zeng Rong Tang (增荣堂), Xian Nv Zhen (仙女镇). When it was published, the Chengxi mosque of Zhenjiang (镇江) got a copy and stored it. Then the

---

[1] This means that the book was collected by the Japanese during the time of their occupation of Northeast China.

[2] See the book mentioned above, 586.

[3] Guang Xu (光绪) is the title of De Zong (德宗) Emperor's reign; he was on the throne from 1875-1909.

publisher published it again in the same year. We don't know what happened between the two editions; however, our conclusion of two separate printings is based on the information on the title page of both editions. On the title page of the first edition, the following information is given: in the top margin, "the second year of Guangxu"; in the right side, "written by Mr. Jin Beigao" and a seal of the Chengxi mosque of Zhenjiang; in the middle of the page, "*Qingzhen Shiyi*"; and on the left side, "stored in Zengrongtang, Xiannvzhen." On the title page of the second edition, Chengxi mosque is identified as the party who stored the edition, but there is no seal for it. This means that this edition was published based on the one mentioned above. In terms of the quality of printing and the form of the writing, the first is better than the second.

The latest edition of the book was published in the tenth year of the Republic of China (1922). On the title page of the edition, the following information is given: "republished in the tenth year of the Republic of China"; "written by Mr. Jin from Shicheng" and "stored by the Islamic Books and Newspapers Office of New Jie in Beijing". The main body of the edition contains the prefaces of each of Ma Shifang (马士芳) [1], Hu Huiyuan, Ma Tingfu, the author and Chen Daoshao. This is followed by the text, followed by a comment of Chen Daoshao and the letter of the author to the senior minister. At the end, Qianlong's comments and instructions for Zhuchun's presentation are attached. On the first page of Ma Shifang's preface, there is the seal of Beijing University, in which the following words are written: "Collected by the Library of Yanching University", which means this edition was collected by Beijing University in the time of the Republic of China.[2]

In terms of contents of the editions we mentioned above, there is no difference between them except in one matter. There is a greater number of

---

[1] He was a Muslim scholar and an Imam of a mosque in Gansu province during the time of Qian Long (1736-1796). The preface was written by him in the 38th year of Qiang Long which was 1774.

[2] It is so because Yanjing University existed before the establishment of the People's Republic of China, which then merged with Beijing University.

prefaces in the later editions than in the early editions, and they are arranged in different orders in various editions. All characters in all editions are in a complex form and arranged vertically. There are no punctuation marks in the prefaces and in the letter to the senior minister, while there are two kinds of marks in the main body (text), i.e. slight-pause marks and full stops but bigger. There are notes done by Chen Dashao beside some sentences of the text.

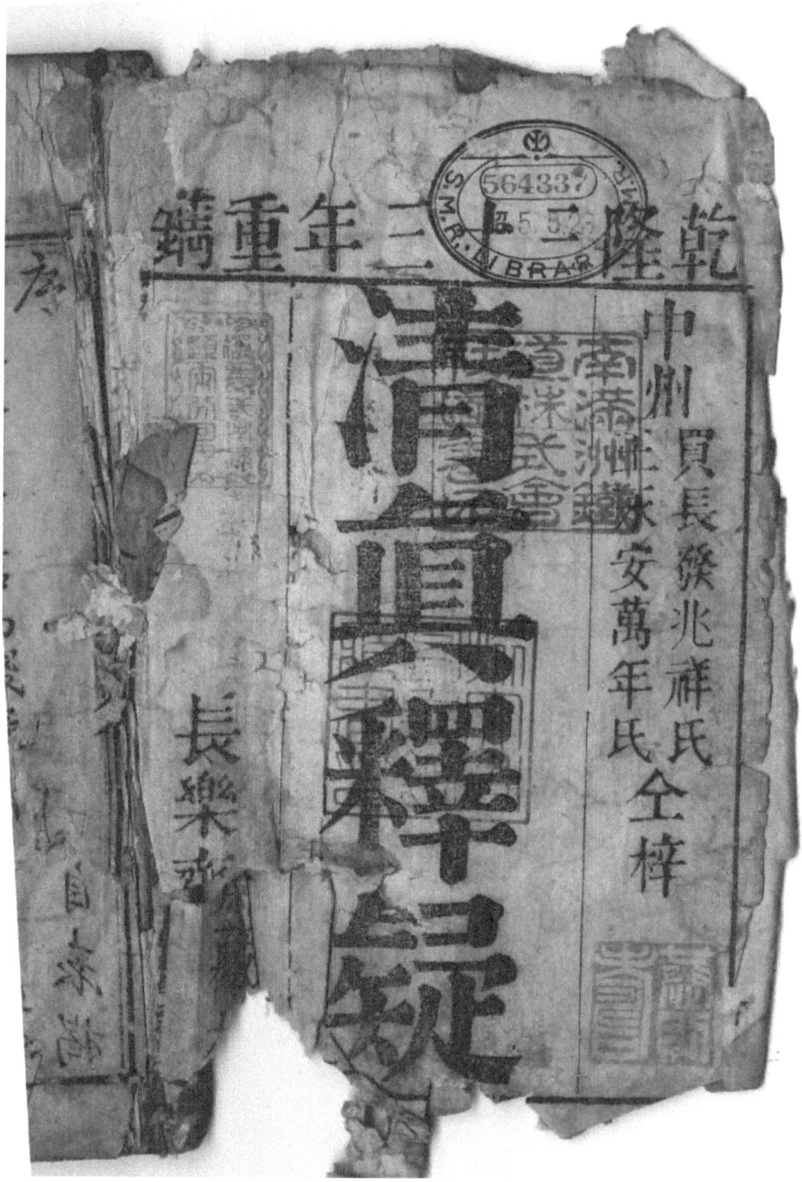

Figure 1. Title page of Qingzhen Shiyi, published in 1769, in the 33rd year of Qianlong.

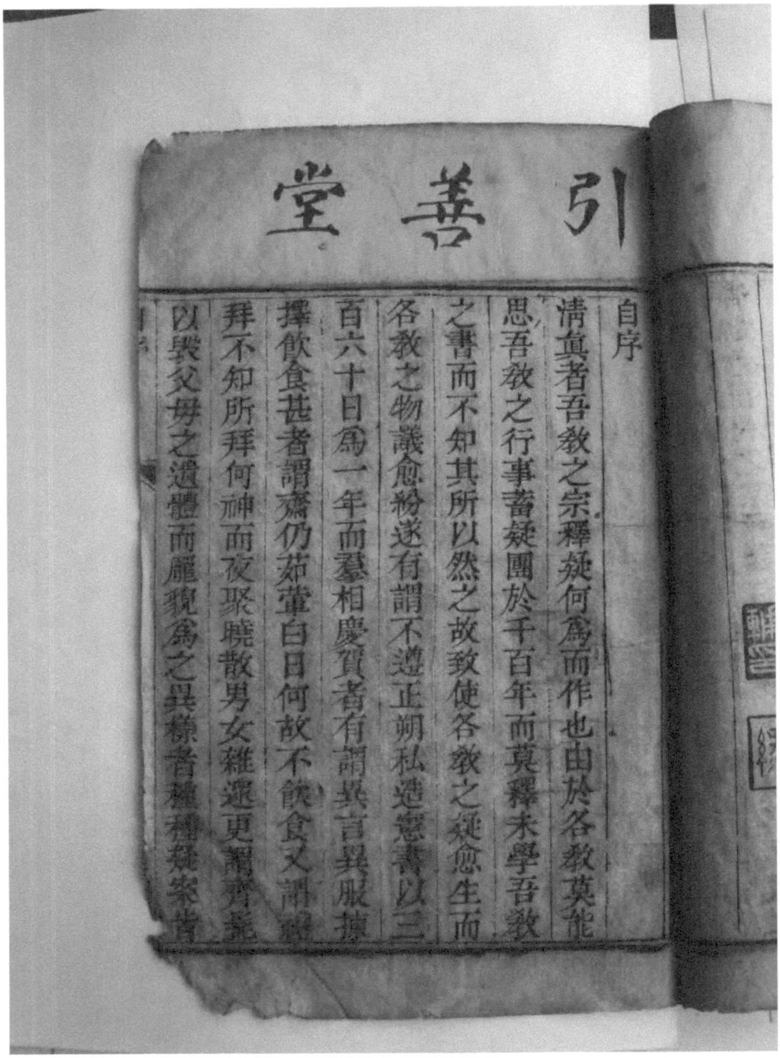

引善堂

自序

清真者吾教之宗釋疑何為而作也由於各教莫能
思吾教之行事蓄疑團於千百年而莫釋未學吾教
之書而不知其所以然之故致使各教之疑愈生而
各教之物議愈紛遂有謂不遵正朔私造憲書以三
百六十日為一年而羣相慶賀者有謂異言異服擁
擇飲食甚者謂齋仍茹葷白日何故不飲食又謂[illegible]
拜不知所拜何神而夜聚曉散男女雜遝更謂[illegible][illegible]
以毀父母之遺體而麗貌為之異様者種種疑案皆

Figure 2. Preface of the author to Qingzhen Shiyi (1769), in the 33rd year of Qianlong.

Figure 3. Title page of the 1st edition published in the second year of Guangxu (1876).

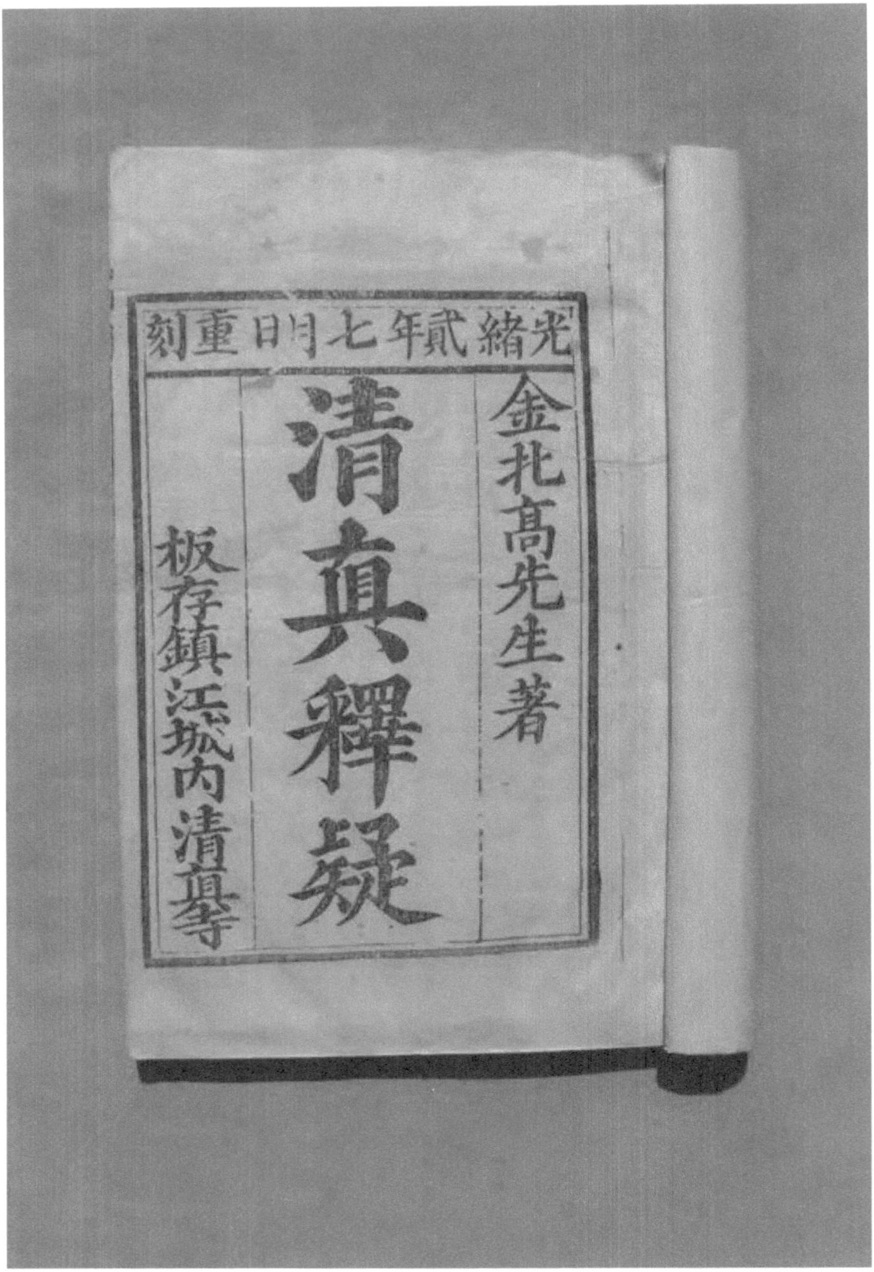

Figure 4. Title page of the 2nd edition published in the second year of Guangxu (1876).

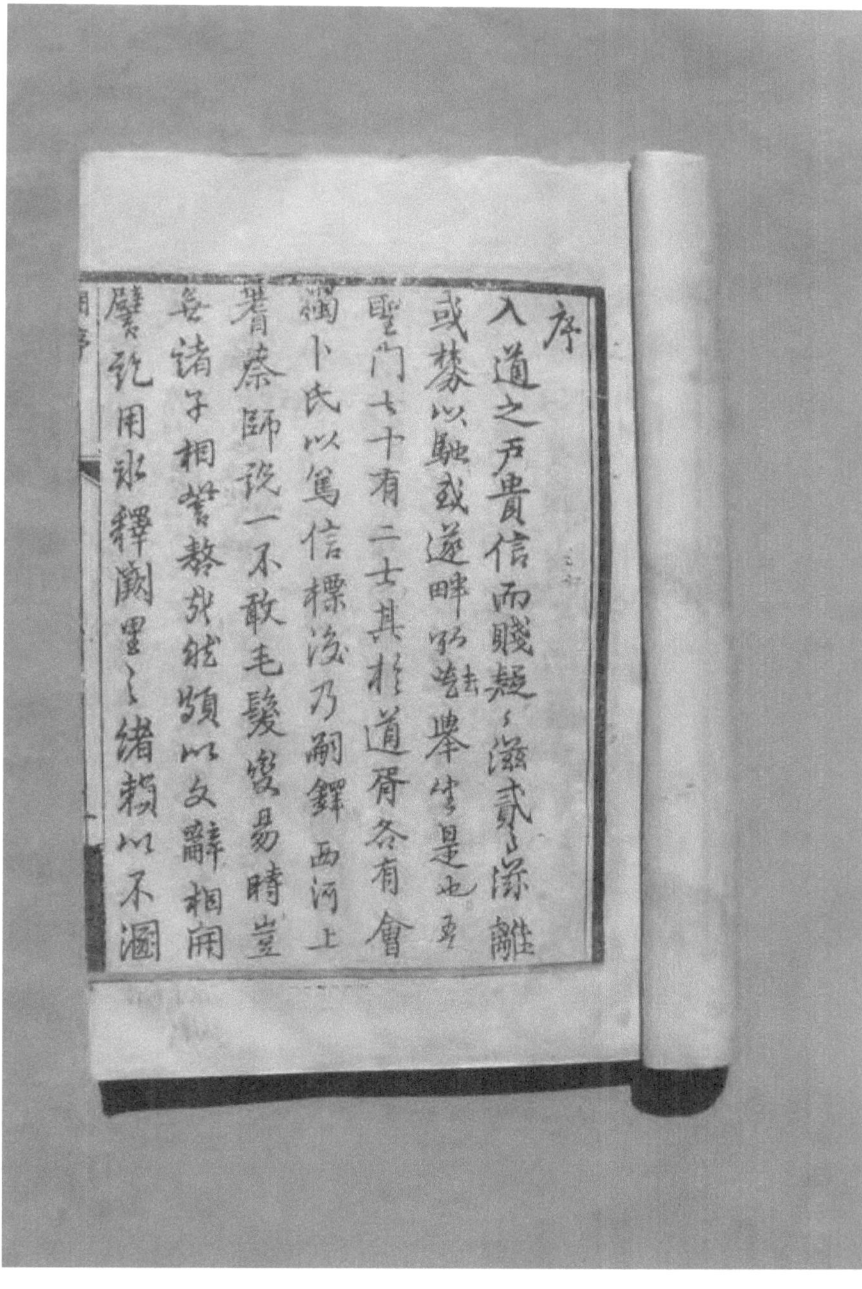

序
入道之戶貴信而賤疑疑滋貳貳滋離
或棼以馳或遯畔於法舉世是也吾
聖門七十有二士其於道胥各有會
獨卜氏以篤信標後乃嗣鐸西河上
耆秦師說一不敢毛髮變易時豈
無諸子相訾謷哉然頗以文辭相角
譬乾用以釋闡異之緒賴以不溷

Figure 5. The first page of Hu Huiyuan's Preface to Qingzhen Shiyi (1876).

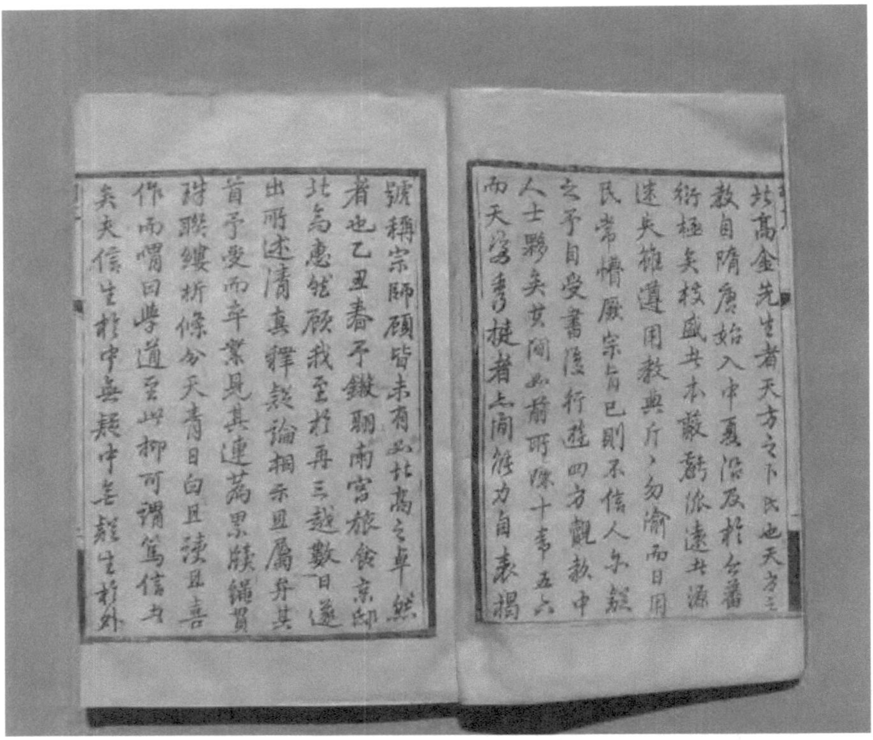

Figure 6. The 2nd and 3rd pages of the Preface.

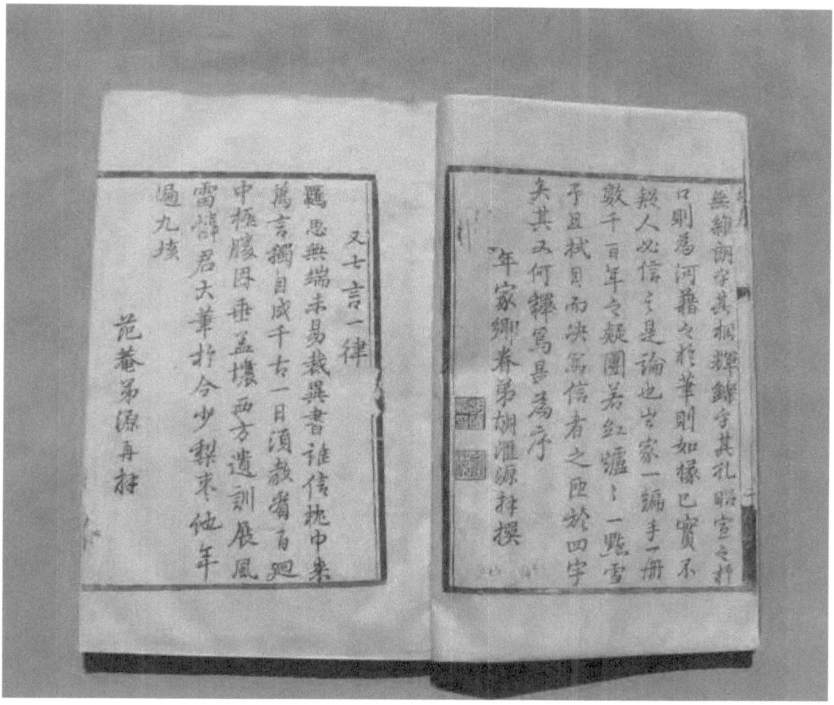

Figure 7. The last page of the Preface with Hu Huiyuan's poem (1876).

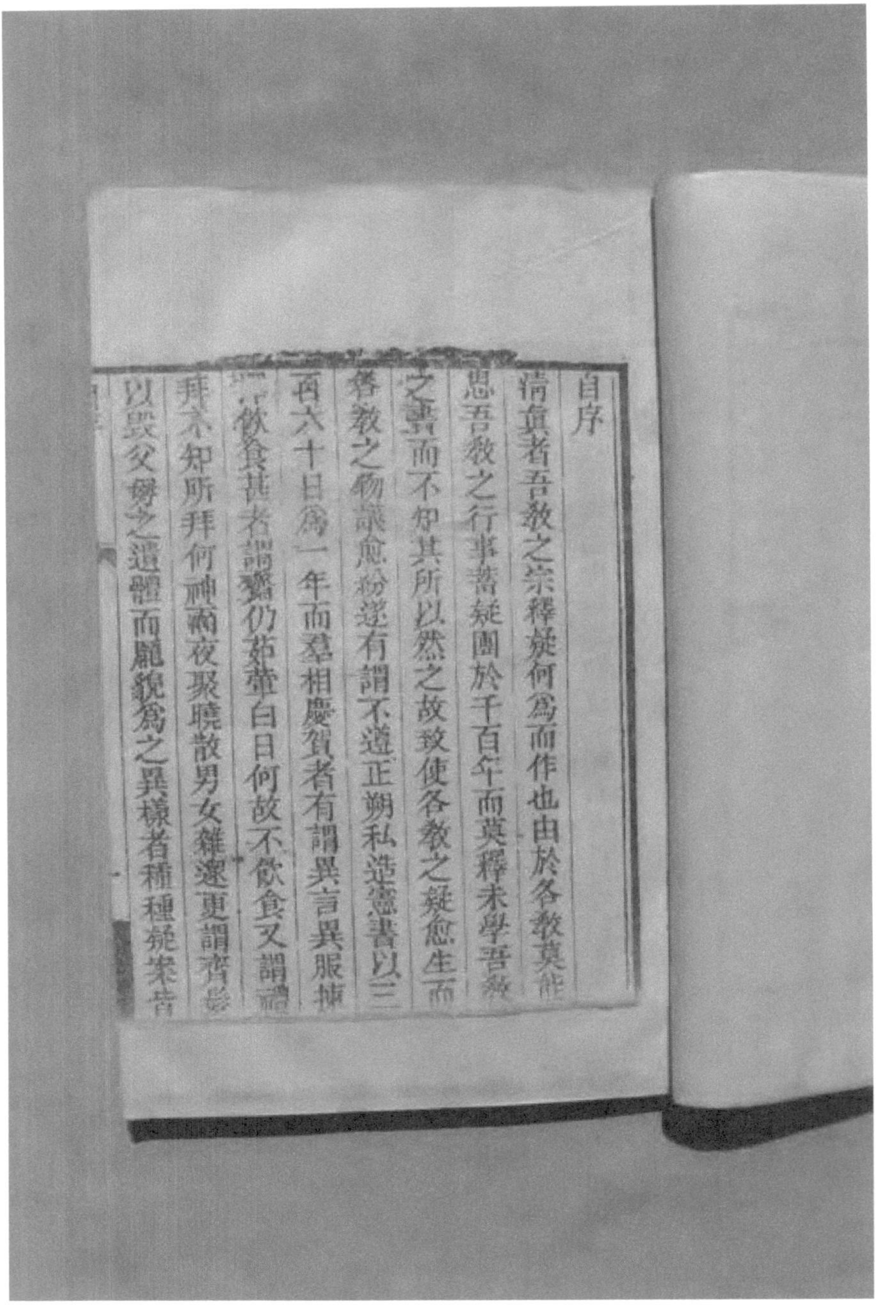
自序
清眞者吾教之宗釋疑何爲而作也由於各教莫能
悉吾教之行事蓄疑團於千百年而莫釋未學吾教
之書而不知其所以然之故致使各教之疑愈生而
各教之物議愈紛遂有謂不遵正朔私造憲書以三
百六十日爲一年而羣相慶賀者有謂異言異服拒
[illegible]飲食甚者謂豬仍茹葷白日何故不飲食又謂禮
拜不知所拜何神黑夜聚曉散男女雜遝更謂齊髮
以毀父母之遺體而醜貌爲之異樣者種種疑案皆

Figure 8. The author's Preface in 2nd edition of the 2nd year of Guangxu (1876).

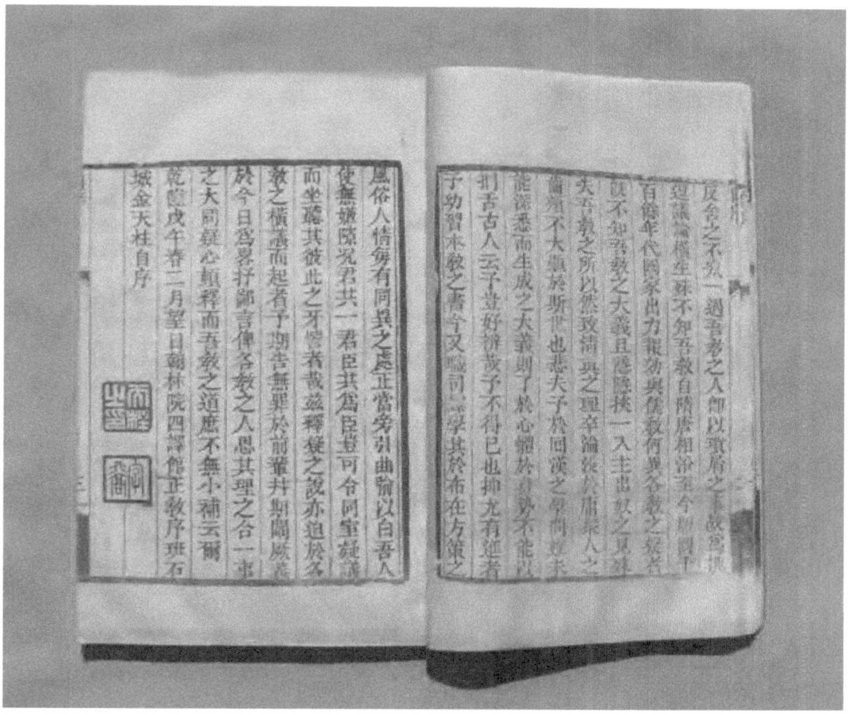

Figure 9. The 2nd and the last page of the Author's Preface with his seal.

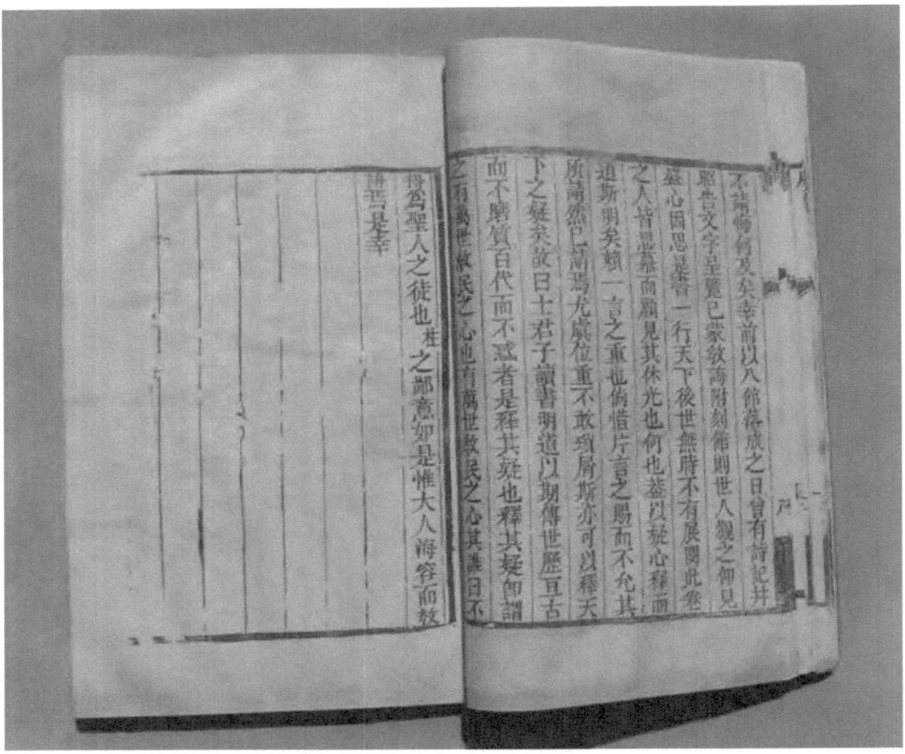
不禱悔何及矣幸前以八飾落成之日曾有詩記并
恥告文字呈覽已蒙敎誨附刻飾則世人觀之卻見
蓋心固思是書一行天下後世無時不有展閱此卷
之人皆思慕而願見其休光也何也蓋以疑心釋而
道斯明矣頓一言之重也倘惜片言之賜而不允其
所請然已辭焉尤擴位重不敢瑣屑斯亦可以釋天
下之疑矣故曰士君子讀書明道以期傳世歷亘古
而不磨質百代而不惑者是釋其疑也釋其疑卽謂
之有萬世敎民之心也有萬世敎民之心其誰曰不
得爲聖人之徒也哉之鄙意如是惟大人海容而敎
誨焉是幸

Figure 10. The last two pages of the letter (1876).

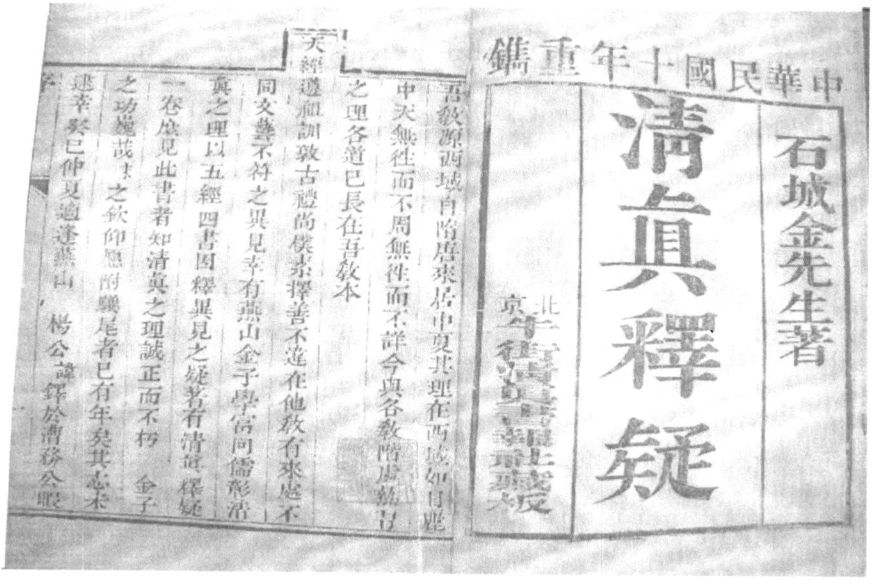

Figutur 11. Title page of the last edition of Qingzhen Shiyi in 1922 and the first page of preface by Ma Shifang to the edition in 1874.

In addition to what has already been mentioned, related references introduced some other editions of the book. Professor Bai Shouyi (白寿彝), a famous historian, said in his *Records of Hui Figures* that Yuan Guozuo republished the *Qingzhen Shiyi* between the fortieth and forty-third years of Qianlong (1776-1779). Li Xinghua and others claimed that they saw an edition published in the sixteenth year of Daoguang [1](道光 1836) and another one published in the third year of Guangxu (1877)[2]. According to the authors of *The History of Ancient Chinese Civilization*, there is a combined edition of the original book and its complement. [3] Wang Jiafan

---

[1] It is the title of Xuan Zong (宣宗) emperor's reign who was on throne from 1821-1850.

[2] This edition is introduced by Yu Zhengui and Yang Huaizhong in their *Abstracts of Islamic Documents and Literatures*, (Yinchuan: Ningxia publishing house, 1993), 183,184.

[3] It will be introduced later.

(王家范), one of the authors, said: "The original work was written by Jin Tianzhu. In the first year of Guangxu, the complement was completed. They were combined in the next year." Based on Ma Shifang's preface in the edition of the tenth year of the Republic of China (1922), there is an edition that was published in the thirty-eighth year of Qianlong (1874). This is known from the preface, which was written when some Muslims were going to republish the book that year.

Moreover, the website of Beijing University mentions that in the library of the Beijing Teachers University there is an edition published in the first year of the Republic of China (1912), and in the library of Nanjing University there is another one without a publishing date. And again, Li Xinghua mentioned an edition published in the second year of Guangxu on which the two characters of "御览" were added in front of the title of the book. This means the edition was republished based on the one that had been glanced at by Qianlong after the Hai Furun incident, which will be discussed in detail in the next paragraph.

Qingzhen Shiyi was confiscated by the government of the Qing dynasty as one of the banned books. In the thirty-ninth year of Qianlong (1775), the emperor issued an imperial edict to investigate prohibited books, and local authorities acted accordingly. A Muslim from Hainan named Hai Furun (海富润) had left his hometown in a search of knowledge that lasted several years. In the forty-sixth year of Qianlong (1782), Hai Furun came from Shanxi (陕西) to Hankou (汉口). He made the acquaintance there of a man from Jinling named Yuan Guozuo (袁国祚) who was managing a shop beside the mosque. Mr. Yuan was eager to promote Islamic culture by printing various Islamic books. He gave Hai Furun some books as a gift, four of which were in Chinese. Three of them were Liuzhi's works, i.e. *Tianfang Zhisheng Shilu Nianpu* (天方至圣实录年谱), *Tianfang Sanzijing* (天方三字经) and *Tianfang Zimu Jieyi* (天方字母解议). The fourth was Jin Tianzhu's *Qingzhen Shiyi* (清真释疑), the subject of this study. Hai Furun took these books with him and went to Guilin (桂林). It happened to be a time that officials were searching for prohibited books. As a result, he was arrested by the government and his books were confiscated by officials. One official, Zhuchun (朱椿), reported to the emperor as follows:

> I am now interrogating the suspected convict. I have sent to Guangdong, his ancestral home, and requested the local officials to search in detail to see whether there are other illegal works or not. At the same time, I have asked officials of other provinces to check and seize all said books, send them to the capital and have them burned, and to arrest all authors, printers, and promoters for interrogation and punishment. I have sent these books to his majesty for his perusal....

The emperor replied to him after perusing those books: "Most of these books are vulgar, but they are not arrogant and do not go against the law...." However, the provincial governors had already begun to implement Zhuchun's official communication. The governor of Hu Bei (湖北) had arrested Yuan Guozuo and collected many books; the governor of Jiangnan (江南) investigated Jiangning (江宁), Zhenjiang (镇江) and Songjiang (松江), and prepared to arrest Liuzhi, Jin Tianzhu and other relevant people. By that time, however, Liuzhi was long dead and Jin Tianzhu was working in Beijing or retired already. We have no information on if he was arrested, but his house in Jiangning was checked by officials.[1] Mr. Yuan Guozuo's elder brother and Gai Shaoxian (改绍贤), who was the author of one of the prefaces to Liu Zhi's book, were also arrested. At that juncture, Zhuchun received another imperial edict in which the emperor said: "Free all arrested people and give back all books...." When he was released, Yuan Guozuo went to Beijing and presented Liuzhi's *Zhishengshilu* (至圣实录) to the emperor to examine. The emperor wrote for him the following words: "*Yuan Er*[2] *is a law-abiding Muslim.*"

Xu Wenyong (许文镛) said in his preface to the Complementary of *Qingzhen Shiyi*: "I heard in Beijing about Mr. Jin Beigao's Qingzhen Shiyi. From my investigations I learned that the book was read by the emperor in

---

[1] Yu Zhengui, *Chinese Past Dynasties and Islam*, 229.

[2] Yuan Er (袁二) is the surname of Yuan Guozuo (袁国祚).

the time of Qianlong. Unfortunately, very few editions remain today. It did not circulate widely." Based on this, it is possible that *Qingzhen Shiyi* was looked at by the emperor.

In the letter to the senior minister, Jin Tianzhu stated that he had written no book before *Qingzhen Shiyi*, but he had written a poem. We tried to find the poem by various means but failed. Thus, we conclude that *Qingzhen Shiyi* is Jin Tianzhu's only published work. It is essential to note that Hu Weiyuan (胡薇元) claimed in his preface to the completion of *Qingzhen Shiyi* that the book was produced by Ma Zhangmin (马章民),[1] Jin Tianzhu and others. This is a baseless claim. In his presentation to the emperor, Zhuchun said that those books were written by Liuzhi. This is, of course, wrong also. Perhaps based on this, Marshall Broomhall, B.A. listed *Qingzhen Shiyi* in his *Islam in China* under the name of Liuzhi, which is an error.

2.2.4 People's Appraisals of *Qingzhen Shiyi*

Since being published, the book received readers' welcome and won much praise from scholars at various times. Mr. Chen Dashao, a contemporary of Mr. Jin, said:

> Beigao (北高) talked with the guest for a long time; his presentation was like a thousand stages or a snake in Changshan (常山),[2] very rich in terms of content and perfect in terms of order; very nice in terms of structure and

[1] Ma Zhangmin (1069-1666) was one of the scholars at the time of the Qing dynasty. He was a writer as well as painter. In 1661, he received a pass with first place in the imperial exam and was appointed as a senior compiler.

[2] Changshan (常山) is the name of a mountain located in Zhengding town, Hebei province. As to Changshan snake, Mr. Hai Zhengzhong quoted from *Sunzi Jiudi* (孙子·九地) the following words: The snake of Chang shan, if you beat its head, its tail comes to bite you; if you beat its tail, its head comes to bite you; if you beat its mid, its head and tail come together to bite you. See: footnotes of his *Translation of QingzhenShiyi in Modern Chinese*, (Yinchuan: Ningxia Publishing House, 2002), 139.

> clear in terms of meaning. He used the way of Yaojie (遥接)[1] to show the similarities of different religions, and the way of analogy (类叙) to point out the shortcomings of other religions, just as artists do. If you say that his talent and learning is like the tide or the sea, well, it is both, which means that he learned from Changli and Meishan (昌黎眉山)[2] for a long time

Mr. Ma Tingfu, his classmate from Yunnan, said:

> When I read the book, I felt that he had used the pens of Han Yu (韩愈) [3], Liu Zongyuan (柳宗元)[4], Ou Yangxiu (欧阳

---

1 It refers to a way of presentation in which one collects things from various places which are far from each other and put them together into one place to show their similarities.

2 Changli (昌黎) is the native place for Hanyu (韩愈) in Hebei province, here it means Hanyu himself. Meishan is the native place for Su Dongpo (苏东坡) in Sichuan province. Here it means Su Dongpo himself. He means that Mr. Jin learned their works for a long time.

3 Hanyu (韩愈, 768-824), his title is Tuizhi (退之), is from a noble family in Mengxian, Henan province of China, and he lived in Changli (昌黎), Hebei province, which was why he called himself '昌黎韩愈'. Hanyu liked to study since his childhood; he went to the capital city to find an official job when he was 19 years old. In 792, he became a Jinshi and since then was appointed to various positions, one after another. In 801, he was given the title of Erudite (四门博士, an official of special broad skill and knowledge) in the state directorate of education. Two years later, he was appointed as an investigating censor and attendant gentleman in Ministry of Personnel (吏部侍郎). He has a work titled *The Collections of Mr. Hanyu*. See Liao Zhongan, *The Dictionary of Ancient Chinese Literature*. (Beijing: Beijing Publishing House, 1989), 129.

4 Liu Zongyuan (柳宗元, 773-819), his title was Zihou (子厚), and he was from Hedong (Yongji, Shanxi (山西) province). In 793, he was raised to the rank of Jinshi, and appointed as a proofreader in the Academy of scholarly worthies (集贤殿书院正字). In the first year of Yongzhen (805), he was promoted to the

> 修)[1] and Su Shi (苏轼)[2] to interpret the profound ancient books of Islam. The book is as clear and easy to understand as watching fire; nothing obstructs your view. It makes the reader feel that he is meeting an old friend. The content of the book is very familiar to his mind, and the words flow smoothly. Not only will this book leave non-Muslims with nothing to argue and suspect about Islam, but it will also help doubtful Muslims to recover their conscience, strengthen their faith, and hold fast to the teachings of their early generations.

After more than 100 years, Ma Anli, a Muslim scholar from Yunnan, said in his preface to the *Complement* to *Qingzhen Shiyi*:

> In 1873, I came back from the west; then I came north to take the exam, where I met Mr. Tang Jinhui. He showed me

---

vice director of bureau of the Ministry of Rites (礼部员外郎). Liu Zongyuan was a famous writer and poet in the time of the Tang, his travel notes made a great impact on later generations. He has *The Collections of Liu Hedong*. See Ibid, 127,128.

[1] His name was Ou Yangxiu (欧阳修, 1007-1072), his title is Yongshu (永叔), and his assumed name was Zuiwong (醉翁), from Jiangxi province. He became a Jinshi in 1030 and was appointed as the Hanlin academician, Vice Military affairs Commissioner and so on. He was one of the eight great masters during the Tang and Song, and had *The Collections of Ouyang Wenzhong*. See Ibid, 168,169.

[2] His name was Sushi (苏轼, 1037-1101), title Zizhan (子瞻), assumed name Dongpo Jushi (东坡居士), and he was from Meishan (眉山), Sichuan province. His official career was full of frustrations. But he was very successful in poetry, writing, Ci (a Chinese poetic genre) and painting. He was another one of the eight great masters during the Tang and Song. He had *The Collections of Su Dongpo*. See Ibid. 173.

> Mr. Jin Beigao's *Qingzhen Shiyi*. In response to his request, I read the book with pleasure and found his quotations to be very full and clear and his discussions definite and precise. Indeed, he expressed what elder generations did not.

In his *Dictionary of Islam*, Mr. Jin Yijiu, a contemporary scholar in this field in China, called *Qingzhen Shiyi* a famous Islamic book.

There are many other expressions of praise from other scholars.

Perhaps because it is a valuable work, people have printed it many times, especially in the time of Guangxu, during which it was reprinted at least three times, according to the data we have.

2.2.5 Literature Review

Many scholars mentioned *Qingzhen Shiyi* in their works, among them Bai Shouyi in his *Annals of Muslim figures,* p. 1066; Jin Jitang in his *A Study of the History of Islam in China*, p. 203; Mi Shoujiang and Youjia in their *Outline of the History of Islam in China*, p. 164; Zhang Xiumin in his *The History of Printing in China*, p. 623; Gao Wende in his *Dictionary of Prominent Figures of Nationalities*, p. 367; Yang Huaizhong in his *Islam and Chinese Culture*, p. 421; Fu Tongxian in his *History of Islam in China*, p. 107; Yu Zhengui in the *Encyclopedia of Islam in China*, p. 448, 449, and some others. However, they did no more than a general introduction; they did not study the book in detail.

A great contribution to *Qingzhen Shiyi* was made by Mr. Tang Jinhui in the time of the Qing dynasty and by Mr. Hai Zhengzhong in the present time. They are worthy of consideration as great contributors to the book. Let us spend some time assessing what they did.

Tang Jinhui was born in 1820 and died in 1900. He was a Muslim from Shandong province. He passed the imperial examination in 1861, and was appointed as the vice director of a bureau in the Ministry of Personnel (吏部员外郎). Mr. Tang served as an official for thirty years. He was well acquainted with the works of Wang Daiyu, Liu Zhi and others. He considered them voluminous and inaccessible works; however, he placed much importance on Mr. Jin's *Qingzhen Shiyi*. According to Ma

Zhonglong's preface to the complement of *Qingzhen Shiyi*, Mr. Tang printed *Qingzhen Shiyi* many times. Perhaps he found some of Jin Tianzhu's words too caustic, necessitating some changes to the text. He spent more than ten years doing so. He invited Ma Kaike, Ma Anli, Ma Jian, Bai Guang Yuan, Ma Chunli, Jiang Runfen, Ha Xianzhao, Zhao Jiaqi, Gong Chuqiao, Wangyun, Makui, Feng Jing, Mu Xingjun, Xu Wenyong, Wang Tingxiang, Ma Dan, Ma Yuanrui, Ding Yuquan, Mi Xielin, Shi Wentian, Liu Jingzhi and other Muslim scholars to consult relevant references. "Anything they find like Confucianism doctrine, they should write it down and add it to the text of *Qingzhen Shiyi*, so that people can understand easily." That is how the book, *A Complement to Qingzhen Shiyi*, came into being.

Compared to the original book, this book is richer in content and smoother in expression. It quotes more evidence from Confucian books, and as a result, it seems more abundant in terms of grounds of argument. However, its shortcomings are also obvious.

First, it changed the original text so much that the reader cannot recognize which is the original text and which is the complement. Some scholars criticized Mr. Tang for this.[1] Secondly, some very important contents of the original text were removed; therefore, the text no longer reveals anything about the political situation that Chinese Muslims were facing at the time of the author. Thirdly, it is not as easy for common people to understand as the original, which contravenes Mr. Jin's purpose. Based on that, we prefer to say that the complement is an entirely new book rather than a variant of *Qingzhen Shiyi* itself.

To have *Qingzhen Shiyi* published in its new form, a valuable study was done in 2002 by Hai Zhengzhong, a researcher at The Hui Study Centre of Ningxia University, Ningxia, China. The text covers varied topics, which should logically be separated from each other, with each topic being given a title. However, the original text has no separations between different topics, leaving aside the given titles for each topic. The punctuation marks in the text are not as easy to understand as modern marks. Moreover, many of the

---

1 See for example: Bai Shouyi, *Brief History of Islam in China*, (Yinchuan: Ningxia Publishing House, 2000), 109.

characters are of complex forms and are read from top to bottom which people are not accustomed to reading today. Mr. Hai edited the text, separated its topics, gave a title to each one, added modern punctuation marks, changed the characters into modern ones, and made the direction of the written language start from left to right. Most importantly, he translated the text from ancient Chinese into modern Chinese, which enables everyone to understand the text. Therefore, we should say that Hai is the pioneer who introduced *Qingzhen Shiyi* in its new form to contemporary readers.

Nevertheless, the edition produced by Mr. Hai has some shortcomings, among which are the following:

1. There are some mistakes in the separation; see, for example, pages 46, 133, 153-154.

2. Mr. Hai translated some sentences incorrectly; see, for instance, pages 90 and 117.

3. Some titles are not suitable; see, for example, pages 4 and 32.

4. Many parts of the text have been deleted. This might have been done by Mr. Hai because of some special considerations. However, as a result, people cannot read those parts, which are regarded as very interesting.

5. More regrettably, Ma Tingfu's preface was wrongly separated into two parts in the edition that Mr. Hai used, so he treated the second part of the preface as the preface of Ma Tingfu because it was accompanied by a stamp, and the first part as part of the letter to the senior minister. As a result, he brought the second part to the front of book and the first part to the back, along with the letter.

Beside Mr. Tang Jinhui and Mr. Hai Zhengzhong, Mr. Wan Jingsen made a valuable study of Jin Tianzhu's life and his thoughts as presented in *Qingzhen Shiyi*, however, he neither said anything about the background of the author and his work, nor did he translate the text into modern Chinese or English. In addition, Mrs. Xuelian wrote an article in which she introduced two editions of the manuscript that are stored in the Dalian library, made an evaluation of them, and criticized some scholars for their opinions regarding the first edition of the book.

2.3 About This Study

2.3.1 The edition on which this study is based

When I presented my initial dissertation proposal, Professor Ajmal Abdur-Razzaq Al-Aidurus, Deputy Dean of ISTAC at that time, suggested to me that I chose a manuscript in the Chinese language. Therefore, I contacted Mr. Hai Zhengzhong, an Associate Professor at Ningxia University and a close friend. In response to my request, he sent me two manuscripts: one, Zhang Shizhong's *Guizhen Zongy*i (归真总义) which is in the field of theology; the other, Jin Tianzhu's *Qingzhen Shiyi*, which became the subject of this study. The edition he sent me was the one first published in the second year of Quangxu (1876) and then republished in 1987 from a photocopy of the original by the Ningxia Academy of Social Sciences. After an initial period of study, I felt that I needed to see other editions of the manuscript.

By that time, I had learned about the existence of two editions of the manuscript in Dalian Library, China. When I told my supervisor, Professor Osman Bakar, about my idea, he encouraged me to go there and see them so I did that. Therefore, this study has been carried out based on the edition published in the second year of Guangxu (1876) compared with the two in Dalian library, the first of which is the one that was published in the thirty-third year of Qianlong (1769) and the second, is another edition published in the second year of Guangxu (1876)

Regarding the physical characteristics of the manuscript, the said edition consists of 140 pages; each page is 250mm long and 155mm wide; the page frame is 180mm long and 135mm wide. On each page there are 9 lines, each of which contains 20 characters. The number of characters on each page is 180; therefore, the total number is: 140 ×180 = 15,200 characters. However, due to the empty spaces, we can conclude that the actual number of characters in this manuscript is around 15,000 characters.

As for the contents, there are 6 prefaces, written by Hu Huiyuan (胡汇源), the author, Shi Kezong (石可宗), the publisher, Ma Tingfu (马廷辅) and Chen Dashao (陈大韶). This does not include Hu Huiyuan's poem, which comes after his preface, and the author's letter to the senior minister that was incorrectly placed as part of Ma Tingfu's preface. This is followed by the main body of the text. On the first page of the text, the following information is given: the title of the book at the top right-hand side of the page; the names of the reviewers, Chen Dashao, Hu Huiyuan and Ma Tingfu, with their places of origin; the author's name and his place of origin, and those of two proofreaders, Ke Yuandu (科元度) and He Yuanjiao (和圆峤). The term, Nan (男), appears on the page before these two names.[1]

2.3.2 What I have done for the study

The contents of the text fall mainly into the category of jurisprudence (*fiqh*) and the objectives of rules (*maqasid al-Shari'ah*). It covers, for example, *taharah*, prayer, fasting, *zakat*, food, drink and so on; and the author gives answers to questions raised by people as to why Muslim practices differ from those of others. In addition, the author discusses with a "guest" some points of the Islamic faith, criticizes other religions, especially Catholicism, Buddhism and Taoism. Moreover, he presents his own opinion on *tasawwuf* and some other matters. In brief, the text contains a variety of topics.

However, the original text is like running water. It has not been separated according to topics, has no titles, no commas, nor any other form of punctuation normally found in modern writing, which makes it difficult to understand. My major task is to introduce this manuscript to English readers. To do that, I had to first understand the text well myself. Therefore, I had to read it again and again. Mr. Hai's study helped me to a certain extent, but I found that he had made many errors of comprehension in his study and, as a result, errors of titling and punctuation. I discussed my observations with him several times and he accepted my opinions regarding those mistakes. Then, I divided the text into various parts according to topic, gave a title to

[1] It refers to one of the two possible meanings: son, which means the two men are the two sons of the author; or the title of the last rank among the five ranks of nobility in ancient China which are Gong (公), Hou (侯), Bo (伯), Zi (子) and Nan (男). I prefer the second meaning rather than first one because their family names are different from the author's which is 'Jin' (金), Chinese people do not change their family names unless in very special or dangerous situations.

each part, separated it into paragraphs, and added punctuation to them. When I was sure that my understanding was good enough, I translated the entire text into English. In addition, I carried out a historical study and made some commentaries and notes on the text, followed by a conclusion. Furthermore, when it was time to edit the whole text, I made some changes to the prefaces and the letter in terms of their order.

2.3.3 Objectives of the study

Throughout this study, I wanted to achieve the following objectives:
(1) To know when Islam arrived in China and the origins of Chinese Muslims in the early eras of their history there;
(2) To know the status of Chinese Muslims at various periods of history;
(3) To show some of the efforts made by Chinese Muslim scholars (*Ulama'*) for the revival of the Muslim Ummah in China;
(4) To show the adverse circumstances that Chinese Muslims went through during the Qing dynasty;
(5) To introduce English readers to the academic achievement of one Chinese Muslim scholar.

2.3.4 Research questions of the study

This study will try to answer the following questions:
(1) When did Islam start to spread and how did the number of Muslims increase in China?
(2) What was the situation and status of Muslims in China during the Qing dynasty and for the one thousand or more years before that?
(3) What kinds of problems did Muslims face in Chinese society in different periods of history?
(4) What efforts were made by Chinese Muslim scholars for the Muslim Ummah in China?
(5) Were Chinese Muslim scholars aware of the comparative study of religions that arose for the first time in the West in the 19th century?
(6) What is the significance of Jin Tianzhu's *Qingzhen Shiyi*?

2.3.5 The Methodology of the Study

To carry out this study, I adopted the following methodologies:
(1) Library research
I conducted library research, not only in Malaysia but also in China, with the view of collecting sufficient data and information about the manuscript and its author.
(2) Editing the manuscript
I edited the selected manuscript that I have translated in this study.
(3) Translation and commentary
This book was written in 1737 in classical Chinese language, which is different from today's Mandarin. My main task has been to translate the edited form of the book into English. It is my hope that this translation will provide a new source of knowledge of classical Chinese thought for those who do not have the ability to read classical or modern Chinese.

2.3.6 Chapters of this study

This study is categorized into six chapters: Chapter One is a historical study; Chapter Two is about the author's life and his works; Chapter Three is the English translations of the edited prefaces; Chapter Four is the English translation of the main body of the edited text; Chapter Five is my commentary and comments on the text; Chapter Six is the conclusion. I also added an appendix which consists of: (1) the English translation of Chen Dashso's commentary on the main body of the text; (2) the English translation of the author's letter to the senior minister; (3) the edited original text of each preface, the main body, Chen Dashao's comments and the letter.

2.3.7. The significance of this study

(1) This study is significant in that it gives us a better understanding of Islam and other thoughts and beliefs in 18th century China.
Islam as a religion and Muslims as a community have existed in China for more than one thousand years. China's Muslim population today has been variously estimated at more than twenty million. The period of the end of the Ming and the beginning of the Qing is the golden age of Chinese Muslim

scholarship, during which the greatest Chinese Muslim scholars lived. Today, however, very little is known about their writings. This study is an attempt to present one aspect of Chinese understanding of Islam in an earlier century.

(2) This study is also significant for highlighting the historic dialogue between Islam and other Chinese religions, namely Buddhism, Confucianism, Taoism and Catholicism. It therefore aims to contribute towards a better mutual understanding between the Chinese people and Muslims, especially in Southeast Asia. In general, the *Ulama'* in contemporary China do not interact with scholars of other religions. This study, however, shows that Chinese Muslims did engage in dialogue with members of other faiths two hundred years ago.

(3) Finally, this study provides indicators of a strategy for Muslims in contemporary China to deal with the government and with non-Muslims.

It seems that the author wrote this book to help solve social problems that had arisen from non-Muslims' misunderstanding and ignorance of Islam. The author tried to show that Islam was not entirely foreign to the Chinese religious consciousness. With that view in mind, he tried to show the similarities between Islam and other Chinese religions, especially Confucianism, the main religion in China at that time. Muslims in contemporary China need to understand how best to handle the relationship with the government as well as with other non-Muslim groups in China. Jin Tianzhu's book may be of value for this purpose.

PART TWO:
THE TRANSLATION OF THE EDITED TEXTS

CHAPTER THREE:

TRANSLATION OF THE EDITED PREFACES

3.1 Preface of the Republishing in the Second Year of Guangxu

The book of *Qingzhen Shiyi* (清真释疑) was published by one of the virtuous men of the past. The main aim of the book is to elaborate clearly and definitively the concept of the True God and His Oneness, and to expound the five religious obligations of Islam and the five constant virtues related to human relations[1] which are in the 30 parts of the Holy Quran. Islam is the noblest religion. It can purify people's hearts and minds, rectify their intentions, and help them to know themselves as well as God. Whoever follows its doctrine will benefit, and those who do not will lose. All who read the book appreciate it. However, the original edition has been lost, and to disseminate it, we decided to reprint it. We narrate this briefly to record the whole course of the incident. If people who are interested in spreading culture, they are allowed to prepare papers and publish this book to spread it widely.

3.2 Preface of Shi Kezong

My first ancestor was from Tian Fang (天方).[2] Islam began in Mecca and is primarily [a call] to obey God's orders and to worship Him. It started to spread in China during the Sui and Tang dynasties (581-907), and is like the overall aim of Confucian doctrine, which is to purify man's mind and protect

---

[1] They are called in Chinese '五常' (five constant virtues), namely: Ren (仁, benevolence), Yi (义, righteousness), Li (礼, propriety), Zhi (智, wisdom) and Xin (信, fidelity). See: *Modern Chinese English Dictionary*, 756.

[2] The term "Tian Fang" means Mecca. See Ma Yuyi, *Historical Records of Islam in China*, (Yinchuan: Ningxia Publishing House, 2000), 28.

his nature. However, very few people can understand the Muslim language,[1] and they have lost their own language because they have been in China for a long time. Furthermore, they are uncertain about Islam. How can they blame the non-Muslims for their suspicion?

Jin Tianzhu (金天柱) was afraid that people would forget Islam, so he wrote this book with the aim that it would be circulated throughout society. In it he presented his ideas by using Confucian terms and principles to facilitate an understanding of Islam. Whoever reads this book and studies it repeatedly will understand its contents and the author's ideas and will believe that all wise men (prophets and others) have the same mentality, even though the world is vast. Furthermore, he or she will not be suspicious of Islam anymore.

Because of war, people were forced to leave their homes and wander about; as a result, nothing remained of the first edition of the book. Some brothers collected money to cut blocks for printing and they asked me to proofread. I agreed because I did not wish for Mr. Jin's good intentions to be forgotten, and that is why I also wrote this preface to record the story of the matter.

---- By Shi Kezong in Zhenzhou (真州), 215, the fifth leap month, Second Year of Guangxu (1876)

3.3 Preface of Hu Huiyuan

It is important for the doctrine of religious schools to be believed in and not doubted, for, if this was the case, its adherents would be disloyal (halfhearted), and they would eventually fracture into groups. They will either lose the right way or rebel against their own religion and join other religions; this phenomenon can be seen everywhere. Our sage's sect[3] had 72 students, each with his own understanding of Dao (principle or truth), except

---

[1] It was mainly Arabic and Persian in the beginning of history of Islam in China and also some central Asia languages afterwards.

[2] It is the name of a town in Jiangsu province, located in delta of the Changjiang River (the Yangtze River).

[3] He means Confucius.

for Bushi (卜氏),[1] who was well known among later generations because of his deep belief in the Confucian doctrine. He carried on his teacher's work and taught beside the western river.[2] He wrote a book titled *Cai Shi Shuo* (蔡师说),[3] in which he presented Confucian doctrine as it was without any change to his teacher's ideas. Do you think that no one slandered him? No, there were slanderers, yet he managed to remove people's doubts using his own language to explain the truth, and the suspicions melted away like dissolved ice, so that the order of Jue Li (闕里)[4] was maintained.

Mr. Jin was the Bushi (卜氏) of Muslims. Islam came to China in the time of the Sui and Tang dynasties and it spread from one generation to another. Because of that, today there are many Muslims in China.[5] If a tree grows luxuriant with branches and leaves, its roots might be rotten. If a stream of water is very long, its source might be lost. Although Muslims followed Islamic doctrine and did not change their minds, they did not understand the purpose and principles of the Islamic obligations and regulations that they practiced in their daily life. Due to this uncertainty, non-Muslims are also suspicious of Islam. Since the time I started my career as lecturer, I have been to a lot of places, where I met many Muslims. Five or six out of ten among them are just like I described above; the intelligent among them studied a few things and presented themselves as masters of great learning and integrity. However, I noticed no one as brilliant as Mr. Bei Gao.

---

[1] He means Bushang (卜商), one of Confucius's students, whose title is Zixia (子夏).

[2] It is located in Wei state (魏国) which was in today's Henan province.

[3] We have tried hard to find information about the said book but found nothing.

[4] It is the name of the place where Confucius was teaching.

[5] We do not have any information about the number of Muslims in China at the author's time. According to Bai Shouyi and Jin Jitang, it was about 50 million in the time of The Republic of China. See their *Essays of Huizu, Huijiao and Huimin*, (Hong Kong: Zhong Shan Book Company, 1974.), 1.

In the spring of 1745, I suffered a setback in the Southern Palace,[1] and so I traveled to Beijing where I stayed at the residence. During that period, Mr. Beigao visited me several times. After some days, he showed me his book entitled *Qingzhen Shiyi Lun* (清真释疑论) and asked me to write a preface. I agreed, and when I read the book I found that it was very detailed with words strung together like beads. Furthermore, he presented his ideas in an orderly and obvious way, just like the sun on a sunny day. The more I read the book the more I liked it, and I thought that if a person studied his religion so deeply, he could be considered as one firmly convinced. Such firm belief comes from having no doubts in one's mind; and this in turn comes from having no distracting thoughts in the society. The ideas that the author presented in this book are as clear as the sun and the moon, and the writing is as lucid and lively as a running river. If you truly believe in something, then people will do the same. When this book is published, the suspicions that have existed for a thousand years will disappear like a little snow falling on a hot stove. I rub my eyes and wait for the day when Islam spreads all over China; at that time, nothing will need clarification. This is my preface for the book.

----By Hu Huiyuan, a country-mate of the author, Fifth month of the Chinese lunar calendar, Tenth Year of Qianlong (1745),

3.4 Hu Huiyuan's poem in seven characters:

The minds of the people have been confined for a long time,
Who could imagine that an unusual book would emerge from beneath a pillow?
Containing tens of thousands of words, all of which will be immortalized,
I read it a hundred times a day.
God's will has been sent down to the earth,

[1] It was an unofficial reference to the ministry of rites. See Li Kairong, *Chinese-English Dictionary of Politics and Laws*, (Beijing: Book Publishing House, 2002), 165. He means that he failed the imperial examination.

It will show the power of the western teaching[1] as much as wind and thunder do.
It is a pity that such works are so few,
I believe that very soon the book will spread all over the country.

3.5 The Preface of Ma Tingfu

Since ancient times, a great path (doctrine and principle of religion) has been handed down, like the sun and the moon moving in their orbits and the rivers running on the earth. There is nothing to be suspected; therefore, there is nothing to dispute. However, the world is wide and there are differences between China and foreign countries. Furthermore, the way people understand doctrines and thoughts and the doors they enter are different; therefore, they consider things that are unfamiliar to them as unorthodox. As a result, they make unfair comments against them, so that excellent words have been neglected and the truth is hidden. Hence, those who set their minds on promoting the truth should clarify and clear the theory in a way that is easy for people to understand. Thereby suspicions will disappear like ice that dissolves when it meets fire. Islam, for instance, began in Mecca, which is in the western lands, and was handed down to Muhammad from the earliest ancestor. Its source was distant, its course was long, and its doctrine detailed and exhaustive.

It was more than one thousand years ago in the time of Zhen Guan (贞观) of the Tang Dynasty (627-650) that Prophet Muhammad sent his companion, Saad ibn Abi Waqqas, to China to disseminate Islam. It is composed of five guiding principles: Recitation (of shahadah or the declaration [of faith]), prayer (salat), fasting, zakah and pilgrimage (Hajj); and four regulations: filial obedience, faithfulness, etiquette and modesty. Islam is a great religion because it requires people to practice these five principles and four regulations at the same time. There is, thus, no difference between Islam and Confucianism in general. However, there are some

[1] In Chinese, the term 'western' (西域) refers to the Muslim world including the Xinjiang area at that time; and 'western teaching' here means the Islamic doctrine.

specific regulations in Islam in relation to drinking, eating, and dress, marriage and funeral ceremonies; possibly because Muslims prefer simplicity and practice cleanliness. These have been handed down from one generation to the next without any change.

The belief of some Muslims who do not practice Islam well and who do not fully understand its teachings is mixed with doubt, and they think that the rules are too difficult to practice. Some of them went so far as to give up their own faith, abandon the regulations of their predecessors and embrace other religions. Such suspicions should be clarified. At the same time, when non-Muslims see the extreme to which some Muslims practice Islamic teachings, they slander Islam and speak badly about it without taking the time to first examine and study [what they attack]. These suspicions, too, should be cleared.

I could not achieve my goal. In the twelfth year of Yongzheng (1735), I luckily passed an imperial examination held in my town. Then, in the tenth year of Qianlong (1745), I traveled to the capital city to take an examination. After the spring examination,[1] it happened that I met Mr. Jin Beigao, who was working in the Translators' Institute (四译馆)[2] of Hanlin Academy (翰

[1] The examination system in the Ming (1368-1644) and Qing dynasty (1616-1911) was as follows: a provincial exam (乡试) was held every three years and those who passed it were called Juren (举人). The following year, they would go to the capital city to take the metropolitan examination (会试) that would be held in the spring and those who passed it, were called Jinshi (进士).

[2] Its original name was '四夷馆', means institute of foreigners. It was established in the fifth year of Yongle (永乐) in the time of the Ming dynasty (1407) as an institute of translation. At the time of the Qing, its name was changed to '四译馆' and subordinated to the Hanlin Academy. It was composed of eight departments: Tatar, Mongol, Nvzhen (the ancestor of Manzu), Huihui (Muslims in mainland China), Tibet, India, Baiyi (Daizu), Gaochang (Ughur) and Burma. There were 20 instructors and 6 interpreter clerks for Korean. See Zhang Zhengliang, *The Great Dictionary of Official Positions in Ancient China*, (Zhengzhou: Henan Publishing House, 1990), 340.

林院)[1]. He is refined, courteous and urbane; he regulates and orders everything: study, work, retiring at night, rising in the morning, and so on. His mind is pure; therefore, he deals with people honestly; his nature is out of the common run, this indicates that he was very much influenced by the Confucian books.[2]

Later, he showed me his *Qingzhen Shiyi* (清真释疑), and when I read the book I felt that he had used the pens of Han Yu (韩愈), Liu Zongyuan (柳宗元), Ou Yangxiu (欧阳修) and Su Shi (苏轼) to interpret the profound ancient books of Islam. The book is as clear and easy to understand as watching fire; nothing obstructs your view. It makes the reader feel that he is meeting an old friend; the content of the book is very familiar to his mind, and the words are read smoothly. Not only will this book leave non-Muslims with nothing to argue and suspect about Islam, but it will also help doubtful Muslims to recover their conscience, strengthen their faith, and hold fast to the teachings of their early generations.

Beigao's book will play a significant role in guiding people to the right path and purifying their hearts. Indeed, it is a bridge to Islam and will be an enduring masterpiece. As for the words that appear slanderous towards other people or religions, they are quoted to refute their arguments, not because the author enjoys doing so. Perhaps he did that because if you do not touch the body of a thing (a religion, for example), the right path will not become manifest. I understand his intention, but would those who read this book be able to excuse Beigao for his embarrassment [of them]?

Beigao entrusted me with writing a preface, and to fulfill his request I wrote these words. I hope our brothers can encourage each other to strengthen our faith and practice Islamic teachings.

---

[1] It is the name of an Academic institution first established at the time of the Tang and continued into the coming dynasties of China with different functions. It was in charge of modifying history, academic writings, and interpreting as well as examinations. See Ibid, 1036.

[2] He means the main Confucian books that we have mentioned before. To know the titles of the books,

----By MaTingfu, Junlushi, a younger brother of the author from Yunnan, in a hotel in Beijing, in the tenth year of Qianlong (1745).

3.6 The Preface of Chen Dashao

Man's heart is the origin of custom, and custom is the final purpose of education. Today, it has become a social trend to care for humanity in our society. Rules and regulations are set out clearly, and education has improved and become more widespread all over the country. However, if you scrutinize our society you will see that people dare to break the rules and regulations and cheat each other. Why have such things not been rooted out?

In the second year of Yongzheng (1724), I was sent as a Jinshi (进士)[1] chosen by my town to stay in the capital city, where I had an opportunity to meet some famous officials and listen to them. I took their words for my guidance and continue to repeat them, expecting that I could become a pure and authentic man, for I think this is the right way to preserve our education. Fortunately, after a year I joined the class of instructors to study with them; the Gonghous (公侯),[2] and the Guizhou (贵胄),[3] are refined and cultivated. During the days that I was studying, I took as my motto "敦伦循纪，清洁真实", which means, "Be faithful in morals, follow the rules and regulations, be honest and upright, pure and sincere." If a guest came to see me, I would present these words as a gift. Mr. Jin is one of my close friends in the office. He is someone who supports traditional education.

I had a very close association with Beigao for a long time. He always brought me to the Translators Institute and taught me personally. He dresses neatly; his food and drink is pure. He appears very gentle and cultivated, and he does not like to listen to the words of Buddhism and Taoism. I got along well with him, and his speech, in which he calls to respecting aged people

[1] "Jinshi" is the metropolitan graduate with honours (designation of the few best graduates of the national civil service recruitment examinations).

[2] It is the second class of five ranks of nobility in ancient China.

[3] It refers to the sons of noble men.

and obeying parents, is very pleasant to my ear. Is this the religion described by some as boundless and meaningless?

One day, Beigao came to me and said, "People are talking about my religion based on hearsay." Then he showed me his *Qingzhen Shiyi* (清真释疑). I found the ideas that he presented in the book to be sensible, and the practices he enjoined in it are in accordance with the doctrine of the [Golden] Mean. There are only a few things that are slightly different from the main culture in our society. Muslims are sincere in studying Confucian books, taking part in official exams, serving the country as officials, and practicing the feudal order of importance and seniority in human relationships. They deal with the monarch, fathers, brothers and friends in the right way.

Fortunately, famous contemporary scholars have guided me for more than ten years, so I have a great interest in studying human nature and customs. While Mr. Beigao was feeling sorry and concerned because of people's suspicions, I said, "Do not feel sad. Very soon, when this book is published, people will be enlightened. Furthermore, it is not only your religion that faces such a problem; even family members have different opinions. Take different prefectures and villages for example. People's attire and foods are different even if they live close to one another. Korea, for instance, is very near to China. Their rules and regulations are handed down from one generation to the next. It is said that they are the offspring of Yin Shaoshi (殷少师).[1] We do not know about their food and drink; however,

[1] He is from the royal family at the time of the Shang dynasty (1600 B.C.-1300 B.C.), and the uncle of the Emperor and one of his subjects. His name is Bigan (比干), he was given Yin Shaoshi (殷少师) as the title of his nobility. Yet he was killed later by the Emperor, and his son ran into the Changlin Mountains. When Shang was replaced by Western Zhou (西周, 1046 B.C.-771 B.C.), the son returned and the Emperor of the Zhou dynasty gave him Lin (林) as his family name. It is popular knowledge that he is the first ancestor of all people in the world whose family name is "Lin". Every year, many members of the Lin family from Korea, Thailand and Malaysia go to Weihui (卫辉), Henan

we know that their headgear and shoes, as well as their attire are totally different from those of our society. People know that their ancestor's regulations were like that, so they say nothing against them. When this book is published, people will know what Islam is all about. It would be not reasonable for them to remain suspicious after that."

Beigao entrusted me to make a commentary, so I have written these words in the front of the book in which I reviewed after the days of our first meeting and our conversations with each other.

----By Chen Dashao from Songzi, Chubei,[1]a selected country magistrate and a student of the author, In the beginning of the third year of Qianlong (1738).

3.7 The Author's Preface

Qingzhen (清真) is my religion's objective. Why did I write *Qinzhen Shiyi*? [I wrote it] because people of other religions do not understand the faith and practices of Muslims, and their doubts and suspicions that have existed for more than 1000 years have yet to be clarified. They do not understand why Muslims do such things[2] because they have not read Islamic books and so their suspicions have increased and they have carried on endless discussions about Islam. As a result, it was said that Muslims do not follow the lunar calendar; [3] instead they make their own with a year of 360 days. They celebrate with each other in groups for their own New Year. Some people

---

province of China to hold a ceremony of their first ancestor and an international conference. From http://www.google.com.my, 18/10/2008.

[1] Chubei (楚北) is today's Hubei (湖北) province; Songzi (松滋) is located in the southern part of the province. See The Editorial Comitee of Etymology Dictionary of Name of Places in China, *Etymology Dictionary of Name of Places in China*, (Shanghai Dictionary Publishing House, 1995), 32.

[2] It means the Islamic obligations like *salat*, fasting and other practices which are different from theirs.

[3] The traditional Chinese calendar was the official one at that time.

said that Muslims speak a different language, wear different clothes and shun certain food and drink.[1]

Furthermore, it is said that Muslims eat meat and fish during the fasting month,[2] and they do not eat and drink in the daytime. In addition to that, we don't know which God Muslims worship. We see them gather at night and disperse before dawn, and men mix with women. Moreover, there are people who say that Muslims cut their hair to destroy the body that was given [to them] by their parents. All these questions have not been answered.

The reason these questions remain unanswered is not because we are short of qualified personnel, but may be because the older generations paid more focus to the main elements of Islamic teachings and they felt that these kinds of questions were not worth clarifying. In the past, Mr. Wang Daiyu (王岱舆) wrote '*ZhengJiao Zhenquan*' (正教真诠, *The Real Commentary on the True Religion*), *Qingzhendaxue'* (清真大学, *The Islamic Great Learning*) and *Xizhen Zhengda*' (希真正答, *The True Answers forthe Senior Asker*). *Qingzhen Zhinan* (清真指南, *The Islamic Guidance*) is the handwork of Mr. Ma Wenbin. Later, Mr. Liuzhi wrote '*Tianfang Xingli*' (天方性理, *Islamic Philosophy*), *Tianfang Dianli* (天方典礼, *Islamic Decrees and Regulations*) and others; I can't mention them all.

The authors' aims were mainly to guide Muslims and to expound the teachings of Islam by quoting from Islamic books. The contents include how to know and worship God, as well as general knowledge on daily life. Moreover, these books are big. Who would spend time reading them? People of other religions had already formed their opinions about Muslims. Such people would deny even pure gold and beautiful jade. Furthermore, the issues mentioned above have not been discussed in those books. As a result, non-Muslims do not have a book [on Islam] that is easy to understand, which is why those doubts exist till today.

---

[1] It means that Muslims differ from other people who eat whatever they want, as long as it is edible.

[2] Acording to their religion, the requirement is to refrain from eating meat and fish; however, they can eat vegetarian meals during the time of fasting.

Older generations did not clarify these doubts, not because they were unable to do so, but because they thought that it was unimportant that non-Muslims talked about Muslims if there was no difference between the former and the latter in practicing the feudal order of seniority in human relationships. They felt that those issues were not that important; therefore, they let people confound right and wrong. Arguing with them [they felt,] was unnecessary.

Who am I? How dare I write to show people that I am more intelligent and moral than older generations? Furthermore, the world is vast; therefore, customs, languages, attires and rules differ. Even in China there are similarities and differences, so surprise is unwarranted, if the guiding principles and discipline is alike except for slight differences. Mengzi said, "Yangzhu (杨朱) doesn't want the monarch[1]; Mozhai (墨翟) doesn't want the father."[2] Also, Buddhism and Taoism combined to acknowledge the respected teacher as a father. Thus, they made the monarch and father nothing but a [superfluous] form. Eventually they abandoned their monarch as well as their fathers.[3] Therefore, they have neither.

On the contrary, while Islam purifies the guiding principles and strengthens discipline, everything still has its own basis and evidence, rendering it completely different from the doctrines of Yang (杨) and Mo (

---

[1] Yangzhu (杨朱) was from the Wei state and one of the great thinkers in the beginning of the warring states, a period of history of China (475-221 B.C.) The year he was born and died is not known. Yangzhu disliked cooperating with the ruling classes and preferred to live in seclusion; this was why Confucius, who called to obey the emperor and serve the state, criticized him and his followers.

[2] Mozhai (墨翟, 476-390 B.C.) was from the Lu state and was the representative of Mohism, a school of thought in ancient China. Mozhai studied Confucianism, then gave up it and established his own theory which advocates people to love and help each other, and the states to coexist and not fight each other.

[3] It means that they abandoned two of three guiding principles which are, "the monarch guides his subjects, the father guides his sons and the husband guides his wife."

墨), as well as Buddhism and Taoism. When people meet those who have rejected the relationship between the monarch and his subjects, abolished discipline, and cut off the relationship between fathers and sons, why do they not investigate and talk about them? This behavior of theirs [seems to be] reserved for their encounters with Muslims.

It should be remembered that Islam has continued to spread for more than a thousand years since Muslims came to China during the Sui and Tang (隋唐) dynasties. During this lengthy period, Muslims have rendered services to the country as much as the Confucians have, with no difference between the two. Those who doubt Islam do not know its teachings, and they refuse to learn because they have already formed their own opinions about it. As a result, Islamic theory, instead of spreading in society, has been lost, disappearing within the lips and teeth of the common people. How sad this is!

Although I have not done a detailed study on the scholarship of the Hui and the Han, I know in my mind how it was created and developed. I also have some experience, so I could not bite my tongue and say nothing. An ancient wise man said, "I speak, not because I want to but [because] I must."[1] Besides, I studied Islamic books when I was a small boy. Now I am an official figure in the Translators' Institute. Whenever I find similarities and differences in the ancient books and records, I like to clarify them for people by quoting copiously from multiple sources and giving examples. In this way I hope to clear up the suspicions and help [people] deal harmoniously with each other. Furthermore, we have the same monarch and government. How can we allow people to be suspicious of each other or to slander one another? How can we sit and listen to words of denigration?

I was compelled by the reproach of people of other religions to write this *Qingzhen Shiyi* (清真释疑). I hope that my explanations are in accordance with the wishes of the older generations; furthermore, I wish to

---

[1] Mencius was asked by one of his students: "People say that you like to argue, why?" Mencius said: "Do I like that? I have no choice but to do that." See Chen Puqing, *Translation and Commentary of Four Books*, (Guangzhou: Huacheng Publishing House, 1998), 341.

interpret the doctrine of Islam for the people. To achieve this purpose, I expressed in this book my superficial view, which may help people in our society to recognize the similarities between Islam and Confucianism. As a result, their suspicions may disappear quickly. It is also a humble supplement to Islamic theory.

----By Jintianzhu, from Shicheng (石城)[1], an instructor of the Translators' Institute, Hanlin Academy. 5th day, the second month of the Chinese lunar calendar, Third Year of Qianlong (1738).

3.8 Chen Dashao's commentary on the author's preface

The sea is wide; the sky is vast, the branches are in length and breadth, and the factions are different. The world is great and therefore, the *Dao* (road, way, principle, doctrine of religion) is great. The sages and the men of virtue gallop (spread) their thinking across thousands of kilometers; the brilliant men use their eyes and their ears to probe different fields of knowledge. They make varied thoughts close to each other and come together. As a result, a right system of thinking would be established. Whoever holds such opinion, he is worthy enough for you to follow him and spread his thought. Mr. Jin Tianzhu wrote a preface in full and clear words after he finished the body of *Qingzhen Shiyi*; it can be compared with the chapter of *Yuandao.*[2] It elucidated the principles of Islam; at the same time, it deepened the theory of Confucianism, and integrated the teachings of the two into one another.

---

[1] It refers to Nanjing (南京) which is the capital city of Jiangsu province.

[2] It was written by Hanyu in the time of the Tang dynasty, in which the author summarised the principles of Confucian doctrine, showed that there is no contradiction between the feudal order in human relationships and ethics, and stressed the importance of both the cultivation of individual characters and the administration of states. See Zhang Dainian, *the Dictionary of Congzi.* (Shang Hai: Dictionary Publishing House, 1993), 656.

CHAPTER FOUR:

TRANSLATION OF THE MAIN BODY OF THE EDITED TEXT

4.1 General Words

The doctrine of my religion is to worship the only God, Allah, and to turn back to Him. This doctrine was clarified by the father of messengers[1] and sincerely practiced by his later generations. Muslims all over the world, whether they are in China or abroad, are like each other in terms of practices and actions. They number more than ten million. Some of them are capable only of following the teaching of Islam. Some can learn Arabic, whilst others can write books. Why? This is because people are different in terms of intelligence. Some of them are worthy, some are intelligent, some are stupid, and some are incompetent. In addition to that, their specializations are also different. How can those who are unable to explain the basic teachings of Islam eliminate people's doubts?

Today, many people in China talk about our religion. They say that Islam is heretical and Muslims are prickly and obstinate people. Muslims who did not learn [about Islam] do not know what it is all about. How will they answer the questions raised by non-Muslims? Even those who are learned only in Confucian doctrine, like my generation, for example; some of them learned about Confucianism in their childhood, but they never studied Islamic books; therefore, they do not have firmly rooted knowledge. How are they to thoroughly understand people's doubts and suspicions or answer them clearly and easily? Similarly, those who studied Islamic books rather than Confucian [sources] are unable to clarify the teachings and basic articles of Islam. It is only those who are learned in both and can compare

---

[1] The author refers to Adam, the first man on the earth.

them that are capable of enlightening others. Suppose there are scholars as I described above who maintain that Islam is a heretical belief and that Muslims are prickly and obstinate people. Today, Muslims follow the three cardinal guides (三纲)[1] and the five constant virtues (五常)[2] specified in the feudal ethical code, as do the followers of Confucius. How do people reject the relationship between the ruler and his subjects and between father and sons? Why do they violate the law of propagation to seek the so-called realm of seclusion and silence?[3]

4.2 Food and Drink

As for the teachings of my religion, they cover fasting, prayer, celebration,[4] food and drink, hats and clothes, funerals and the offering of sacrifices to the spirits of the dead.[5] They have different degrees and forms and should not be misused. People of other religions have spoken about Islam without knowing the details of its doctrine. Oh, how they misunderstood! These people did not read the book of Confucius, in which the chapter of *Xiangdang* (乡党)[6] describes several circumstances in which animal meats cannot be eaten. These are when meat is slaughtered improperly; when the right condiments have not been added to it; it is putrid and spoiled, when the colour of the food and its smell have changed; when it is cooked incorrectly

---

[1] They are: 君为臣纲: emperor or king guides subjects; 父为子纲：father guides sons; 夫为妻纲, husband guides wife.

[2] Which are: 仁, benevolence, 义：righteousness, 礼：propriety, 智：wisdom, 信: fidelity.

[3] He means Buddhism and Taoism which encourage people to not get married and live in temples as monks and nuns.

[4] It means the celebration of Eid al-Fitri.

[5] Chinese Muslims never use this term to express this meaning, instead, we call it Guo Amal or Guo Niyyati which means to make charitable deeds by inviting Ahongs (normally Imams of mosques) and some religious men to recite Quran and make Dua; providing good food for them to eat; giving them some money as sadaqah (charity).

[6] It is the title of one of the chapters of *Lunyu* (the analects of Confucius).

or at the wrong time; alcohol as well as jerked (dried) beef that are bought from market, and meat offered as a sacrifice to a god or the ancestors when it is more than three days old. These prohibitions are meant to protect people's property and lives and to embody the good intention of Tian (天) and Di (地)[1] that likes living things to live rather than be hurt or killed.

Most people in the country respect Confucius and realize that his doctrine should be followed. However, how many of them refrain from eating what has been forbidden? The Buddhists are even stranger; their teachings are very strict in forbidding the consumption of meat, and in front of people they adhere to this; however, when they are alone, they break the regulation. Regardless of whether they follow their doctrine or not, we can see that there are some foods that are forbidden according to their religion. Why are they not questioned about this? All people are aware and believe that Buddhism prohibits eating meat because in their view that will damage the nature of mankind. This is the same reason why Islam forbids some foods, but very few people know this. Even those who do, have only a superficial knowledge of things. They say, for example, that this is *halal* (permissible) and that is *haram* (forbidden); yet they are unaware that some parts of the permissible things are *haram*. This rule embodies a profound knowledge of hygiene. For example, cattle, sheep, chicken and duck are *halal* for Muslims, according to Islam, but their blood, eyes, brains, waists[2] and kidneys should be thrown away because they accumulate filth, smell bad and hurt our nature.

Another example is about dogs and pigs. They like to eat filth and stay in low-lying land; their nature is turbid and their breath muddy. It is

---

[1] Literally, *Tian* means sky and *Di* the earth, but they also refer to the Creator especially in the view of people in ancient times. This is why the Chinese emperors called them selves Tianzi (天子) which means the son of God, in order to make known that their power is given by God.

[2] This is a problematic term, we don't know what the author means by it. Mr. Hai ignored it in his translation.

recorded in Bencao (本草)[1] that the temperament of the pig is such that it prefers this land, which is why it is named "豕" (*shi*).[2] Islam strictly forbids the eating of pigs and dogs, but also animals that have died a natural death, for their illness makes them harmful to our health, just like pigs and dogs. Also forbidden are birds with talons, land carnivores, aquatic animals with scales and shells [and bodies] of strange shapes and sizes, and all intoxicants like alcohol. Do people know this?

All types of fruit, vegetable and food crops are permissible for consumption except things that make people crazy and muddle-headed. I can only discuss the rules of food briefly here. These things are forbidden because they hurt the nature and life of humans and eating them is bad for the propagation of human beings. These rules are not meant to impose restrictions on eating and drinking without any proof or evidence. Muslims decide what they can and can't do based on what is stated in the Islamic book, which has been clarified by our prophet and presented by our scholars. As a Muslim, my mind is aware of that and my eyes touched by it.

At this moment, a man of official appearance emerged before me and bowed with his hands folded in front to show politeness. He sat down and said, "You are wrong, Sir. As Islam has spread in China, Muslims should follow the rules of the current government in eating and dress. However, they are choosy. They have many rules in food and drinking. They say that pigs and dogs are dirty because they like to stay in low-lying land so that their natures are turbid and their breath is muddy. Muslims are to keep away from such turbid and muddy things and not eat them. If these animals were really like what you said they are, then why did Yao (尧), Shun (舜), Yu (禹), Shangtang (商汤), Wenwang (文王), Wudi (武帝),[3] Confucius (孔子),

---

[1] The full title of the book is Ben Cao Gang Mu (本草纲目, the Compendium of Material Medical) written by Li Shizhen (李时珍, 1518-1593).

[2] It means pig.

[3] Yao and Shun are two of the five emperors and leaders of tribes in ancient China; Yu was the first emperor of the Xia dynasty (2070-1600 B.C.); Shangtang was the first King of the Shang dynasty (1600-1046 B.C.) while Wenwang and Wudi were the Kings of the Zhou dynasty (1046-256 B.C.).

Mencius (孟子),[1] as well as wise kings and their intelligent subjects not describe them similarly? Do you mean that those people were not as intelligent as Muslims? Mencius said: 'I heard that foreigners can be changed to be like Chinese, but I never heard that Chinese should be changed to be like foreigners.'[2] Though you are Muslims, you have been in China for a long time. Why are you still strict about religious rules? Flexible people are not like this. You said that Muslims know how to preserve their nature, correct their behavior, reform their spirit and prevent anything from hurting their lives. It is not really so."

I replied: "Not so. Ancient generations possessing virtue used to have etiquette and regulations of their own, according to which everything was treated. The system of the three cardinal guides and five constant virtues, as specified in the feudal ethical code, human relations and disciplines and the rules and regulations for food and drink, was the standard which wise men urged people to follow. Virtuous men educated them accordingly. So, all people, without exception, must follow it, just like the saying, "Everything, the inner and the outer, its dross and essence, will be well known and all [the] contents of our heart will be made crystal clear."[3] It would not be in

---

These men managed their societies successfully and thereby, they were considered wise men and admired very much by later generations of Chinese people, especially Confucius and his followers.

[1] Mencius (372-299 B.C.), whose name was Ke (轲) and title was Ziyu (子舆), studied Confucian thought, then traveled to states in his time to persuade the rulers to follow ancient Emperors and Kings in terms of governing societies. Unforunately he failed. In his late age, Mencius returned to his home town and started to teach. He wrote "Mengzi", only 7 chapters of which are left. See Wang Jiafan and Xie Tianyou, *Chinese Ancient Civilization*, (Zhejiang Ancient Books Publishing House, 1999), 462.

[2] This is taken from the *Four Books.* "Xia" (夏) refers to China and "Yi" (夷) to the minorities around China. See Chen Puqing, *Translation and Commentary of Four Books*, 321.

[3] It is taken from Zhuxi's Interpretion of "Zhizhi Zai Gewu" (致知在格物) which means: study things hard, then you will know the principles of everything.

accordance with the above saying][1] if we followed only the guiding principles and neglected the minor regulations and rules of food and drink. Another example is recorded: "To make harmony and try hard to mediate, without being restrained by any regulation, is also not commendable." Therefore, gentlemen do not ride their carriages in front of the gate of the capital city and honest people do not drink water from the Tanquan (贪泉),[2] which shows their extreme scrupulousness. You said that foreigners should change to be like the Chinese. I think you may not have understood well what exactly Mencius meant by these words. Muslims should be changed, or would have been changed long ago, if they were to separate between the monarch and his subjects, fathers and sons, husbands and wives, brothers and friends; or were to stop paying taxes for government, or if they were to give up etiquette between the old and the young, or stand against righteousness and justice. If this were the case, they would have been changed long ago. The matter would not have waited for your reminder. What is the behavior of the Muslims in the matters mentioned above? Why do they need to change? Why did you not think deeply about this before saying that, because they did not read Confucian books, Muslims are strict and obstinate.

"I was told that the older generation of all well-educated clans leaves advice and instructions for their families to educate the later generations. We Muslims are observing the instructions of our older generations. Zengsifu (曾思父)[3] said in his interpretation of Zhangyinshi (章尹氏), [1] "If it is a

---

The author quoted it here to demonstrate that although food and drink are minor things but they should be paid attention to. See, Department of Chinese philosophy, faculty of philosophy, Beijing University, *History of Chinese Philosophy*, (Beijing Publishing House, 2003), 288, 289.

[1] The coming sentence is problematic without the added part in square brackets.

[2] It means: the spring of greed. It is located in Shimen (石门), Guangdong province; it was said that the honest person will become greedy if he drinks water from that spring.

[3] We attempted to find information about this person but failed.

right way, it should not be changed for life; if it is not, why you would wait three years to change it?"[2] When we do not eat certain foods and abstain from some things, it is to follow the advice of our older generations. The early Muslims started to do this approximately one thousand years ago, and we, the later generation, will not change it. Because of this, we are denounced by people instead of being praised. This means that, in their view, those who do not follow the advice of their old generations are orthodox. I think that intelligent people should not do this. What would you make of the following?

> Why has Wuling Zhongzi (於陵仲子)[3] not been killed till now? He does not like to be [the] subject of [the] monarch, or to manage his family's property, or to associate with the princes under the emperor. This means that he wants people to do nothing and be useless. [4]

From this, we can see that ancient wise men denounced this kind of person;[5] yet Muslims should not be [denounced], because we freely give our loyalty to the monarch, manage our families' properties and socialize with other

---

[1] This is the name of one of the scholars who interpreted *Lunyu* (论语). These words are taken from Zhuxi's *Variorum of the Four Books,* (Yue Lu Book Publisher, 2004), 58.

[2] *Ibid.*

[3] Wu Ling (於陵) was the name of a place in Qi (475-221 B.C.), one of the seven states in the history of China. It was in the south of Changshan town, today's Shandong province. Zhongzi (仲子) was one of the members of the royal family, who didn't like to get involved in politics due to corruption, and preferred to live in seclusion in this place, hence why he was called "Wuling Zhongzi".

[4] This is taken from the *Four Books*, see Chen Puqing, *Translation and Commentary of the Four Books*, 344.

[5] It is so because his actions are against the Confucian doctrine which encourages people to get involved in society and production.

people. I have never heard of anyone that was criticized by wise men for not eating certain foods. Why has it become a cause for doubt today?

"You said that Muslims do not read Confucian books; therefore, they do not know the truth and principles of things. Let us disregard the percentage of Confucians as well as Muslims who do not read Confucian books. I think that not all the Confucians who recite his poems and read the [right] books are men of moral integrity. It was said in ancient days, "Moral conduct is the root, while literature and the arts are its branches." It was also said, "To brighten virtue is the most important moral act." To brighten virtue is to expand one's natural conscience, so that one will complain neither to God nor to people. The natural law, by which God creates things, should be realized. People should not imitate those who indulge in empty talk. If you examine the number of Confucians that conform to these words, you will find them very few. Our religion guides us to recognize the oneness of God and to return to Him, which means to go back to God, who created everything.

"Let us put aside the concept of God in Islam. The term God was mentioned many times in the Confucian books. The clearest and easiest way to understand is what Zhuxi (朱熹) [1] said when explaining the sentence of "*Ke Pei Shang Di*" (克配上帝) found in Shijing (诗经), 'Shangdi is the dominant of Tian (天, the heavens).' He also said, 'The heavens and the earth are changing all the time because they have a dominant.' 'Be reverent, so that you can converse with Shangdi.' These words are not from Islamic books but from Confucian ones. If God does not exist, it would mean that both the ancient people's poems and Zhuxi's interpretation were wrong. Islam prohibits things that hurt people's nature and life. Muslims comply with [divine] regulations even if they do not know the reasons for the prohibition of certain foods because they remember God in their hearts

[1] Zhuzi (朱子) is Zhuxi (朱熹, 1130-1200), he was originally from Huizhou (today's Jiangxi) yet grew up in Fujian. Zhuzi was appointed to several official positions. He wrote many works, the most famous of which is *The Variorum of the Four Books*. For more information on him, see *History of Chinese Philosophy*, 283.

always. This is the rule that Islam requires following to save man's nature; it is not a minor thing such as literature or art."

4.3 God and Jesus

The guest said, "According to what you just said, although Muslims did not read Confucian books, they still understand the will of God and, therefore, in order to expand man's natural conscience, they do not eat foods that hurt man's nature. This is so because they were guided and influenced by their grandfathers and fathers when they were small. After they grew up and became adults, they were educated by teachers and guided by friends for a long time. In other words, they grew up in an Islamic environment; therefore, they were not influenced by different [cultures]. This could be a natural phenomenon and nothing surprising. Yet, you mentioned the Dominant and that it is He who created all things. Is it not like the Catholic God?"

I replied, "Again, you are wrong. The Dominant of the Catholics is an idol for people to worship, and they do not prohibit [certain] food and drinks as Muslims do, therefore, how can they be like us? They are confused about the Dominant; for example, they said that Tianzhu (天主) was born, and Mary had been pregnant. These two statements are widely divergent. If He is Tianzhu, why is His mother called Shengmu (圣母)?[1] Why do they not refer to her directly as the mother of God? It is contradictory, and, clearly, Catholics do not know the foundations of their own doctrine at all.

"Everything in the cosmos has its own Dominant. If there were no dominant, things would conflict with each other. Let us take the human world as an example: the monarch is its dominant; therefore, common people do not dare to strive for power. Similarly, the dominant should not be like the common people. Catholics say that Tianzhu (天主) can create everything, which means that he also created his mother, Shengmu (圣母). If this is the case, how he could have been born to her? This is enough to identify whether the doctrine is true or false.

---

[1] It means the mother of a prophet or sage.

"They said that Jesus came down for persuading people to believe in him and to do good; this was why he was not afraid of being exhausted. This statement is most absurd. They did not realize that if He could create the heavens and the earth and everything between them, then why could He not send down rain, wind, thunder and lightning and make them prevalent in human society. Floods, landslides and earthquakes are signs by which God warns people; therefore, why would He have to take on human form and be born [into the world]? Today, the King issues his orders, and requires people to obey them. To those who refuse, he either sends some officials or an army, if necessary, to punish them to maintain control. If Tianzhu came down to persuade people to give up evil and return to good, then it is like a King, who personally leads the army. Is this reasonable?

"The Dominant whom Muslims believe in does not leave the heavens and the earth even for a moment. Why? It is said that heaven is a macrocosm and man is a microcosm. The former has its own Dominant as does the latter.

"The Dominant of the macrocosm is the one who created the heavens and the earth and everything between them. He lets the four seasons come and go every year and makes the day bright and the night dark, and He sends the wind and rains, while the Dominant of the microcosm lets our hands and feet move, our ears listen and eyes see. It is our life (命). It might be said that our heart is the dominant ruler of our body but this is not entirely correct. It is acceptable if it means that the heart contains the spirit and makes the decisions. Suppose that the heart is the dominant ruler of the body, no one would die because everyone wishes to live forever. If the heart dominates, it will prefer the body to live forever. Then, why do the four limbs (arms and legs) and bones separate suddenly and the heart disintegrate after a person dies? This proves that the heart is not the dominant ruler of the body; rather its ruler is the life-force, which does not separate from the body even for a moment.

How, then, could the ruler of the cosmos leave it? Zisi (子思)[1] said, "The Dominant of the cosmos cannot be heard or smelt." Dongpo (苏东坡) also said, "Haotian (昊天) [2] is dusky, so we could not know its nature; therefore, we could not name it." The God that we believe in has nothing like Him or a form, just like the life in a person's body. Is it like anything? Has anyone seen it? Therefore, we are required to be aware of Him in every moment, not only during prayer. This is like what Confucius said, 'A gentleman should not go against benevolence, even in the time after his meal.'

"Sir, how can you compare Catholicism to Islam? According to its doctrine, Jesus is considered God, yet we do not know whether this has been scrutinized or not. In the Islamic books, Jesus was a wise man as well as a messenger of God. There were some people in his time who refused to follow his doctrine. They slandered him privately and even wanted to kill him. In order to achieve their aim, they hired some robbers, framed him and nailed him to a cross. This explains why Catholics cross themselves whenever they do something, to show their precious remembrance of Christ's suffering and death. Jesus disappeared that day and most of his followers suffered because of him. Those who knew Jesus were fearful. They called him Lord, and later generations followed them till today. Their situation is just like an army that has won a war; they regard their general as emperor, yet as an honest and respectful subject of the emperor, he rejects such treatment. On the other hand, those people who witnessed [Jesus's] situation had it engraved on their bones and hearts so that they transmitted the idea [of Jesus as lord)] to later generations until today."

The guest said, "Since God created prophets to guide people, He should arrange matters so that people follow and not slander them. Why did He allow them to come to harm? Why didn't He clarify the real situation, clear

---

[1] Zisi (子思, 483 B.C-402 B.C.) was a grandson of Confucius. See Wangjiafan and Xie Tianyou's *History of Chinese Ancient Civilization*, 461.

[2] It refers to the sky and the heaven.

[Jesus] of the charges and let his followers be exonerated of the framed charges? Why did He cause so much trouble?"[1]

I answered, "Shun (舜) was a great wise man; am I right? He fell down a well and escaped from death in a great catastrophe;[2] Confucius (孔子) was in a difficult position between Chen (陈) and Cai (蔡),[3] but his doctrine continues to spread till today. It is normal for such things to happen to wise men. You said what happened with Jesus was to make trouble; then Chinese wise men should not meet such difficult positions. According to Islam, Jesus was a messenger sent by God to western lands, and he was not God. Isn't the concept of the Dominant ruler in Islam and the one stated in Catholicism different?"

---

[1] Mr. Hai Zhengzhong separated this question and its answer from the last paragraph and made them as an independent paragraph and therefore, titled it as "Sheng" (圣人, prophet). I think they should be under the title of God and Jesus as part of the paragraph.

[2] It is said that his father was blind; his mother died when he was small; his stepmother gave birth to his brother named Xiang. The father, stepmother and Xiang tried to kill him several times. One day, they let him to go down into a deep well. Shun did as they wanted him to do, but he went down into the well with a thing that would save him. When they left, he came out from the well successfully. See, Stanley Chodorow, *A History of The World*, (Harcourt Brace Jovanovich, Publisher, 1986), 61; Hai Zhengzhong, *Translation of Qingzhen Shiyi in Modern Chinese*, 47.

[3] "Chen" (陈) was one of the states of princes in the time of the Zhou (11th centry B.C.-256 year B.C), its location was in southeast of Henan and north of Anhui. "Cai" (蔡) was another state at that time, its location was in the area of Shangcai and Xincai, Hennan. The story is like this: Confucius was traveling between states to persuade rulers to follow Zhouli (周礼). When he and his companions arrived to an area between Chen and Cai, the King of Chu state (楚国) issued an letter to invite him to come. When the rulers of the two states heard about it, they sent an unknown ministry to lay siege to *Chu* state. Due to this, there was no food provided for Confucius and his companions for seven days. See Chen Puqing, *Translation and Commentary of the Four Books*, 489.

4.4 Calendar, Fasting and *Zakah*

4.4.1 Calendar

The guest said, "Indeed, Islam is different from Catholicism. However, Muslims came to China during the time of the Sui and the Tang (隋唐), so they should follow Chinese laws and rules. However, you follow a foreign calendar that has 360 days a year and does not differentiate between the four seasons, spring, summer, autumn and winter. [You use it] for fasting and move [the fasting month] back one month in every three years. Why do Muslims do all this? People are very surprised."

I said, "What kind of words are these? Why are Muslims accused of breaking the dynasty's laws and rules? It is to make people suspicious of them. Who would dare to deviate from the dignified calendar when the entire world is now under China and the emperor's rule? If the accusations are true and we do not use the lunar month of 30 days and an intercalary month, it would be another world. Is that possible?

"In Muslim society, people live in peace and harmony and are not estranged from one another. If the population increases, they establish schools for those who cannot attend because of distance or financial problems; furthermore, wealthy men among them provide students with food and clothes, so that they may continue their studies and focus on them without wasting time. After several years, they complete their studies, and some of them might be excellent while others are average.

"As for the Islamic book, Chinese characters are not used [to spell the Quran] because we are afraid of deviating from the original phonology of the book and losing its original style. Therefore, we have maintained the pronunciation as it was in early times. They (non-Muslims) do not know the way of the Muslims, so it is not surprising if they consider the timetables for prayer and fasting as a calendar.

"Today, the government makes a calendar every year, and in addition to that, Tai Changsi (太常寺)[1] makes timetables in the form of slips for religious activities and the anniversary of the death of parents, which are selected by Qin Tianjian (钦天监)[2]. These are usually stacked in government offices. In recent years, they have put circles on the calendars to make it easier for people to know the dates. They did all this because books are always closed and are more difficult to consider compared to slips. In this way, the government makes people aware of the time.

"An analogy of this is when ordinary people hang their own timetables of the anniversary of their parents' deaths in their houses. Is it reasonable to consider these timetables calendars?

"In Islam, the daily prayers and the yearly fast (Ramadan) have fixed times and days [respectively] which must be written clearly, just like the timetable slips for religious activities and death anniversaries of parents, which are conveniently stacked in people's houses [to make it easy to see and to respect those occasions]. Instead of keeping an open mind, non-Muslims have accused Muslims of making private calendars. If the emperor had not [personally] considered this, Muslims might have fallen into a very dangerous situation. Please, think carefully about what I have said.

"Let us consider the accusation that the Muslim year has 360 days and their practice of congratulating each other. This originated from the fasting, which is an obligation in all religions. The fasting in Islam is different from that of other religions. Our prophet understood and sympathized with the poor. He said that monarchs and their subjects, as well as rich people, do not lack food and drink and, therefore, do not suffer as hungry people do. Their conditions have never been as difficult as those of widows, widowers, orphans and the childless, even if they experienced a year of crop failure. Therefore, Islam set a month for fasting in which Muslims are required to

---

[1] The Court of Imperial Sacrifices is the most prestigious of the Nine Courts in the central government. See *Chinese- English Dictionary of Politics and Laws*. Beijing: Book Publishing House. 2002. P.184.

[2] It is the Directorate of Astronomy. *Ibid.,* 171.

eat *sahar* (a predawn meal) at the hour of the cock's crow and break the fast when the stars brighten. During the daytime they are not allowed to eat a single grain or to drink a drop of water, regardless of whether it is the bitter cold of winter or the intense heat of summer.

"Muslims are not allowed to choose the month for the fasting, and it moves back one month every three years.[1] Islamic law permits Muslims to eat meat, which is a significant difference from religions that forbid this. Again, nobody can say that he or she never made any mistakes, knowingly or otherwise, in words and deeds in their daily life.

"In the fasting month, people make amends for their mistakes and they realize from their experience of fasting that God likes people to live well and that they are lucky compared to the poor. Furthermore, it can help dukes and princes to understand their emperor and to be just in making political decisions. Also, senior officials can understand dukes and princes and try to find a proper way to use the power of punishing and interrogating plaintiffs. Finally, it helps the common people to understand the Dominant (God), the emperor, princes and senior officials, so that they may purify their thoughts, decrease their desires, correct their mistakes, improve themselves to be better people and help them to know and empathize with the tricky situation of helpless people. Muslims fast for a whole month with these intentions. When it ends, they have a special bath, put on new clothes, and go to the mosque for prayers. Afterwards, they congratulate each other on completing the month-long obligatory fast in which they closed their doors, unlike the other months. This is the reason for the felicitations.

"Islam requires Muslims to fast because it leads them to contemplate hardship, which might make them more compassionate. On the contrary, a situation of ease might lead to excessive, causing them to forget to be kind, and possibly resulting in evil and eventually forming a vicious cycle. People ridicule Muslims without thinking about the profound meaning of fasting. Ignorant Muslims cannot explain why they fast and even some scholars are unable to give a detailed explanation with abundant quotes from the right sources. Till now, there are still many people who maintain that the Muslim

---

[1] It is because of the difference between the Muslim and the Chinese calendars.

year has 360 days; they do not know that our yearly celebrations are for the completion of the fast and not for the New Year. Is my explanation clear?"

4.4.2 Fasting and *Zakah*

The guest said, "I understand what you mean. According to what you said, revered persons, their Excellencies and rich people must imitate hungry people. Doesn't this mean that Islam requires people to be inflexible and trouble themselves? Is this reasonable?"

I answered, "The ancient emperor tilled the earth; his wife fed silkworms. Government officials of various levels, as well as common folk were all intellectual and physical laborers engaged in heavy work. The emperor was the leader (owner) of the country, and his wife was regarded as the mother of the people. Did they need to till the earth for food and to weave clothes? Did they not know that they should spend time holding the memorial ceremony for the ancestral temple of the ruling house? Instead, they wanted to experience for themselves how hard it is for farmers to produce grains so that people might take diligent care of them.

"I used to read a story which said that in the 21st year (444 C.E.) of Yuan Jia (元嘉), in the time of Liu Song (刘宋, 420-589), the King of the Song dynasty sent a prince named Yiji (义季) to Yanzhou (允州)[1] to be its feudal official. He prepared a farewell dinner for the prince in a place named Wu Zhanggang (武帐冈).[2] Before they left, the King told his subjects that there was a feast in an official location, and he asked them not to eat until they arrived there. They walked for a long time, but by sunset they still had not arrived, and everyone was hungry. At that moment, the King said, 'You grew up in plenty, so you do not know the difficulties of the common people. Today, I allowed you to experience hunger so that you may know how to save grains as well as other goods and materials.'

---

[1] It was one of the nine states at the time, located in the middle part of Shandong province. See the Editorial committee of *Dictionary of Etymology of Names of Places in China*, (Shanghai: Dictionary Publishing House, 1995), 298-299.

[2] It was the name of a place in which all kind of weapons were put up.

"What he said is in accordance with the meaning of fasting in Islam. Furthermore, I checked the ancient writing of the term Zhai (斋)[1] and found that it was formed by combining two Chinese characters, Bu (不, meaning: do not), and Shi (食, meaning: eat). This is the meaning of fasting to the ancient Chinese people: 'do not eat'. This is what is termed 'Quyi' (取义, etymology)[2] in the critical interpretation of ancient texts. Mencius used to say: If a person in the world drowned in water, Yu (禹) felt that he was the one who had caused him to drown; when he was told that someone was hungry, Ji (稷,)[3] felt that he was the one who had caused his hunger."

"Was this to make trouble for themselves? Muslims not only think about hunger but experience it, too. In this way, they pay attention to people's lives. So, [fasting] allows the emperor, revered persons, their Excellencies and rich people, to remember [the plight of] widowers, widows, orphans and the homeless, to know, through experience, the favors and charity provided for them by God. This is the general significance of fasting in Islam.

4.4.3. *Zakah*

"Muslims have businesses everywhere. If their capital increases to 20 Liangs (两) [4] it is called Manguan (满贯)[5] and if it has remained for one year after it reaches this amount, Muslims must pay 5 Qians (钱)[6] in charity (*zakah*). This is called 'Tianke'(天课),[7] which is an obligation upon the rich to [help] support the poor in the name of God and prevent them from being homeless. It is also good for our emperor to alleviate his burden.

---

[1] It means fasting.

[2] It means to take two characters of different meanings and combine them to make a new character with a new meaning.

[3] He was a wise man and people regarded him as the god of grains.

[4] Liang (两) is a unity of weight; one Liang is equal to 50 grams.

[5] This is called in Arabic "niÎÉb" which means the full amount of money, and the owner of which is required to pay zakah.

[6] It is a unity of weight, 10 Qians are equal to one Liang.

[7] It means 'zakah'.

"This money is given willingly to helpless people in the town without pressure from the government. If some people have extra clothes, houses and daily necessities, they must give 'Tianke' only once, because these goods do not inherently increase. If someone has farmland, he must pay one-tenth of the grain to others after he has paid some to the state as income tax. It must not be hidden privately. Islamic law states that God will punish those who are greedy and refuse to pay 'Tianke'. Furthermore, those obligated to pay *zakah* have no right to receive it from others, unless they are facing difficulties on a journey, in which case they may receive *zakah* to survive.

"Islamic rules pay much attention to sympathizing with humans. Muslims must follow every single word of the Prophet, and they dare not ignore them. Therefore, the emperor, revered persons, their Excellencies, as well as rich people fast for a whole month till today. In Muslim society, people fast together regardless of whether they are rich or poor. They all wish to decrease their mistakes and faults. Therefore, fasting is widely practiced by the public. Have you heard about this, Sir?"

4.5 Funeral

The guest said, "I understand the meaning of fasting. However, for the funerals, you Muslims neither clothe the dead nor use a coffin; you just bury the dead in the ground. This is a deplorable way to treat loved ones, and it goes against the taboo of not allowing earth to touch the skin of the deceased."[1]

I said, "The theory of preventing the earth from meeting the body sounds as bright as the sun and stars. However, our Prophet and men of virtue said that everything is created from the earth and they will be buried in it. There are four ways to bury the dead: gold (金), wood (木), water (水) and fire (火). Any way that is used will return the dead to the earth in the end, as there is no other place to cover their bones. As no one can escape the earth, why we do not bury the dead directly in the ground? Therefore, it is not in accordance with Islam to wrap the dead repeatedly nor is it necessary.

---

[1] See for example *the Translation and Commentary of the Four Books*, 303.

"According to the sayings of our Prophet, man is nobler than any other living thing. People are equal before birth and after death although they differ in wealth during their lifetimes. Islam prescribes funerals this way for equality, so that the rich will not waste money and the poor can bury their beloved ones with dignity. Without a fixed way, people would not have rules to follow when they bury their dead. Therefore, there is no difference in Islam between rich and poor in terms of funerals.

"[In Muslim society,] when someone dies, a hole is dug that is approximately one *zhang* (丈)[1] in length, and inside, to one side, there must be a cavity two *chis* (尺)[2] high and wide, and seven *chis* in length. It should be hollow and emptied of earth.

"Non-Muslim people have never witnessed the way Muslims bury their dead; when they heard that they put them in the ground, they assumed that there are no burial rules except to fill the hole with earth. They do not know that this kind of hole will not fill up with earth for about 100 years and it will not touch the bones of the dead for about 3 to 5 years. How do we know this? A Muslim died and was buried in a place far from his hometown. When his children grew up, they moved their father's remains back there. Approximately 20 to 30 years had passed since the man died, yet, when they opened the grave they found that earth had not filled the cavity.

"In areas with sandy soil, it is not possible to hollow out a cavity in one side of the grave. In this case, a vertical hole of 7 to 8 *Chis* deep is sufficient. Several planks should be placed inside and along the sides to prevent it from collapsing. Finally, the hole should be covered with some planks or flagstone. Some people place in the cavity a square box from either wood or stone.

"Muslims do not prepare ready-made-clothes or coffins for the dead. This is to show that, just as people are not different from one another in wealth at birth, when there is nothing with them but the afterbirth, likewise, when they die, they should be just like the day they were born.

---

[1] It is a unity of length, one *Zhang* = 3.33 meters.

[2] It is a unity of length, three *Chi* = one metre.

"The deceased is washed in clean water; then wrapped in layers of white sheets; three for men and five for women. According to funeral regulations in Liji (礼记),[1] the living must trim the fingernails of the dead and, for men, the moustache. For Muslims, these two things are also done regularly [when alive]. They place the body of the dead-on sheets and perfume it with safflower, camphor and musk. They also put some perfume inside the rectum to drive away snakes and insects and to remove the smell of decay. This is good for both the living and the dead. Then they put the body of the dead inside the niche of the grave, seal it up and fill the hole with earth. Once the person who placed the body comes out, the grave will be filled, a gravestone erected, and the funeral is over. If a poor person died while traveling, the Muslims in that area will bury him according to the way mentioned above; they will not leave his body out in the open.

"However, it may be argued that this still does not prevent dead bodies from meeting the earth. This sounds correct. However, consider the case of a person who died on a very hot summer's day; his body is dressed and placed inside a coffin. Then, yellow lime is used to prevent any dirty water and foul smells from escaping. Isn't lime from the earth? The dead body will decompose quickly. Although the beloved of the dead cannot bear the body to be touched by earth, it is already mixed with the mud lime. How do you explain this? After all, not all non-Muslims are rich enough to spend around one thousand *liang* (两) of gold to buy a coffin and those who can afford more than ten *liang* are no more than 4 or 5 percent. Those who have no one to depend on can only spend 2 to 3 *liang*, or they may not even have that much. Even if they bought a very humble coffin for a small amount of money, it would not protect the body from wind and rain. Furthermore, if they could not bury it, or if they did, but not carefully, after a few days the body would be exposed and the limbs separated from each other. Anyone who saw this would be grieved. People who pass by would have to hold their

[1] It is one of the Confucian books written by Daisheng (戴圣). It includes the regulations and rules, as well as social organization, customs and morals at the time of the pre-Qin (秦) and Han (汉) and is an important reference to study Confucian thought.

noses, and how would they feel looking at this? Are poor people not worth any respect? Even if the deceased had children who had no money to spend, what would the situation be? In this case, which would be better, to let the body encounter earth by burying it in the ground or to leave it exposed because of a lack of money?

"Man is the most noble among all living things in the world. If people did not exist there would be no bridge (?) on the earth and even if there were one, it would be useless. Nowadays, the rich spend as much money as they like on funerals while no one cares whether the bodies of the poor are buried or not. Kind-hearted people do not do this. It is strange that rich people put gold and pearls on the dead—they call it "Xunzang" (殉葬)[1]—hoping to prevent the body from rotting. It has already been returned to the earth, so it is useless to do this even if the dead body had been preserved for a thousand years. Not only that, but also a door has been opened for thieves, because funerals such as this will be well-known and wide spread. As a result, brigands will think of ways to steal; then they will loot those treasured objects. If these "heroes" are caught, they will be beheaded for merely opening the coffin while the punishment will be twice as severe if they stole the objects. Such lavish funerals entice the living to wrongdoing and cause disturbance to the dead.

"Here, I remembered Mr. Du Shaojun (杜少俊，杜甫)[2] who recited a poem that said: "*Yesterday the jade-fish was buried in the grave; this morning the gold bowl has appeared in the world.*" Do you not believe this? If you went to the markets in the main cities, you would find curio sellers holding copper or jade objects in their hands, saying, 'This jade was made in

[1] It was a custom in ancient China, according to which the wife and servant of the dead were forced to be buried with the dead man. It also refers to things that were buried with the dead.

[2] Du Shaojun (杜少俊, 712-770) whose name was Fu, was well-known as *Dufu* (杜甫). He was a very famous poet and had a work entitled *Collections of Du Shaojun*. See Liao Zhongan and Liu Guoying, *Chinese Clasical Literature*, (Beijing Publishing House, 1989), 112-114.

the time of the Han Dynasty[1] and buried with the dead. This is an antique mirror that's been around for ages.' However, people do not stop to think that if such things were buried with the dead, why are they for sale? Yet vendors sell them with an easy conscience.

"Even though the sellers are not asked where they got the objects from, intelligent people should think carefully: If I bought an object and buried it with the deceased and later the object appeared in the possession of antique dealers, just like what we saw today, I should wake up and stop preparing objects for burial. Of course, I do not mean that every grave will be robbed, but why do we not guard against it before it is too late? Islamic funeral [rules] prohibit people from burying objects with the dead; therefore, it does not provide an opportunity for thieves. This is beneficial for both the living and the dead, yet people are unable to accept it as something positive.

"This is the Islamic funeral; it neither leaves the dead exposed nor opens the door for thieves. No Muslim's grave has ever been robbed even once in a thousand years. If Confucius and Mencius had been asked to evaluate the Islamic funeral, they would probably say that it is perfect. Is it correct to bury the dead in the ground or not?"

4.6 Wearing White Caps and White Clothes

The guest said, "The Islamic funeral is worthy of affirmation. However, Muslims always wear a white cap, even when there is no funeral. They do not mind at all.[2] Why they do that?"

I said, "Since ancient times, people have preferred distinct colors in different periods. During the Xia (夏) Dynasty,[3] it was black; during the

---

[1] It existed from 206 B.C. till 220 A.C.

[2] According to Chinese custom, people wear white hats and clothes only during funeral arrangements. To do that in ordinary times is considered a propitious thing.

[3] Xia was one of the earliest states in China, which existed from the 22nd century B.C. to the beginning of the 21st century B.C.

Zhou (周) Dynasty,[1] it was red, and during the Shang (商)[2] Dynasty, white was the preferred color of their clothes, jewelry and vehicle curtains. Imagine that we are following the Shang system and all people prefer white; would you be suspicious of this?

"Today, people use white for funerals, yet we do not know what color the people of the Shang dynasty used when they arranged their parents' funerals nor what was taboo for them. We Muslims do not uphold white; we wear white caps only at the time of prayer. Those Muslims who do not know the cardinal principles of righteousness wear white caps all the time in order to distinguish themselves from non-Muslims, and it has become a custom and a habit.

"According to Islamic rules, both caps and clothes should be white. Perhaps this is to show that there is no difference between [Muslims'] outward show and inner thoughts and that their hearts are pure, without any pretense, just like the color white. Furthermore, it is the origin of other colors and it is not mixed with any other, therefore it is the purest. In addition to that, the emperor, revered persons, senior officials and common people belong to separate classes; they wear different official caps and clothes at various levels. Mr. Liu Jielian (刘介廉) recorded this in detail in his Tianfang Dianli (天方典礼) and it should not be ignored."[3]

4.7 Knowing God and Performing Prayer

4.7.1 How to Know God

The guest said, "According to your statement, all practices of Muslims are based on evidences. Nothing is open to doubt. Well, which god do you

---

[1] Zhou was the name of a state; it was divided into two namely the Western Zhou and the Eastern Zhou. The former existed from 11th century B.C. till the year 256 B.C. The latter existed from year 770 B.C. till year 256 B.C.

[2] Shang (商) was the name of one of the early states in China; it existed from 17th century B.C. till 11th century B.C.

[3] See Liu Zhi, *Qingzhendianli* (the Islamic rules and regulations), reprinted in 43th year of Zhonghuaminguo (1954), 167.

worship when you pray? What idol do you erect? The concept of God in your statement sounds acceptable, but you said that the heavens and the earth and everything between them were created by Him. Instead, why do you not ask [yourself], considering the immensity of heaven and earth, their infinity: who would be able of creating them? According to Confucius, heaven and earth and everything between them were created by the air of Yin (阴) and Yang (阳).[1] The coming and passing of spring, summer, autumn and winter, the movement of the sun and the moon, the passing of time, the rise and fall of nations and every action of drinking and eating follow the natural law. They were designed by a certain will. Again, in Islam, there is the theory of rewarding those who do good and punishing those who do wrong. God is the only one who conducts this, and nobody else is involved, which means that God works hard and must be very tired. In addition, Muslims build mosques all over the country and pray inside them, with men and women mixing with each other. It is said that you Muslims gather at night and disperse at daybreak; such behavior incurs the comments of people."

I said, "Yes, your interrogation is in accord with Islamic books, in which there are related questions and answers, because people all over the world have similar hearts and principles, even though the world itself is very wide. However, every country has its own book and every religion its own theory. Only the one that is in accordance with the feudal order of priority in human relationships (纲常伦纪) is the orthodox one.

"The differences in spoken and written languages are signs on earth of God's greatness. He wants careful men to realize that there is more than one theory in the world, although some people want them to be the same; but who can achieve that? A friend used to argue with me that for Muslims to claim that they have their own prophet is fantastical; there have only ever

---

[1] Yin (阴) and Yang (阳 are two terms of ancient Chinese philosophy which refer to the sky and the earth, or the airs of the two which caused the creation of everything. See
http://blog.sina.com.cn/s/blog_4de7c08601007 uw3.html.

been prophets in China, therefore, how could there be any in other countries?

"I said. 'How can you say this? Haven't you heard that God is just absolutely? The [One who is] just has no partiality. Is it reasonable that God would only focus on China, create prophets to guide the Chinese people, and not do the same for people in other countries? Suppose that other countries never had any prophets; where did people get their languages and books from?'

"You said that every single action of drinking and eating has been designed. For example, say there was a lot of gold to be distributed to the public but no manager in charge. In such a case, who would take less than the others? They would necessarily fight each other to own as much as they could, and the consequences would be too horrifying and uncontrollable. On the contrary, if there was a manager, he would apportion it for them at the appointed times according to their deeds, regardless of whether they were near or far, old or young. There would be no dispute.

"As for things being designed, it means that everything has been decided and prearranged. My question is: Who is the designer? It is God, who created everything. Suppose that heaven and the earth were created by the air of Yin and Yang; then let us take the human body as an example; it contains Jing (精), Qi (气) and Shen (神).[1] The Jing has its own form, while the air and spirit do not. Regardless of how the congenital conception was, if there is no physical body, where would these three elements be located? The Qi (air) and Shen (mind) may not do anything unless there is first a place for them to be preserved. Now, I would like to ask you, before the heaven and the earth came into existence, where were the airs of Yin and Yang

[1] "Jing" (精) means the subtle liquid material; "Qi" (气) means the very active air which supports all functions of human body; "Shen" (神) means the shows or signs of functional activities of human body, or psychological spiritual activities of human. The three terms formed the main contents of traditional Chinese culture and became a theory that discusses the relation between Jing, Qi and Shen in the process of human life. For more detail, please see http://www.ms-health.com/cms/Article/tsyl/bdft/ctyx/200707/5032.html

preserved? All religions are ambiguous and vague on this issue; they do not want to make it clear; therefore, it has caused big disasters for people.

"Let us take as an example the calendar, which is issued every winter. Who would dare to issue it before the appointed time? We must wait for the time to come before the calendar can be handed out. Because of the existence [and authority] of the King, people's actions are unified. If there were no craftsman to cut and print the calendar and no King to issue the order with regards to the calendar at the beginning of each winter, no one would believe that it could be cut and published by itself.

"It was proposed that it is the air of Yin and Yang, and not God, that creates the heaven and the earth, that causes the coming and going of the four seasons, the changing of the times, the movement of the sun and moon and the rise and fall of nations in history. It is the natural law. At the same time, it was also stated that everything has been prearranged. Please realize that the air of Yin and Yang needs to be preserved by the heaven and the earth, as I stated above; [only] then they can play their roles. Even if the air of the two could cause effects [without being preserved somewhere in the heaven and the earth], they cannot play their roles by themselves; just like the calendar that cannot be published without cutting, printing and issuing by the king.

Hence, it is said in the Islamic book that king of the world is the shadow of the Dominant (God).[1] He is the monarch who rules all the worlds; supports living things, safeguards the mountains and rivers, allows the worthy person to get close to Him and pushes the bad one away, rewards those who do good and punishes the wrongdoers. Man is unable to do these things; indeed, it is His will that He wants us to recognize this principle and not be confused by it. Even each species of bird, beast, insect and fishes has its own king. That was why Mencius said, 'Kylin (麒麟, the Chinese unicorn) is the king of the beasts; the phoenix (凤凰 in Chinese) is the king of the birds.' How many people can (or have the chance to) see the emperor

---

[1] The author refers to the saying "The Sultan is the shadow of God on the earth, whoever is devoted to him will be guided, whoever cheats him will lose his way." See, Al-Shaokani, *Al-Fawaid Al-MajmËÑah*, p. 623.

every day? Yet, everyone respects and fears him. According to what you said, you would not believe in his existence unless you saw him; then, all people can say that there is no order issued by the King regarding reward or punishment, let everything take its own course. Is it practical?"

4.7.2 Performing Prayer

"Prayers in Islam are like this: there are five daily prayers and a congregational weekly prayer (Jumah). Wherever Muslims live there is a mosque, in which they worship the Dominant. Muslims who did not acquire Islamic knowledge do not know its rules; therefore, they are not able to embody them well.

"Our *'ulama'* publicize the Islamic rules and general etiquette and explain them systematically; however, those who are busy the entire day with their business and have no time to listen to talks, attend once every few days or once a month.

"We worship God because it is said in the Islamic book that everything in the past and the present was created by Him. People usually say that wealth and children are predetermined, yet they do not investigate who did that. According to Islam, the Dominant (God) is the Creator; He is detached and unending (超然无极),[1] and every existing thing that has ever come into existence, together with the heaven and the earth, is His creation.

"Daily prayers are [intended] to worship God, who is profound and unseen; He has no direction and form; like the spirit that is contained in a person's body. Those who live east of the Kaabah face west when they pray. And those who have not learned do not know the reason for this.

"Knowledge is everywhere in the world but it cannot be understood without a teacher. We may use our body to understand the concept of God; as mentioned earlier, the human body is a microcosm, and its Dominant is the life in it. Who among us has seen it? What does it look like? Where is it located in the body? If we say it is in the head, then there is no life in the body and feet. If there were no life there, they would not feel pain, which would mean that they are dead. On the other hand, if we say it is in the lower

---

[1] It means unlimited by time and space.

part of the body, then there is no life in the higher part. From this we know that life has no space and direction in the body; it occupies the whole corpus, this explains the sensations and feelings in every part of it. The Islamic book says that God is everywhere in the world but we are not able to determine His position and form.

"Non-Muslims burn paper on Chinese New Year's Day, and they enshrine and worship the memorial tablet, on which the following words are written: "The real Dominant of all living things in three worlds and ten directions." We should think about the meanings of these words so that we will realize that the existence of heaven, earth, man and all living things in ten directions must be managed by a real Dominant. People did not perceive this and reflect on it; they thought that everything is as it was a long time ago. They are wrong, yet they slander others.

"You said that the Dominant (God) will reward those who do good and punish those who do wrong, and asked me: how does He know the doers of good from the wrongdoers? Think about the thick clothes that people wear in winter that totally cover their bodies so nothing can be seen. Their eyes are in their heads. However, they know whenever there is a louse[1] on the body and they can catch it easily, regardless of where it is. How are the fingers that have no eyes able to catch such a small thing that is under our clothes? It is due to the light of life, which envelops the whole body. This is an evidence for reward and punishment.

"God is with everything in the heavens and the earth, He knows every single movement of every man, and therefore He rewards and punishes him or her.

"Another example would be people who live in a village far from the capital city; they do not know that there is an emperor and a strict system of law. However, if they break the law and are discovered, they would be investigated. If they committed a grave crime they would be punished according to the law; they would not be let off just because they have not seen the emperor or because they were ignorant of the law.

---

[1] It is a small invertebrate animal.

"In order to know and worship God, intelligent people should embrace these two examples and not wait until the last moment to repent, for it will be too late. Muslims know that there will be reward and punishment, so they fear God. As a result, they follow the rules of Islam and rarely commit a sin. If non-Muslims could study Islamic doctrine sincerely and follow Islamic rules, they might commit fewer crimes and therefore they would not be punished by the law of the state.

"Islam's concept of the Dominant is very certain and clear to understand. Some people said God is the heaven above what we can see. This is wrong. That heaven is what everyone can see; it is limited and, therefore, it cannot be compared to God. The concept of God is very subtle, so you cannot understand it unless you make a careful and hard study of it. It is just like *Wuji* (无极), which was mentioned in *Tian Fang Xing Li* (天方性理).[1] What does it mean?[2] This term endorses the concept of God in Islam. Most of the Confucian books contain principles of the truth and guidance to the right path. However, followers of the Confucian doctrine either abandon the difficult contents and follow the easy ones or mix it with other religions, so that they end up believing in the superstitions of Buddhism and Taoism, which attract people's minds by promising them good fortune. They are unaware that God does not have any relatives, therefore He assists only the moral people. Whosoever seeks fortune from those men loses everything, including their consciences. Briefly, you must be sincere to have faith, for if you are not, you will be confused as to whether you have it."

4.8 Gathering of Men and Women in Mosques

"As for saying that men and women are mixing with each other, it is most unfair to impute this to Muslims. According to the Islamic book, boys and girls are not allowed to eat together in the same place when they are seven

---

[1] It is an ancient Chinese philosophical term which refers to the origin from which everything derives. Because it has no taste, smell, sound, colour, beginning, and end, nothing can be used to describe it.

[2] There might be something lost here, as a result, the sentence looks problematic.

years old. This regulation might be imitated from *QuLi* (曲礼).[1] Furthermore, that part of a man's body from the navel to the knees is not allowed to be seen by others. For the female it stretches from the head till the feet. Women are not allowed to meet other men except seven categories: grandfather, father, brothers, husband, children and grandchildren, mother's blood brother and father's blood brother. It is also stated there that females are not allowed to meet anyone whom they could theoretically marry. They are required to wear *hijab* (a scarf) to cover their heads down to their heels when they come out of the house or take a sedan chair or carriage; nothing of their bodies should be seen. This is the best way for Muslim women to practice.

Why, then, would people say that Muslim men and women mix together and that there are mosques everywhere that Muslims dwell where they have been seen mixing together? In fact, according to the Islamic book, females are not allowed to go to mosques to pray; and they are not allowed to visit graves, even for their parents' burial. Females are not allowed to meet males. Therefore Islamic regulations require them to stay at home to pray and remember God. Occasionally, at prayer time, there might be a helpless old lady who comes to the front of the mosque to beg. In this case, she will only be allowed to stay at the entrance; she will not be allowed to pray with males. This is the helpless Muslim who lives in eastern lands.

In western lands (Muslim countries), however, they can get living allowances from certain welfare organizations, and they are not allowed to enter the mosque. In addition to that, mosques must be kept clean, which is why people must purify their bodies (by making *wudu'* and *ghusl*) before they pray, while women might pollute the mosque with their menses. Furthermore, if a man and woman mix together, licentious actions might take place out of the view of others. That would encourage evil instead of

---

[1] *Quli* is the title of a book in which there are many regulations for daily life, some of them are like Islamic regulations. See, *Sishu Wujing* (The Four Books and The Five Classics, edited by Chen Xuguo, Yue Lu Book Publishing House, 2002), 432, 433.

promoting good. That is why Islam is against it. In conclusion, I say that there is definitely no mixing between males and females among Muslims."

4.9 Gathering at Night and Dispersing at Daybreak[1]

"As for saying that Muslims gather at night and disperse before daybreak, it is most incredible. I would like to ask: Do they do that every day and every night, or only sometimes? It would be impossible for them to gather and then disperse every day and night, because among Muslims there are educated people, farmers, laborers and businessmen. Everyone has his own business, even though some of them are diligent while others are lazy. However, they have aged parents and young children to support, so they would not able to delay their business or neglect it; otherwise, their family members will suffer from hunger or cold. People have limited energy, therefore, how they can gather continually? Furthermore, when they gather and disperse, they will not be silent. They must do something and say some words; why would they gather if there was no speech or activity? If they were busy every night, they would be very tired; yet they need to conduct their business. I doubt that they would have enough energy to manage everything, so they would die within a few days. This proves that they could not gather and disperse every day and night. If they gather and disperse sometimes, [it would be more reasonable] because the world is vast, with many people. If Muslims gather and later disperse, it could be because they must attend a marriage or burial ceremony; or a Muslim had come from another part of the country, died, and the local Muslims must carry his body to the mosque to prepare for burial the next day. On a night like this, there would be some people at the mosque preparing for the funeral.

---

[1] To gather at night was prohibited at that time because there were some deviating religions like Bailianjiao (白莲教) trying to overthrow the Qing dynasty; they were gathering at night and dispersing in the early morning. As the author said, there were some official men who wanted to imply a similar case for Muslims, and if the emperor accepted their report, they could take action to eliminate Muslims and abolish Islam.

Non-Muslims do not know this, so they accuse the Muslims of gathering at night and dispersing in the morning. Or, during the fasting month, the number of people who come to the mosque to pray will increase many times more than on ordinary days. Also, educated people, farmers, laborers and businessmen may not have time to pray on time, so they might make up the lost prayers in the mosque after sunset. They start to do that from the time it grows dark till the first watch (初更);[1] then, after prayer, they will return home to have a rest. At cock's crow, they rise again. Those who accuse Muslims of gathering at night and dispersing in the morning want people to suspect that Muslims are conspiring to commit crimes.[2]

It is said in the Islamic book that it is forbidden to take anything that does not belong to you. Moreover, the aim of the prayer in the fasting month is primarily to repent, and Muslims do not dare to have any presumptuous intentions. Instead of that, they submit to the will of God, regardless of whether they are rich or poor, in ease or difficulty. In brief, most Muslims practice their religion earnestly.[3] Confucian books require people to cultivate their moral character. For example, it is said: "Do not see what is against propriety; do not listen to what is against propriety; do not say what is against propriety; and do not touch what is against propriety."[4] Those who said, do not try to stop illegal things by themselves. Muslims pray five times a day and a Jumah prayer once a week; they always fear God; the sincere in their prayers turn directly to God, the creator of all things. They are so pious that they forget and devote themselves to worship God. Sir, are you aware of this?"

---

[1] First watch (初更) is one of the five two-hours-periods into which the night was formerly divided.

[2] Such as conspiring to kill the emperor and subvert the government.

[3] As a result, they will not commit any crime.

[4] It is taken from *Lunyu. Yanyuan* (论语·颜渊), see: *The Translation and Commentary of the Four Books*, 148.

4.10 To Maintain the Integrity of Muslims on Certain Occasions

The guest said, "I have talked with you at length, and it appears that you have read some Confucian books. Why are you still such a stickler? [Why are you not] talented and romantic? Why do you not cultivate your feelings by reciting poems and drinking alcohol? I once saw and heard a Muslim who had changed and become like a non-Muslim in that his educational attainments were impressive, he drank alcohol whenever he came across it and ate whatever food he was provided with. If he could enter upon official circles successfully, he would not be a stickler like some persons are when dealing with people. Distinguished personages in the past were not sticklers at all. They knew how to deal with different people in the right way. In fact, to make friends with great officials is nothing more than joining in the fun on occasions. Why do you take matters so seriously? In the days to come, you should be flexible, be out of the three worlds.[1] This is the right appearance that a real hero should have."

I said, "You are wrong, Sir. The most important trait for a man is honesty (loyalty) and filial obedience. That is why the kings enlist subjects from families that are well known for their worthy progeny, because if a person obeys his parents and makes them happy, the parents trust that he will not change their right way of behavior. He is the right person who can be trusted by the emperor to take care of young orphans, and to run a country. He will not lose his will when he suffers setbacks. Through one's drinking and eating, we can see whether a person is honest and obedient or

---

1 The term *three worlds* is a Buddhist term, which means three worlds with different levels: the first level is the world of appetite and sexual desire in which majority of common people live. The second level is the world with little desires, it is dwelled by those who have given up the most desires and enjoy only perfect and excellent things. The third level is the world that belongs only to those who have given up material enjoyment completely and only have spirit left in them. The guest indicates the regulations of religion in trying to persuade the author to be a carefree man who does whatever he likes.

not. The one you mentioned as being a [lapsed] Muslim, I don't know how many generations of his ancestors were Muslims.

It surprises me that he would drink alcohol whenever he came across it and did not mind at all what he ate. I guess, although he did so, his mind was not at peace and his face was not pure. He may not even have liked people to call him Muslim, but he could not stop them. He tried but was unable to conceal his identity as a Muslim. During the time that he was drinking and eating, he must have felt as if he was sitting on a bed of nails. Although he might look relaxed, he would be on guard and afraid that people may dig up his Muslim background. When a Muslim faces such situations, why does he not reject it openly? Perhaps he thinks that he could gain a position and make a fortune by pleasing the high officials (VIPs) who might accept him to join a group of ministers like theirs. Furthermore, his children could join the ranks of civil and military officials.

"He thought that in the past many people divorced their wives and abandoned their children to gain a prominent position and make a fortune. [He thought,] 'They did not feel ashamed of that. I could please high officials by drinking and eating with them without divorcing my wife and abandoning my children. What is the sense of not doing so?' He ignored one thing: that time will soon pass away, and everything that he gained in the present will end. His children could neither be promising by themselves nor carry on their father's position by association with high officials, and they might divorce their wives and abandon their children. Even though dead, it is not impossible that he knows the retribution visited upon his late generation today. These people are aware that their grandfathers and fathers were Muslims and are afraid of their backgrounds being exposed. Whenever they feel ill at ease, not peaceful and look back and forth for fear of their cover being blown, when they feel this is due to their disobedience of their grandfathers' religion and their going against their fathers' way, this is the right time in which their conscience can be regained. If someone could repent at this moment, it is hopeful that he will return to the right way again.

"A generous person would think: This guy is a Muslim who has disobeyed his grandfather; he does not feel ashamed, nor does he not care for filial piety (孝道) due to concern for position and fortune. If his grandfather were to see or know what his grandson had done, he could not accept that, because what he did is against the morality of filial piety. People who forget their own origin cannot be entrusted with the care of orphans and the management of a country. Furthermore, they shouldn't have a place to stay between heaven and the earth. If there is a minor post in the government that needs to be filled, he should not be appointed to it, because if he could disobey his beloved ones today, he will disobey the emperor tomorrow. Based on this analogy, don't expect him to be an honest subject. It is impossible that he could follow Boyi's (伯夷) [1] style. From this, we know that those who have no scruple in drinking and eating together with non-Muslims cannot really be accepted by Muslims. Not only that, but they also are shameless sinners between the heavens and the earth!

"They do not realize that alcohol is very harmful, which is why it was forbidden even by Chinese wise men. Yu (禹) hated drinking alcohol and liked to hear good advice; Zhougong (周公) made an official warning to forbid alcohol, according to which if people drank together in a group, they should be killed. To drink alcohol is a minor sin,[2] while killing is a major punishment, and Zhougong insisted on punishing minor sinners with capital

---

[1] It was the name of an honest man in the late Shang dynasty, who was well known because of his filial piety. His full name was Yun Gongxin (允公信). His father appointed his brother Shuqi (叔齐) to be the successor. When the father died, Shuqi abdicated the position to Boyi, however, the latter rejected because to accept it was to go against the father's will. Then, he escaped and left from Shang; Shuqi, his brother, followed him to the Zhou dynasty. It was chanced that Zhou was planning to send armed force to suppress the Shang; the two brothers tried to stop the war by persuading the emperor of Zhou but they failed, because of the war, Shang was destroyed; the two brothers refused to eat the food that was provided to them by the Zhou, regarding it as a disgrace. In the end, both of them died from hunger in a place named Shou Yang Shan (首阳山). See *History of Chinese Ancient Civilization*, 456.

[2] It might be acceptable to say this comparing to other serious sins like killing people; or according to Chinese law at that time. However, drinking alcohol is counted in the seventy big sins according to the Shari'ah.

punishment because drinking alcohol leads to killing many persons. He thought that if he did not do so, he could not unite the hearts of the people and govern the country properly. This was the way that Chinese wise men ruled people, which also contained such prohibitions. As to those who canceled the prohibition, I don't like to say anything against them, for I would be blamed and censured.

However, there are some non-Muslims who are either classmates of Muslims, or took the imperial examination together with them, or are their co-workers in the same office who lure them to drink alcohol. As a result, Muslims of weak faith might be lured by them. When they disperse, they will talk to others and mention, as a joke, that so-and-so drank and ate [with them]. If a fight occurs, they forget the promise that they would not tell anyone else. It becomes an empty word.

Though the lured Muslim is blameworthy, his friends who lured him, instead of stopping him, let him go against his grandfather's religion, forget his origin, and lose his integrity as a Muslim. After luring him, they enlarge the matter and spread it to others. They don't realize that it is possible in the future for other people to lure their children into going against their grandfathers' principle of dealing with people, which consisted of *Xiao* (孝, filial piety for father), *Ti* (悌, showing respect to elder brother), *Zhong* (忠, being loyal to the emperor) and *Xin* (信, being honest with friends). Why would that happen? Because if you dealt with others in a certain way yesterday, today they will deal with you in the same way. That's life. Hence, someone reflecting upon the death of Caoman (曹瞞)[1] wrote, "In the past, when he was helping the Han (汉), Caoman mistreated their widows and orphans. Who could imagine that, after forty years, his widow and orphans would be mistreated?" Why do intelligent people not reflect on this?

I say these words today, not only to persuade Muslims to strength their roots, but also to persuade non-Muslims not to lure ignorant Muslims when they meet them and not to let them fall into wrong actions. What benefit do they reap from such [seductions]? They give themselves a bad reputation which might cause harm to their following generations. If you persuade

[1] Caoman (曹瞞, 155-220) was a famous politician, strategist and poet.

others not to forget their principles, there will be someone who does the same for your children in the future; as a result, they may be exemplary in dealing with people according to the principles of *Xiao* (孝,), *Ti* (悌), *Zhong* (忠) and *Xin* (信). I expect that you will accept my advice and not do that in the future. If there was a good official in charge of the security of society, he might rectify the situation strictly when meeting a Muslim drinking alcohol; such actions would be in accordance with morality and ethics.

4.11 Trimming the Moustache and Shaving Body Hair

The guest said again, "Body hair is given by parents and should not be damaged. However, Muslims trim their moustache and shave the hairs of the lower part of the body. After removal, it grows back several days later. Isn't this a trifling and troublesome matter? Furthermore, it is trivial and has nothing to do with the principle of truth; so why do you do so?"

I said, "In ancient times, men combed their hair as women do. However, now, people follow the royal regulation [to plait their hair]. Muslims trim their whiskers, not only to follow Islamic rules, but also to look presentable and to feel refreshed and comfortable. Furthermore, affairs are either primary or secondary (some are very important and some are less important); some things should be preserved while others should be removed. What would be the situation of the world if there were no difference between the primary and the secondary and no difference [recognized] between what should be preserved and what should be removed? It was said that if weeds are removed, it lets crops grow; if the emperor and his subjects are settled,[1] people will live in peace and safety.

"As for the mouth and whiskers, [assume that] the former is the emperor. When a person eats food, his mouth, which is the emperor, has the right to eat. How can his subjects disturb the emperor while he is eating? Obviously, the whiskers should be removed; but they should not be removed too much. We keep those in the middle of the upper lip, and the hair at the sides of the mouth should be preserved for impressiveness. Not a single

[1] He means that each of them is in their rightful place.

hair on the temples should be touched. By doing so, the positions of the emperor and his subjects will be settled.

"There should be no interference when a person eats and drinks. [After the hair is trimmed] it does not get in the way of eating and drinking; even soup will not drip, and others will not think ill of you. People feel disgusted when they see soup dripping from someone's whiskers, so why they should not be trimmed? In your opinion, these minor whiskers should not be damaged; however, people nowadays cut their hair;[1] why do people do so? People do not make scathing comments about that because it is a royal decree to cut them and, in their view, the law is perfect. However, they do not know why it is so. It is perfect because there is some hair that remains in the plates and it is an enduring symbol of removing evil and maintaining good.

"Muslims remove the hair of the lower body to make it easy to clean when they bathe. We cannot pray to God unless our body has been cleaned and refreshed, so we must remove filth from our body first. It is like farmers removing weeds before they sow the field with seeds. In ancient times, in the time of *Shangtang* (商汤),[2] people made inscriptions on everything, especially on bathtubs. A bathtub is nothing but an implement; however, they did this to remind people to prepare their bodies and make them clean, inside and out. Chinese wise men used inscriptions on the bathtub to remind people to be good in thoughts and deeds. Our prophet taught inner and outer cleanliness of the body by removing the unnecessary hair of the body. This

---

[1] The Qing dynasty required people to follow the custom of the royal race which was the Manzu, and plaiting the hair was one of the requirements. As a result, most people in the hinterland of China practiced this. They cut hair on the front part of the head and plaited the back part.

[2] He was the founder of the *Shangtang* (商) dynasty, which existed from around the 17th century B.C. till the 11th century B.C.

is more advanced; is it not? There is a saying with a similar meaning: "There is no 'Dao' out of the body."[1]

4.12 Why Muslims Do Not Worship Idols

The guest said, "According to you, all the practices of Muslims are in accordance with principles and truth, but you do not worship idols, and this seems unreasonable."

I said, "There are not two suns in the sky; and there cannot be two kings to rule the people. For a long time, it was widely accepted that people should revere nothing but God. In short, non-Muslims speak much but practice little. They say that they do not placate ghosts and gods (supernatural beings) to seek fortune, yet they worship them. You do not remember this saying: "If you offend God, you will have nothing to pray to." In *Fogubiao* (佛骨表)[2] of Changli (昌黎), there is a very detailed discussion about this. He said in his letter to Meng Dongye (孟东野):[3]

> Who was the Buddha? Did he behave like a gentleman or a dishonorable person? If his behavior was that of a gentleman, he should not allow his followers to wallow in misfortune. If he was a dishonorable person, he is dead and his soul is no longer able to act. There are so many angels in heaven and the earth, and every one of them has its own position and cannot be replaced by anyone else. How could

[1] "Dao" is a philosophical term which means morality, the principle of things and the way or path of life. The author means here that one must start by cleaning his body when he wants to be clean in terms of deeds.

[2] It was said that Tang Xianzong (宪宗, 806-820) supported Buddhism very much. He wanted to bring the so-called finger of Buddha into the palace to worship. One of his subjects called Hanyu (韩愈) tried to stop the emperor, he wrote an article for the purpose and titled it *Fogubiao* (佛骨表) in which he criticized Buddhism and showed no mercy.

[3] Meng Dongye (孟东野, 751-814), was a poet in the middle of the Tang dynasty. He had a work titled *Collections of Meng Dongye's poems*.

his ghost be allowed to ride roughshod over others and do whatever it wants?

There is no evidence at all to believe in him; however, many people do. At the same time, they are confused. These words are from Confucian books, not from Islamic books, but they are very reasonable and acceptable. Some people are doubtful of these so-called gods, but they are deceived by them and sacrifice themselves to seek benefits.

"Islamic books say that the heavens, earth, ancient prophets and wise men were created by the Dominant. He has no image to hang up, but we venerate Him. As for commandments, prohibitions and other regulations, Muslims must follow them. We do not exceed them; thus, we improve ourselves and become advanced people.

"Mencius said (孟子): 'Everyone can be as great as Yao (尧) and Shun (舜).' He also said: 'Shun was a man, I, too, am a man.' If people do not follow Yao and Shun's actions, but hang their images in the living room and worship them while disobeying their parents and older brothers, God will send down misfortune on them, and the spirits of Yao and Shun would be unable to save them, even if they are with them. Furthermore, what benefit could you derive from worshipping these so-called gods for which there is no evidence? If they could send down wealth, there should be no beggars among their followers. If they could send misfortune then all Muslims should be dead without exception, because we do not worship them. Only wise men can understand truth such as this. Stupid people believe the deceiving words of Buddhism and Taoism, seeking fortune and honor.

"If such gods can send down good fortune, why haven't devout Buddhists who prayed to them every day been repaid? For example, Liang Wudi (梁武帝)[1] starved to death, and Buddha did not save him. From this we know that Buddha is not worthy of worship. Buddhists explain this story[2]

---

[1] His name was Xiaoyan (萧衍, 464---549), the founder of the Liang dynasty (梁). He was on the throne from the year 502 to 549. He built many Buddhist temples and in 549, he died from hunger and illness.

[2] The story tells how Liang Wudi died.

by saying that even though Liang Wudi starved to death, he became a Buddha. Is there any substantial proof for this explanation? Even if we agree that he did, it only proves that Buddhism is a religion that calls on people to be lowly and degraded. How do we know this? Buddhists always say that a certain emperor was reincarnated from a certain Buddha.

"Let us analyze these words: [Someone became a Buddha first,] then an emperor, after suffering many difficulties and much trouble. Based on this, an emperor is much more honorable than a Buddha. If he is not, why are people encouraged to cultivate their morality and character to become a Buddha, after which they could be reincarnated as an emperor. As to why he became an emperor, Buddhists say it is because he suffered many difficulties before he became a Buddha. Therefore, he can enjoy his karma[1] without limits, for after he becomes an emperor he can do whatever he likes. If this is true, why did the King of Liang starve to death at a time when he could do whatever he wanted? These words contradict each other; they make no sense except to deceive the foolish.

"By examining this, it is evident that Buddhism is without any basis. Is there something more laughable in Buddhism? It is said that Guanyin Dashi (观音大士)[2] helped many people. However, when she became a Buddha, she had no avenue for reincarnation as a commoner, let alone as a king. As for seeking fortune and honor from Buddha, nothing can be seen after you have spent money to build temples to satisfy those lazy people. I am afraid that by doing this, you have spread evil instead of good. Is Liang Wudi's matter not enough evidence for that? If you asked Buddhists, they will always say, 'Nobody can escape from the decision of Tian (天) and his arrangement.' They have no choice but to say this, and they should state it in the beginning. Therefore, Muslims worship nothing but the one God."

---

[1] Hindus and Buddhists believe that the quality of people's current and future lives are determined by their behaviour in this life and past lives.

[2] She is one of the four great Buddhas according to the Buddhism propagated by the Chinese. She was imagined by them in order to save people from disasters.

4.13 Slaughtering Animals

The guest said, "To revere [one] God has been clarified. However, Muslims do not eat vegetarian food; on the contrary, they consume beef and mutton. Furthermore, you refrain from eating such foods unless certain incantations are recited at the time the animals are slaughtered. It should be the same regardless of who slaughtered the animals, Muslim or non-Muslim. Why are you so strange?"

I said. "When we slaughter animals, we mention God's name, not incantations. Before we do anything, we mention His name, and when people hear this, they think it is unusual. I used to see an admonition in certain official departments, which said: "Omit any punishment that could be omitted, because even plants are living things created by Tian." If we are not encouraged to abuse plants, which are God's creations, then how can we abuse animals? They have life, so how can we not be cautious? People who slaughter animals for a job are wrongdoers; gentlemen dislike mentioning them. Whoever is preparing a wedding or arranging a funeral, will recite a Qur'anic verse [Tasmiyah] before slaughtering. "The emperor does not slaughter cattle without a reason, and senior officials do not slaughter sheep without an excuse." This was to instill a sense of the importance of living things and sympathy for animals. We are not allowed to satisfy human wants indiscriminately. The regulation stated in Li (礼) and the rule of Islam are the same.

"You only know that Muslims recite a verse before they slaughter, but you do not know that they must also choose a faithful and practicing Muslim to slaughter animals; otherwise, the meat is not lawful.[1] In Li (礼), it is stipulated that animals should not be slaughtered without a reason; however, there was no specific rule, which meant that anyone could do it.

"The Islamic rules for slaughter are difficult to comply with. As a result, people are not able to satisfy their powerful desire for decent food,

---

[1] What he stated here is in accordance with Chinese Muslims' behaviour. However, there is no such regulations in Shari'ah law. On the contrary, Muslims can eat the meat of animals that are slaughtered by Christians and Jews in their own way as long as they mention the name of God.

even though they may have many birds and beasts, if they could not find a person qualified to slaughter or the time is not suitable for slaughtering. This is the way in which slaughtering without reason could be forbidden.

"However, people can slaughter if they are preparing for a wedding or inviting people for food after a funeral, and they should not be stingy. If someone wanted to slaughter an animal without a reason, the one who is asked to do that on his behalf should refuse, although he can recite Quranic verses. This must be taken seriously, even though it is a minor matter."

The guest said, "Sir, you are wrong. Tian (天) and Di (地) created [living] things for human beings. If there were so many regulations for slaughtering a single bird, making it difficult to conduct, wouldn't it be against their will?"

I said, "Have you never heard that things in heaven and the earth are limited, while the desires of men's hearts are endless? If we do not nip an evil in the bud and are not very careful [in using natural resources] to meet men's desires, the consequences will be uncontrollable. That was why people said, 'If a given behavior has not been regulated, it is impracticable.' Do you believe that?"

4.14 Cleaning the Body by Taking a Bath

The guest continued, "All practices of Muslims are based on principles and evidences. However, I still have something to discuss with you. I was told that if a Muslim couple had sex at night, they refrain from eating and drinking until they have taken a bath and use a water pitcher[1] to hold the water. Although they are a couple, they should not let others know that they had sex at night. However, people will come to know that by means of the bath, and they will taunt them. Again, before Muslims go to the mosque for prayer, they must wash the seven orifices of their heads, using water from a pitcher too. This is tiring and laborious."

I said, "The Islamic way of life, starting from major matters like the relationship between the monarch and his subjects and that between fathers

[1] The water pitcher makes a noise when someone takes a bath with it, so the neighbors will know that the couple had had sex at night.

and sons, and ending with minor things like daily regulations of drink and food, is recorded in the Islamic books without exception, therefore, even lazy people examine their own consciences before they do anything. When it is the time to perform devotional activities like prayer, fasting and so on, they will not go if they have not had a bath. The reason for this is that Islamic doctrine teaches us, as Muslims, that we should not deceive ourselves. For example, if a man did not make *wudu'*, he would not dare to pray. Why? Because the angels are above his body,[1] so he cannot deceive himself. He will be extremely careful. If someone wants to pray to God without having a bath and cleansing his or her body and heart, that is because they were taught to do so in their childhood. When they grow up, [the habit] has already had been established, so they will not change their way of life upon seeing diverse ways.

"In addition, everything concerning sex must be dealt with carefully. Thus, Muslims are very vigilant not only in arranging a match by the parents' order and on the matchmaker's word,[2] but also in dealing with wet dreams. Marriage is a primary concern in human affairs. If there were no married couples, how could there be future generations? Who, then, would attend to offering sacrifices for our ancestors?

"Everyone wishes to have wise and gentle future generations. This can only be realized if their parents give them an excellent education and if many previous generations of their forefathers had refined their own conduct and had good morals and ethics. According to a theory in the Confucian books, the fetus can be educated while it is still in its mother's womb. This is a less advanced understanding, for such education cannot be performed unless there is a baby in the womb. This is less superior to the Islamic practice of bathing; whereby illegal sexual actions are prevented and the

---

[1] He may mean the two angels, namely RaqÊb and AtÊd, who oversee recording the actions of mankind.

[2] According to Chinese culture, sons and daughter can not get married without their parents' permission and their order, and there must be a person who acts as a matchmaker and goes to the female's father to ask his permission.

human body and heart are cleaned and purified. Even youths who have strong sexual desire will refrain in very chilly weather for fear of the cold.

"When people take a bath, they feel light and relaxed and there will be no dirt on their bodies anymore; as a result, their minds will be clean. If the wife were to become pregnant now, it is more advanced than the Confucian way mentioned above. People said, "If you want to make a stream of water clean, you must clean its source first." In the Islamic way, the source of the stream is already clean, therefore, how can the stream not be clean?

"Islamic books mention a number of situations in which Muslims must take a bath to clean their body: after sexual intercourse or a wet dream; at the end of the menstrual period; and forty days after childbirth. Only then can they fast and pray to God. This is the Islamic way of life.

"Let us see what non-Muslims do. If a couple had sex at night, they will not dare to go to the temple the next day to worship their gods. If you asked them the reason for this, they will say, "My body is not clean, so I dare not worship God, [for] I am afraid I will blaspheme it, in which case, I would be guilty." Everything must be washed with water and starch; then it will be clean. Without being washed, nothing could become clean by itself with the lapse of time. They dare not worship God because their body is not clean, yet they feel ashamed to take a bath. Their body is already dirty because they did not take a bath. They should know that this will lead to a continual accumulation of dirt, and when dirt accumulates it must become foul. Furthermore, sexual relations can not be stopped between a couple, so the dirt will accumulate more and more, and the body will be dirty for their entire lives, during which they will not clean themselves.[1] So it is ludicrous to say that one does not dare to worship God because the body is not clean.

"I find it strange that non-Muslims understand minor things while ignoring key issues. Let us have a look at Tian (sky, heaven) and Di (the earth); they are so great and powerful. Furthermore, they were neither sculptured by an artisan nor painted by a painter in the five colours (blue, yellow, red, white and black). The sky is a canopy above our heads and the mountains stand beside us; therefore, people should fear having a dirty body

---

[1] As a reason, they will not worship God for their whole life.

in this world. Non-Muslims can still carry the blue sky on their heads, step on the earth, inhale the rain and dew and enjoy the grace of the five cereals.[1] They do not feel fear at living in such a world. This is what I mean by "ignoring major things". As for the idols in temples, they are nothing but sculpted mud and carved wood. Although they are green-faced and long-toothed, red-haired and gold-bodied, still, they are nothing but dirty mud and rotten wood fashioned by men. However, non-Muslims dupe and deceive themselves; they fear these things made of mud and wood. This is what I mean by "understanding minor things". They do not know that early generations made these idols to warn stupid and obstinate people, and that is the whole story.

"Therefore, whenever they have had sex, Muslims do not drink, eat or leave home unless they have had a bath. They use a pitcher to hold water so that the dirt will go together with the water and not remain anymore. If a man bathed in a river of running water, there is no need for a pitcher. As for why we do not use a bathtub to hold water for a bath, it is a place that is easily dirtied; fresh water will become dirty whenever it is poured in it; as result, it could not be drunk. This leads to a waste of the water. Muslims use the water stored in a pitcher when they take bath because, according to Islamic rules, used water is dirty. On the other hand, water stored in a pitcher is clean, and everyone knows this, so it can be consumed. Since people know that water could be stored cleanly in this way, why do they reproach the Muslims for using pitchers?

"You said that having a bath is a shameful act. If a girl gave birth before she got married, everyone would consider that shameful; if she gave birth after she got married, everyone would say it is a happy event. If taking a bath is a shameful act, then giving birth is the same, isn't it? The important consideration is whether the act has been done in a legal or illegal way. Therefore, why do people have any objections to taking a bath?

"Prayer is a ritual in which Muslims worship God. How are people to show their devotion by facing God with ears, eyes, mouth, nose, hands, feet, and body that have not been cleaned? Therefore, Muslims must wash the

---

[1] They are: rice (稻), millet (季) /(稷), wheat (麦) and beans (豆).

seven openings in their heads[1] as well as their body to make the inner and outer parts of the body clean and fresh; then they can pray to God. This is what Mencius meant when he said, "Even a bad person, if he fasted and had a bath, can still worship God."

4.15 Why do we not offer sacrifices to the souls of the dead?

The guest said, "I have apprehended the reason for bathing. However, after a parent dies, when holding the memorial ceremony for their death, you Muslims do not burn paper money or offer food. How, then, do you express your respect for the dead? Also, on the New Year you do not stick antithetical couplets [written on scrolls] on your doors. Why?"

I said: "Everyone has parents. They should be attended, supported and respected before their deaths, and it is natural and reasonable to hold a ceremony after they die. However, burning paper money and offering sacrifices to the dead are only to show a modicum of kindness by living persons, such as sons or daughters, toward the dead. If you traced the practice to its source, you will find that burning paper money was a way of Buddhism and Taoism. It was not in accordance with Confucian doctrine. The Confucian method of ceremony is to spill wine on the earth and burn cotton and silks, and then the ghost comes to consume the smell. Now it is mixed with the way of Buddhism. I think the dead forefathers do not like to receive it. Eighty to ninety percent of Confucian people join in fasting and ceremonies in the way of Buddhism and Taoism. This means that they have inclined to the teaching of the two religions, although they claim to be followers of Confucian doctrine. Are these the students of wise men who say "no" to the theory of Yang (杨朱) and Mo (墨翟)? Moreover, Buddhists fast and arrange special rites, which they call 'Yingfu' (应付).[2] This means that they have lifted the ban from wine and meat, which is why Chan Hezi (禅和

---

[1] They are the eyes, ears, nostrils and mouth, which are called by Chinese people as Qi Qiao (七窍), meaning: the seven apertures.

[2] It means they do that only to satisfy people's wishes; it has no any effect on the dead in fact.

子)[1] doesn't accept it. They defame each other, but all of them are on wrong paths.

"In the early times in which Muslims came to China, they did not understand the Chinese language; they did not speak or read it. When local people saw them following a completely clean way in their life and dealing with others honestly and sincerely, they named Islam as "Qing Zhen Jiao" (清真教).[2] When their predecessors noticed that Islam is able to remove improper thoughts and help people to revere the one God and return back to the true One, they called it as "Hui Jiao" (回教).[3] It might be because they saw that Muslims engage in self-examination, and that their prayer and fasting, giving money to poor people are all to release their hearts so that they return back to God. We do not know the real reason that the great thinkers of early times called Islam by this name. It is possible that the piety of early generations of Chinese Muslims was accepted by God and, as a result, He sent down this name. We do not know. Otherwise, why has this name been used for such a long time and has still not disappeared?

Islam can remove improper thoughts from people's minds, so Muslims do not do meaningless acts. On the anniversary of a parent's death, Muslims prepare food for people to eat, and they give some money to widowers, widows, orphans and the childless. If the parent left clothes and caps, they will be given to the parent's close friends as souvenirs. It is beneficial for both the dead and the living, and God sees them when they do that. Offspring who like to do good things, how [can you say] they do not attach importance to the spirits of their parents? Furthermore, when a person dies,

---

[1] It is also called 'Chanhe' (禅和) referring to the followers of Chanzong (禅宗), which is one of schools of Buddhism. See Ren Jiyu, *Dictionary of Religions*, (Shanghai: Shanghai Dictionary Publishing House, 1998), 1053.

[2] "Qingzhenjiao" means 'the pure and the true religion.'

[3] "Huijiao" means the religion of Huihui (Chinese Muslims). However, these names of Islam have been replaced by the term 'Yisilanjiao' (伊斯兰教, religion of Islam). It was stated in "Notification regarding to the name of Islam" issued by the state council of China on June 2, 1956, that the term 'Huijiao' should not be used any more. See Hai Zhengzhong, *Translation of Qingzhen Shiyi*, 116.

he will move to the other world, where he will be ruled, just as it was before he was born. How could human beings have no origin [from which they came] and be ignored [after they died]?

"Buddhism deceives people. It requires offspring of the deceased person to fast and hold memorial ceremonies. But people do not observe and do not know the reality. If a man went against the law and committed a minor infraction, he can ask someone among his friends and relatives who has a high social position to beg the official in charge of the issue for leniency, and the official might show leniency. If a person who has no position in the society at all says that he can do that for the transgressor, I think he will harm him instead of helping him. Buddhism claims that it can exempt people from punishment through fasting and holding ceremonies for the dead in a certain way. In fact, the so-called fasting is nothing but [an appeal to] wish fulfillment, by which they can recruit stupid people and collect money from them. This was why Chan Hezi (禅和子) disliked the practice. If I were to accuse them of destroying the natural bonds and ethical relationships between family members, would they be innocent of the charge? As to transgressions committed by the deceased that cannot be retrieved and forgiven, the money paid for that purpose is extracted from [the family members] by swindling.

No good impact is made upon the situation of the dead forefathers. The burnt paper money and the storehouses are gone with the wind. Nobody knows where they are. Even if the forefather wishes to stay in the [paper] building, spend the money, and use the articles, he cannot, because everything has been burnt and damaged already. How could they return to become like they used to be? Is there any lying word that deceives people more than this? Getting to the bottom of the matter, this is not the Confucian way. It is not as good as giving the money to poor people in the town, which would benefit not only their forefathers, but also several generations of their offspring who will enjoy the goodness left by their forefathers, by which they might be increased in number, honor and splendor. Some of them might gain high positions. Do they need to spend so much money to buy so-called

Feng Shui Bao Di (风水宝地)?[1] Is it not stupid to consider the location of a house or grave? Is it not a pity to do so?

"Those masters of Feng Shui always say, "To bury the dead, you must choose such-and-such a time on such-and-such day. If the day he appointed is very hot or comes two to three days after the death of the deceased, the dead body will start stinking, and its limbs will separate from each other. Such cases are always happening. Their aim in doing that is to improve the prospects for the prosperity of the offspring of the dead. In fact, they are trying to use human power to change God's will. If they can do that, let all the pregnant ladies in the world ask them to choose a lucky day for them to give birth. It would be better, would it not? They do nothing before a person is born, but talk nonsense after he dies. Their way is wrong.

"Muslims do not burn paper money, they do not offer sacrifices to the dead, they do not seek so-called lucky locations to build houses or bury the dead, because everything has been prearranged by God for everyone. If the dead can still eat the food of this world, they should be provided with three meals a day; if they are provided only several times a year, they will have no food to eat and no clothes to wear for hundreds of days. How can their flesh and blood forget them? It is not reasonable. If a person still needs food and clothes of this world after death, then where did he get food and clothes from before he was born and had no offspring to fast and hold ceremonies for him? Buddhists will say: humans are born by way of reincarnation. Before they were born, they could get food and clothes from the offspring of the previous generations who fasted and held ceremonies for them."

4.16 Reincarnation

I was thinking silently: Confucius and Mencius taught people not to turn human relations upside down. All of us know that the heaven and the earth were created first; then, human beings appeared on the earth. It is said in

---

[1] Chinese people believe that the right location of a house or tomb has an influence on the fortune of a family, therefore, when they chose a location, they invite special people to see whether the location is good or not, which they call "Kan Fengshui".

Gangjian[1] that Pangushi (盘古氏)[2] was born in the age of waste, but we do not know when that was. Islamic books say that God created a couple of human beings. [Every time the wife gave birth to a pair of twins, one male and one female]. The couple let [each pair] marry separately. Their number reached 72 pregnancies; every pregnancy yielded twins, making for a total of 144 persons. According to the theory of reincarnation, let us ignore where the first couple reincarnated from. I would like to ask: where did the spirits of the 144 persons start from? If they need reincarnation to exist, it must be like this: the first person dies and reincarnates into the second; the second dies and reincarnates into third, and so on. One person only reincarnates into one other, so how could there be so many people in the world now? They are like the sand in Henghe (恒河沙数).[3] Let us say that the 72 pairs of twins were the beginning of reincarnation. Please try to infer like this: the oldest brother died first; then he reincarnated into his younger brother's wife's stomach. When she gave birth, the baby [who was the oldest brother of the husband] is the son of his brother. If you continue to extrapolate, the grandfather must be his own grandson. This is a turning upside down, which could not be [logically] acceptable! How could God allow such a thing to happen? How can wise men feel at ease with this kind of saying! Even if we took Pangu (盘古氏) as an example, he must go down to succeeding generations in the same way till today.

---

[1] It is a kind of historical book in 8 volumes, covering the history of China for five thousand years. Resource: http://www.Baidu, Encyclopedia knowledge, 16th May, 2008.

[2] He was considered as the first man to emerge on the earth according to Chinese history. It said that he changed nine times and grew up one Zhang (more than 3 metres) every day. His life lasted 8 thousand years. See Wang Jiafan and Xie Tianyou, *History of Ancient Chinese Civilization*, p.454. According to some Chinese Muslim scholars, Pangushi was Adam. See for example: *Zhengjiao Zhenquan* (正教真诠), 151; (Qing) Tang Jinhui, *Qingzhen Shiyi Buji* (清真释疑补辑), (Hong Kong: Lan Yue Publishing House, 2006), 21.

[3] It is a term in Buddhism, meaning the number that is so big that nobody could count it, just like the sand in the Henghe River.

Therefore, it is stated in the Islamic book that mankind cannot conjecture how the real Dominant creates everything. It is also said that the real Dominant is the creator. Everything is created by Him. God's creatures can be great or small or many or few, depending on His will. Let us take a fictional character as an example. The character is like a creature; the writer is like a creator. In writing the character the writer can make it big or small, much or little, beautiful or ugly. Everyone knows that the writer is the only one who decides; the characters cannot control the right of the writer. Everything follows the same principle. I just gave you an example. This is an example for creation, not for reincarnation. As for an analogy for reincarnation, let us say the following: a person writes the character "天",[1] no matter whether it is big or small, and someone wanted him to write another "天", or many such "天". The writer said, "There is no need to write any more. The one can reincarnate to be an innumerable number of "天", as many as the numbers of grains of sand in the Heng River." Would you believe him? Does it still need further discussion?

For as long as the heavens and the earth have existed, all people, no matter if they were wise or average, have come forth from the wombs of their mothers. Parents do not know whether the embryo is male or female. How can they know whether it will be wise or average? Even if the embryo is wise, he cannot do remarkable things in his mother's womb. In this way, God shows the greatness of His creation, to help people to think about it and not to ignore it. Moreover, it has happened that some wise men died when on the verge of fulfilling their enormous potential. Their deaths could not be postponed even for a moment to let them complete their work. This also shows the greatness of God's creation. It proves that nobody has the right to give and deprive. The one who said, "Between the heaven and the earth, I am the only senior"[2] could not escape from death in the end. Otherwise, why does he not appear in the world to call people to be monks? I think he did not say these words, because monks and nuns do not talk wildly. It was his followers who exaggerated the words to make their doctrine to be more

---

[1] This character has several meanings like: sky, heaven and God.

[2] He refers to Sakyamuni, the founder of Buddhism.

famous and popular. If this is the case, it is not fair to attribute these words to him. If he said these words, it means that he was not a humble man. How could his words be considered an admonishment? Where did he place his own father and grandfather? Is it not a fallacy if he was the only senior, and everyone except him is less important, and he forgot where he came from? These are the reasons why Muslims reject the idea of burning paper money and offering food to the dead, as well as reincarnation.

As for hanging up antithetical couplets written on scrolls, I have talked about it in detail already. As to bells and drums, Muslims do not use them when they pray. That is to prevent disturbance to their devotions. Nor do they use music when they arrange for marriages and funerals. That is to rectify the general mood of society by removing vulgarity and promoting propriety, and [in the case of funerals] it lets people remember those who passed way and their deeds in a serious atmosphere. These are also things that have people confused and which they want to understand. Islam aims to remove all irregular ways to focus upon worship of the only Dominant. Muslims avoid man-made images because they cloud and confuse their innate dispositions (*al-fitrah*).

4.17 Taoist priests and Their Magic Arts

As for the Taoist priests,[1] every angel has its own duty. Wind, cloud, thunder and rain; sun, moon and stars; frost, dew, snow and hail; mountains, water, fire and earth, are all managed by the powers of angels. In obedience to God's order they neither increase nor decrease even a little without His permission. Like ministers who never disobey the orders of their emperor; each enjoys his salary according to his position and duty, and none dares bend the law for personal benefit. Therefore, a case like this would definitely never happen: One man is a grade nine official [a very low position], but he gets a first-grade salary because he knows how to satisfy the court's chief minister of national granaries; while another person who should receive very high pay because he is a first-grade official does not

[1] They are people who claim that they can bring fortune for people and control the forces of nature which is, in the Islamic perspective, the duty of angels.

know how to win minister's approval by flattery, so the minister dislikes him and, thus, does not pay him anything.

Here, I remembered what Zilu (子路)[1] said: "A person talks with others while his aspirations and interests are different from theirs; because of that, he looks shame-faced. Such a person I do not understand." The person looks ashamed because people do not talk to him. He means that several people live in a room; they can talk to each other about whatever they like, but there is only one person who they never talk to. It is not appropriate for that person to speak to them. That was why Zilu said that he himself could not understand him. The principle of both human beings and angels is the same. First, people who beg without due cause are too trivial to settle; next, their demands should not be met if they have no approval. For example, the court's chief minister of national granaries sits in his office every day to handle tax matters from all over the country and pay the salaries [of bureaucrats and] soldiers. He makes disbursements according to approved official letters. He cannot give anything to those who have no approval. He cannot even meet them; otherwise, self-seekers will come to meet him one after another.

The minister will not meet these people, first, because they have no order issued by the emperor; second, he doesn't have enough energy to do so. He would not be able to handle their endless petitions even if he worked day and night. The case of Taoist priests should be understood in this way. Then people will stop begging them. All government decrees must be approved by the emperor, even in the face of public wrath. It would be absurd for the underling to disobey the order of the emperor to satisfy the public. These are the reasons why Muslims do not beg Taoist priests. Islam upholds a firm and clear stand on the matter to protect Muslims from deviation.

In my view, it is most heretical if someone claimed that he or she has magic arts. It is not only Muslims who do not believe in them, Confucius

---

[1] He was one of the students of Confucius. See: Chen Puqing, *Translation and Commentary of the Four Books*, 146; Mr. Hai, the *Translation of Qingzhen Shiyi in Modern Chinese*, 127.

and Mencius also did not like mentioning them. Let us see whether priests really can send angels to do whatever they want and if they know the past and future. This country is vast, the responsibility of the emperor is very weighty, and there have been brutal and domineering men in every period of history. With their transcendent knowledge, the priests should know their whereabouts. If they have true magic arts and can command angels, why do they not send five bolts of thunder to kill them? If priests did that, it would not only save money, but also avoid arguments and lawsuits. How pleasant that would be! By doing this they could also gain the virtue of a loving human. In addition to that, there are many benefits for [the priest], as the emperor will be pleased, and society will be stable.

Likewise, when the country encounters drought or excessive rain, food crops do not grow, and people are anxious and weary, those who have the true arts should not sit back and let the people suffer nor allow the emperor to be forced to draw on stocks and send more than ten thousand Dan (石)[1] of grains from the national treasury to relieve people in stricken areas. If they really have that kind of ability, they should be able to foresee all such imminent disasters; if they could not foresee one before it happens, they must surely know after the fact and get angels to send rain to the dry land and make the seedlings of cereal crops suddenly grow. Had a priest done this, surely the people would be deeply grateful to him. Angels could also be sent to flooded areas to disperse the clouds and mist, make the sun shine and the water recede. Farmers would be happy, and both the public and private individuals would be filled with exultation. If you observe carefully you will find that no priest has appeared to do as proposed. They are as helpless as the common people in the face of calamity. If you ask why they do not deliver the people, they reply, 'That is God's will.' I say the same. Now it is clear that magic arts are unable to wrest God's power. If His decree is so mighty that it cannot be challenged by any force, one may question why non-Muslims believe in magic arts over belief in God, and obey the words of certain individuals over those of God? If Muslims believe in the magic arts and worship priests, then we are the same as those who seek personal gain.

---

1 "Dan" (石) is a unit of weight: one Dan equals 60kg.

Those who claim to venerate the emperors and follow the old ways are pedants with high-sounding ideals and impracticable views.[1] How sad it is!

There were once extraordinary entities[2] who could touch a stone and turn it into gold and even summon wind and rain [i.e., control the forces of nature]. However, since then, they no longer associate with society. If a person [with claims to such powers] associates with the people and eats and dresses like common people, he must be a crook who comes to defraud them of their money and belongings. This is one of the ways in which we can distinguish between true and false possessors of supernatural powers. One may say that he does not eat any cooked food and that he only needs several bowls of water every day. In fact, he needs water to soak beads that are made from cattle bones.[3] If you meet such a person, remove his clothes and deny him access to them, you will find that he is a crook.

4.18 Leaving Family to be a Monk or Nun

As for leaving one's family to be a monk or nun, it is perfectly regulated in Islamic sources. In this regard, Muslims are unlike Buddhists and Taoists, who wear hemp cloth in summer and fur coats in winter, drink whenever they feel thirsty and eat whenever they feel hungry. They neither weave cotton cloth nor plough the earth; they live in high and wide buildings [temples] and play in the mountains and forests together with wild birds, or sleep leisurely and carefree, leaving the difficulties of cultivation and farming, spinning and weaving to the public. There is an ancient saying that goes: "Already, the sun has risen to 3 *zhangs* (丈) but the monk has yet to rise. It seems that freedom from engagements is better than honor and interests [money]." It is said that these words have deep and positive meanings, but I am afraid that they might encourage people to go against the

---

[1] There were emperors in history of China, cheated by some priests and took the so-called elixir trying to live for ever.

[2] The author means by "supernatural beings" awliya of Allah (friends of God) some of which have the Karamat (unusual abilities). Sunni Muslims believe in their existence in the world.

[3] Then, the bones can be edible.

emperor and their parents. We understand those who were forced to hide in temples to escape from troubles and disasters. They were not like Buddhists and Taoists, who were used to delicious food on the table and colourful silk fabrics in their room, oblivious that they should be grateful to the emperor for his favors and to God for His grace. Do they not consider the source of their food and clothes? They do not know that these things are achieved by other people through challenging work, not their own magic arts. They are unaware that only three or four-tenths of the common people earn their pay from their own contributions.[1]

Let us take military and civil officials as an example. They sacrifice their own lives and those of their families to protect and develop the country; however, they do not enjoy the carefree lives of monks and priests who bear no responsibilities and, as a result, do not contribute to the country. People are easily deceived by their words because they hanker for good fortune. Only wise men can recognize them [for what they are], hence the saying, "The sun has risen to 3 Zhangs but the monk has yet to rise."

Upon deeper reflection, one will find that these words were nothing but a voice of protest. I always do desultory reading of historical books. During ancient times, there were some emperors who were deceived by alchemists and swallowed so-called elixirs. They could not bear the poison of alkali metals that caused them to become dehydrated and thirsty and feel unbearable pain. There was not even one successful case. Had there been, Qinhuang (秦皇)[2] and Hanwu (汉武)[3] would still sit somewhere stately today. However, they disappeared totally. That which I have stated above is

---

[1] In other words, 30-40 percent of common people work hard but gain less.

[2] Qinhuang (秦皇, 246-209 B.C.). His name was Yingzheng (嬴政), and he was the first amongst the Kings of Qin who eliminated the Han (韩), Zhao (赵), Wei (魏), Chu (楚), Yan (燕) and Qi (齐) from 230-221 B.C. and united China, calling himself the Emperor. To unify thoughts and opinions, he burned a lot of books and buried many scholars alive in pits.

[3] Hanwu (汉武, 156-87 B.C.) was the emperor of Xihan (西汉, The Western Han, 206 B.C.-25 A.C.), and his name was Liuche (刘彻). See Wang Jiafan and Xie Tianyou, *Ancient Chinese Civilization*, 489.

not more than a fruit pit, spat upon by older generations.[1] They are not my words, and I hope you can understand me.

If a Muslim develops the inclination to leave his family, he is not allowed to do so unless he fulfills the following: he must wait until his parents die first,[2] to avoid causing them pain and heartache; second, he should wait until his sons and daughters get married, so they can replace him to support the family; and third, he has to pay off his debts. If someone owes debts, he must give the bill signed in acknowledgment of debt back to the person and clear himself from all obligations, and then he can leave his house and family. Once a man leaves his family, many of his worldly concerns will be replaced by a desire only to be close to God. It is neither like the art of flying in the daytime[3] nor nirvana.[4] To check erroneous ideas at the outset, our Prophet outlined the above regulations to discourage individuals from abandoning their families for the solitary life of a monk. If a person does not fulfill the above conditions, he is not allowed to leave. At the same time, it is stated in Islamic texts that to serve one's emperor and be honest to him; to serve parents and show respect to them; to make friends and be honest to them; to support your wife and servants; to show tender care for the widower, the widow and the childless; to maintain one's prayer and fasting and not leave them; and to perform honorable deeds, is a thousand times better than leaving one's family for devotion. In brief, Islam attaches more importance to human relations, and does not encourage people to withdraw from society and live in solitude.

If a Muslim decides to leave his family, he must gradually consume less drink and food, until he eats only one meal per month after about one year; then he must settle all his affairs. Upon fulfillment of these criteria, he can leave his family and society and go to a wooded mountain where he can look

---

[1] He means that what he said is not his own words but taken from others.

[2] This opinion is correct because to support one's parents is an obligation (wajib) while leaving family for devotion (Ibadah) is not compulsory.

[3] It refers to the Taoists who claim that they can fly.

[4] Nirvana is a term in Buddhism and Hinduism meaning a state of perfect bliss in which the individual becomes absorbed into the supreme spirit.

at Bavid's deer (麋鹿) in the morning; listen to the cries of apes and cranes at night; drink the water of springs, eat the fruits of trees and wild vegetables and, lastly, cover his body with the setting sun and make the fragrant grass his mattress. Whatever the weather is: cloudy or fine and clear; windy or rainy, he never gets influenced by the coming and going of rolling clouds; he cuts off thinking about worldly pursuits, no matter if the day is long and the night short. He can walk on top of a mountain and along the water's edge; he can sleep inside a stone cave as well as on top of the mountain. At this moment, his mind is detached; everything in nature is quiet and silent. A moment like this is equal to thousands of years in the man-world, within which everything is changing: advancing and being demoted; nations' rising and falling; gaining and losing. All that has been totally united with Tian and Di, and the Muslim travels amongst the creation without any space between the two. No one has the chance to glimpse the pleasure that he enjoys. To leave one's family in Islam is something like this.

4.19 Conclusion

Everything in the world, regardless of whether it speaks or is silent, moves or is still, is like what we have discussed above; and Islam has been clearly distinguished from other religions. How do I dare to speak about the behaviour of non-Muslims? You asked me, Sir, so I have had to speak about them in detail to tell you the reality of Islam.

The guest[1] thanked me repeatedly, and then he said, "Islam has not been clarified since it came to China, where it has been handed down from one generation to the next, and the later [generation] does not dare to change even a single word. I have never heard anyone that has explained and publicized it as you did today, to help people to know that Islam is a theory based on its own basis and evidences. In the days to come, I will no longer survey the sea of Islamic theory with my superficial view. Although the theory will not be understood well unless we read many books and suspicions will not be clarified unless we have rich knowledge, still, I have

[1] The word 'guest' is the last word in the edition published in the 33rd year of Qianlong (1769), which means it is an incomplete edition.

suddenly been enlightened during exchanging thousands of words with you this entire day. There are many people—myself now excepted—who do not understand Muslim behaviour. Why don't you write down our questions and answers and turn it into a book? This will benefit the suspicious and those who make [ignorant] comments and will help give them about a comprehensive view of Islam; and the book might be followed and handed down by them to coming generations. Next year, I will come to ask you for a copy of the book. Please do not forget this."

Then, the guest left.

As my talent is scant and my learning modest, and as I am occupied with official affairs, I was afraid that I would not be able to do it well and, as a result, people would not like to read it. However, the guest earnestly asked me to write it down, so I cannot refuse him, [especially since] the purpose of our dialogue was not to show a style of writing but to clarify Islamic teachings. Although my language is very common, it is to remove suspicions of people who doubt Muslim practices. [They do] not [doubt] their language, so why should I mind so much what people may say about my language and, thereby, hesitate and not write? [I would be] like one who is building himself a house, but he keeps [stopping to] discuss with passing travelers how to build.[1] To avoid later regret, I decided to stop caring whether people would make comments or not and give it to those who share my goal for the purpose of printing and publishing it. In the future, if people find some shortcomings in the book and think it needs rectification, they may do so; or if people from distant places who share my goal find the book to be beneficial but not widely spread, they can reprint it. This is my long-cherished wish; it is also the reason that I wrote "*Qingzhen Shiyi*".

[1] He means that it is not necessarily at all. He said this to show his humbleness.

PART THREE:
COMMENTARIES, COMMENTS AND CONCLUSION

CHAPTER FIVE:

COMMENTARIES AND COMMENTS

Qingzhen Shiyi was written mainly to clear up the doubts of Chinese society towards Muslims' behavior, therefore, the author's focus is on issues relevant to Islamic law or Shariah. However, since faith impacts on the behavior of man, he also explained some theological matters pertaining to religious doctrine (*kalam* or *aqidah*). In the coming pages, I would like to make some commentaries and necessary comments on the significant issues that the author presented in his book.

5.1 Theological Thoughts (الأفكار العقائدية)

The major matters Mr. Jin discussed in this regard are the following: God and His existence, oneness, names, position (or direction), creation and punishment; differences between Islam and Catholicism; the reason Muslims do not worship idols. He criticized Buddhism for its theory of reincarnation and Taoism for its magical arts. Let us see what he said in these matters.

5.1.1 Regarding God

It is well known that Islam is a monotheistic religion which believes that there is no god but Allah, therefore, the oneness of God is the key idea of Islam. As a Muslim, Mr. Jin strongly believes in the existence of God and it is because of Him that the universe keeps changing. He demonstrated his idea by quoting Zhuxi's words: "there is a dominant in heaven and the earth that is why they continually change." He also believes that there is only one God, in this regard, he said: "there is only one sun in the sky, and there is one king for people, it is clear since long time that only one should be respected." He also quoted a Confucian scholar's words which say: "If you made Tian angry, you will find nothing to pray" to demonstrate his idea. In terms of the name of God, he used several terms, with the exception of

"Zhuzai" (主宰, the dominant), he called God "Zhenzai" (真宰, the real dominant), "Shangdi" (上帝, God), "Tian" (天, sky, but it refers here to God) and "Shangtian" (上天, meaning: the heaven, providence, God).

5.1.2 About the position and direction of God

The issue of the position or direction of God is an important matter in Islamic theology about which Muslims' theological schools have argued with each other for a long time. When discussing this issue, Mr. Jin said: "We may use our body to understand the concept of God; as mentioned earlier, the human body is a small world and its Dominant is the life in it. Who among us has seen it? What does it look like? Where it is in the body? If we say it is in the head, then there is no life in the body and feet. If there is no life there, it will not feel suffering, therefore, they are dead. On the other hand, if we say it is in the lower part of the body then there is no life in the higher part. From this we know that life has no space and direction in the body; it occupies the whole corpus, this explains the sensations and feelings in every part of it.

The Islamic book says that God is everywhere in the world but we are not able to determine His position and form." What he presented here is the opinion of majority of Chinese Muslims. We agree with him in saying that there is no specific position and direction for God, but we do not agree with him that God is located everywhere in the world because to say so is somewhat against the oneness of God. If we read the Quran carefully, we will find that there are three kinds of verses: 1. some of them say that God is above the "Arsh"; 2. some say that God is in the heaven and on the earth; 3. others say that God is with mankind or very close to them.

After analyzing these verses, we find that the issue of the position of God is beyond our intellectual ability, it is too great for us to discuss. Therefore, we do neither say that God is in a certain place in or above the universe, nor He is everywhere in the world. Instead of that, we believe that God exists in a form that is suitable for Him, and we have no any idea about the form.

5.1.3 Creation of everything in the universe

With regards to the existence of everything in the universe, it is all created by God in the view of Islam, as Mr. Jin stated several times. He argued for the theory of Confucianism in this regard, which says that everything exists because of the airs of Yin and Yang. According to him the two airs need a place to lay (store) in; his question is: where were they laying before the existence of the heaven and the earth? He thinks that even if they do not need a place to be stored, the airs of Yin and Yang are unable to do anything by themselves without a power coming out of them. He took the calendar as an example, "Let us take the calendar as an example, which is issued every winter.

Who would dare to issue it before the appointed time? We must wait for the time to come before the calendar can be handed out. Because of the existence (and authority) of the King, people's actions were unified. If there is neither the craftsman who cuts and prints the calendar, nor the King who issues the order with regards to the calendar at the beginning of each winter, no one would believe that it could be cut and published by itself." Mr. Jin pointed out some self-contradictions of Confucianism, he said: "It was said that it is the air of Yin and Yang and not God that creates the heaven and the earth; that causes the coming and going of the four seasons, the changing of the times, the movement of the sun and moon and the rise and fall of nations in history. It is the natural law.

At the same time, it was also said that everything had been prearranged." He asked them and then answered his question: who makes the predetermination? It is the dominant which created everything. According to him, if everything exists naturally, there wouldn't be a prearrangement, however, Confucianism admits the prearrangement; since they admit that, then, they have no choice but to admit the pre-arranged is the creator.

5.1.4 Reward and punishment from God

Muslims believe in the theory of reward and punishment of God, while non-Muslims do not. They think that there are so many things for God to do, therefore He is not able to know who is a good doer and who is an evil maker. Jin Tianzhu gave them an example, he said: "Think about the thick clothes that people wear in winter where their bodies are totally covered and nothing can be seen. Their eyes are in their head. However, they know whenever there is a louse on the body and they can catch it easily, regardless of where it is.

How are the fingers that have no eyes able to catch such a small thing that is under our clothes? It is due to the light of life, which envelops the whole body. This is an evidence for reward and punishment. God is with everything in the heavens and the earth, He knows every single movement of every man, and therefore He rewards and punishes him or her." As to why ignorant people will be punished, Mr. Jin said: "People who live in a village far from the capital city; they do not know that there is an Emperor (King) and a strict system of law. However, if they went against the law and were discovered, they would be investigated. If they committed a grave crime they would be punished according to the law; they will not be let off because they have not seen the Emperor or because they were ignorant of the law."

I would like to point out here that according to Islam, ignorant people's punishment will be lighter than others. For the impacts of this theory on one's behaviors, Mr. Jin said: "Muslims know that there will be reward and punishment so that they fear God, and as a result, they follow the rules of Islam and rarely commit a sin." He advised non-Muslims to know God and worship him before it is too late, and told them the significance of this: "If Non-Muslims could study Islamic doctrine sincerely and follow Islamic rules, they might commit fewer crimes and therefore they will not be punished by the law of the state."

5.1.5 The nature of Jesus

Both Catholicism and Islam declare that God created everything and therefore, some people think that the two religions are the same. Mr. Jin denied this, and he listed the differences between two as the following: 1. Catholicism worships God facing an idol or image of Jesus and Mary while Muslims do not worship any idol; 2. There are no regulations of food and drink for Catholics to follow while Muslims must. In addition to that, about Jesus in Catholicism, he pointed out the following self-contradictions:

1. They call him "Tianzhu" (天主, the dominant of heaven or God), however, they call his mother "Shengmu" (圣母, the mother of prophet); why do they not call him "Tianzhuzhimu" (天主之母, the mother of the dominant or God) directly?

2. They said that God created everything, which means that Mary also was created by God. If this is the case, how could God have been reborn by her?

3. They said that God came to the earth for persuading people to believe in Him and do good things. This, according to Mr. Jin, is more absurd, and he said in this regard: "They did not realize that if He could create the heavens and the earth and everything in between them, then why could He not send down rain, wind, thunder and lightning, and make them be full in human society.[1] Floods, landslides and earthquakes are symbols, with which God warns people; therefore, why would He have to take on human form and be born (into the world)?"

4. Mr. Jin believes that God does not leave the heavens and the earth for a single minute, however, Jesus did, which means he is not God, "The Dominant whom Muslims believe in does not leave the heavens and the earth even for a moment. Why? It is said that heaven is a big world and man is a small one. The former has its own Dominant as has the latter. The Dominant of the big world is the one who created the heavens and the earth and everything in between them. He lets the four seasons come and go every year and makes the day bright and the night dark and He sends the wind and rains, while the Dominant of the small world lets our hands and feet move, our ears listen and eyes see. It is our life (命)...which does not separate from the body even for a moment, therefore, how could the ruler of cosmos go away?" Since Jesus left the earth and human society, it means that he is not God.

[1] As a result of this, they dare not do any evil.

5.1.6 The reason Muslims do not worship Buddha

Because Confucianism's focus is on worldly affairs rather than man's spiritual life, Buddhism occupied people's spiritual world in China, and as a result, most people worship the image of Buddha and other Buddhist idols. They do not understand why Muslims do not do like them, and feel strange about it. Mr. Jin gave them following explanations: 1. There is only one sun in the sky and one king for people in the country. If Muslims worship Buddha, that means they believe in him, which makes God angry. 2. Buddha is not worth being believed in as a god at all. To demonstrate his statement, Mr. Jin quoted what Hanyu (韩愈) said regarding Buddha:

> Who was the Buddha? Did he behave like a gentleman or a dishonourable person? If his behaviour was that of a gentleman's, he should not allow his followers to wallow in misfortune. If he was a dis-honourable person, he is dead and his ghost (spirit) does not work anymore; there are so many angels in heaven and the earth and every one of them has its own position that cannot be replaced by anyone else. How could his ghost be allowed to ride roughshod over others and do whatever it wants?

According to the author, the most important thing for a man is his behavior,

> If people do not follow Yao and Shun's actions, but hang their images in the living hall and worship them, meanwhile, they disobey their parents and older brothers, God will send down misfortune on them and the spirits of Yao and Shun would be unable to save them even if they are with them.

Buddhists worship Buddha to ask him to bless and protect them, and however, they are not in peace and good fortune while others may not be in misfortune and disaster.

In addition to this, the author argued against Buddhism regarding its concept of reincarnation and against Taoism about its magic arts.

5.2 Legal thought of the author (الآراء الفقهية)

As we have pointed out before, the main purpose of the author was to remove people's doubts and suspicions toward Muslims' behavior, therefore, the matters of jurisprudence (Fiqh) occupied most pages of the book. The discussed matters in it are: food, clothes, funeral, bathing, prayer, fasting, charity (zakat). He tried to explain why Muslims do these things and what the significance of them are. [1]In a sense, the book falls into the field of Maqasid Al-Shariah.

5.2.1 About the regulation of food

In Islamic law, there are some regulations and limitations regarding food. Chinese Muslims were following those regulations as specified by the Hanafi School, which is very strict in terms of judgment. Therefore, non-Muslims slandered them and described them as sticky and obstinate. According to them, since they have lived in China for a long time, Muslims should change their way of life and should not follow their religion anymore. Mr. Jin listed some regulations of food reported in the chapter *Xiangdang* (乡党) of *Lunyu* (论语) to demonstrate that Confucianism also has such regulations. He also said that Buddhism prohibits eating meat, this means that it is not only Islam has such regulations and limitations in terms of food, therefore, people should not talk about them in this regard.

As to prohibited food in Islam, Mr. Jin listed the following: pig, dog, naturally died animals, sharp-clawed birds, carnivorous beasts, aquatic animals with scales and shells of strange shapes and sizes and all intoxicants like alcohol. According to him, the reason these things are forbidden is because they hurt the nature and life of humans and eating them is bad for

---

[1] This is what Iz Al-din and some other scholars did, see, Al-Sulami, Iz al-din Abd Al-Aziz Abd Al-Salam, *Qawaid Al-Ahkam Fi Masalih Al-Anam*, (Beirut: Dar Al-Kutub Al-Ilmiyyah, 1420/1999).

the propagation of human beings. In addition, although cattle, sheep, chicken and duck are Halal for Muslims according to Islam, their blood, eyes, brain, waist and kidneys should be thrown away because they accumulate dirt, smell bad and hurt our property.

When the guest asked him that if this is the case, why did the ancient wise men not say anything regarding this? The guest also quoted words of Mencius, "I heard that foreigners can be changed to be like Chinese, I never heard that Chinese should be changed to be like foreigners." and argued against him that Muslims should change their way of life and be like others since they live here in China. Mr. Jin said: "Not so. Ancient generations of virtue used to have the etiquette and regulations of their own according to which everything was treated. The system of three cardinal guides and five constant virtues as specified in the feudal ethical code, human relations and disciplines and the rules and regulations for food and drink was the standard which wise men urged people to follow, as virtuous men educated them accordingly." As to the guest's argument, he said:

> Muslims shouldn't have changed, or it would have changed a long time ago if they separate between the monarch and his subjects, fathers and sons, husbands and wives, brothers and friends; or stop the tax payment for government, or give up etiquettes between old and young people, or are against righteousness and justice. If this was the case, they would have changed a long time ago, it would not have waited for you to remind them. What is the behaviour of Muslims in the things mentioned above? Why do they need to change?

He quoted words of a Confucian scholar to support his statement, "If it is a right way, it should not be changed for life; if it is not, why you would wait three years to change it after?" According to him, ancient wise men denounce people who do not like to be (the) subjects of (the) monarch, or to manage their family's property, or to associate with the princess under the Emperor. Muslims are not this kind of people, so why they are questioned?

5.2.2 Why Muslims use their own "Calendar" and celebrate their own "New Year"

Chinese Muslims put up in their house time tables written in Arabic or Persian, they congratulate each other when it is Eid al-Fitr, which arouses the suspicions of people and causes doubts of officials. As a result, they frame the case against Muslims that the latter use their own calendar rather than the official one, and celebrate their own New Year rather than Chinese New Year, which, as Mr. Jin said, was against the royal rule at that time. In his answer to the guest's question, the author came straight to the point and then started to explain why Muslims do all this,

> As for the Islamic book, Chinese characters are not used in pronunciation (to spell the Quran) because we are afraid of deviating from the original phonology of the book and losing its original style. Therefore, we have maintained the pronunciation as it was in early times. They (non-Muslims) do not know the way of the Muslims, so, it is not surprising if they consider the time-tables for prayer and fasting a calendar.

To help people to understand what he meant, he took the official calendar as an example,

> Today, the government makes a calendar every year and in addition to that, Tai Changsi (太常寺) makes timetables in the form of slips for religious activities and the anniversary of the death of parents, which are selected (decided) by Qin Tianjian (钦天监). These are usually stacked in government offices. In recent years, they have put circles on the calendars to make it easier for people to know the dates. They did all this because books are always closed and are more difficult to use compared to slips. In this way, the government makes people aware of the time. An analogy of this is where ordinary people hang their own timetables of

> the anniversary of their parents' deaths in their houses. Is it reasonable to consider these timetables as calendars?

Regarding the New Year, Mr. Jin said: "This originated from the fasting that is an obligation in all religions. The fasting in Islam is different from that of other religions. Our prophet understood and sympathized with the poor. He said that monarchs and their subjects, as well as the rich, do not lack food and drink and therefore do not suffer as hungry people do. Their conditions have never been as difficult as those of widows, widowers, orphans and the childless, even if they experienced a year of crop failure. Therefore, Islam set a month for fasting in which Muslims are required to eat Sahur (a pre-dawn meal) at cockcrow time and break the fast when the stars brighten. During the daytime, they are not allowed to eat a single grain or to drink a drop of water, regardless of whether it is the bitter cold of winter or the intense heat of summer.

Muslims are not allowed to choose the month for the fasting and it is postponed for one month every three years. Islamic law permits Muslims to eat meat, which is a significant difference compared to other religions that forbid this.

Again, nobody can say that he or she has never made any mistakes, knowingly or otherwise, in words and deeds in daily life. In the fasting month, people make amends for their mistakes and they realize from their experience of fasting that God likes people to live well and that they are lucky compared to the poor. Furthermore, it can help dukes and princes to understand their emperor and to be just in making political decisions. In turn, senior officials can understand dukes and princes and try to find a proper way to use the power of punishing and interrogating plaintiffs. Finally, it helps the common people to understand the Dominate (God), Emperor, princes and senior officials, so that they may purify their thoughts, decrease their desires, correct their mistakes, improve themselves to be better people and help them to know and empathize with the inconvenient situation of helpless people. Muslims fast for a whole month with these intentions. When it ends, they have a special bath, put on new clothes, and go to the mosque for prayers. Afterwards, they congratulate each other on completing the month-long obligatory fast in which they closed their doors unlike the other months. This is the reason for the felicitations."

We can see here that the author clarified the reason why Islam required people to fast, the time and some rules of fasting, the purpose and some significance of fasting. Very interestingly, he pointed out the impact of fasting on the spirit of the officials, princes and the Emperor, therefore, each of them tries his best to do his job, because of that, the society will be in peace and harmony. As to the reason why the fasting has such an impact, he said that it is "because it leads them to contemplate hardship, which might make them more compassionate. On the contrary, a situation of ease might lead to excessiveness; causing them to forget to be kind and possibly resulting in evil and eventually forming a vicious circle." At the end, he clarified that Muslims congratulate each other because they have completed the fasting, not because it is their New Year.

When the guest was confused why revered persons like his Excellency and rich people should imitate hungry people, Mr. Jin enumerated three evidences to support his statement:

1. Ancient emperors tilled the earth; his wife fed the silkworm; government officials of various levels, as well as common folk were all intellectual and physical laborers engaged in heavy work. They did this in order "to experience for themselves how hard it is for farmers to produce grains so that people might take diligent care of them."

2. The story of the King of Nan Song (420-479) who asked his subjects to experience hunger to let them know how to cherish grains and materials.

3. Etymology, according to which, the character "斋" (fasting) was formed by laminating two Chinese Characters together, Bu (不, meaning do not), and Shi (食, meaning eat); this was the meaning of fasting for the ancient Chinese people, which means that ancient Chinese people fasted.

4. Mencius said, "If a person in the world drowned in water, Yu (禹) felt that he was the one who caused him to drown; when he was told that someone was hungry, Ji (稷,) felt that he was the one who caused his hunger." If the fasting of Islam is to make people be inflexible and trouble themselves, those wise men's actions would be regarded in the same way, yet no one says this.

5.2.3 *Zakah* and its significance

Zakah (obligatory charity) is one of the five primary obligations in Islam. According to a famous *hadith* (saying of the Prophet Muhammad) which enumerates the five pillars, *zakah* comes before fasting,[1] which would apparently indicate that there is no connection between the two. However, Chinese *ulama'* changed the order of the two and mentioned *zakah* after fasting when translating the *hadith*, so that the order of the five obligations in their works is: Nian (念, *shahadah*), Li (礼, prayer), Zhai (斋, fasting), Ke (课, *zakah*), and Chao (朝, hajj),[2] which establishes a certain connection between the two. Mr. Jin did the same in his work when he mentioned the *niÎÉb* (the minimum amount of property which causes *zakah* to be due), the purpose of *zakah*, the kinds of properties upon which *zakah* is due, the recipients of *zakah*, and some exceptional cases.

Then he said: "This is why the emperor,[3] revered persons, his Excellencies, as well as rich people fast for a whole month till today." He means that these people fast to experience hunger; as a result, they pay *zakah* easily. A more interesting point is his mention of the significance of *zakah* to the state, "It is also good for our Emperor to alleviate his burden." *Zakah* is an obligation in Islam and, therefore, the Islamic state appoints people to collect *zakah*. However, Mr. Jin said, "This money is given willingly to helpless people in the town without pressure from the government." From this statement, one might understand that *zakah* is voluntary and not an obligation. We don't think that this is what he means. We think that he said this concerning the political situation of the time.

---

[1] There is a difference in terms of the order of zakat in the hadith. In Al-Bukhari, zakah comes after prayer and before hajj, while fasting comes at the end of the five pillars. See Al-Zubaidi, *Mukhtasar Sahih Al-Bukhari, Kitab Al-Iman,* (Riyad: Daru Al-Salam, 1417/1996), 24. It comes in Sahih Muslim after prayer and before fasting, and hajj comes at the end. See Abdul-Azim, Zakiyyi Al-din, *Mukhtasar Sahih Muslim*, (Riyad: Daru Al-Salam, 1417/1996), 39.

[2] See Da Pusheng, *Islamic Six Books*, (Beijing: Religious Culture Publishing House, 2003), 105.

[3] He means *khalifah* or *Amir al-Muminin.*

5.2.4 Comparing Muslim and non-Muslim funerals

Chinese people, I mean non-Muslims, pay great attention to their dead, especially dead parents. To protect the body of the deceased from the earth, they make a coffin and bury the corpse in it. Muslims do not do that; rather, they bury the deceased directly in the earth after enshrouding it. As a result, they were censured by the society for not respecting their beloved ones. Mr. Jin's response to that was: whatever way is used to bury the dead, the dead will return to the earth in the end, so what is wrong with burying the corpse directly in the earth?

Furthermore, the Muslim method does not necessarily lead to the earth touching the body of dead. He clarified the way Muslims bury their dead (placing it in a niche at the bottom of the grave) and pointed out that this way could prevent the body from the earth for a long time. On the other hand, burying the dead in a coffin may not necessarily protect the corpse from the earth. Be that as it may, it will cause two negative results:

1. Poor people may be unable to buy a coffin; therefore, their dead would be exposed.

2. Rich people normally put valuable things like gold, silver, etc. into the coffin together with the body, and they like their funerals to be well publicized. This will inspire thieves to rob the grave and steal those treasured objects. If those thieves are caught, they will be killed for merely opening the coffin. The punishment will be twice as severe if they steal the objects.[1] Such ostentation entices the living to wrongdoing and causes disturbance to the dead. Then he mentioned the advantages of the Islamic way of doing a funeral:

> It neither leaves the dead to be exposed nor opens the door for thieves. A Muslim's grave has never been robbed even once in a thousand years. If Confucius and Mencius had been asked to evaluate the Islamic funeral, they would probably have said that it is perfect.

[1] His family might be involved and killed because of him, for example.

5.2.5 The reason Muslims wear white skull-caps

Chinese Muslims observe many traditions about clothing. One of the more distinctive is to wear a white skullcap. The *ulama'* and common Muslims, especially those who practice the daily prayer, wear the white skullcap all the time. However, non-Muslims wear white clothes only while making funeral arrangements during the mourning period for the death of a family member. Therefore, wearing white clothes violates one of their taboos. This became one of the excuses the officials presented to the Emperor when asking him to force Muslims to give up Islam and to destroy their mosques. Mr. Jin's first tactic in this regard was to reduce the sensitivity of the issue by telling people that,

> Since ancient times, people have preferred assorted colors during different periods. During the Xia (夏) Dynasty, it was black; during the Zhou (周) Dynasty, it was red; and during the Shang (商) Dynasty white was the preferred colour of their clothes, jewelleries and vehicle curtains. Imagine that we are following the Shang system and all people prefer white; would you be suspicious of this?

The answer of course, is no. He said that Muslims wear the white skull-cap and clothes only at the time of prayer, not because they prefer this colour, but because Islamic rules require them to do so, which may be,

> To show that there is no difference between their outward manifestation and inner thoughts and that their hearts are pure, without any pretence, just like the white colour. Furthermore, it is the origin of other colours and it is not mixed with any other thing; therefore, it is the purest. [However,] those Muslims who do not know the cardinal principles of righteousness wear white hats all the time to distinguish themselves from non-Muslims, and it has become a custom and a habit.

According to the author, the Emperor, revered persons, senior officials and common people belong to separate classes; therefore, each class should wear hats and clothes which are suitable for them. At this point we need to make the following observations:

1. The author mentioned that people in different periods of history preferred assorted colors and that during the time of the Shang dynasty they preferred white, which means that there is nothing wrong for Muslims to prefer this colour. Furthermore, when explaining why Islam requires people to wear white, he mentioned some distinctive features of this colour, which means that it is proper for Muslims to prefer white over other colors. However, he denied that Muslims wear white hat and clothes at the time of prayer because they prefer this colour. My question is: if Muslims do not prefer this colour, why would they choose it over other colors?

2. His judgment that common Muslims who wear white skullcaps all the time "do not know the cardinal principles of righteousness" is unfair to them. On the contrary, perhaps among those who observed this practice, are great scholars who know the principles better than him.

3. We do not agree with him in his statement that every class should wear different clothes to reflect their status. There is no such regulation in Islam, to the best of my knowledge. The most that could be said about it is that it is an opinion of some scholars or a school. In Islam, people are not encouraged to distinguish themselves from others by wearing distinctive clothes or hats; instead, we are encouraged to have a simple life, although there are, no doubt, differences between one man and another in actual Muslim societies. What the author stated in this regard is in accordance with Confucian doctrine, which divided people into varied classes and prescribed distinct dress styles and professions for each class in perpetuity.

5.2.6 Do Muslim men and women mix with each other?

In traditional Chinese culture, men and women were not allowed to gather with each other. Perhaps being influenced by that, Chinese Muslim women do not generally go to mosque for prayer.[1] However, some officials pressed the case that Muslim men and women gathered in mosques and interpreted it as an offence against decency. Mr. Jin vigorously denied the accusation. "As for saying that men and women are mixing with each other, it is more unfair to impute this to Muslims." He listed four reasons for his statement:

1. According to the Islamic book, boys and girls are not allowed to eat together in the same place when they are seven years old. That part of a man's body from the navel to the knee is not allowed to be seen by others. For the female it stretches from the head till the feet. Women are not allowed to meet other men except seven categories: grandfather, father, brothers, husband, children and grandchildren, mother's blood-brother and father's blood-brother; it is also stated there that females are not allowed to meet anyone whom they could theoretically marry. They are required to wear *hijab* (a scarf) to cover their heads down to their heels when they come out of the house or take a chair (sedan) or carriage; nothing of their bodies should be seen.

2. Women are neither allowed to go to mosques for prayers nor to their parents' graves for visiting; are they required to stay at home to pray and remember God.

3. In addition to that, mosques must be kept clean, which is why people must purify their bodies (by making *wudu'* and *ghusl*) before entering the mosque for prayer. However, women might pollute the mosque with their menses.

4. If men and women mixed together, licentious actions might take place out of the view of others. That would encourage evil instead of promoting good. Based on the above-mentioned arguments, Mr. Jin concluded that there is no mixing between males and females among Muslims.

It is necessary to note here that the author made an incorrect judgment when he said that women are not allowed to go to mosques for prayer. According to the relevant *hadith* of the Prophet, although women are not

[1] The situation is changing now, with more and more women going to pray in the mosque.

encouraged to go to mosques for prayers, they are also not prohibited to do so. In fact, the Prophet (pbuh) explicitly prohibited men from preventing women from attending mosques. What the author presented here might be an opinion of some scholars in China or abroad, but it is not in accord with the evidence; therefore, it is not acceptable in my view. And also, to say that the mixing of men and women might lead to licentious actions out of the view of others is to make a negative assumption about Muslim men and women (سوء الظن) while we are required to maintain a positive opinion of them (حسن الظن) unless we have concrete evidence to the contrary.

5.2.7 Why do Muslims gather at night and disperse in the early morning?

During the Qing era, there were some people who tried to overturn the dynasty in the name of certain religions. They would gather at night to lay their plans. As a result, people's freedom of speech and assembly were severely curtailed. The Muslim practice of gathering in mosques for congregational prayers attracted the attention of some officials, who suspected that Muslims might be up to something against the government. In response, Mr. Jin analyzed the case as follows: a gathering will either be every night or on some nights. If those officials mean that Muslims gather every night, it is impossible, because every one of them has a family to support; therefore, he should do his business. If he works all day and then gathers with other Muslims every night, he will soon die, because a man's energy is too limited to maintain such a schedule.

If they mean that Muslims gather at certain times, there is nothing wrong with that. Muslims may gather for weddings or funerals; or, if a person died far from his own town, local people may arrange a funeral for him at night to bury his body the next day; or some people may not have prayed on time during the day, so they make up the missed prayers at night; or it might be the fasting month, during which the number of people who come to mosques for Tarawih prayer (صلاة التراويح) will be ten times more than in other months. All these cases are possible and reasonable; therefore, Muslims should not be doubted and questioned for that. To convince people that Muslims have no negative intentions against the government when they gather, Mr. Jin said:

> It is said in the Islamic book that it is forbidden to take anything that does not belong to you. Moreover, the aim of the prayer in the fasting month is primarily to repent, and Muslims do not dare to have any presumptuous intention. Instead of that, they submit to the will of God, regardless of whether they are rich or poor, in ease or difficulty.

In other words, Muslims do not have the intention to take power from the current ruling class and therefore, they will do not do anything against the government because Islam taught them to do so, especially in the fasting month.

5.2.8 The harms of drinking alcohol

Public drinking has been a social phenomenon in China since ancient times till today. When they gathered on ceremonial occasions, officials would drink alcohol together and clink glasses with each other. Anyone who did not join in would be ostracized for not being “a regular guy”. Mr. Jin adhered to the Islamic regulation, which prohibits drinking alcohol and, as a result, he faced great social pressure. Some people tried to convince Mr. Jin to change his lifestyle and be like others, but he rejected this. He contrasted drinking alcohol with honesty to the Emperor and filial piety to the parents, which are two of the three cardinal principles of Confucianism. According to him, whoever drinks alcohol is not respectful or obedient to his parents and “if he could disobey his loved ones today, he will disobey the Emperor tomorrow.” Therefore, “if there is a minor post in the government to be filled, he should not be appointed to it.” Mr. Jin also pointed out that drinking alcohol is harmful and it was because of that that the ancient Emperors strictly prohibited it. He requested non-Muslims not to entice Muslims to drink alcohol because it may prevent them from eventual retribution.

> I say these words today, not only to persuade Muslims to adhere to their root principles, but also to persuade non-Muslims not to lure ignorant Muslims when they met them and not to draw them into wrong actions. How do they benefit from doing so? They give themselves a bad reputation, which might lead to harm for their following generations. If you persuaded others not to forget their roots, there will be someone who does the same for your children in the future; as a result, they might be perfect ones who deal with people according to the principles of Xiao (孝, filial piety to father), Ti (悌, showing respect to one's elder brother), Zhong (忠, being loyal to the emperor) and Xin (信, being honest to friends).

We have noticed here that the author used the Buddhist theory of karma to support his own statement which is in accordance to Islam as it is stated in some hadith.

5.2.9 Slaughtering animals

Except for vegetarians, there are no limitations for Chinese people regarding meat. They eat whatever animal they like, if it is edible, regardless of whether it died naturally or was slaughtered by someone. If it was slaughtered, it doesn't matter how or by whom it was slaughtered. However, Muslims normally eat beef and mutton slaughtered by a Muslim in the name of God. This seems strange and incomprehensible to non-Muslims. They say that Muslims recite certain incantations, which is a mistake, of course. Mr. Jin corrected that mistake first and informed them that Muslims mention the name of God when they slaughter animals. He pointed out that Muslims are required to do that in order "to attach importance to living things and exercise sympathy for animals." According to him, even a plant should not be abused, so how can we abuse animals which have real life? Therefore, we can slaughter them only if there is an important occasion like a wedding or funeral arrangement, and it must be done by a pious man. As to those who slaughter animals for a job, they are evil-doers (wrongdoers). There are three points in the author's presentation that we must comment on:

1. He did not answer the question of the guest as to why there are no Muslim vegetarians.

2. We do not agree that Islam allows us to slaughter animals only on important occasions. It is stated in *the Holy Qur'an* (2:29) that God created everything on the earth to meet the needs of mankind; therefore, we have the right to enjoy so-called natural resources, the only restriction being that we are not allowed to waste resources by killing or consuming them unnecessarily.[1]

3. With regards to the slaughter of animals, there is no regulation in Islam that only a pious Muslim can conduct slaughtering;[2] instead, it is stated in *the Holy Qur'an*, as well as in the books of jurisprudence, that Muslims can eat the meat of animals that are slaughtered by the People of the Book, if they mention the name of God before doing so.

4. Regarding his judgment that those who slaughter animals for a living are evil-doers, it might be argued that since the animals are lawful for mankind and not everyone knows how to slaughter, there must be people who conduct slaughtering as a job. It might be acceptable to say that to slaughter animals is a permitted job (*halal* or *mubah*) which is last on the list of those encouraged by Islam.[3]

5.2.10 The reason Muslims take a bath after sexual intercourse

Whenever they have had sexual intercourse, Muslim couples must wash their bodies (*ghusl*) with water before they do anything which may let

---

[1] See chapter 7: 31, 32.

[2] Practically speaking, common Muslims (al-Awam) in China prefer to invite Imams of mosques or their students to slaughter animals.

[3] It is somewhat like divorce (Al-talaq) in terms of Jurisprudence of *Shari'ah* which is the most among the lawful things that God dislike according to the hadith, "أبغض الحلال عند الله الطلاق." Which is narrated by Abu Dawud and Ibn Majah, see Al-Shawkani, Muhammad Ali Muhammad, *Nail-Al-Aotar*, (Beirut: Daru Al-Marifah, 1423/2002), vol. 2, 1386, No. 4.

people know that they had recently had sex. Intercourse is a shameful act in the view of non-Muslims. When it is time for prayer, Muslims wash the seven orifices in the head using water in a pitcher. All of this seems very burdensome and difficult to non-Muslims. Mr. Jin explained:

> The Islamic way of life, starting from major matters like the relationship between the monarch and his subjects and that between fathers and sons and ending with minor things like daily regulations of drink and food, is recorded in the Islamic books without exception; therefore, even lazy people examine their own consciences before they do anything. When it is time to perform devotional activities like prayer, fasting and so on, they will not go if they have not had a bath. The reason for this is that Islamic doctrine teaches us, as Muslims, that we should not deceive ourselves....In addition to that, everything that concerns sex must be dealt with carefully. Thus, Muslims are very vigilant not only in arranging a match as per the parent's instructions and on the matchmaker's word, but also in dealing with wet dreams.

Very interestingly, the author tried to show the impact of bathing on the coming generation. He said that by the Islamic way of bathing illegal sexual actions are prevented and the human body and heart are cleansed and purified. If the wife becomes pregnant now, the baby will be a wise or gentle man, because it is said that, "If you want to make a stream of water clean, you must first clean its source." In the Islamic way, the source of the stream is already clean and, therefore, the stream must be clean.

As for the non-Muslims' concern that bathing may let people know that the couple had had sex at night, Mr. Jin's response is that it depends on whether the act was done legally or illegally. If it was done illegally, it is a shameful act; if it was done legally, then it is not. That is just like a woman giving birth; if she gave birth before getting married, people will consider it shameful; if she did so after marriage, they will call it a happy event.

Concerning the reason that Muslims use a water pitcher rather than a bathtub when they take bath, it is because according to Islamic rules, used water is dirty; on the other hand, water stored in the pitcher is clean, so it can be used for purification. As for the reason Muslims wash the seven orifices of the head, it is because prayer is a ritual in which Muslims worship God, and show their devotion to God, therefore, they must make their ears, eyes, mouths, noses, hands, feet and bodies clean.

5.3 Some other thoughts

During his discussing with the guest the author presented some ideas which are brilliant and therefore worthy of paying attention to.

5.3.1 Humanity

Islam's view of humanity is one of its distinctive features. According to Islam, God created everything on the earth before mankind, and then, he created man as a vicegerent (*khalifah*),[1] to let him carry the Trust (al-Amanah)[2], and made him among the noblest of creatures.

> We have honored the sons of Adam; provided them with transport on land and sea; given them for sustenance things good and pure; and conferred on them special favors, above a great part of Our creation.[3]

Mr. Jin was fully aware of this and, therefore, he stated several times that mankind is the most honourable thing on the earth. For example, when talking about funerals, he said: "According to the sayings of our Prophet, man is nobler than any other living thing. People are equal in terms of birth and death, although they differ in terms of wealth during their lifetimes." Again, he said: "Man is the noblest among all living things in the world. If

---

1 *Quran,* 2, 29,30.

2 *Quran,* 33: 72.

3 *Quran*, 17: 70.

people did not exist, there would be no bridge on the earth and even if there was one, it would be useless."

According to him, Islam prohibited some things to protect mankind, "These things are forbidden because they hurt the nature and life of humans and eating them is bad for the propagation of human beings." This is one of five purposes of Shariah.[1] Another example of this is that, according to the Shariah, a rich man who has enough money to pay *zakah* has no right to take *zakah* from other people; however, if the man faced difficulty and danger because of a subsequent lack of money, he can take *zakah* from others. This judgement is in accordance with the principle of jurisprudence that the prohibited becomes permissible due to necessity. It seems that Mr. Jin was very aware of the principles and purposes of Shariah and, therefore, the importance and position of mankind in Islam.

It is necessary to note that there is a crucial difference between the view of humanity in Islam and the Western view, which emphasizes the importance of mankind against God and the right of the first against the latter. On the contrary, the view of humanity in Islam is very similar to that of ancient Chinese culture in its emphasis of the importance of mankind compared to the rest of creation. According to Islam, God is the creator, and mankind is His creation. They cannot be compared at all; therefore, there is no conflict between them at all. However, modern Chinese scholarship has been influenced by the West and as a result, their concept of humanity is that "everything is for the benefit of mankind and everything is dependent on mankind." It is, in fact, a denial of God's status and function. At the same time, it justifies the release of all limitations on human desires, allowing people to do whatever they like.

---

[1] The five objectives of the Shari'ah are: to prevent (or preserve) the life of man, his faith, property, intelligence and propagation. See for more details: Yusuf Hamid Alim, *Al-Maqasid Al-Amah,* (Cairo: Dar al-Hadith, 1997); and also Mohammad Hashim Kamali, *Principles of Islamic Jurisprudence*, (Ilmiah Publishers, 2nd ed., 2004), 395-408.

5.3.2 Limitation of natural resources

As late as the twentieth century, most of mankind thought natural resources to be unlimited and inexhaustible. It was only in the 21st century that more and more people began to realize that resources are limited. Interestingly, in the 18th century, there were some people in China who already knew that. When the guest asked Mr. Jin about Muslim conditions for slaughtering animals, which the guest considered unreasonable, Mr. Jin responded:

> Have you never heard that things in heaven and the earth are limited, while the desires of men's hearts are endless? If we do not nip an evil in the bud and are not very careful (in using natural resources) to meet man's desires, the consequences will be uncontrollable.

This means that there were people who knew that and that Mr. Jin had accepted that view, which led him to conclude that man's actions should be regulated and his desires limited; otherwise, it would bring profound consequences. What he stated has taken place since the so-called Industrial Revolution and is still happening today because of the ignorance and arrogance of mankind.

5.3.3 The outlook of the author towards life

The outlook of most ancient religions towards worldly life was negative to varying degrees. One of the important manifestations of this view is withdrawal from social life to become monks. Most Chinese ulama' at the end of the Ming Dynasty and the beginning of the Qing were Sufis to various degrees, and Mr. Jin was one of them. When talking about prayers in Islam, he said:

> Muslims pray five times a day and a Jummah prayer once a week. They always fear God. The sincere in their prayers turn directly to God, who is the creator of all things. They

> are so pious that they forget and devote themselves totally to the worship of God."

The terms "they forget and devote themselves totally to the worship of God" is an expression of the concept of *fana* (الفناء), which is one of the highest degrees of devotion to God in Sufism. This indicates that Mr. Jin was a Sufi. However, he was against Buddhist and Taoist monks,

> Who neither weave cotton cloth nor plough the earth; they live in high and wide buildings [temples] and play in the mountains and forests together with wild birds, or sleep leisurely and carefree, leaving the difficulties of cultivation and farming, spinning and weaving to the public.

According to him, if a man had the intention to leave his family for devoting himself to God with his heart and soul, he must first satisfy some requirements; otherwise, he is not allowed to do so. Even if the man fulfilled those conditions, he is not encouraged, according to him, to do that, because,

> to serve one's emperor and be honest to him; to serve parents and show respect to them; to make friends and be honest to them; to support your wife and servants; to show tender care for the widower, the widow and the childless; to maintain one's prayer and fasting and not leave them; and to perform honorable deeds, is a thousand times better than leaving family for devotion. In brief, Islam attaches more importance to human relations and does not encourage people to withdraw from society and live in solitude.

We agree with the author in this view and believe that it is the right view of Islam in this regard, which is supported by the sayings of the Prophet Muhammad, "A believer who mixes with people and bears their harm with patience is better than a believer who doesn't mix with people and doesn't bear their harm with patience."[1] Moreover, there is no monasticism in Islam at all. [2] Furthermore, according to Islam, mankind came to the earth as a vicegerent whose job is to worship God and build this earth physically and spiritually in accord with His will. To guide mankind and help them to successfully complete their duty, God sent down His revelations to prophets and sent them as messengers to people at different periods of history, which required them to involve themselves and not to run away from their societies. Also, mankind came to earth to undergo God's test, and that test must be related to the substance of our lives in all their aspects. If we leave our society and stay in solitude, it, in a certain sense, means that we have tried to escape from the test of God. This is against God's purpose of creating mankind. And God knows best.

---

1 Al-Tabarani, Abu Tahir Ahmad Muhammad Ahmad Ibrahim Al-Asbahani (360), *Makarimu Al-Akhlaq*, (Beirut: Daru al-Ilmiyyah, 1421/2000), 323.

2 *Quran*, Chapter 57: 27. Monasticism is a way of devotion initiated by some religious men before Islam in which people devote themselves to worshiping God by staying away from society. See Al-Saadi, Abdur-Rahman, *Taisir Al-Karim Al-Rahman Fi Tafsir Kalam Al-mannan*, (Beirut: Muassasat Al-Risalah, 1417/1996), 782.

CHAPTER SIX:

CONCLUSION

6.1 Achievements of the Study

Muslims came from Arab world and other areas to China during the early years of the Tang Dynasty, started to settle down during the Song, increased in the period of the Yuan, and became identified as a new race, the "Huihui" (回回) in the time of the Ming. However, by the time the Qing Dynasty was established, 1000 years after their arrival in the country, Chinese Muslims were still facing two problems caused by the differences between the two cultures.

The first problem was social. Most Chinese people of the Ming and Qing eras were Confucian in terms of philosophy; however, they practiced aspects of Buddhism and Taoism in their daily lives. For example, except for vegetarians, there was no limitation upon them in terms of food and drink. They would eat and drink whatever they liked, if it was consumable. They would stick antithetical couplets (written on scrolls) at the top of their doors on the Chinese New Year. If someone died, they would cover the body with clothes and place it in a coffin before burial; to save the body of dead, they put some gold and silver or other valuable things in the grave. When a year had passed from the date of the death, they would burn paper money and provide food for the dead. In terms of faith, they believed in Buddhism and would worship idols for seeking good fortune. They also believed that Taoist priests could help them and fulfill their requests. They would ask those self-proclaimed masters to find the right location for them to build their houses. Such things are rejected by Muslims.

At the same time, Muslims have certain regular practices that non-Muslims do not. Muslims, for instance, wear white hats and clothes, while non-Muslims do so only when a family member dies. Muslims cut their hair and shave some parts of their bodies while non-Muslims do not, because, in their sight, all hairs on the human body were given by parents and, therefore, should not be hurt at all. Muslims take a full bath (*ghusl*) after sexual intercourse while non-Muslims feel shy to do so.

The second was a political problem deliberately instigated by certain government officials and motivated by cultural chauvinism. Convinced of the unfailing superiority of their own customs, any divergent customs had to be changed to conform to their ways. To realize their objectives, those officials took some cases related to Muslims as their means and presented them to the Emperor petitioning him to issue decrees against Islam and permit them to destroy mosques, and force Muslims to give up their identity and faith. They accused Muslims of the following:

1. Muslims do not follow the official calendar; on the contrary, they have their own calendar with a year of 360 days; and they celebrate their own New Year, an occasion on which they congratulate each other.

2. They dress differently from others.

3. They do not eat non-Muslims' food.

4. They do not eat anything during fasting times; when they do eat in the early morning (*suhur*) and after breaking the fast, they eat meat.

5. They pray, but their god cannot be seen.

6. They gather at night and disperse in the early morning.

7. Their men and women mix together when they pray in the mosques.

8. They trim their whiskers and shave the hairs of their bodies to look different from others. With these problems, as a minority, Chinese Muslims were facing excessive pressure from Chinese society to assimilate and as a result, some of them gave up their Islamic beliefs or concealed their Muslim identities.

Qingzhen Shiyi, in fact, was Mr. Jin's reaction to those problems in general and to the second one in particular. He attempted to alleviate the political and social pressures Muslims were facing by removing people's doubts and suspicions. In the light of Mr. Jin's discussion, the differences between the two cultures could be divided into two kinds: those which can be harmonized and those which cannot. Based on this, he adopted three approaches.

As we pointed out before, Confucianism was the foundation of the mainstream culture and the orthodox ideology in China at that time. The acceptance by the society of any religion or culture was proportional to its similarity to Confucianism. Those which were close would be accepted, while those which were different would be rejected or forced to change. Mr. Jin was fully aware of this; therefore, the first strategy he adopted was to show non-Muslims the similarities between Confucian doctrine and Islam, which might reduce the distance between Muslims and non-Muslims and allow them to live together in peace and harmony.

The most important subject Mr. Jin always mentioned in this regard was *Sangang* and *Wuchang* (三纲五常) which were the main principles of Confucian doctrine, according to which the relationship between the Emperor and his subjects, fathers and sons, husbands and wives, brother and friends is regulated. It is, indeed, like Islamic doctrine, which requires common people to obey the ruler (walÊ al-amr), sons to obey fathers, wives to obey husbands, younger brothers to defer to elders, and friends to treat each other with respect and loyalty. However, for Muslims this principle is subservient to another principle: obedience to the creation is only allowed when it does not entail disobedience to God. As to the aspects that could not be harmonized, Mr. Jin explained the reasons for them and the significance of the Islamic practices. It is obvious that his aim in doing so was to show the advantages of Islam compared to Confucianism in those matters and the reasonability of Muslims maintaining their own identities.

To follow the teachings left by forefathers was another principle accepted by most Chinese people at that time. Therefore, the second way adopted by Mr. Jin was to tell non-Muslims that certain Muslim practices which seemed different from majority practices were due to Muslims following the teachings of their own forefathers. For non-Muslims to criticize Muslims for doing so would mean contradiction of their own principle that people should follow the teachings of their forefathers. Intelligent people would never do that.

We have seen that Confucian doctrine underwent change over time and became a new ideology by mixing with Buddhism and Taoism after an initial period of conflict with them. Therefore, although most people at the time claimed to be Confucians and considered it an honour, in fact, practically, they were following many teachings of Buddhism and Taoism knowingly or unknowingly. Taking this as a starting point, Mr. Jin repeatedly pointed out for Confucians that they themselves were following doctrines of religions other than Confucianism, so they had no basis to criticize Muslims for following their own religion's teachings. These are the main strategies the author adopted to remove people's doubts about Muslim practices.

Considering the impact of theology upon human behaviour, Mr. Jin also touched upon some theological issues in his discussions. First, he stressed the oneness of God and that He created everything, that God has no direction, is unseen, and that there is nothing like Him. He affirmed that God knows everything and will, therefore, reward doers of good and punish wrongdoers. In his view, Jesus is not God but one of the messengers of God. The author criticized Buddhists for worshiping Buddha and believing in reincarnation, and, likewise, he criticized Taoists for their magic arts by which they cheated not only common people but also some emperors.

As for Confucianism, Mr. Jin criticized its school of idealist philosophy that attained prominence during the Song and the Ming eras and taught that the existence of everything is caused naturally by the airs of Yin and Yang and that there is no God to create anything.[1] His argument against Confucianism in this regard is that before the airs of Yin and Yang fulfill a function, they need a locus. If this is the case, then where were they before the heaven and the earth? He took the concept of "Ding Shu" (定数, predestination) of Confucianism as a starting point and pointed out its self-contradiction: if there is prearrangement, then there must be a pre-arranger, which, according to him, is God. Therefore, the conclusion is that if Confucians admit predestination, then they must accept the concept of God and His function. To support this conclusion, Mr. Jin quoted words of some representative Confucian scholars that demonstrate that ancient Chinese sages believed in God and that He created everything.

[1] See for example, *The orders of Everything, The life and the death of man, and Yin Yang in "Zhouyi"*, http://blog.sina.cn/s/blog_4de7c08601007uw3.html

A question frequently asked by people in China and abroad is whether Confucius was a prophet or messenger of God or not. Before we go into details, it is necessary to first clarify the term "Sheng Ren" (圣人, prophet). In brief, the term has two meanings:

1. A wise man or outstanding figure;

2. An ancient emperor. It seems that there is no connection between the term and prophethood or messengerhood.

However, the term came to be used to refer to prophets and messengers also. Mr. Jin, in his discussions with the guest, mentioned the term "Sheng Ren" many times, and when he referred to Prophet Muhammad (peace be upon him), he used the phrase "Wo Jiao Sheng Ren" (吾教圣人), which means "the prophet of my religion" or "Muslims' prophet".[1] He also used the term in referring to ancient Chinese wise men in general; however, when he referred to Confucius specifically, he never used it; instead, he called him "Kong Zi" (孔子) alone or blended with "Meng Zi" (孟子), to say "Kong Meng" (孔孟). He never used the term "Kong Sheng" (孔圣) or any other term that would indicate that Confucius was a prophet or a messenger. This, if it can prove something, would prove that Confucius is not a prophet, in his view. At the same time, it tells us that the author did not deny the possibility that there had been one or more prophets in ancient China.

If this is what he meant, it is supported by the following dialogues: Taizai (太宰)[2] asked Zi Gong (子贡)[3]: "Is Confucius a Sheng Ren? Why he is so knowledgeable?" Zi Gong replied: "It must be that God sent him as a Sheng Ren and made him versatile." When Confucius heard this, he said: "Does Taizai knows me? I was poor when I was small; that was why I learned some superficial skills."[4] This means that people at that time were familiar with the concept of prophet and messenger and that it meant one sent by God, who bestowed upon him knowledge of many things.

---

[1] Literally, "wujiao" means "my religion". However, the author is referring to the term as "we Muslims" .

[2] It was the title of an official position at the time of Confucius.

[3] He was one of the students of Confucius.

[4] See Chen Puqing, *Translation and Commentary on the Four Books*, 121.

However, Confucius denied Zi Gong's statement by telling people that he acquired knowledge by learning. In another dialogue, he denied being a prophet: "Speaking of prophet-hood and kindheartedness, how dare I accept that?"[1] From the Islamic perspective, however, a prophet is the one who has received revelation from God and the messenger is the one who proclaimed himself as such and showed people *muÑjizat* (miracles) as evidence of his claim. However, Confucius stated that his knowledge is received from hard learning, which means it is not received from God. Moreover, he neither claimed that he is messenger nor did he show any *muÑjizat*. Furthermore, although he believed in God and claimed that he knew "Tian Ming" (天命),[2] Confucius never called people to believe in God nor did he emphasize His oneness and uniqueness as the prophets did throughout human history; rather, he encouraged them to respect "Gui Shen" (鬼神)[3] but be far away from them.

When Zi Lu asked him how to worship "Gui Shen", Confucius said: "You haven't yet [properly] served the living; how would you serve the dead?" When the former asked him again about death, he replied: "You don't know about life yet; how can you know about death?" [4] This means that although Confucius did not deny the hereafter, his focus was on worldly issues. He deliberately downplayed the ultimate destination of mankind. If he were a prophet or messenger, he would not have done so. Based on this, we conclude that Confucius was neither a prophet nor a messenger, but a wise man and a great thinker.[5]

---

[1] *Ibid*, 109.

[2] "Tian Ming" means the mission from God and His prearrangement.

[3] "Gui Shen" means the spirits of the dead and, sometimes, supernatural beings in general.

[4] See, *Translation and Commentary on the Four Books*, 37.

[5] Osman Bakar mentioned that the well-known Malay-Indonesian scholar Hamka holds the view that Confucius may be accepted by Muslims as a prophet, and that Indonesian Confucians refer to Confucius as a *nabi*. To him, Confucius's *Analects* would be the evidence if he were indeed a prophet. See his book, *Islam and Confucianism, A Civilizational Dialogue* (Kuala Lumpur:

In addition, Mr. Jin presented some brilliant opinions that could be considered valuable contributions not only to the society of his time but also to today's society. The first of these ideas is the limitation of natural resources. In his conversation with the guest about the slaughtering of animals, Mr. Jin listed some regulations which, in his view, are Islamic. He stated that Muslims cannot slaughter an animal whenever they feel like it. The guest argued that such a restriction must be against God's will, since He created everything for human benefit and therefore, people have the right to do with animals whatever they like. The author responded by pointing out that natural resources are limited; therefore, human desires should be limited and their actions regulated; otherwise, it will create grave consequences to the detriment of humanity. Mankind today needs to pay heed to such an opinion more than in any previous era.

The second point that the author presented in this book is the nature of humanity, a subject which has been the focus of much scholastic attention. Unlike western scholarship, which emphasizes the importance of mankind and neglects God's role in the world and in human affairs, the human being, in the Islamic view, is created by God and, as such, he has no choice but to obey God's will in certain aspects (natural laws and biological imperatives).

However, he has also been endowed with moral choice and, as such, should follow God's will in choosing good and shunning evil, and he will bear the responsibility of his choice. This is on the one hand. On the other hand, man is the noblest of all living things; his life is the most important, and his personality must be respected and protected, regardless of whether he or she is rich or poor, an emperor or a common person. This, according to Mr. Jin, is the main reason why Islam required people to bury the dead in a straightforward way without coffins or funerary objects, so that poor people

---

University of Malaya Press, 1997), 72. We hereby, would like to share that it is well known that the source of Confucianism is the thoughts of Yao, Shun, Yu, Wenwang and Wuwang; what Confucius tried to do was to revive *Zhou Li* (the rites of the time of Zhou dynasty). In this sense, it will be reasonable if we considered one of those people as a prophet and Confuius as *Mujaddid* (reviver) of his teaching.

can bury their dead. It is also because of this that Islam allowed a rich man who would normally have to pay *zakah* to take *zakah* from others if he happens to face financial difficulty while travelling.

The third point of the author, which is brilliant in my view, is his outlook on worldly life. As we have pointed out before, all religions in the world have a negative attitude towards worldly life. Some of them discourage people from marrying, some prohibit their followers from eating meat, and so on.

Tasawwuf, or Sufism, is a tendency in Islamic thought which started in the time of Prophet (peace be upon him) and spread all over the Muslim world soon after. We do not know enough to form a judgment about the exact time in which Sufism first came to China, but there are stories of some Chinese *Ulama'* in the Ming and Qing eras who had some miraculous experiences known as *karamat* in Arabic.[1] Furthermore, in the list of teaching books in mosques of China, we can find some books that introduce and interpret the doctrine of Sufism. One important Sufi concept is *zuhd* (disinterest in fame and wealth). Based upon their interpretation of this concept, some Muslims prefer to withdraw from society and live away from it.

Our point here is that, although he was a Sufi, Mr. Jin did not encourage people to do so. This can be seen through his arguments against Buddhists and Taoists and his presentation of the conditions for a Muslim to leave his family and live in the mountains. To him, even if the conditions are fulfilled, people should not be encouraged to do that; instead, they should involve themselves in worldly affairs, manage their families, support their parents, help people in need, and so on. At the same time, they should worship God as well as they can in an easy and uncomplicated way, like performing prayers, fasting, etc. Mr. Jin held such an opinion at a time when many Muslims had deviated from the real teaching of Islam in the name of Sufism. This means that he understood the Holy *Qur'an* and the Sunnah of the Prophet (peace be upon him) and, therefore, Islam and the *Shariah* very well.

---

1 Li Xinghua, *History of Islam in China*, 540-544.

6.2 Evaluation of Qingzhen Shiyi

Human works, without exception, cannot be free from mistakes and shortcomings. During my study of *Qingzhen Shiyi*, I noticed some points in the author's presentation which are open to debate and criticism.

1. Some of his answers are irrelevant; see, for example, page 52, where he mentions education in Muslim areas and why Muslims do not use Chinese characters to pronounce Islamic books (the Quran for example), while the guest never asked about that.

2. Disorganization; see, for example, pages 54 and 56, where he argues with the guest regarding Yin and Yang's function in the creation of everything. His argument is repetitious and, therefore, appears disordered.

3. Self-contradiction; see, for example, page 55, where he mentions that people in various periods of history preferred unusual colors, and that white was the preferred colour in the Shang era, which means that there is nothing wrong with preferring the white colour. However, the author denied that Muslims wear white hats because they prefer this colour. A questioner could ask him: if you Muslims do not prefer the white colour, then why do you not wear hats of other colors? The self-contradiction becomes more obvious in the following passage:

> According to Islamic rules, both hats and clothes should be white. Perhaps this is to show that there is no difference between their outward manifestation and inner thoughts and that their hearts are pure, without any pretence, just like the colour white. Furthermore, it is the origin of other colors and it is not mixed with any other thing; therefore, it is the purest.

This is a more reasonable explanation for why Muslims prefer white.

4. He imposes certain views on the other party; see, for example, page 51. The guest never mentions God, one way or the other. However, the author quotes some words of ancient Confucian sages and then asks the guest: "If God does not exist, wouldn't it mean that both the ancient people's

poems and Zhuxi's interpretation were wrong?" It would be right to ask such a question if the other side had denied the existence of God.

5. Erroneous judgments; see, for example, 58, where he says that women are not allowed to enter mosques for prayers. This is wrong, of course, because the Prophet (peace be upon him) never prohibited them from going to mosque, although he did not encourage them to do so. Another example is his statement on page 58 that drinking alcohol is a minor sin, while it is considered one of the 72 major sins (al-kaba'ir), according to the consensus of the entire Ummah.

6. Far-fetched and unconvincing comparisons; see, for example, page 59, when talking about the reason why Muslims trim the mustache, he compares the mouth with the emperor and the mustache with his subjects and said that when the emperor eats, subjects should not disturb him, and if they do so then they should be removed. This comparison is very far-fetched in my view.

7. Incomplete answers; see page 60, where one of the questions of the guest is why Muslims prefer to eat the meat of cows and sheep and are not vegetarians. The author did not answer it at all.

8. Digressions from the subject; see, for example, page 64, where he mentions stories of some ancient emperors who had been deceived by alchemists and swallowed so-called elixirs which poisoned them, causing dehydration, intense thirst and unbearable pain. This, in my view, should have been mentioned when discussing Taoist priests and their magic arts, not in the context of leaving one's family to be a monk, because it was the Taoist priests who concocted those so-called elixirs and provided them to the emperors as the greatest achievement of their magic arts.

These questionable points led me to doubt the completeness and accuracy of the editions I saw and, therefore, I believe it necessary to find the first edition of the book or the original manuscript of the author and make further study of it.

However, these shortcomings of the book are insignificant when compared to its advantages:

1. The author uses many examples familiar to readers which would help them to understand his ideas well.

2. His presentation is very simple and brief and, therefore, readers will not feel bored or tired.

3. His arguments against other religions are strong in most points, which may show readers their shortcomings.

4. His exposition of Islamic beliefs and practices is convincing in general, which is why, when their conversation ended, the guest asked him to collect their dialogue in the form of a book and publish it; and when his friend Chen Dashao read the book, he was convinced and repeatedly urged him to publish it as soon as possible.

5. His language is beautiful in general and wonderful in some places of the book, which gained much praise for him, as we quoted before. 6 He presented some brilliant ideas, as we have summarized above.

Finally, there is one more matter which increases the value of the book, in my view. It is, to the best of my knowledge, the first book that aimed to defend the religious rights and identities of Muslims and, thereby, their subsistence with their Muslim identity in China.[1] The author could not have done so without very strong faith and great courage, especially in a period of history when there was no freedom and democracy in the modern sense.

---

[1] See Yu Zhengui and Yang Huaizhong, *Abstracts of Chinese Islamic literature*, Ningxia Publishing House, 1993.

6.3 Suggestions for Further Study

In conclusion, I would like to suggest institutions and individuals interested in Islam and Muslims in China studying this topic further, particularly the following points:

1. To get more information about the early and late periods of the author's life as well as the lives of the prefaces' writers;
2. To ascertain whether "the guest" was a real man or an authorial device;
3. To find the first edition of the book or the original manuscript of the author;
4. To look for and find the poem of the author.
5. To introduce the book to Arabic readers.

With this, we conclude our study of *Qingzhen Shiyi*.

APPENDIXES

As parts of *Qingzhen Shiyi,* there are two contents including Chen Dashao's commentary on the book and, a letter written by a minister both of which, we believe, are worthy enough for english readers to know about an therfore, we have translated them into English language. We also think that it is necessary to put the original text of *Qingzhen Shiyi* in Chinese language infront of our respected readers to injoy and so, this part of our study include three appendixes namely: The English translation of Chen Dashao's commentary on the text; The English translation of the letter to the senior minister and the edited Chinese texts of *Qingzhen Shiyi* in classical Chinese language which include: the prefaces, the main body, Chen Dashao's commentary on the text and the letter to the minister.

I. Translation of Chen Dashao' comments

According to the chief commander of Huaiyin (淮阴),[1] the more soldiers there are, the better it will be. This was because his knowledge of the principles of things [in general] was good and his [knowledge of] military law was perfect. Based on that, he did what must be done and stopped what should be stopped. Beigao (北高) talked with the guest for a long time. His presentation was like a thousand stages or a snake in Changshan (常山), very rich in content and perfectly ordered; very fine in structure and of clear meaning. He used the way of Yaojie (遥接) to show the similarities between different religions and the way of analogy (类叙) and to point out the shortcomings of other religions, just as artists do. If you were to say that his talent and learning are like the tide or the sea, well, they are both, which means that he learned from Changli (昌黎) and Meishan (眉山) for a long time. As for the rules and regulations that he presented, they are based on

[1] His name was Hanxin (韩信) and he was a very successful military leader (general) in the time of Liubang (206 B.C.-194B.C.).

sympathy for humanity and are in accord with [universal] principles. He did nothing but call people to follow their forefather's regulations when they wanted to do their business. There is nothing strange and unreasonable at all.

Fuzi from Nishan (尼山夫子)[1] followed people at his time when they began to use silk to make hats instead of flax.[2] A self-willed man from Muchun (暮春狂士)[3] liked to eat *yangzao* (羊枣) but gave it up.[4] People did not know the reason why they did that. How did they know that they should not chip in those people and slander them? This tells us that everything has its reality and that our job is to find the reality, nothing more. By following the principles of things, searching for their true situation, and going back to their source, you can arrive at the original status of phenomena. This is what we call their reality. If the reality of a thing were known, there would not be anything for people to talk about. Though Beigao is a Muslim, he is familiar with Confucian doctrine and is, additionally, a master poet. His two sons, who are being trained in the institute, are very good at writing poems. They will take part in the imperial examination. That

[1] Fuzi (夫子) means man, husband etc. Students of Confucius addressed their teacher as Fuzi respectfully. Nishan (尼山) is the name of a mountain in which Confucius was born. It is about 25km from Qufu (曲阜), Shandong province in China. See Shan Shumo, *Dictionary of Famous Mountains and Great Rivers in China*, (Shandong Higher Education Publishing House, 1992), 519.

[2] Confucius was extreme in following the rite of *Zhou* and was trying to publicize it. To make hats using flax was in accordance with the rite of *Zhou*. However, when people changed this and started to use silk to make hats, he followed them, because to make hats using silk was cheaper than flax at that time. See: Chen Puqing, *Translation of Commentary of the Four Books*, 120.

[3] Muchun (暮春) might refer to a place named Lu which is Qufu (曲阜) in Shandong; the man was one of Confucius's students whose name was Zengzi (曾子). See Ibid, 498,499.

[4] Yangzao (羊枣) is a kind of fruit, small in size, and black in colour. He gave up eating it because his father also liked it, so he did that in order to show his respect to his father. See Ibid, 498.499.

is why I admire Mr. Jin and why I wrote this commentary with my little talent and little knowledge.

----By Zongshan Chen Dashao, From the country of Hubei Songzi

II. Translation of the Letter

It is said that gentlemen seek knowledge to know the truth well and spread it in the world, they hope that their theories will never be obliterated or repudiated by coming generations. Is there more than one truth? [No, but] they establish their theories to help people learn what they do not know and are clear what they doubt. By doing so, their theories can be transmitted to future generations. Those who were engaged in the transmission [of these theories] were different peoples.

What they transmitted is nothing more than the Three Cardinal Guides (三纲) and the Five Constant Virtues (五常), as specified in the Feudal Ethical Code, as well as the relationship between God [or nature] and mankind. Their transmissions could be divided into two types of knowledge: one is morality and ethics, while the other is science and technology. The most popular and the most famous among these people were Confucius and his students.

Why? Before they established their theory, people did not know how great and how strong the way of the Two Emperors (二帝) and the Three Kings (三王) was,[1] such that it has not been obliterated until now. Therefore, [people] doubted their doctrine and felt that their writings were obscure. However, when Confucius and his students clarified [their work], people's suspicions disappeared. That was why those who followed the way of the Two Emperors and the Three Kings not only admired Confucius and his students, but wished to be their students as well. Mencius said, "I did not have a chance to be a student of Confucius, but I learned from gentlemen in

[1] The Two Emperors were Yao (尧) and Shun (舜); the Three Kings were Xiayu (夏禹), Shangtang (商汤) and Wen Wu Wang (周文、武王) of Zhou. See Chen Puqing, *The Translation and Commentary of the Four Books*, 449.

private." He said such words because his suspicion was removed after he read their books.

I was thinking: When Confucius was teaching in Queli (阙里),[1] many students followed him and travelled together with him. He was nothing but a poor teacher; but people liked to stay with him in a very humble house and endure the torments of hunger. At that time, Confucius had neither a prominent position nor plenty of money. Why did so many people want to follow him? It was because they admired him for his good intention of educating people with eternal knowledge that could not be weakened or obliterated.

I had an enjoyable time, the like of which did not come in a thousand years. However, I had not yet written a single word to clarify the truth and clear people's suspicions. [If that is so,] it is as if I had not lived at all. Ancient wise men valued practice instead of superficiality, which was why Confucius used to teach people and say: "It is good enough if your words express what you mean." He also said: "I am as good as others in terms of diction, however, when it comes to practice as a gentleman, I have not yet reached that state."[2] This means that Confucius was encouraging people to be practical, does it not?

In the fourth year of Yong Zheng (1726), I came to the capital city to clean my father's grave.[3] It so happened that the former Chief Minister of the Institute of Translators was giving a public notice for entrance examinations. I passed the exam and was employed. So far, I have worked for 19 years. I knew the circumstances of the Institute very well and I

---

[1] Queli (阙里) is the name of a place located in Qufu (曲阜) city, Shandong province where Confucius taught his students.

[2] He said this to show his modesty.

[3] According to Chinese custom, the offspring of the deceased go to their dead father or mother's grave at Qingming (清明) to clean it and hold a memorial ceremony. However, Muslims in China do not do this if they are practising Muslims. I think the author means that he visited his father's grave, but he used a term which is familiar and easier to understand for the person he was writing the letter to.

realized that, as a minor official, I could not serve my country as I wished. What I could do was to obey the regulations and not fall into the wrong way; otherwise, the emperor would be disappointed in me. However, if your behaviour is different from others, they will slander you. You can neither follow the unhealthy habits of those smooth and evasive people to satisfy them, nor bear to change the direction of the right way that you are following.[1] If you appear like a pure man in the morning and do something dirty at night, not only will gentlemen say no to you, but lowly people will do the same.

One day, Your Excellency came to the institute and asked us about any long-standing abuses. You enlightened us and gave guidance with the following words:

> Since we have been appointed as officials for the government, our bodies no longer belong to ourselves. Have you not heard a saying that says, 'You should share in the cares and burdens of the one whose food you eat'? More than a hundred persons are working in this institute; their payments every year are more than one thousand Liangs (两) of silver. This means that you are trusted by the public. As lecturers, you are carrying responsibilities for them, so you must present everything that relates to them and the state. Unfortunately, people are not aware of that. If you do not speak when you are able to do so, the hidden trouble will be very dangerous. Do not think that it is enough for your job to examine and distinguish situations of the Han and other races and to write reports with excellent penmanship. You must know that ancient wise men did not pay much attention to whether you are a master in literature and arts, whether

[1] He is talking about the difficulties of dealing with officials, many of whom have such habits. As one of them, if you follow them, they will be satisfied with you, but you have to go against the principles of religion or morality; if you do not, you will be in an isolated position and face problems. The author is talking about his experiences with those officials.

> you are good in writing Chinese characters or not. In their views, these things are nothing but the mastery of a skill. [Rather,] you must clarify the principles according to which we know how to purify our hearts and minds, how to cultivate our bodies, how to harmonize our family relationships, how to govern our state and make the world peaceful. When we are successful in overcoming our selfishness, and restoring our primordial nature (*fitrah*), we should practice the principles. This is the factual knowledge. These types of essays are useful for one's body, mind and life. They are also very helpful in spreading virtue and in raising the quality of people. You should learn from wise men. Those who only have one skill are not worthy enough to learn from.

When I heard your guidance, all my doubts and fears were removed and, therefore, I reported several affairs, which led to certain reforms. As a result, the situation became better than before such as the expenses for the exams were decreased, a lot of welfare was canceled and falsely received and excessive payments were eliminated. Some of the remaining funds were given back to the higher department. Thus, those who used public office for private gains could no longer be imperious and despotic. As a result, the dignity of the law was defended; and some of the funds were used to support the weak and poor people so that they could be independent. The education aimed at preparing qualified personnel improved noticeably. As for the examination system, only those who scored well could be accepted and employed. Thus, poor participants from far places found a home to turn to.[1]

They visited each other, and their looks were elegant. However, they used to miss their schoolmates and were always mentioning them. I was told that they sighed with regret ever since they came to the capital city. These

---

[1] Before being employed, they were either staying at hotels or in their friend's houses. However, when they got jobs, the government provided them with houses.

participants showed mastery in writing articles and poems; their works are invaluable. We chose some of the works for editing and printing. Many people came to buy books; as a result, the price of paper in the markets rose. At the same time, many people came to request manuscripts from those participants, most of whom were youth. At that time, our institute became a place where all good and propitious things converged. How happy we were then!

As to those who spread rumors and slandered [us], winning some to their side and pushing others out, that is a widespread practice. Fortunately, the supervisor treated them fairly. "He took back the land which was stolen and cleared it out." These words seem to indicate that people were praising the supervisor, while in fact they were criticizing him.[1] It is impossible to avoid people's slander totally. It is said that words of warning [or advice from] gentlemen might educate many coming generations, but slander coming from lowly people is not to be feared. You can listen to the latter, but you should not fear them. They do not know that God is there; He sends down either fortune or disaster whenever He wills. Those people want others to ingratiate [themselves] with them, obey and fear them. The lowly are satisfied when people do what they ask of them. However, honest and pure men do not do that. As a result, those people did not welcome them, which was why they were missing the land of their ancestors.

Islam was called *Qing Zhen* (清真). "*Qing*" means to avoid dirty things when doing business. Whoever wants to join Islam must not try to ingratiate himself with multiple false gods for gaining fortune from them. He must serve and obey the One God, so that he can come close to the truth and be far from falsehood. Then he will know how to deal with God.

Muslims have been in China since the Sui (隋) and Tang (唐) dynasties and they became citizens a long time ago. They have no negative ideas. They follow the ethical regulations of human relationships, support the living and bury the dead. They do not differ from the society in this regard.

---

[1] Because when he took back the 'stolen land', they lost much interest and therefore they criticized him.

They do so out of sympathy for humanity. Moreover, educated Muslims take part in policymaking, just like other people.

As to why Islamic books are not transliterated into Chinese, this is because, if this were done, the pronunciation would be changed and the book may lose its original sound. This is like Chinese books: to save their original sounds, we must know how to read and pronounce. As for Muslims' fasting, prayers, cultivation of moral character, harmonization of family life, serving the country, as well as the way they purify their hearts and natures, non-Muslims have not had time to study all these things, so how could they deeply understand them?

But also, the world is wide, and there are many states in the world today. In our institute, there are books from eight countries. [There is a department for every country.] Each department has less than 4000 characters; there are only 800 or so words of minorities from the western areas.[1] I think the number of characters for other nations is probably the same; they would be around one thousand. Compared to Chinese characters, theirs are not enough to use. As a great nation, its books and documents should be true and detailed.

However, I think that those states must have rules and ethical regulations if they have their emperors. Of course, their rules and regulations were not made by one person. Since each state has its own language and alphabet, it must have its own way of behaving. I think that people's behaviours in different states might be different from each other in terms of minor details, but they are like each other in terms of the cardinal guides and the constant virtues. Otherwise, there would be no difference between honor and disgrace, old and young; there would be no etiquette, no punishment and no order in society. If so, how could the state be ruled? How could families be managed? How could people live in peace? How could the power of state be continued? We can conclude through this that if there were no languages and alphabets in other states, no books and documents, then those states would be like the world of the birds and beasts.

---

[1] This indicates India.

Everything has its principle, which was why Daxue (大学)[1] started with *zhizhigewu* (致知格物), the term *zhizhi* (致知) means to know the principles of dealing with one's self, one's heart, life, the state and the world. The second term, *gewu* (格物), means to study the concept of public favors and people's interests; to know what is right and what is wrong; to recognize what should be rejected and what should be accepted, what should be given and what should be taken, so that public and individual affairs are not dealt with wrongly. That is called *zhizhi* and this is called *gewu*. People who do not know these principles doubt, therefore they slander however they please. Although some Muslim scholars have written some precious books, those books are too detailed and too deep for people to understand. Furthermore, their purpose was not to eliminate doubts such as those we face today. Because of this, I have felt regretful for many years.

I learned Islamic knowledge for a long time, and I have always thought of interpreting the teachings of Islam using the Chinese language. But I was afraid that I would not be able to do it well or to explain deeply and, as result, that people would look down upon me. Until the second year of Qianlong (1737), in which I was appointed as the head of translators, I was simultaneously an instructor in the department of Huihui (回回馆). My job was to interpret textbooks, teach alphabets and pronunciation, explain their meanings, and to clarify customs and daily etiquette. I did these things, firstly to render service for the state; secondly, to publicize my religion and dispel people's suspicions about it. That was the right time for writing a book.

I thought that when people open and read it they would feel as though they are communicating with me face to face. Then they will know that Islam is in accord with the Cardinal Guides and the Constant Virtues, and they will not doubt Muslims' behaviour anymore. If people's suspicions are

---

[1] Daxue is the title of a book written by Zengzi (曾子) and it means great learning. It was one chapter of Liji (礼记) and then it was separated into a book in the Song (宋) and was considered one of the four Confucian books namely Zhongyong (中庸), Lunyu (论语), Mengzi (孟子) and Daxue (大学). See: *History of Ancient Chinese Civilization*, 1500,2499.

removed, Muslims and non-Muslims all over the land could live together in harmony and peace. This book was written at that time, and it was as if it fell from the sky. I completed it within one month and then spent several more months modifying it. I named it "*Qingzhen Shiyi*" (清真释疑). I mean by this title that people's doubts about Islam were not removed for a long time. To remove it, it is better to write a book, because to answer questions orally is useful for a short time, but answers in a book will continue for many years. It can be spread throughout the world. How great it is! We should follow the teachings of the ancient wise men who encouraged us to write books.

The book was completed a long time ago, but I did not publish it. I have a friend named Chen Daoshao (陈大韶) who came from Song Zi (松滋), Hubei. He was admitted as a student at the institute after taking the exam. After a while, we became friends. One day, he saw this book by chance and read it for a month and then he made some comments with warm feelings. He said:

> I am wondering whether Islam is like Buddhism or Taoism. If it is like Buddhism, why do Muslims not worship ghosts and gods to seek good fortune as Buddhists do? If it is like Taoism, I heard that Muslims do not try to fly as Taoists do. If you look at their religion, you would find that it requires people to retain relationships between the emperor and his subjects, father and sons, husband and wife, brothers and friends; I see that Muslims can be scholars, or farmers, or laborers, or business men. They are not different from Confucian people. And, I admire Muslims for their religion, which can strengthen their faith and make it firm that no Muslims convert to Buddhism or Taoism, for their deep and clear understanding of the disadvantages and falsehoods of those two religions. However, many of my Confucian people not only joined Buddhism and Taoism, but also wrote books and constructed theories to promote them. They say that Buddhism, Taoism and Confucianism were

> originally one religion. They did not think, for Confucius said: "To study heretical beliefs is harmful." Mencius said: "Whoever can speak against the theories of Yang (杨) and Mo (墨) could be considered a student of wise men." Changli (昌黎) said: "Buddhism and Taoism are more harmful than Yang (杨) and Mo (墨)."[1] The doctrine of the so-called three in one[2] is familiar to me; [but I do not think so, for] if they were one, those wise men would not have said the words that I quoted above. However, since they said such words, it means that the three were not one religion. Now, to remove people's suspicions, you presented the version of two-in-one. Buddhism and Taoism do not encourage people to get married, so how could their numbers increase? Since they do not bear children, their doctrine should disappear. I would like to ask the followers of the two men:[3] Who amongst you are not children of Confucians? Today you joined their religions.[4] Sometimes people might rediscover their consciences. If they thought seriously, they would know that to say that the three religions are one is in fact to say that their followers are Confucian. It does not mean that the doctrines of three religions are the same or like each other. My suspicions have been removed after reading your book. You should publish it as soon as possible to clarify people's suspicions.

But I did not publish it. On the contrary, I kept it with me for many years until I had almost forgotten it. Yesterday, Dashao (大韶) came and urged me again. Some Muslims who were filled with exultation when they read this

---

[1] See: *History of Chinese Philosophy*, (Beijing: Beijing University Publishing House, 2003), 232.

[2] It means the three religions were one in their origin.

[3] He means Buddhism and Taoism.

[4] He means by two persons the founders of Buddhism and Taoism.

book; some of them were educated in an Islamic background and some in a Confucian background. All of them wanted to help me print it. I was somewhat touched at those moments, yet could not bear to do so. I thought: why do I not submit the book to your Excellency to make corrections and to write a preface so that I could include it at the beginning of my book as an honor? Thus, the suspicions and doubts of all people who do not understand Muslim behaviour will be cleared and eliminated totally. Your Excellency will be respected and admired not only by me, but also by all readers of this book forever.

I was taught that every banquet in the world will break up at the end（天下没有不散的筵席）. To make preparation for my life after retirement, I ordered lecturers and students in the Institute to copy the thirteen books[1] to enjoy in my late age. They are on my table now. When I am available, I open and read them till the last page. The name of the transcriber is at the

---

1 According to Mr. Hai, the Thirteen Books were Islamic books which were normaly taught in mosques of China. However, I think that the author means by the term the thirteen Confucian books which were familiar to educated people at that time. My ground for this statement is the following: 1. To mention Islamic books which are in Arabic and Persian to the person makes sense only if he was a Muslim; however we have no source to tell us that he was a Muslim. 2. The Islamic books are called '*Shi San Ben*' (十三本), see for example, Jin Yijiu, *Dictionary of Islam*, (Shanghai Dictionary Publishing House, 1997), 118; while the Confucian ones are called '*Shi San Jing*' (十三经), see Ye Shaojun, *Index of Shisanjing*, (China Book Press, 1957), the author said here *Shi San Jing*, he didn't say *Shisanben*. 3. In the translation centre, there would not be many people who knew Arabic so that they could transcribe those books; but every one could write in Chinese very well so that they could fulfil the request of the author, who was their boss. Based on that, I believe that the thirteen books mentioned by the author here in his letter were the Confucian books namely: *Zhou Yi* (周易), *Shang Shu* (尚书), *Shi Jing* (诗经), *Zhou Li* (周礼), *Yi Li* (仪礼), *Li Ji* (礼记), *Chun Qiu Zuo Zhuan* (春秋左传), *Chun Qiu Gong Yang Zhuan* (春秋公羊传), *Chun Qiu Gu Liang Zhuan* (春秋穀梁传), *Lun Yu* (论语), *Meng Zi* (孟子), *Xiao Jing* (孝经) *and* *Er Ya* (尔雅).

end of each book; when I see the name, I feel that I see the person himself. At this moment, I have mixed feelings of grief and joy in my heart. I feel grief because [one day] I will not see and talk with them face to face as I do today. Then, why do I not try to treat the future grief before it becomes reality? Ancient people used to say, "The style of handwriting is just like the writer himself." When I look at these names in the future, the case that we were working on together appears in front of my eyes. This is the best way to enjoy life after retirement. Even if one sits alone in the future, he will have the same feeling that he had during the days two or three others were working together with him. Won't that be nice?

Now, our emperor is holding an unprecedented ceremony. He personally came to the office of Han Lin Academy (翰林院), calling on scholars to compose poems together; then carve those poems on stone and set the stones in the office, so that people in the future will remember the celebration. He hopes his contributions will be eternal. This means that the emperor would like to educate this world forever, but I do not know whether those who come after him will want to carry on his undertaking in perpetuity. This is like what was said: "Later generations will look at today like today's people look at yesterday." It is because our emperor simultaneously has great virtue and morality as well as a high-level understanding of the theory of Confucian knowledge and diction that we have had this flourishing age.[1]

Today, I submit this book to you, asking you to make corrections and to write a preface. I do this to prepare something that might remind me of the days in which we were in your company. Although the situations will have changed, I can get abundant enjoyment from the reminder. If I do not ask this of you, it will be too late to repent. I have written a poem on the day the eight halls were completed, and I submitted it to you with an introduction that you kindly taught me. The poem was carved inside the institute.[2]

---

[1] The time of Qianlong was considered as the flourishing (golden) age in the history of China.

[2] Thus far, I have not been able to obtain any information related to this poem written by the author.

Whenever people see it, they admire and praise it. I guess, if this book is published, there will always be some people to read it in the future. They will remember and admire you and appreciate your great brilliance. Why? Because their doubts will be eliminated and the truth will become obvious through your words. If you dislike writing, I have already asked you to do so. If you are greatly concerned about your position and do not want to become involved in such minor things, the book can still can remove people's doubts. That is why it is said that gentlemen seek knowledge to know the truth well and spread it in the world. They hope that their theories will never be obliterated or repudiated by coming generations since they have successfully removed suspicions and doubts. Whoever can do that will be considered as one of those with the intention of educating people forever. If someone has such an intention, none can say that he could not be the student of wise men.

This is my humble opinion. It would be my pleasure if Your Excellency could be tolerant with me and teach me.

III. The Edited Texts of *Qingzhen Shiyi*

再次重刻《清真释疑》序

窃观《清真释疑》一书，刊自前贤，阐发真主，贵人极品。承领天命五功，人伦五典。天经三十册，明命至真。以事了目，教门至贵。与夫正心诚意、认己认主之学，遵守者得矣，自欺者失矣。是书也，其于好道阅之，无不赞赏。为板遗失，其广播重刻，略叙片言，以志始末云耳。如有同好道者，自备纸张印刷，以广流传，可也。

石可宗序

予始祖，天方人也。天方之教，以奉主命朝拜为务，自隋唐传入中幅。一切明心见性之旨，足与吾儒相表里。第国音世罕能识，且附居内地者，为日既久，沿诵失真。己则不能无疑，又曷怪人之疑之者？

天柱金先生，恐教之中湮，爰著《释疑》一篇，以行于世。其中词旨显豁，大率取儒家道理，以证其说之旁通。读是书者，反复研求，了如指掌，始信四海之大，千圣同心，复何疑于天方之教乎？

顾兵燹流离，版片尽失。同人延鸠赀付梓，嘱予校雠。诚不欲没金先生一片婆心也，因为叙其颠末如此。

光绪二年闰五月望日，真州

也园氏石可宗谨叙

胡汇源序

入道之户，贵信而贱疑。疑滋贰，贰滋离，或梦以驰，或遂畔以去，举坐是也。吾圣门，七十有二士，其于道，胥各有会，独卜氏以笃信标后，乃嗣铎西河上，著《蔡师说》，一不敢毛发变易。时岂无诸子相訾嗷哉？然颇以文辞相开譬，讫用冰释，阕里之绪，赖以不溷。

北高金先生者，天方之卜氏也。天方之教，自隋唐始入中夏，沿及于今，繁衍极矣。枝盛者本蔽亏，派远者源迷失。虽遵用教典，斤斤勿渝，而日用民常，懵厥宗旨。己则不信，人亦疑之。予自授书后，行游四方，睹教中人士伙矣。其间，如前所陈，十常五六。而天姿秀挺者，亦间能力自表揭，号称宗师。顾，皆未有如北高之卓然也。

乙丑春，予铩翮南宫，旅食京邸，北高惠然顾我，至于再三。越数日，遂出所书《清真释疑论》相示，且嘱弁其首。予受而卒业，见其连篇累牍，绳贯珠联，缕析条分，天青日白。且读且喜，作而谓曰：学道至此，抑可谓笃信者矣！夫信生于中无疑，中无疑生于外无杂。朗乎其相辉，铄乎其孔昭。宣之于口则为河，借之于笔则如椽。己实不疑，人必信之。是论也出，家一编，手一册，数千年之疑团，若红炉之一点雪。予且拭目而决，笃信者之匝于四宇矣，其又何释焉？是为序。

乾隆十年乙丑仲夏之吉年
家乡眷弟胡汇源拜撰

又七言一律

羁思无端未易裁，异书谁信枕中来？
万言独自成千古，一日须教看百回。
中极胜因垂盖壤，西方遗训展风雷。
怜君大笔于今少，梨枣他年遍九垓。
范庵弟源再抄

马廷辅序

从来大道昭垂，如日月经天，江河行地，奚必疑之，亦奚必谆谆辩之？然宇宙廖阔，中外攸分；人之体道者，各有从入之路，捷径之门。自不习其事者，以为奇异之端，遂从而非议之，将使微言大义，掩晦莫彰，而其真不出。有心斯道者，当申明其说，使人易知共晓，彼疑之者，自涣然冰释矣。如清真教典，始于西域天方国，乃至圣绍鼻祖心传，其源远，其流长，其道广大悉备。

自唐贞观时，高贤塞尔德·宛噶思奉至圣之命，传教中土，至今千有余年，以认、礼、斋、课、游为纲领；以孝悌、忠信、礼仪、廉耻为条目。其道之大者，五伦五事之必遵，与儒教无异。但饮食衣服之制，冠婚丧祭之典，大概从朴素之风，取清真之义。世世率由，无敢擅易。缘教中有行之不著，习焉不察者，遂至疑信相参，以为拘而难行，甚且有忍心悖畔，坏祖宗之良规，而入于他途者，此疑之当释也。亦有他教之人，见其遵守严密，不考原委，从而非议多端，此疑之又当释也。

予有志未逮，幸乙卯中式，乙丑公车北上。春闱试后，适逢翰林院四译馆教习，北高金先生者，言论风采，彬彬乎诗书礼乐；起居动静，恂恂然清洁真诚。知其性天高迈，得于经书之义蕴者深也。继而以《清真释疑》示予，予读其文，皆本韩、柳、欧、苏之笔，发清真奥妙之典，洞若观火，毫无障翳，能令观者如逢其故有，了然于心，了然于口。不但他教之人无所疑议，即教中之游移莫定者，亦可感发其天良，坚定其志气，永守祖训于不衰。

是北高之《释疑》集，其为功于世道人心者，岂浅鲜哉？斯诚本教之津梁，可以永垂不朽。至其言之援引辩驳，非好为訾议。盖体夫不直，则道不见。我且直之之意也。世之睹斯集者，其见谅于北高之苦衷乎？

北高嘱予为序，于是约略陈词，亦望同志诸君子，共相笃信力行云尔。

乾隆乙丑清和月谷旦，滇南弟
马廷辅君禄氏题于京邸之旅舍

陈大韶序

人心者，风俗之本；风俗者，教化之著。今天下人文蔚起，纪纲罗列显烁。薄海内外，陶淑日上。顾不规不洁，我虞而诈，往往沿袭，故常而不能尽革，何也？

雍正甲辰，予以乡选进士游京师，得谒缙绅先生谆谆，以此为训，谈论往复，期归于清洁真实，是维持世教者之良法。逾年，忝列教习官学。公侯贵胄，多彬彬儒雅。讲习之下，即以“敦伦循纪，清洁真实”为训。偶与宾客晋接，亦本此为赠答。若翰林院四译馆教习，北高金先生，与旅署最密迩，所借以扶树道教之一友也。

北高与予往来久，几至忘形，携予译署，亲自训课。衣冠常整，饮食常洁，仪礼节度秩如雅，不乐闻佛老语。聚首经年，尊亲大义，恻然动听。此岂漫无所得，而好为矫异者乎？一日，北高顾谓予：“我教门也，世人闻而口道之。”因以《清真释疑》一集出示，言焉而正，行焉而庸，只一二末节，略与世殊。读儒书，应科目，登皇路，率伦常事，笃乎；君父兄友者，不爽分毫。

予幸十余年来，得接当世士大夫，启迪指画，于人心风俗，讲究日上。而北高先生犹以世疑为隐憾。予曰：无憾也，是集出现者，自豁然矣。且家居之不能尽同，非独而教为然也。即州县此疆彼界，被身服口，安得一辙。今朝鲜逼近东土，之纲之纪，子弟授学。都门世传，殷少师之裔。饮食不可知，而冠履裳衣，尽与世违。人知其祖制如斯，是以无词。今是集出，人群知之。知而犹疑，必非人情。

北高嘱为点次，予以相知久，即以往复之语书之简端。

时值乾隆三年戊午孟秋月
教习拣用知县楚北松滋同学弟
陈大韶顿首拜撰

作者自序

清真者，吾教之宗。《释疑》何为而作也？由于各教莫能思吾教之行事，蓄疑团于千百年而莫释。未学吾教之书，而不知其所以然之故，致使各教之疑愈生，而各教之物议愈纷。遂有谓不遵正朔，私造宪书，以三百六十天为一年，而群相庆贺者；有谓异言异服，拣择饮食；甚者谓斋仍茹荤，白日何故不饮食；又谓礼拜不知所拜何神，而夜聚晓散，男女杂沓；更有谓齐发以毁父母之遗体，而庞貌为之异样者。种种疑案，皆莫能释。

然不能释者，非吾教之无人，盖缘吾教疑前辈只自作大言，而不屑白此目前疑案。昔岱舆王先生著有《正教真诠》、《清真大学》、《希真正答》；而《清真指南》，则文炳马先生之笔也；迨其后，介廉刘先生又著《天方性理》、《典礼》之类，不可枚举。皆集吾教之经，以阐吾教之义。其事，则认主、拜主、民常日用；其言，则指点教内之人者居多。且书册浩繁，谁肯究心探讨？乃各教之人，先存己见，虽有美玉精金，尽行抹煞。而前此数事，为之特殊者亦少，各教无从一览而便知，而疑卒以不释。夫前辈之未释其疑者，非不能也，抑以为伦常不异，议论何伤。故无足重轻，任世人之颠倒，不必为此口争舌辨也。

予何人？斯敢为妄作，而以贤智多前辈然？而天地之大，五方风气之异，语言、衣服、制度之殊，即中夏论之，皆有同异，何足乖张？惟是人纲人纪，悉归于大同。孟子曰："杨无君，墨无父"；释老又用保举恩父，则又举君父而假之，遂置其君父于不用，均之无耳。吾教振纲常，饬伦纪，般般可据，与杨墨、释老大相径庭。今于害仁义而废君臣，灭纲常而绝父子者，反舍之不究，一遇吾教之人，即以琐屑之事，故为挑逗，议论横生。殊不知，吾教自隋唐相沿至今版图，千百余年，代国家出力报效，与儒教何异？各教之疑者，既不知吾教之大义，且隐隐挟一入主出奴之见，殊失吾教之所以然，致清真之理，卒沦没于庸众人之齿颊，不大显于斯世也，悲夫！

予于回汉之学问，虽未能深悉，而生成之大义，则了于心，体于身，势不能以扪舌。古人云："予岂好辩哉，予不得已也。"抑尤有进者，予幼习本教之书，今又职司译学，其于布在方策之风俗人情，每有同异之处，正当旁引曲喻，以白吾人，使无嫌隙。况君共一君，臣共为臣，岂可令同室疑议，而坐听其彼此之牙眥者哉？兹释疑之说，亦迫于各教之横议而起者。予期告无罪于前辈，并期阐厥义于今日。为略抒鄙言，俾各教之人，思其理之合一，事之大同，疑心顿释；而吾教之道，庶不无小补云尔。

乾隆戊午春二月望日

翰林院四译馆正教序班

石城金天柱自序

陈大韶点评

海阔天空，支分派别，此世之大，故道之大也。贤知驰才思于万里，高明极耳目于殊途。引而近，会而归，斯道之能事毕矣。存此见者，乃可与遵之道之。金子于《释疑》而有序，浑灏详明，堪与《原道篇》并驾齐驱。宗回教，深儒学，其一以贯也哉。

宗山

纲领

吾教之道，敬一归真，开天之圣祖明之。后之子孙，谨循恪守，跬步不离。迄于今，凡四方六合，无问海内外，言同教者，其事不异。乃同教奚啻千万，止能行，而习莫克言，而著者，何故？因有贤、智、愚、不肖之殊，与学之偏全不一。彼不能阐吾教之大义，奚以释各教之疑议无惑乎？

议吾教之偏异拘执者遍寰区也。吾教之不学者，己尚不明，何由对答？且学不能以兼该，如吾辈幼习儒书，未读本教之书，是无本之学，于各教问答，焉能晓畅？即专习吾教之书，而置儒书于不问，亦不能引经释义，大白其衷。两两比议，使问者即为豁然。设有之矣，其谁又复曰偏异拘执者乎？今日三纲五常，子臣弟友，毫无异于儒生。岂弃而君臣，去而父子，禁而相生相养之道，以求其所谓清静寂灭者哉？

论饮食

至吾教所论斋拜、庆贺、饮食、冠裳、丧葬、祭祀，原有等威，不得滥用。各教未得其详，遂生物议。噫，误矣！未读孔子书矣。《乡党》篇中不食者甚多，如割不正不食，不得其酱不食，食饐而餲，鱼馁而肉败不食，色恶、臭恶、失饪、不时、沽酒、市餔皆不食。至于祭肉，亦不出三日，出三日，则不食。凡此皆摄其性，固其命，体天地生物之心，不致有伤性伐命之咎。世之人多知尊孔子，敬孔子，其能行孔子之言，而不食其不食者，果有几人？更可异者，释教之人不食生牢，律法大戒，虽阳奉于昭昭，而阴违于冥冥。且无论违与不违，而自号曰“食”与“不食”，是释教亦有所不食矣，而士君子遇而不问者，其谓之何？释所论肉食伤人之性，世人皆知之而皆信之。

吾教之所言不食者，亦曰伤性，而世人多不知。即一二知者，亦不过曰：“若者回教之所食；若者回教之所不食。”而不知，食者之中，犹有不食者在，其卫生之精妙，更有进焉。如牛、羊、鸡、鸭之类，乃吾教所必食者，其血、眼、脑、腰、两肾，奚为弃置？因有聚秽与恶气相冲，故皆不食，亦以其伤性故耳。他如犬、豕之甘食秽物，喜居洼下，其性最浊，其气最昏。《本草》备载其浸下名豕之义。吾教之所忌者，于此独严。然亦不特此，凡物自殁者，因病知毒，恐致戕贼，亦与犬、豕同戒。即飞禽之有利爪者，走兽之食肉食者，鳞甲之不成正形者，酒醴之醉人者，一概不食，人知之否？其果蔬五谷，出自地脉，除无狂惑人者，未有不食。此亦言食物之大略，不能备载周详。其所以不食者，实以伤性、戕命，害其生生不息之理而，然非漫无考凭，而故为此矫情之论。总以吾教经书所载，圣贤所言，学者宣讲行止，斯须敬守无遗。予警于心，而触于目也。

忽有缙绅之客，揖予而前，坐而诘曰：子言过哉！子之教，既流行中国，则食物、冠裳当遵时制。子教中人动为拣择，一饮食间，有如许议论，尝言犬、豕秽污，喜居洼下；又言其性最浊，其气最昏。子教之人，皆能避昏浊而不食，胡以尧、舜、禹、汤、文、武、孔、孟，以及历代之圣君贤相，未有言及犬、豕若此者？今以子言，是前古圣贤，皆不如子教之人乎？孟子曰："吾闻用夏变夷，未闻变于夷。"子辈虽回教，久居中夏，仍如此之拘执，善变者当不若是。而子且言，教中人皆知性理之学，正心修身之事，决不至有伤性命，是未必然。

予曰：不然。古先圣贤各有礼制，小大由之。纲常伦纪之道，日用饮食之条，圣以之敦，贤以之学，务纳其人于轨物之中，斯须不可或去，正所谓"众物之表里、精粗无不到，而吾心之全体大用无不明"者，若专事乎纲常之大，而偏废乎饮食之小；又所谓"知和而和，不以礼节之，亦不可行也"。是以君子不受国门之御，廉者不饮贪泉之水，皆谨小慎微之意。今子言用夏变夷，恐亦未详所言之宗旨。使吾教之道无君臣，无父子，则当变；无夫妇，无昆弟、朋友，则当变；无贡税，无长幼，无仁义礼智，不待子言，宜变之久矣。今回教于君臣、父子、夫妇、昆弟、朋友、贡税、长幼何如者？而何变之有？而子乃曰：回教之人未读儒书，流于拘执，何未之思也？

尝闻大家祖先莫不垂有家训，以示子孙，吾教守祖训兢兢。曾思父在章尹氏注云："如其道，虽终身不改；如其非道，何待三年？"吾教所不食之物，与不行之事，皆遵祖训于千百年后而不改，延之子孙，终身守之。乃反以不逊之语，斥遵祖训为异端，将以非祖训为正学，吾恐智者不若是也。吾不知，"於陵仲子，上不臣于王，下不治其家，中不索交诸侯，率民而出于无用，何为至今不杀者"，此又何说也？由此观之，古圣先贤，不过以此数事责人。而吾教之人，臣于王者自若，治其家者自若，索交于人者又自若。自古未闻以不食某物之故，而见责于圣贤，何独至今而疑之？

子言吾教之人不读儒书，罔知义理。且不论儒教之不读儒书，与吾教之不读者等。吾恐儒教之诵其诗，读其书，亦未必人人皆君子也。古人云："德行本也，文艺末也。" 又云："德行之本，莫大乎明德。"明德者，明其自有之天良，不怨天，不尤人，凡天之所以生生不息之理，实当体认，勿效空谈。此数语者，隐而察之，而儒教之坐言起行者，果几人哉？若吾教之道，言敬一归真。归真者，归于造物之主宰。

今姑无论吾教之所谓主宰。即就儒书所言上帝者不少矣，而其最易明白者，莫如《诗》"克配上帝"之朱注云："上帝者，天之主宰也。"朱子又曰："天地亦是有个主宰，方始恁地变易无穷。"又言："毋不敬，可以对越上帝。"是非回教之言，而儒教之书也。将谓真宰之言为虚诬，则朱子之注，与前人之诗皆非与？吾教于乱性者不食，纵未知义理之人，其心中能时具此真宰，故不至伤性。此吾教不能伤性之说，非所论于文艺之末也。

论主宰与耶稣

客曰：如子所言，教内之人未读儒书，而能知上帝之义，不食戕性之物，而能明德者是矣。何也？子教之人，幼而祖父，长而师友，熏陶渐染，终日闻之，见异不迁，抑或自然之理。今子言主宰，天地万有惟其所生，毋亦近于天主教之谓乎？

予曰：是又不然。彼天主教之所谓主宰者设像而祀，饮食不择，恶得与吾教相似？彼所言主宰，似是而非，自认不的。即以天主降生，圣母受胎之说，大相天壤。既曰"天主"，其母又称"圣母"，何不直称"天主之母"？此自相矛盾，不知根柢之甚也。

天地间一物必有一主。物无定主，则起而争。以世界论，君为世界之主，而民勿敢争，即不得与凡民同类。彼天主教曰：天主能造化万物，则圣母之有生，亦被其造化，明矣。其母既被造化，彼行造之主，复投于受造之腹中。即此一语，真伪立分。又曰：天主降生，欲劝世人信彼为善，故不惮劳瘁，则更谬矣。全不思，彼能造化天地，生成万物，何难以风雷之号令，布满于人间？即如洪水滔天，或山崩地陷，无一不非上天示警之意，岂有降生投胎之理？今天子发政施令，遇有梗顽，大则征伐，小则惩创，无往不宜。若天主降生劝人为善，则是天子复自为连帅方伯，而行征伐惩创，有是理乎？

吾教所言主宰之理，斯须不离天地之内外。何则？世人皆云天一大天，人一小天。天一大天，即有一大天之主宰；人一小天，即有一小天之主宰。大天之主宰，为造化天地万有之主，能使四时往来，晦明风雨。小天之主宰，能使吾身之手足运动，耳目听闻，即吾身之命也。或曰，心为此身之主宰者，未尽然也。谓心以藏神，而为用事之主宰，其说近是。假使心为主宰，则人皆长生。何也？世人孰不欲其长生？心既可为主宰，皆主此身之不死。乃人于死后，何以四肢百骸，忽然涣散；心当此时，亦块然乎？以是知，心非人身之主宰，是此命焉，不可须臾离也。天地之主宰，又岂可离乎？子思云："上天之载，无声无臭。"东坡亦谓："昊天冥冥，不可得而名。"吾教之论主宰，无似无像，亦如人命之在人身，有何比似，孰能见诸？故吾教经中，有申如在其上之敬，非惟拜时宜申如在，欲时时具有此心，正孔子所谓："君子无终食之间违仁"。

子何以天主教律吾教耶？且天主教有所谓耶稣，彼乃奉之为主宰者，不知尝考。吾教经中，耶稣实西方之圣人，亦主宰之差使。当其时，有叛道不遵者暗加非议，欲致之死。复买盗攀害，国法钉死十字架上。彼教凡所行事，皆画十字者，以此所钉耶稣，当日不见，与谋之辈多被其殃。当时知者深为畏惧，即号耶稣为主宰，相沿至今，以讹传讹。若辈之喻，亦犹大军平复之后，彼即以方伯连帅认为天子，然纯臣知敬，自不敢当。无如若辈，目睹其事，遂铭心刻骨，世传为真，直至今日。

客又曰：主宰既生圣人劝世，应使世人尊崇，勿许非议，何又任人加害，而不明正其与谋之罪，使后来见殃，多费周折？

予曰：舜，大圣人也，浚井而出；孔子厄于陈蔡，斯道今传。圣贤当厄，往往而有。子言多费周折，则中夏诸圣人，即不应有此危厄也。

今以吾教之书籍参之，耶稣实西方之圣人，非主宰也。则吾教之所谓主宰，与天主教之所谓主宰，不大可见乎？

论历法与斋课

一、历法：

客曰：子教不同于天主教，固然。然汝教来中夏，自隋唐始，凡事俱当遵制。何得自外宪书，以三百六十日为一年，不讲春夏秋冬，三年一转？世人甚骇。

予曰：恶！是何言也？胡陷吾教乐触王章，计启众惑，以至于此？今天下一君，四海一国，煌煌宪书，孰敢不遵？如以三百六十日为一年，总不计月之小大，与春夏秋冬之往来，是别有一天地耶，其然乎？夫吾教所居之地，本无隔膜。若教内人蕃衍，必开设义学，听远方单寒，不能延师者就学焉。学者饮食衣服，皆此地之有力者供给，不使他累，致废时日。数载后，学业有成。还乡日，大以成大，小以成小，幸渊源之不绝。在吾教字书不假汉字音译，恐音韵背离，有失旧章。故经千百年之久，仍如一日之初者，此也。彼不知吾教之大义，又安知不以吾教家贴户晓之斋拜日期，指为宪书者？

今夫国家每岁制造宪书外，太常寺又刻钦天监选择祭祀日期，及忌辰日期，印刷单条，贴于公署。近年，宪书于日期之上，新例刻有圆圈，使知忌辰斋戒之期。何必另刻祭祀与忌辰单条？盖缘书册常掩，未若单条易见。此国家觉民之道也。由此而推，士庶人自有应祀祖考之期，照式贴于内室，若此亦指为宪书，可乎？吾教每年斋拜，各有日期，必应刻明，亦如祭祀、忌辰日期之单条格式，贴之各家，使人望而即知，便于遵行。胡各教之人不体此情，即以私制宪书之名加之？苟非天意普垂，几何不为此语陷也。子其慎之，吾为子解。

二、斋课：

以三百六十日为一年，而群相庆贺之故，缘各教规，皆有斋之一条。吾教之斋，则与各教不同。吾教圣人思宜体恤穷民，言君公王侯卿大夫，下至士庶富厚有力者，自是饮食无亏，饥寒罔觉。纵岁遇荒歉，未必如鳏寡孤独，倍加之困苦。方于每年之中，设斋一月，均令鸡鸣而食，星灿而开，白日颗粒不入肠胃，滴水不下咽喉。无拘祈寒盛暑，挨次三年，遵照前设之月举行，勿许拣选。是不禁茹荤，而较之茹素者，不大有间乎？又谓，人生日用、语言、行事，孰能保其无过？或无知，或故犯。于此斋戒之月，各加内省，悔过迁善，体上天好生之心，自知四民之困苦，得遂爱养之至意。使诸侯体君王之意，布政施令，务期于至公；使大夫体诸侯之意，用刑鞫讼，必期于各当；使士庶人体上帝、君王、诸侯、大夫之意，清心寡欲，改过自新，亦知无告之困苦。如此存心设想，敬待期满，沐浴重新，以祀上帝。拜后各相庆贺，谓此经月之内，闭户虔修，不比平日，故有庆贺之举。其所以然者，以人劳则思，思则善心生；逸则淫，淫则忘善，忘善则恶心生，踵而行之而已。今人不思此义，妄为讥刺。吾教之未学者，固不能道答；间有学者，又不能详细援引解说。相传至今，谓吾教以三百六十日为一年者众矣。殊不知，吾教之庆贺者，谓斋戒之功成期满也，非年也。吾子其释然否？

客曰：此意诚得矣。子言君公大人、富厚有力，皆效饿夫，毋乃固执自苦，而不通于人情乎？

予曰：古者天子躬耕藉田，后妃亲治蚕桑，下至士庶人，莫不皆有纺绩之劳，胼胝之职。今如子言，则天子躬为万乘，后妃尊为国母，岂必待耕而食，自织而衣，不知欲供宗庙祭祀之用？因以识民间稼穑之艰难，自广爱民之术。吾观刘宋元嘉二十一年，宋帝以衡阳王义季为兖州刺史，亲饯于武帐冈。将行，敕诸子且勿食，至会所设馔。日旰不至，皆有饥色，乃谓曰："汝曹少长丰佚，不见百姓艰难。今使汝曹识有饥苦，知以节食御物而。"此与吾教斋戒之意，正自符合。又查古写"斋"字，原以"不食"二字叠架为之，是古人之斋，亦取"不食"之义。不然，即不得谓字有取义之训耳。孟子不云乎："禹思天下有溺者，犹己溺之也；稷思天下有饥者，犹己饥之也。"毋亦固执自苦乎？吾教于民间困苦，曲意仿为，非特自思，而并以己身效之，大有重于民命，使君公大人、富厚士庶，不忘此鳏寡孤独之无告者，故多方拯救，以体好生之心。此斋之大凡也。

更有进者，吾教内贸易四方，有本至二十两者，名曰"满贯"。约经营一周，除去日用已费，仍存本二十两，即应施散银五钱，名曰"天课"。何为天课？意使富厚之人，代天养育蒸黎，不使失所，亦稍能释我君之忧。此项之银，推本递算，并无传唤催科，胥役扰责，均系己身自算，暗给乡族之无告者。外有衣服住房、动用什物，只散天课一次，其后免议，盖以再无滋息耳。至于田亩所收，除输纳正赋官粮外，仍有什一之天课，照例给人，不敢私匿。间有下愚悭吝不出，吾教经律明有天谴。其有满贯，应散天课者，不得复受他人之天课。万一是人远出窘迫，不妨受天课以全生。吾教之规，总以恤人为重。凡先圣所言，兢兢自守，不敢忽略。故君公大人，富厚士庶，必虔斋一月者，此耳。延至今日，贫富同斋，均期寡过，广众大行。吾子不闻乎？

论丧葬

客曰：斋之一事，日知之。然子教殡殓，无衣衾棺椁，惟用土葬。是薄待其亲，与无使土亲肤者，左矣。

予曰：然，无使土亲肤之言，炳如日星。但吾教圣贤垂训：万物土中生，万物土中埋。今葬法有四：金、木、水、火。推之尽头，同归土内，未必别有天地，以贮其骸骨耶。既不能离土，何不直归于土？故反复缠裹，重袭累赘，吾教葬法不取。吾教圣人之训，以人贵于万物，富贵虽有殊分，死生原同一致。始酌定葬法，勿使富贵有厚葬之侈，而贫者受暴露之惨。倘不预为筹画，则无所适从。故葬法无分贫富贵贱。

死之后，挖坑丈余，旁开一穴，高二尺余，宽亦如之，长七尺零，其内空虚，非实砌掩覆可比。各教未睹吾教之葬法，一闻土葬，皆以为用土实掩，并无规格。殊不知，此等坑墓，延至百年，方能长满，非三年五载即充洞，而洽其骸也。百年长满何以见之？尝有客死他乡，待子成立，搬回本地，或二三十年，比及复开，所洽未几。抑有沙地，不宜作此旁穴，只挖直坑，亦深七八尺零。另用厚木作四方围墙，以防陷塌。止用木盖，间有用石板者。其旁穴内，亦有用四方匣，木石无拘，皆可置造。

不具衣衾棺椁者，意如人之初生，不分贫富，惟具衣胞，别无他物。今原始反终，仍如来日。惟用新细白布，缝若被单，男三层，女五层。将亡人用净水洗过。而《礼记》之丧礼，于洗后方为剪甲齐须。此二事者，吾教用之于平日。今将洗过之亡人，放被单上后，撒攒香细面、朝脑、麝香等物。坑内亦用香料，使逐蛇虫而却病味，存亡俱赖。将死者入毕，先用土坯砌实旁开坑门，外以竹木作门搪塞。俟收殓之人上出，然后倾土坚筑，做冢立碣，以完葬法。设有旅终外境，贫无以葬，同教辈必为代葬，仍依前法，亦不暴露。

议者谓，难免土之亲肤。其说似矣。吾不知，人当盛暑仙游，既有衣衾棺椁，又多用黄泥石灰，意取渗秽水，而殓气臭。泥灰非土乎？俄顷，发变消化，虽不忍使亲肤，而泥灰与尸骸已合为一，此又何说焉？今以各教论，未必人人富厚，且不论千百金之购求沐椁，即数十金之棺椁者，止百有四五。而贫无告者，俱二三两之薄皮烧材，甚至此皆不可得。即得之，其材不蔽风雨，再如不能埋葬，或掩之不固，不数日间，尸骸暴露，肢体解裂，见者酸心，过者掩鼻，于人心何如？岂贫乏之人不足论耶？虽其人之子孙，亦付之无可，如何而已？当此之际，土亲肤乎？不亲肤乎？掩为是乎？非乎？

大抵天地生物，人为至贵。倘世界无人，则亦无圯之土壤耳，有之何益？今富贵之家，听其厚葬；贫贱之人，任其暴露，有心者当不如是。可怪者，富贵之家多用金珠穿戴，名曰"殉葬"，惟期尸骸不朽。夫已归土中，纵千年不朽，何益于事？且即不朽，已伏开门揖盗之端。凡此大葬，庸众盛称，播扬既远，而绿林中豪客已生心矣。宝物冠戴，尽行盗去。一经缉获，开棺者斩，盗物加倍。是生人招厚葬之陷，而死者亦被厚葬之惨。始叹杜少陵诗云："昨日玉鱼蒙葬地，早时金碗出人间。"不信然乎？今五都之市，货卖古玩者，每执铜玉旧器，大其言曰："此殉葬之汉玉，此殉葬之宝镜，历年多矣！"而世人不察，既言殉葬，何复售于人间，恬然货卖，相安无事？纵不以王法论究竟彼物之来历，有心者亦当三思：如我以千金购求殉葬，倘后日之出，亦如今日，即可以自悟，而不为殉葬之谋矣。盖殉葬者，未必家家有失，而何可不预防其失也？何如吾教，禁用殉葬，不启小人之盗，存亡俱受其益，人心反无恔乎？是吾教土葬，首无暴露之惨，次免盗葬之患，虽千百年不能一见。以吾教一体葬法质诸孔孟，又未必不获尽善尽美之称矣。土葬之法，然与？否与？

论穿戴

客曰：子教葬法可矣。但子教中人，究无丧事，常戴白帽，全不忌讳，何也？

余曰：自古以来，各有所尚，夏则尚黑，周则尚赤，商则尚白，言衣服、垂戴、车帏皆白也。倘如至今，悉遵商制，皆尚白色，子复何疑？今日丧制用白色，不知商时，于父母之丧，曾用何色？又何忌讳？吾教之戴白帽者，惟礼拜时用，非尚之也。吾辈之不明大义者，欲以别于各教，时戴白帽，则固矣。以教条论，礼拜服色，非止白帽，衣皆白色。盖取对越上帝，神明交谛，有表里如一，纯白无伪之义。且白为本色，不假染造，以全天真。除此，则君公、大夫、士庶人，各有大小品级之制，朝衣朝冠，具有等威，介廉刘先生于《天方典礼》中，备载明白，焉可小视。

论认主与礼拜

一、认主：

客曰：如子所言，子教行事，般般可考，毫无疑议。吾不知，子教礼拜，所拜者何神？所设者何像？如言主宰之说，凿凿可据。乃云天地万物，俱彼造化，不思天地之大，无有穷极，谁能造化？儒教论天地万物，为阴阳二气所生，春夏秋冬，日月往来，四时明晦，古今盛衰，一饮一食，皆天地自然之理，莫非定数。汝教又有赏善罚恶之说，俱出主宰之独断，毫不假手于他人，则主宰亦劳且苦矣。且于各方建设礼拜寺，每日五时入寺礼拜，男女杂沓，人传夜聚晓散。似此举动，自招物议。

余曰：然，子所诘。皆合吾教之经内，具载有是问答，盖天下之大，心同理同。而各国有各国之书，各教有各教之论，要以不废纲常伦纪者为正教。虽语言异韵，字画各样，皆造物之大能，显著于天地，欲有心者，时相参证，非止一家而已。虽欲齐之，谁能齐之？向有友人与予言，吾教之有圣人，言殊虚诳。夫圣人唯中国有之，而化外何得有耶？余曰：子何小言至此？汝不闻"天道至公"？至公者，无私也。岂天独厚中国，而生圣人，以教中国，即不复生圣人，以教各方乎？使无圣人，则各国之书籍文字，何自而有乎？

子言一饮一食，皆有定数。今有万金于此，欲给众人，设无主持，谁肯取少？势必群起而争，争之不已，后将何极？有主之者，量亲疏远近，老少大小，自为分派，约期给发，可无争端。夫"定数"者，预定之词，预定为谁？造物之主宰也。若以天地万物，皆阴阳二气所生，以人身论之，精气神三者，精为有形之物，而气与神皆无形。且无论先天之受胎若何，假无此肉身，则精气神收贮于何方？是气与神，必得有收贮之所，而后有生发之处。试问：未有天地，阴阳二气收贮于何方何所？其意具欲渾说，不肯明言，祸天下之苍生者大矣！即如冬至时，天下皆颁宪书。未至其时，孰敢私发？必于是时，然后分发，谓有天子，然后可以统一。今使言，宪书总无刊刻印造之工匠，又无君命之颁发，于立冬日，而宪书自出矣，人必不信。

又常言：天地万物，总无行造之主宰。春夏秋冬，四时往来，日月晦明，古今盛衰，皆归于阴阳二气，天地自然之理，又言莫非"定数"。试思，阴阳二气，必待有天地收贮，而二气始能发生。纵二气之当行，亦未有自己行之者，如宪书之无刊刻，无君命，而自为颁发，自为印刷者无异。故吾教经云：世界之君王，即主宰之影射。彼为天下之君，爱养群生，保障河山；贤者进，不肖者退；善者赏，恶者罚，非人所能为，实主宰之判断。意使世人，体认此理，不致溷淆。虽飞禽走兽，虫鱼之类，皆有君长，故孟子云：麒麟之于走兽，凤凰之于飞鸟。世人日见天子者有几何？天下无不尊崇，无不畏惧。如子之言，必待见而后信，举天下之人皆曰，君王并无赏罚号令，一听于自然之理，可乎哉？

二、礼拜：

吾教礼拜之说，七日大拜，每日五时朝拜主宰，于各方建设礼拜寺。诚然，因不学之人，罔知教规，不能体认。吾教内有学业者，逢期宣讲教条与日用五常之节，各有次序；于认主拜主之学，日日新之。彼经营之士，终日奔忙，不能静心，逢期听讲，可日月至焉。其所以朝拜主宰者，因吾教经云：古往今来，天地万物，皆受主宰之造化。世人多云，财帛儿女，俱是前定，不究所定为何主？故吾教经典，实指主宰，超然无极。凡同天地万有而生，皆为受造之物，独主宰为行造之主。一日五时礼拜，申如在其上之敬，盖无方所，无似像。居东土者，惟向西礼拜而已。此种理路原因，未学自不知根。天地间无往而非学问，未有无师指点，而能自明者。主宰之喻，如人身然。前所云，人一小天。小天之主宰，即人身之命也。命之在身，曾有何人见本身之命？何似像？何方所？使人言命在头，则身与足皆属无命。无命之处，痛痒无知，即为死物。言命在下，上身亦然。以是知，人之命，无方向，无定所，通乎人之一身，无处不在，无处不有。则一身之内，更无处不知，无处不觉。经云：真宰同乎天地万物，亦无处不在，无处不有，且不可以色象、方向，定主宰之所在。各教人于元旦烧纸，其所供牌位上书“天地三届，十方万灵真宰”，此等语意，尤须参究，是天地人三届之有，与十方万灵之生，必有真宰之所主持。而世人不察，以为故套，当前错过，反诋他人。

子言，真宰之赏善罚恶，何以能知？子当思，人于冬日，服饰重重，周身遮蔽，皆不能见。虽有二目，位居上方。一有虮虱，知在何处，伸手即得，无微不照。虮虱，微物也，衣为之遮蔽。十指无目，何以一伸即获？盖以命之灵光，笼罩乎全体。此即赏善罚恶之一明证。真宰同乎天地万有，凡有蠢动，莫不周知，岂无赏罚乎？又虽穷乡僻壤，如素不知有君父之尊，王法之严，任意胡行，一经发觉，自必究竟；倘犯大辟，按律何差。并不以彼之无知，与从未见君而释之。赏罚之严，一至于此。世之有心者，当即此触类旁通，以进于认主拜主之道，勿至临期而悔，思无及矣。故吾教之人，心知赏罚，有所畏惧，至能坚守教规，鲜为非理。若他教之人实心讲论，踵而行之，自能少过，刑措无用矣。

吾教所论真宰之理，具载经书，炳如洞著，绝无游移影响之谈。有谓，即此昭昭之天。非也，昭昭者，人所共见，亦有限量，乌能可比。此理甚微，非细心研究，与割尽畏难苟安之习，不能有得，即如《性理》所云'无极'。无极之言，实指何物？即此一语，可以证吾教言真宰之实据。大抵儒教之书，多见道之语；而儒教之人，多舍难而就易。或有以神道相乱，信释老之诬，而以邀福动人。彼不知，皇天无亲，惟德是辅。凡一求福，则无往不失，岂特天良。总之，信道欲笃。苟信道不笃，焉能为有，焉能为无？

论男女杂沓

至言男女杂沓，更无可加于吾教。吾教经言：男女七岁不同席。此盖仿于《曲礼》。再言，男子从脐至膝，不可令人见；妇女则从头至脚皆不可现，以至除七等人外，概不相见。七等为谁？祖、父、兄弟、丈夫、子孙、亲生母舅、亲生伯叔是也。又云：男女之内，可与联姻者，即不可以相见。又云：凡妇女出门，或坐轿，或乘车，皆用罩头，以纱绸为之，从头笼至脚跟，丝毫不令人见，方为至理。今云男女杂沓，不知何见，而出此言？吾教礼拜寺，所在皆有，曾于何处，见有此等行事？况吾教经中，断定不许妇女入寺礼拜；虽有父母丧事，亦不准其到坟，总以不可与人相见之故，致有是禁。惟令各自在家潜修暗祝，悉遵条约。间有老朽孤贫无告之妇，每逢礼拜日期，叩寺求讨，以度残喘。然麾之大门之外，听人施给，并不许入寺同班礼拜。此东土无奈之回民。一在西域，另有养膳，决不听其入寺。且寺内之义，原宜洁净，大凡礼拜，必定预为沐浴。恐妇女辈，于天癸之讲究不清，反致亵渎。况一经男女溷杂，势必淫行潜滋，将欲为善，实乃长恶，故吾教不取。男女杂沓，吾教之所必无。

论夜聚晓散

至言夜聚晓散，更属荒唐。试问：夜聚晓散之说，不知每日夜聚晓散耶，抑或有时聚散耶？将谓每日夜聚晓散，则士农工贾，各执一业，虽勤惰不同，而仰事俯给，皆不能或废。稍有懈怠，则啼饥号寒，在所不免。人身精力有限，何能朝朝连连？且夜聚晓散，不得默默，必有所言所行。使无言行，此聚何为？夫晓不闲，夜无暇，而本业又资待理，吾恐精力衰惫，不数日，即登鬼录。此每日之不能夜聚晓散，明矣。将谓有时夜聚晓散，天下之大，谁无婚姻丧葬？或吾教之孤客死于异乡，势必扶入寺内，众人代为安排，次日埋葬。是夜，寺内有人置办，他人不知，即谓夜聚晓散者。又于斋戒之月，礼拜者十倍其常，而回教之士农工贾，或按时不及交还拜课，乃于日落后，入寺还补白日之拜课，燃灯时至初更。拜毕归家休息，以待鸡鸣复起。夫倡夜聚晓散之言者，意欲人以异谋妄图疑之。吾教经言，苟非己之所有，虽一毫莫取。而斋月礼拜，尤为省愆悔过之要，不敢妄涉意念。即衣食之丰歉，事物之顺逆，一听于冥冥之天。总之，吾教身体力行者居多。儒书不云修身乎？如"非礼勿视，非礼勿听，非礼勿言，非礼勿动。""勿"之云者，实用其力，禁止其非也。是以吾教一日五时礼拜，与七日之拜，时形敬畏，而拜内之虔诚，直归于造物之主宰。其无我忘己之念，与之俱化。吾子亦识之乎？

论保持气节

客曰：与子言已久，似略晓儒书。既读儒书，何仍如此拘执？风流洒脱，诗酒陶情。吾曾目睹耳闻，某某名列子教，读书有成，毫无回教气象，遇酒即饮，遇物即食。使一旦身入科名，鹿鸣琼林，执教固辞，或者不可再如某某。当时名流行事亦如之，总无拘执，世路明白。交接当道，不过逢场作戏，何必认真？今而后，还须圆通于三界之外，方是英雄本来面目。

余曰：子言过矣。世间好事惟忠孝，故征忠臣于孝子之门，谓其人能孝于亲，使亲心豫悦，即一颜面之承，不为亲所疑虑，不改亲之正行，他日之能忠于君，可以托六尺之孤，可以寄百里之命，临大节而不可夺者，必此其人。夫今以些微口腹，而即可以验人之忠与不忠，孝与不孝必矣。如子言某某者，实系回教，若辈祖父，身列回教，不知几世？而其人竟可以遇酒即饮，遇物无忌。彼虽同人饮食，吾揣，其心必不安，色必不正。或且恶人称彼为回教，又必自掩其回教。然恶之，亦不能显恶；掩之，又卒不可掩。当饮酒食物之际，此人必如坐针毡，虽强为色笑，其心左右堤防，常恐旁人提出根本。实有无可如何者，奚不直言而显拒乎？谓其可以求富贵利达，可以取贵人色喜，而直至于卿相之班；其子若孙，亦可达于鸳行之列。

彼以为，前世求富贵利达者，出妻见子，不以为耻，吾一饮酒食物间，即可取贵人之喜，尚未至于出妻见子，何乐不为？殊不知，不数年间，忽焉没兮；其子若孙，即不能振作有为，并不能以饮酒食物，而承祖父之故套，下而出妻见子，未可知矣。作俑之人虽在九泉，未必不知其有今日之报。且若辈当恶人提出，与不能掩时，明知若祖与父世为回教，一旦舍祖父之教，背祖父之行，而其跼蹐不安，瞻前顾后，恐人提出根本者，此正良心不昧之时，倘能即此改悔，尚可期望。

设有心者，从旁计议：此子原系回教，今以求富贵利达之心，则祖父可悖，廉耻可无，孝道可亏。设彼祖父见之，或被知觉，自不乐承，此大不孝之罪也。如是忘本之人，奚云六尺可托，百里可寄，天地间应不可容。虽朝廷有不甚爱惜之官，亦不可苟与若辈。盖以今日能悖其亲，他日必悖其君。以此进推，难期忠干。欲若辈效伯夷之高风，万万不能。此知，与外教饮酒食物，全无忌讳者，非止吾教之不容，实天地间无耻之罪人。

彼不思，酒之害人多矣。虽中国圣人，亦屡禁之。故禹恶旨酒，而好善言；周公作酒诰，群饮则杀之。夫酒小罪也，杀大刑也，以小罪而加之于大刑，周公直忍而不疑者，盖以酒之生害，而至于杀人者众矣。以为不如是，不足以一民心，而成吾治道。此中国圣人之教民也，亦有是禁。而后世之驰之者，吾不敢多言，以获其咎也。抑尤有外教之人，或因自幼同窗，或同名科第，或同堂办事，乘间引诱。无本者被其煽惑，分手后，即以某人前日饮酒食物为口实，为快谈，两人誓不外言之约，皆成虚诳。虽受惑者自应诋诽，然前之同窗同第同朝之谊，业已不加劝阻，反引人入套，使悖其祖教，忘其根本，失其同气。及受其哄，离席即侈张之。殊不知，彼虽畅谈于一时，吾恐，彼后日之若子若孙，亦受他人引诱，使悖其祖父之孝悌忠信者多矣。何也？昔以此施，今以此报，往往而然。所以，士君子吊曹瞒诗云："昔日曹瞒相汉时，欺他寡妇与孤儿。谁知四十余年后，寡妇孤儿亦被欺。"有心者，胡不自思？

吾今此言，非惟劝本教人自固根本，亦且兼劝各教，倘遇吾教无知之辈，且不可故为引诱，陷人不义。其实何益于己？徒留此不美之名，以致遗祸子孙。倘汝今日，劝人子孙不忘根本，后日即有仁人义士，劝汝子孙为孝弟忠信之全人。今而后，子其勉夫？亦或有膺民社之责者，遇有回教酗酒事发，更祈加倍整饬，方为有德。

论修剃毛发

客又曰：身体发肤受之父母，不可毁伤。子教之人修剪髭髯，与下身毛孔，今日去之，迟日如故，岂不过为琐屑？亦未尝大关义理。

余曰：古者男子梳头，若妇女然，今日遵王制也。吾教所论剪髭，非独敬守教规，亦以为整饰仪容，清爽身体。且凡事皆有君臣，凡物皆有去留。岂可君臣无定，去留不分，成何世界？如稂莠去而嘉禾植，君臣定而上下安。今以口与髭论之，则口为君，如人饮食，皆归其权于口。岂有君尝饮食，而臣尝为之阻挠拂乱？则髭当齐也，明甚。虽曰齐髭，亦有界限，无容过克，齐止上唇之中。其口辅之两角，仍留长髭，以示威仪。至鬓髯胡须，秋毫无犯，君臣之位定矣。饮食岂能阻挠？纵遇汤水，不致淋漓，可免厌污。倘同人饮食，见此景象，难免憎恶，何所吝而不齐？此些微之髭，夫不可毁伤，今之剃头，独非发乎？奚为徒同以去？子教之人，卒不置喙于其间，盖以为王制也，法尽善也。而不知其法之所以尽善者，非尽去发，仍留辫子，以为存善闲邪之道，万世不易者也。

其所以修剃下身之毛孔，使沐浴之时，不能藏垢，则身清体洁，方可以交神明，而禋祀上帝，故等诸去稂莠之法。如上古之时，凡物皆刻铭文，而汤盘为最。夫盘不过沐浴之器，何以铭为？其意欲人，以此进修身之法，有表里皆沐之意。中国圣人，既已借盘铭，欲人为表里如一之人；吾教圣人，即就本身修剪之法，为表里如一之教，岂不更进一层？语云：身外无道，是也。

论不拜偶像

客又曰：如子所言，教中之事，皆有义理。独不拜神道，似属矫强。

予曰：天无二日，民无二王，敬一无二之理，昭著久矣。总之，各教多口头之学，而少笃实之行。既曰不谄媚鬼神以要福，又曰拜神。独不思“获罪于天，无所祷乎。”昌黎之《佛骨表》言之详矣。其与孟东野书内云：“且彼佛者，果何人哉？其行事，类君子邪？小人邪？如君子也，必不妄加祸于守道之人；如小人也，其身已死，其鬼不灵。天地神祇昭布森列，非可诬也，又安肯令其鬼作威福、行胸臆于其间哉？进退无所据，而信奉之，亦且惑矣。”此亦儒教之书，而非回教之言也，至理可信。有时疑二，复被其惑者，是以利而自徇之也。

回教经言：天地万有，古圣先贤，皆出主宰之造化。惟有尊敬，并无迹像可设。所制礼乐、禁令、行止，大小悉遵，不敢殒越。自是，日进于高明。孟子云：“人皆可以为尧舜。”又云：“舜，人也；我亦人也。”倘不行尧舜之行，而设其像于高堂之上，终日潜修礼拜，所行皆不孝不悌，天必降殃。虽尧舜之神灵具在，岂能为之护哉？况无据之神灵，事之奚益？若谓彼能降福，则各教之事神者，不至有乞丐；将曰彼能降祸，则吾教之不事者，应无孑遗。此等理路，惟智者能行。愚人怀富贵利达，信释老之谎谈。

据言神能降福，胡终日事佛，而不得一报？若梁武帝，饿死台城，佛不之救。由此观之，佛不足事可知。彼释教人，又为之说：梁皇虽云饿死，其实成佛。成佛之说有何实据？即曰成佛，是释子从而贱之者。奚以明其然？彼常云：某帝王是某佛转世。试参此语：成佛之后，又费许多周折，方能转世为一代帝王。如此说来，是帝王之贵于佛也，奚啻什伯。倘曰帝王不贵，何故又劝人修炼成佛，转世即可以为帝为王？其所以为帝为王之故，谓其人当未成佛时，受尽辛勤。及转世为帝王时，将以报其昔日之辛勤，得以遂其所欲为，而受享之无际。何正有为之时，而又饿以死？是自相矛盾，欺愚掩饰之辞，进此一追，自无着脚之地。余静思之，更可嗤者，若观音大士，度尽世间男女。彼成佛之后，虽欲转世为一平人，竟无门路可以投托，尚云帝王。至于求富贵利达，佛之降赐，未见些许，先破己囊，修盖庙宇，以助懒人之恶。吾恐善未曾有，殃或倍之。梁武帝之事，非明证与？如是持此，以穷究释子，彼将曰：难逃天定。是所谓技穷力屈，无可如何之语。独恨其言之不早耳。吾教之敬一无二者，此也。

论屠宰牲畜

客又曰：敬神之说无疑矣。但子教全不茹素，反食牛羊；又必自己念咒宰割，方食其肉。既云食肉，则各教之宰割均属一般，何异怪若此？

余曰：吾教念经宰物，非念咒也。体上天好生之德，凡用一物，必可以告上天者。人闻此语，似属矫强，吾尝见官司自箴，有云："刑罚可省者省，草木皆天生命。"草木亦云天生，不可滥用，何况禽兽？实为有命之物，何不慎诸？至有以此为业，而食其利者，是教中之罪人，君子不齿。其有婚姻、丧葬之当用者，皆念经宰割。其意有在，"天子无故不杀牛，大夫无故不杀羊"，盖重命恤牲，不敢率意，以滋口腹之欲。礼在则然，而吾教之规亦然。

子今知吾教念经宰牲，更不知吾教必择遵行者，方可宰割，不遵此训，仍然不食。《礼》云无故不杀，其实奉行者无几。规矩无定，谁不可举手宰割。若吾教之法，难以便行，纵口腹人，素爱饮食，即鸟兽成群，苟不得宰割之人，与昏夜而非宰割之时，竟难便食。实所以禁无故之宰耳。至婚丧大事，不得吝惜，听其宰割。倘无故滥宰，虽代宰之人，亦不为念经，以操刀凛凛乎，虽小必严哉！

客曰：子言误矣。天地生物，原以为人。今欲食一鸟兽，反制多少难行之例，不欲其便行，与天地之心，不大相悖乎？

余曰：子不闻"天地之生物有限，而人心之好欲无穷"？倘不防微杜渐，谨小慎微，则人心之放，竟至莫可究诘。故云："不以礼节之，亦不可行也。"子其信之？

论沐浴净身

客又曰：子教之事，章章可考。抑尤有可议者，闻闺门晏寝，次日必然沐浴，方为饮食。其沐浴之器，又用壶罐。虽夫夫妇妇，人之大伦，须自避忌。似此沐浴，岂不众人周知，未免令人含笑？又礼拜时，亦用壶罐，洗濯其七窍手足，然后入寺。如此行事，可谓劳且苦矣。

余曰：吾教之道，大而君臣父子，小而日用饮食，莫不具载经典。虽有怠惰偷安之人，究其心以自问。实有难于自处者，倘遇礼拜斋戒，一切举行教规之处，此人必不敢违心以自赴，何也？吾教之学，总以勿自欺为主。如人未经洗濯，必不敢礼拜，何也？[申] 如在其上也，故不敢自欺。以未经洗濯之身心，而对越乎上帝，慎之至也。是以童而习之，长而安焉，不见异物而迁焉。又于人伦大典之事，在在慎重，非特父母之命，媒妁之言，即一同梦之欢，未有不为警惕。盖以夫妇为人伦之首，不有夫妇，何有子孙？不有子孙，谁接禋祀？

人谁不欲生圣贤之子孙？固恃父母栽培，而其祖若宗，不知几代端方，几辈修省，方能得此圣子贤孙。儒书曾有胎训之说，此后一著法也。有何体验？得胎之后，方有胎训，不若吾教沐浴之法，可以止淫行，可以洁身心。苟严寒酷冷，虽顽夫少子，竟有以畏寒而止者。凡沐浴后，孰不知其为轻身而便体者。身不朦垢，心方清洁。万一受胎，是先一著胎训之法。此所谓“欲洁其流，必清其源。”今源则清矣，而流有不洁者乎？吾教经云：凡夫妻交媾，或梦入阳台，或天癸净后，及生产四十日后，必为沐浴，以净此身，方可以治斋戒，祀上帝。此吾教之道也。

又以各教论，凡夫妻交媾，次日竟不敢入庙祀神。及问其故，则曰身子不净，不敢祀神，恐有亵渎，致遭罪谴。凡物之不净，必用水浆洗濯，然后能净。未有不为洗濯，迟之日久，而能自净者乎。今日身子不净，不敢祀神，而又耻于洗濯。夫不洗濯之身，已经朦垢。彼且不思，垢多必然生腐。而况夫妻之间，岂能断绝？则是以垢致垢，莫可究诘。是终身朦之，而不知去。乃云今日不净，不敢祀神，不亦谬乎？余又哂焉，何各教之人，皆明于小，而暗于大？以天地论之，一大神祇，其威灵赫擢，非工匠之雕塑也，非五彩之涂绘也，严严在上，赫赫在旁，不净之身，居此当畏。各教之人，身多朦垢，昂然戴天覆地，食雨露之恩膏，享禾黎之大德，睹此不惧，是暗于大也。至庙中之神像，不过泥塑木雕，虽青面巨齿，红发金身，实污泥朽木，人力之所作为。而各教自愚自欺，反畏此土木造作之物，是泥于小也。殊不知，前辈之人，原以神道设教，欲以儆吓愚顽，非实有其事也。

故吾教规，一有房事，即不可饮食出外，必为沐浴，然后饮食行动。其所以用壶罐盛水之意，使水过污流，不存毫末。倘沐浴于江河长流水内，则不须壶罐之小器矣。至若盆盛浴水，盆内为受秽之处，水一倾入，概成秽污，即不堪以杯饮，未免过用而多败。独吾教用壶罐洗濯之义，盖取用出之水为秽，而所存贮之水皆净也，尽人皆可以饮食，皆知其净。既知其净，又以壶罐为非，何哉？

夫妻沐浴，却言含耻。设处女未嫁而生育者，人皆以为羞；既嫁而生，人皆曰喜。今以沐浴为耻，则生长亦非耻乎？独归于正不正耳，又何嫌于沐浴乎？

至于礼拜，乃祀上帝之礼。以未经修饰之耳目口鼻、身体手足，昧昧而对上帝，以修跪拜之诚，可乎哉？故必先为洗濯七窍体肤，务使内外俱新，然后可以对越。是孟子有云："虽有恶人，斋戒沐浴，则可以祀上帝。"亦此意也。

论祭祀亡灵

客曰：沐浴之故明矣。子教于父母故后，每逢时节，全不烧化纸钱，供奉食物，何以申如在之敬？又于元旦，不用门神对联者，何故？

余曰：天下之人谁非人子，谁无父母？服劳奉养，尊敬不懈；故后四时禋祀，情所必致。但子教之烧化纸钱，供奉食物，不过欲尽人子一时之心。究之烧化纸钱，是释老之行，而非儒者之教。儒者之祭，用酒灌地焚帛而已，鬼来食气。今又杂以释老之行，吾恐若祖若父有灵，必不愿来格来享。世之修斋设醮者，十有八九，是口言孔孟之教，心向释老之行。所称能言距杨墨，即圣人之徒者，固如是耶？况释子之与人修斋设醮者，名之曰"应付"，是不禁荤酒，又禅和子之所不取，且有自相诋诽，皆非正道。

当吾教初来，与中夏言语不通，文字未识。人见吾教有彻底澄清之道，真实无妄之行，遂别其名曰"清真教"。前人有鉴吾教能除诸妄，敬一归真，又名之曰"回教"，盖见吾教之行，多自省之意，其礼拜把斋，散财济贫，均属放心收回之道。当其始来之时，实不知中夏先哲命名之义，或为至诚感昭上帝，特降是名乎，未可知也。不然，何以其名不泯于后世耶？故吾教乃能除诸妄，于父母生死忌日，量力置办饮食；却以钱财，散给乡党邻里之贫民，与鳏寡孤独之无告者。其有衣帽什物，量给父母之最契旧好，以为遗记。此存亡俱受其益，上天亦鉴临之。岂有好善乐于之子孙，其祖父之神灵，反有不重者乎？且人于死后另有世界，另有管束，亦若未生之初。岂无来历，昧昧者乎？

彼释教之荒谈，死后修斋设醮，名为救拔祖父，世人多不之察，昧于义理。如人微犯罪辜，托亲友中之贵显者，向该管官司而求，自必从轻。倘无籍之徒，言彼能往求饶恕，吾恐非徒无益，而又害之。在释教放言修斋免罪，修斋一事，乃应付之经营，以为网罗钱财，招致愚人之具，即彼禅和子所憎恶。今吾以若辈灭其天伦律之，则乌得无罪乎？即以生前过衍，亦无凭空挽回，而竟宽贷之理。所费银钱，空被若辈哄去；祖父之事，仍莫可必；所化纸钱楼库，灰飞而去，莫知其乡。纵祖父欲居是楼，用其财，而享其物，尽已烧毁，何得再成？欺人之甚，夫亦何益？穷源极底，又非儒者之道。何如即将此项银钱，散给乡党邻里之贫民，非惟祖父受益，虽数世之子孙，更延绵其祖父之余德，尤必硕大蕃滋，阀阅簪缨，荣昌并茂，何须购求地理，讲论风水？岂不可惜，岂不真愚？又尝观风水家言：入殓下葬，必用某日某时。致有炎天盛暑，或过二三日者，尸骸腐臭，肢体解脱，往往有之。意望子孙家道，必然兴旺，此乃用人力，夺天意者。若果能之，竟使天下孕妇，求彼选择吉日良辰，令子降生，岂不更美？彼不于未就时求必胜，而乃于已坏时为妄说，计亦左矣。

吾教之所以不为烧化纸钱，供奉食物，求觅地理风水，盖由学业之有定衡也。夫人于死后，再能衣食世人之衣食，亦必每日三餐，方为尽心。若一年之内，只供数次，彼于数百日之内，竟为无食无衣之人而，在世之骨肉，何忍忘之？是必无此理。若于死后，仍然衣食费用人间之财物，而未生之前，尚无有子孙之斋醮祭祀，则衣食费用，又于何处取觅？彼释子之论，必曰：人皆转轮而生，彼于未生之时，尚有前世子孙之斋醮祭祀，费用伊家。

论投胎转世

余窃泯目自思：孔孟教人，伦常不可倒置。各教之人皆知，天地既有之后，方有人物。而《纲鉴》首云：盘古氏生于大荒，莫知其始。而吾教经云：上帝首造夫妇二人，男女隔胎而配，如是者七十二胎，胎皆双生，计百四十有四人。若云转轮，且不问彼夫妇二人从何处转来，即彼一百四十四人之灵，又自何方而始？若云必待转轮，则是甲先死而转乙，乙又亡而转丙，挨次轮转，一人止转一人，何得至今天下之人，奚啻恒河沙数，今概不论。即以前之七十二胎为转轮之始，汝试推之：今以长房夫妇先死，必投胎于弟妇之腹中，及之生育，是为兄弟之子矣。一再而推，祖必转而为孙。似此伦常倒置，天理岂容，圣贤岂安！即以盘古氏例之，亦必如此相传，方有今日。

故吾教经云：真宰造化万有，非人心可以测度。又云：真宰行造也，万有受造也。彼造物之能欲大则大，欲小则小，其多少、有无亦然。今以人之写字譬之，字犹受造之物，人即造字之主。是人欲书其字之大小、多少，妍媸、丑俊，尽随其写字之人；字之必不能操写字者之权衡，人皆知之。凡有工作，悉同是理，举一隅以为例也。然此云行造之喻，而非转轮之比。转轮之喻，如人书一"天"字，且不拘大小，今有人欲再求一"天"字，或千万"天"字，其人曰：不必书，待彼一字转轮，可为百千亿万，无数恒河沙之"天"字也，汝其信之乎？抑亦辨之耶？

自有天地以来，圣凡之身同出母腹。为父母者，并不知所怀之为男女，何能知其为圣凡？即圣人在母腹中，必不能制作有为者。此即真宰显行造之大能，使世人参详识认，不使错过。然亦不特此也，千古圣贤，正于制作有为之际，不免升遐而杳适，并不能缓须臾之分，以补救其未完者。此亦造物之大能，不使有予夺之操也。彼"天上地下，唯我独尊"者，究未出于生死之路也。不然斯人胡不出世普度众人耶？吾想，"唯我独尊"之言，并非若人之语。此必门下后人侈张其说，为光大门庭之柄。第修行之人，不敢妄语。今以是言坐之，岂不冤哉？若果有之，是无辞让之心也，尚可为训乎？而生彼之祖父，又置之于何地位？彼独尊矣，万有皆不足数，并忘所自矣，无乃大谬乎？故烧化纸钱，供奉食物，转轮投胎之说，吾教之所悉除也。

若张挂门神对联，前已尽言。至于不用钟鼓于礼拜之时，使致其对越之诚，不为声音之所拂乱；不用音乐于婚丧之际，是方可正关雎之雅化，慎追远之孝思。此亦人所尝疑，而欲问者。故吾教之道，总以扫却诸邪，惟敬独一无二之主宰，必不以世人造作之假像，而乱我之真性也。

论神道与法术

一、神道：

神道之说，各有专司，不敢越分。如风云雷雨、日月星辰、霜露雪雹、山水火土，凡所作为更置，莫不寓于神道之大权，要皆主宰之使令，非敢妄施毫末之增减，而夺主宰之衡量。亦如百司，总听命于君，有应受之俸禄，则必有应办之执事，不敢顺情涉私。若谓可以行私，能邀司农之盼，则是九品之俸，竟可与一品之恩耶；设应一品之俸，斯人拙于逢迎，司农恶之，而不给与毫末，断无此理。因思子路之言，有云：

“未同而言，观其色，赧赧然，非由之所知也。”此言未同之语，尚有惭色。彼未同者，是共处一室，与他人言，而未与若人言，彼强与之言，宜与夫义若不相合，故子路言非其所知。今人神一理，彼无故之拜祷，首则惮烦而厌其琐屑，况不能施无据之告求。且如司农，日坐高堂，出纳天下钱粮税课，支放俸禄兵饷，皆凭文印散给。而无籍小民，终日拜祷阶前，岂能滥给毫末？何况，不能任彼接见，抑或营谋钻刺之人接踵求见。殊不知，彼司农者，盖不与闻，何也？首无君命，次少精力。苟非然者，将夜以继日，坐以待旦，亦不能胜其无厌之求也。神道之理，应如是而参之，自可绝其拜祷矣。大凡天下之政令，总听命于君王，无敢殒越，虽众怒无伤。倘违君命而善媚，虽众喜何荣？吾教不拜神道，恃此而已。心有主张，外物不能摇撼。故无据之神灵，万不能惑吾教以动听。纵有法术，愈为邪道，非独吾教之所不信，而亦孔孟之所不齿也。

二、法术：

试论彼法真传，能遣天神诸将，能知过去未来。即如国家之大，君父之重，何代能绝跳梁之贼？或内或外，彼自知之。既有真法，能遣天神诸将，何不专使五雷，击死其贼？致免多少财用、议论，何为不快！在彼，亦可延好生之德，更有无穷妙处，上而君父喜悦，下而百姓安堵。抑或天时旱涝，五谷不生，人民焦劳，彼有法真传之士，不当坐视其疾苦，致君父发帑赈济，动经万余留粮给散，在处有之。吾想：彼于已发未发之时，自必先知。抑或不能先知，即于已发之时，多遣天神诸将，使被旱之地，广布甘霖，则苗勃然兴之，人民感戴，以为何如？抑经涝之处，亦遣天神诸将，速之拨云雾而见青天，捧红轮而疏赤水，田父欢欣，公私鼓舞。予窃视之，竟不出此，亦如平人之束手。及问其故，胡不为之救拯？彼将曰：“天意故也。”我亦曰天意故也。直追到此，法力固不可以攘夺天意，明矣。天意既不可攘夺如此，胡各教之人不信天而信法，不听命而听人？尚非吾教不拜神道，不信法术，亦何异惯为钻刺营谋之人？而自敬君，行古道者，为迂阔之士哉，可慨也夫！

且世间原有神仙，自能点石成金，呼风唤雨，断不肯复与人世交接。若仍与往来，无异平人之衣食者，明系哄骗银钱，吊取财物，此即观假神仙之一大法也。抑有言不食烟火之物，每日惟用白水数碗，是欲渗牛炒之念珠也。若遇此辈，将彼衣物另封别处，丝毫不许随身，则真情露，而诳不行矣。

论出家修行

即出家修行之学，吾教方策，条理井然，各有程限。其出家也，非若释老之流，仍然夏葛冬裘，渴饮饥食，不织不耕，居高粱大厦，玩野鸟山林，以衣食之艰难，寄托于众人，守寂高枕，任其所之。古云：“日高三丈僧未起，算来名利不如闲。”此语世云高旷，吾恐教人悖其君亲，必自此语始之。其有逃避祸患，借匿于此，世皆为便，古今同辙，究难置啄。犹有罗珍馐于案上，拥锦绣于屋中，自以为常，而恬然不知君父之恩，上天之德。彼竟忘其所自，不知珍馐锦绣，皆他人所致之物，并非彼法术仙传之所得。殊不知，天下四民，能食其报者，十无三四。即如文武两途，为国家出力报效，实皆拚弃身家，且不能如彼之安享，而又毫无责任，毫无考成。听彼妄言天上地下之语，世人贪福，易受其哄，惟达人知之，故有“日高三丈僧未起”之语。进而思之，是亦不平之鸣也已。予常涉猎史鉴，自古帝王受方士之惑，食长生不老之药，后皆不能胜金石济药之毒，以致燥渴攻体，其势难当，讫无成者。若果有之，则秦皇、汉武今日尚然高拱，而何杳然无闻也？今予之言，亦前人吐去之果核，非我言也，吾子谅诸。

若吾教之有出家者，首则，必待父母天年，使生我之人无憾；其次，则男婚女嫁，可以代我成立；再次，则债务清还，外无挂碍。倘人负我债，又必拣券还人，清白己身之事，毫无沾滞，然后出家。其出家也，乃了尽万缘，独契真宰，亦非如白日飞升之术，玄谈寂灭之流也。吾教圣人防微杜渐，恐人仿效相率，而为高远避世之行，乘所立数事，方好出家。非此，决不可行。又云：人能事君忠，事亲孝，交友信，养育妻子、奴仆，爱恤鳏寡孤独，斋拜不缺，好事忙行，较之出家之功德，奚啻天壤。总之，吾教经书，全以人伦为重，不求隐僻为先。

吾教内人，一有出家之念，先渐减少饮食。年余之后，至于一月一食，始能出家。预了己身之事，然后离人世，入山林，朝看麋鹿，夜听猿鹤；饮流泉而食果蔬，卧夕阳而眠方草。晦明风雨，任云影之往来；昼长夜短，绝世人之继思。山巅水涯，信步所之；石洞天台，听其酣息。斯时也，心境超然，万籁俱寂，瞬乎一刻，上下千古。其间之升降俯仰，得失兴衰，齐天地浑然之理，偕造物而游于无间也。独得之趣，谁能见诸？吾教出家大概如此。

而凡语默动静，持已涉世，亦无不类乎此矣。而吾教与各教，其亦可以晓然矣。余宁敢较量各教之行事，适承吾子问，不得不缕悉实告，而以吾教之真，共白于此日。

结束语

客乃唯唯而谢曰：子教入中国，素未讲明，止以祖父相沿行事，子若孙不敢擅改为词。并未有人焉，大发议论，而知为有本之学，乃如斯也。今而后，谨受教，愿无以浅见探海矣。虽然学非众著不明，疑非洞悉不解，今吾与子对谈竟日，奚啻千言，予豁然矣。而子以外不乏人也。子盍记此问答，刊刻成书，使疑者议者，一览了然，庶几均有所益，可法可传。逾年，予将于子索问答书籍，谨志之，慎勿忽。

客遂飘然而去。

予以后学菲质，又值王事鞅掌，深惧夫言之不文，行之不远。第客命谆谆，问答之间非以求文，盖明教内之规条，纵言鄙意质，不过以释各教之疑议，非疑论于词藻之工也，何必筑室道谋，以滋后悔？故不避指摘，请教同人，付之剞劂。后之君子，有可教我之处，再加补益。或远方同志诸君，观其言或有可采，此书不能遍传，不妨重栽枣梨，以博知闻，是则我之素愿也，夫是则我更欲释疑之意也夫。

陈大韶点评

淮阴专阃，以多而善，理明法备，行所当行，止所当止，故也。北高与客反复坐论，如千层台，如常山蛇，曲尽神明，变化条理，秩然意贯。用遥接法事同，用类叙法非精，于艺者莫辩。曰潮曰海，兼而有之，意其服习于昌黎眉山久矣。至所论条规，亦本人情，准物理，惟遵祖制以从事，绝无矫戾之为。

尼山夫子，于麻冕之变而从之；暮春狂士，于羊枣之嗜而却之。不知其故，安知不可置喙而横议？可知凡事惟其是而已。衡诸理，按诸情，溯其本来源流，归于平正，斯之谓是。既是矣，何辞焉？且北高虽宗清真，而深于洙泗，诗文淹贯，流于既溢，何啻千百。其二郎，亦于官署受庭训，而挥毫如意，行将列科筮仕矣。余故钦服，不揣固陋而妄评之。

宗山

教习拣用知县楚北松滋年家眷弟

陈大韶顿首拜

上馆卿余公请序书

盖闻士君子读书明道，以期传世，历亘古而不磨，质百代而不惑。其道岂有二哉？是明其所不知，而释其疑也。释其疑，乃可以传，传之者固不一。而其所以传之者，不外于三纲五常，天人之事，交尽而已。推其类，则有以道德传者，有以事功传者。而其最传而最著者，究无出于洙泗之师生。何也？当其未经讲明道统之日，天下之人，未知夫二帝三王之道，为如是之经天纬地，不可磨灭，几何不疑于心，而涩于口。一经讲明，则疑者释矣。是以至今人，知遵二帝三王之道者，即知慕为孔氏之生徒。故孟子云："予未得为孔子徒也，予私淑诸人也。"亦以疑心释，而有是见道之言也。窃念阙里从游之时，二三子追随杖履，不过一讲学之布衣，相与株守衡门，乐饥泗水。斯时之人，非谓其有万乘之尊，千驷之富也，而何以从游者之众也？是慕其有万世教民之心，而不至于衰且竭也。

然而，千载一时，究难幸遇，竟遇矣，而又未得有只字片言，以明其道，解其惑，犹之乎未遇，而空此一幸耳。且圣门之教，皆尚躬行，不务浮夸。故孔子尝诲人曰："辞达而已矣。"又曰："文，莫吾犹人也；躬行君子，则吾未之有得。"是，非望于躬行乎？

以柱于雍正四年，因祭扫父墓入都，适逢前任馆卿许出示招考，收录行走，迄今十九年矣，其中事迹，熟睹深知。自愧下僚末吏，不能如志，以报国恩。惟兢兢拙守，不敢自陷匪僻，以遗君父羞。然而，行与世违，人因毁异，初不能效脂韦之习以取容，终不忍变正道之趋而改辙。苟朝云清白，暮藏垢污，小人且知非之，况君子乎。

如蒙咨访馆中积弊，极为开导诱掖，谓："吾人既已委质当朝，则此身不为已有。汝不闻，食人之食者，当分人之忧乎？观此馆中百十余人，每年俸廪，动支千数，此所谓有人民社稷之寄者。汝亦身列教师，与有人民之责。凡有人民社稷之区，岂能一一无议？惜人未之察耳，今及而不言，隐恶大焉。勿谓甄别番汉，端楷奏为一等，足以尽汝之职守。纵文艺精工，字画整齐，不过为人生之一美技，圣贤素所不重。必欲讲明格致诚正，修齐治平之理。至克去已私，复还天理之后，尤必实心行出，方是真正学问，文章方有益于身心性命，明德新民亦在于此。吾人当以圣贤为师，一节之士不足学也。”

当时闻训，疑惧偕释，急白数事，以谢愆尤。其后，稍为更置，觉有生色，论考费之少裁，恒多利益定执，照之不发，冒滥全消。其他，或归权于上，使谋利者不敢复专，则朝廷之法以尊；或拯救于下，使柔懦者可以独立，而育材之教自长进。召考之条，示约诗文而取人，远方寒士暂得依归。谒拜之际，风雅可观。无何，侍侧寡俦，常忆负笈之众；及门未久，屡闻去后之嗟。而珠玑灿烂，频搜月课之选；文字辉煌，顿兴梨枣之工。求稿填门，长安之纸价倍昂；问字盈庭，座中之英俊良多。当是时，千祥集而百福臻，庆何如也？

至于叠颁手论，委用连施，幸督工之不徇，“夺盗地而清还。”是公云利矣，而私实尤之。人之谮也，其能免乎？且云君子之鉴，百世新之；小人之恶，何足畏也？敬而听之，汝其勿惮。彼不知有天者，日蒙一可以祸福。斯人之态，而欲人之趋附之，私之，畏之，之为遂也。而清操之士，无敢视焉，故尝念祖籍。

回教素名“清真”。夫所谓“清”者，凡所行事，远避其浊。求入于清真者，不媚诸邪以邀福，独事真宰以听命，存真去伪之义，明天道也。而回教之来中夏，自隋唐始，代为编氓，绝无异念。亲亲而尊尊，生养死葬之礼，不爽分毫，尽人道也。且读书入仕，亦与世同。缘教内书籍，未经汉字音译，恐音韵背离，有失旧章。即如国书之必识其字，叶其调，固根本之意也。至教内斋拜、修齐治平之理，与存心养性之学，外人无暇讲论，何由深知？

今天下之大，奚啻万国。而八国之书，现存署内。每馆之字不满四千，独西天番字，仅八百有奇。度各国之所存，谅亦百千之毫末。较之汉书之便利，自不足以敷用。而大国之典，应无不核。然想其大概，既有君长，自有制度，文为不待一人之造作。故各国有各国之字画，必有各国之行事，节末虽有殊分，纲常原同一致。不则，竟无尊卑、长幼、礼乐、刑政，则国何以治？家何以齐？人民何以安？社稷何以久？由是思之，使各国尽无书籍文字，几皆为鸟兽之墟矣。

凡事皆有义理，是以《大学》首言“致知格物”。致知者，知其身心性命，家国天下之理；格物者，格其公私、是非、辞受、取与之义，则人己之事，不至错淆。此之谓致知，此之谓格物。今人不知其理，遂疑其事；疑其事，即乱其心，故每加横议，任其所欲。虽教内之前人，亦曾著有书籍类，皆大经大法，深文厚意，而不屑白此目前疑案，以是而憾者有年。

然素习本教之讲，贯常欲以汉书文字，明回教之义意。深惧夫言之不文，行之不笃，为当世者鄙。至乾隆二年，叨沐皇上豢养之深恩，得受译学之掌教，而又身隶回回馆师，训课本，教字书；其于风俗人情，伦常日用，正当讲明。上以报效朝廷，次以显扬祖教，不为世人所疑。使天下之人，展卷观之，如觌面谈，知其不外于纲常，自然无疑于事迹。疑心一释，四海同居。编纂是书，正此时之所当为者。乃上天降临，未期月而书成，经寒暑而修饰，命其名为《清真释疑》，意谓世人疑清真之理，久不能释。思其所以释之者，莫若成书计。口之答人，不过一时，书之答人，可以百世，可以天下，大哉！先圣立书之训，令人遵之无已也。

昨书成已久，藏不敢出。有湖北松滋拔贡生，考授官学教习，陈姓名大韶者，素与友善。忽检是书阅之竟月，操管直批，鼓掌大悦，随发论曰："予向者尝疑，回教之近于释也，乃言不祀鬼神以邀福；又以近于老也，乃云不求白日以飞升。观其教，是仍然君臣、父子、夫妇、昆弟、朋友之教也；[观其人，] 依然士、农、工、贾之人也，无以异于儒也。予又羡回之为教，坚定其心志，从未有流而入于释老者，盖以深明其弊，而实知其伪也。而吾儒之人，日流入于二氏，而且为之著书，而且为之立说。且助彼曰：儒释道三教，原来是一家。彼亦未之思也，孔子曰：'攻乎异端，斯害也已。'孟子曰：'能言距杨墨者，圣人之徒也。'昌黎始谓：'释老之害，过于杨墨。'三教一家之言，我知之矣。果一家耶，则圣贤不当有是言。既有是言，必非一家。子今进解一家之言，以释世人之惑。彼二氏者，首无夫妇，何能生育？既无生育，其道必亡。试问崇二氏者，孰非吾儒之子孙？今则流入二氏。世人亦有天良不昧之时，若辈凝神自思，深知源本。故言之曰：三教原来一家。其意实云：皆儒教之人也。是一家也，非言道也，是言人也。观子之书，予之疑释矣。子速成书，以释天下之疑。"

终未敢疾行，藏之数岁，几至湮没。昨大韶复来催督，又教中之读回书，读儒书者观之，莫不欢欣鼓舞，皆欲代为鸠工付梓。忖虽心动，仍未敢行。而曷可不敬录是编，恭呈斧政，并请一言之序，以耀夫简端，使天下万世之疑回教者观之，莫不尽释于无涯矣。钦仰之思，何容已焉！

又尝闻教诲谓，天下之事，无不散之局。今于未散之先，而预营散后之思，特命在馆师生，分写《十三经》一部，以为归老之娱。置之案头，于会心得意之时，开卷展观，直至终篇。又见书尾之末，落写某人敬书，凝眸之际，如见其人，想亦悲喜交集，不能已于怀者。悲其不能如今日之对晤一堂，宁不先其心，而预伤之矣？古人有云：字如其人。澄心观之，亦若当日之气概，如在目前，此亦寿享林泉之佳况。虽后日独坐之时，亦犹夫二三子共侍之日也，岂不快哉？

今如我皇上行旷古未有之典，亲幸翰林院衙门，诏诸学士联韵赋诗，刻石于署，以垂永久。是圣天子乐育斯世于无穷也，而不知万世之圣子神孙观之，亦将乐大业于靡尽矣？诚所谓"后之视今，亦犹夫今之视昔"耳。以道高德重之身，而又兼理学文词之望，是以得逢此千载一时之盛。

柱今冒昧呈书，并陈请斧政、改削而恳序者，亦预谋归老之一日，而兴侍坐之思，虽得失不同，然优游则一。使忽而不请，悔何及矣。幸前以八馆落成之日，曾有诗记，并昭告文字呈览，已蒙教诲。附刻馆，则世人观之，仰见盛心。因思，是书一行天下，后世无时不有展阅此卷之人，皆思慕，而愿见其休光也。何也？盖以疑心释而道斯明矣，赖一言之重也。倘惜片言之赐，而不允其所请，然已请焉；尤虞位重，不敢琐屑，斯亦可以释天下之疑矣。故曰：士君子读书明道，以期传世，历亘古而不磨，质百代而不惑者，是释其疑也。释其疑，即谓之有万世教民之心也；有万世教民之心，其谁曰不得为圣人之徒也？

柱之鄙意如是，惟大人海容而教诲焉，是幸。

BIBLIOGRAPHY

General References

Bai, Shouyi (1983). Preserved Essays on History of Islam in China. Yinchuan, PRC: People's Publishing House.

Bai, Shouyi (2000). Brief History of Islam in China. Yinchuan, PRC: Ningxia People's Publishing House.

Bai, Shouyi (2000). Records of Hui Figures. Yinchuan, PRC: Ningxia People's Publishing House.

Bai, Shouyi (2001). The Collections of Essays on Nations and Religions. Shijiazhuang, PRC: Hebei Educational Publishing House.

Bakar, Osman, (1997). Islam and Confucianism, A Civilizational Dialogue. Kuala Lumpur: University of Malaya Press.

Broomhall, Marshall B. A. (1966). Islam in China, a neglected problem. New York, NY: Paragon Book Reprint Corp.

Chen, Puqing (1998). Translation and Commentary of the Four Books. Guangzhou, PRC: Huacheng Publishing House.

Chen, Xuguo (2002). The Four Books and the Five Classics (2nd edition). Changsha, PRC: Yuelu Publishing House.

Chodorow, Stanley, Hans W. Gatzke and Conrad Schirokauer (1986). A History of the World. Harcourt Brace Jovanovich. (HBJ) Publishers.

Da, Pusheng (2003). The Six Islamic Books. Beijing, PRC: Religious Culture Publishing House.

Department of Chinese Philosophy, Peking University (2003). History of Chinese Philosophy. Beijing, PRC: Beijing University Press.

Ding, Jun (2006). Outline of History of Arabic Education in China. Beijing, PRC: Academy of Social Sciences of China.

Fu, Tongxian (2000). History of Islam in China. Yinchuan, PRC: Ningxia People's Publishing House.

Gao, Yongjiu (2001). Summaries on Islam of Western Region in Ancient Time. Beijing, PRC: Nations Publishing House.

Grun, Bernard (1982). The Time Table of History of People and Events. New York, NY: Simon and Schuster, First Touchstone Edition.

Ha, Decheng (year information is missed) .). Preliminary Introduction to Islam. Publisher is not known.

Hai, Zhengzhong (2002). Translation of Qingzhen Shiyi in modern Chinese. Yinchuan, PRC: Ningxia Publishing House.

Hong, Xiuping (2006). Selected Famous Works of Confucius, Buddhism and Taoism.

Jin, Jitang (1972). Study on History of Islam in China. Taiwan, China: Guiting Publishing House.

Jin, Qihua (1984). Translation of the Whole Shijing. Nanjing, PRC: Jiangsu Publishing House of Ancient Books.

Jin, Tianzhu (1769). Qingzhen Shiyi. Stored in Changlezhai in the past and in Dalian Library at present.

Jin, Tianzhu (1876). Qingzhen Shiyi. Stored in Zengrongtang, Xiannvzhen in the past and in Dalian Library at present.

Jin, Tianzhu (1876). Qingzhen Shiyi. Stored in Zhenjiang mosque in the past and in Ningxia Social Academy at present.

Jin, Tianzhu (1922). Qingzhen Shiyi. Stored in Book and Newspaper Office of Beijing Niujie Mosque in the past and in Beijing University Library at present.

Jin, Yijiu (1997). Dictionary of Islam. Shanghai, PRC: Shanghai Dictionary Publishing House.

Jin, Yijiu (2006). History of Islam. Nanjing, PRC: Jiangsu Public Publishing House.

Kamali, Mohammad Hashim (2004). Principles of Islamic Jurisprudence. Selangor Malaysia: Ilmiah Publishers, Second Revised Edition.

Li, Canjin, and Lin, Conglong (1990). Brief Dictionary of Literature and Historical Knowledge. Shanxi Public Publishing House.

Li, Jinxin (1999). Outline of History of Islamic kingdom in Xinjiang. Wulumuqi, PRC: Religious Culture Publishing House.

Li, Kairong (2002). Chinese-English Dictionary of Politics and Laws. Beijing, PRC: Book Publishing House of China.

Li, Shen (2005). Confucianism and Confucian Religion. Chengdu, PRC: Sichuan University Press.

Li, Xinghua et al. (1998). History of Islam in China. Beijing, PRC: China Social Sciences Publishing House.

Li, Ziran (2005). Policy of Qianlong towards Hui People, in Collection of Essays on Hui Studies. Beijing, PRC: Nationalities Publishing House.

Liao, Zhonganand Liu, Guoying (1989). Dictionary of Chinese Ancient Literature. Beijing, PRC: Beijing Publishing House.

Lin, Yin (1993). Confucian Culture and Traditional Chinese Medical Science. Fuzhou, PRC: Fujian Scientific Technology Publishing House.

Liu, Jielian (1955). Islamic Rules and Regulations. Publisher is unknow.

Liu, Jielian (1978). Philosophy of Arabia. Taiwan, China: Liming Cultural Inc.

Liu, Yihong (2006). Dialogue between Islam and Confucianism. Beijing, PRC: Religious Culture Publishing House.

Ma, Enxin et al. (1989). Translation and Commentary on Qingzhen Zhinan. Kunming, PRC: Yunnan Nations Publishing House.

Ma, Fulong (publishing time unknown). Preliminary Introduction to Islam. Publisher unknow.

Ma, Tong (2003). Outline of Islamic Thoughts. Yinchuan, PRC: Ningxia Public People's Publishing House.

Ma, Yiyu (2000). Historical Records of Islam in China. Yinchuan, PRC: Ningxia People's Publishing House.

Mou, Zhongjian and Zhang, Jian (2000). Comprehensive History of Religions in China. Beijing, PRC: Social Academy Publishing House.

Murata, Sachiko (2000). Chinese Gleams of Sufi Light. New York, NY: State University of New York Press.

Ningxia Academy of Social Sciences (2002). All Articles, Hui Race Study, 2002 (2).

Qiu, Shusen (1996). History of Hui Race (2 volumes). Yinchuan, PRC: Ningxia Publishing House.

Ren, Jiyu (1998). Dictionary of Religions. Shanghai, PRC: Shanghai Dictionary Publishing House.

Shan, Shumo (1992). Dictionary of Famous Mountains and Great Rivers in China. Jinan, PRC: Shandong Education Publishing House.

Sun, Kean, (1838). Observe and Study on Islam. Peking, China （Qing Dynasty）:Guangwen Publishing House.

Sun, Zhenyu (2000). Study of Wang Daiyu and His Islamic Thoughts. Lanzhou, PRC: Lanzhou University Press.

Sun, Zhenyu (2005). Study of the Relation between Islamic Philosophy and Confucian Theology in the time of Song and Ming. Beijing, PRC: Literature and History Publishing House.

Tang, Jinhui (1876). Qingzhen Shiyi Buji, proofread and republished by Hai Zhengzhong in 2006. Hong Kong, PRC: Lanyue Publishing House.

The Committee of the Brief Ethic Dictionary. (1988). Brief Ethic Dictionary. Chengdu, PRC: Sichuan Publishing House.

The Editorial Committee (1989). Oxford Advanced Learner's Dictionary of Current English with Chinese Translation (4th Edition). Taiyuan, PRC: Shanxi Public Publishing House.

The Editorial Committee for the Encyclopedia of Islam in China (1994). The Encyclopedia of Islam in China. Chengdu, PRC: Sichuan Dictionary Publishing House.

The Editorial Committee of Etymology Dictionary of Name of Places (1995). Etymology Dictionary of Name of Places. Shanghai, PRC: Shanghai Dictionary Publishing House.

The Editorial Committee of Modern Chinese-English Dictionary (1988). Modern Chinese-English Dictionary. Beijing, PRC: Foreign Language Teaching and Studies Publishing House.

The Editorial Committee of the Ancient Chinese Character Dictionary (2005). The Ancient Chinese Character Dictionary. Beijing, PRC: International Trade Limited Company.

The Editorial Committee of the Ancient Chinese Dictionary (1998). The Ancient Chinese Dictionary. Beijing, PRC: Business Affairs Publishing House.

The Editorial Committee of the New Edition of Chinese Dictionary (1988). The New Edition of Chinese Dictionary (3rd edition). Changsha, PRC: Hunan Publishing House.

The Institute of Philosophy and Social Sciences in Ningxia (1981). Collections of Assays of Islamic Study. Yinchuan, PRC: Ningxia People's Publishing House.

The Research Centre of Hui Studies (2005). Collections of Essays on Hui studies, Volume1, Beijing, PRC: Nations Publishing House.

Ugi, Suharto (2005). Kitab al-amwal: Abu Ubayd's concept of public finance. Kuala Lumpur: International Institute of Islamic Thought and Civilization (ISTAC), International Islamic University Malaysia.

Wan, Jingsen (2004). A Study of Qingzhen Shiyi's Thought. Master Thesis, Beijing, PRC: Central University of Nationalities.

Wang, Daiyu (1988). The Real Commentary on the True Teaching, The Islamic Great Learning and The True Answers, edited and punctuated by Yu Zhengui. Yinchuan, PRC: Ningxia People's Publishing House.

Wang, Jiafan and Xie, Tianyou (1999). Chinese Ancient Civilization. Hangzhou, PRC: Zhejiang Ancient Books Publishing House.

Wu, Shuping et al. (1996). The Thirteen Books. Beijing, PRC: Beijing Yanshan Publishing House.

Xia, Zhaoyan (1999). General Study of Chinese Culture. Haikou, PRC: Nan Fang Publishing House.

Xue, Lian Textual Research of Qingzhen Shiyi's Editions. Dalian: Dalian Library, no. 116012.

Yang, Huaizhong (1991). Essays on History of Hui Race. Yinchuan, PRC: Ningxia People's Publishing House.

Yang, Huaizhong (1995). Islam and Chinese Culture. Yinchuan, PRC: Ningxia Public Publishing House.

Yang, Zhanwu (1996). Linguistic Culture of Hui Race. Yinchuan, PRC: Ningxia People's Publishing House.

Ye, Shaojun (1957). Index of Thirteen Classics. Beijing, PRC: China Publishing House.

Yu, Zhengui (1996). Chinese Past Dynasties and Islam. Yinchuan, PRC: Ningxia People's Publishing House.

Yu, Zhengui and H Yang, uaizhong (1993). Abstracts of Islamic Literatures of China. Yinchuan, PRC: Ningxia Publishing House.

Yue, Nan et al. (2007). Legendary Stories of Robbing Graves in China. Beijing, PRC: Pictorial Publishing House of China.

Zhang, Dainian and Fang Keli (1994). General Study of Chinese Culture. Beijing, PRC: Beijing Teachers University Press.

Zhang, Xiumin (1989). History of Printing in China. Shanghai, PRC: Shanghai Publishing House.

Zhang, Zhenglang (1990). Great Dictionary of Officials Positions in Ancient China. Zhengzhou, PRC: Henan Public Publishing House.

Zhu Xi (Song Dynasty), (2004). Interpretation of the Four Books, proofread by Zhu Xuguo.

Zhu, Pengshou (2005). Figures in of The Qing Era. Beijing, PRC: Beijing Library Publishing House.

Zhu, Zuyan (2000). Dictionary of Quotations. Wuhan, PRC: Wuhan Publishing House.

References in Arabic

الأندلسي، أبي الوليد محمد بن أحمد بن محمد بن أحمد بن رشد القرطبي. (2002م). **الكشف عن مناهج الأدلة في عقائد الملة**. بيروت: دار الكتب العلمية.

التويجري، محمد بن ابراهيم. (1423هـ/2002م). **مختصر الفقه الإسلامي**. الرياض: بيت الأفكار الدولية، الطبعة الرابعة.

الحلبي، إبراهيم بن محمد بن إبراهيم. (1409هـ/1989م.). **ملتقى الأبحر**. تحقيق وهبي سليمان غاوجي الألباني. بيروت: مؤسسة الرسالة.

الحنفي، عبد الباسط. (1992/1412). **تاريخ الأنبياء الأكابر وبيان أولي العزم منهم**. تحقيق الدكتور محمد كمال الدين عز الدين علي. بيروت: عالم الكتب.

الحنفي، كمال الدين محمد بن عبد الواحد السكندري المعروف بابن الهمام. (1415هـ/1995م). **شرح فتح القدير**. بيروت: دار الكتب العلمية.

الذهبي، محمد بن أحمد بن عثمان. **كتاب الكبائر**.(1422هـ/2002م). القاهرة: دار السلام للطباعة والنشر والتوزيع والترجمة، الطبعة الخامسة.

الزبيدي، زين الدين أحمد بن عبد اللطيف. (1417 هـ / 1996م). **التجريد الصريح أحاديث الجامع الصحيح** للإمام البخاري. الرياض: دار السلام للنشر والتوزيع.

زيدان، عبد الكريم، (1418هـ/1998م). **موجز الأديان في القرآن**. بيروت: مؤسسة الرسالة.

زيدان عبد الكريم. (1424هـ/ 2003م). **المدخل لدراسة الشريعة الإسلامية**. بيروت: مؤسسة الرسالة للطباعة والتوزيع، الطبعة السادسة عشرة.

سانو قطب. (1423هـ/2002م). **معجم مصطلحات أصول الفقه**. بيروت: دار الفكر المعاصر، ودمشق: دار الفكر، الطبعة الثانية.

السعدي، عبد الرحمن بن ناصر. (1417هـ / 1996م). **تيسير الكريم الرحمن في تفسير كلام المنان**. بيروت: مؤسسة الرسالة، الطبعة الثانية.

السلمي، أبو محمد عز الدين عبد العزيز بن عبد السلام. (1420هـ/ 1999م). **قواعد الأحكام في مصالح الأنام**. بيروت: دار الكتب العلمية.

الشوكاني، محمد بن علي بن محمد. (1423هـ/2002). **نيل الأوطار شرح منتقى الأخبار من أحاديث سيد الأخيار**. بيروت: دار المعرفة.

صدر الشريعة، عبيد الله بن مسعود. (1426هـ/2005م). **مختصر الوقاية** مع شرحه اختصار الرواية لنجم الدين الدركاني. بيروت: دار الكتب العلمية

العسيري، أحمد معمور. (1424هـ/2004م). **موجز التاريخ الإسلامي**. الدمام: الطبعة الثالثة.

الغزي، أبو الحارث محمد صدقي بن أحمد بن محمد البورنو. (1416هـ/ 1996م). **الوجيز في إيضاح قواعد الفقه الكلية**. بيروت: مؤسسة الرسالة، الطبعة الرابعة.

فتاح، عرفان عبد الحميد. (1420هـ/2000م). **النصرانية**. عمان: دار عمار للنشر.

الكاساني، علاء الدين أبو بكر بن مسعود. (1421هـ/2000م). **بدائع الصنايع في ترتيب الشرائع**. بيروت: دار إحياء التراث العربي، مؤسسة التاريخ العربي، الطبعة الثانية.

المنذري، زكي الدين عبد العظيم. (1417هـ/1996م). **مختصر صحيح مسلم**. الرياض: دار السلام للنشر والتوزيع.

يوسف حامد العالم. (1417هـ/1997م). **المقاصد العامة للشريعة الإسلامية**. القاهرة: دار الحديث؛ الخرطوم: الدار السودانية للكتب، الطبعة الثالثة.

References from Websites

1. http://www.zhidao.baidu.com/question - Accessed on: May 17, 2008
2. http://www.zhidao.baidu.com/question/38054261.html - Accessed on: May 17, 2008
3. www.cnair.com - Accessed on: May 17, 2008
4. http:www.crosses.org/history.htm: History of Crosses. - Accessed on: May 1, 2008.
5. http://www.google.com.my - Accessed on: October 18, 2008
6. http://blog. sina.com.cn/s/blog 4de7c08601007 uw3.html. Accessed on: October 18, 2008
7. http://www.Baidu.com Encyclopedia knowledge, Accessed on: May 16, 2008.
8. http://www.ms-health.com/cms/Article/tsyl/bdft/ctyx/200707/5032.ht ml Accessed on: May 16, 2008.

Index

A

B

C

D

E

F

G

H

I

J

K

L

M

N

P

Q

R

S

T

V

W

X

Y

Z

About the Author

Dr. Ma Zhan Ming was born in 1966 in Ningxia, China. After graduating from high school, he began to learn Arabic and Islamic studies in Ningxia Islamic Institute. In 1989, he obtained a diploma of Islamic studies from the Institute and was appointed as a teacher. After 4 years of teaching, he was admitted to Madina Islamic University, Saudi Arabia, where he obtained his bachelor degree in 1998. He then returned to China and continued teaching at Ningxia Islamic Institute. In 2003, he started his post graduate study at the International Islamic University, Malaysia.

He obtained an M.A degree in *Shari'ah* in 2006 and PhD degree in Islamic and other civilizations in 2009. In January 2010, Dr. Ma Zhan Ming returned to China and continued his teaching career as an Associate Professor and then full Professor at Ningxia University. In 2015, He worked at Cambridge university UK as a visiting scholar within which, he visited Oxford university. In Septemger 2017, He was behited by Guangzhou university as high-level personnel and now he is working as a full Professor of the university. Professor Ma Zhan Ming is the author of 4 books and 30 articales published in Chinese, Arabic and English, He is now undertaking 3 academic projects in the field of Muslim Issues and Islamic Studies.

Contact Information:

School of Foreign Studies, Guangzhou University
Guangzhou Higher Education Mega Center
No. 230, Outer Ring West Road, Panyu District, Guangzhou
Guangdong Province, China 510006
Phone: 0086-18122107161
Email: dsufuzi@163.com

COMMITTEE ON
POPULATION AND DEMOGRAPHY Report No. 8

Trends in Fertility and Mortality in Turkey, 1935-1975

Frederic C. Shorter
Miroslav Macura

Panel on Turkey
Committee on Population and Demography
Assembly of Behavioral and Social Sciences
National Research Council

NATIONAL ACADEMY PRESS
Washington, D.C. 1982

NOTICE: The project that is the subject of this report was approved by the Governing Board of the National Research Council, whose members are drawn from the councils of the National Academy of Sciences, the National Academy of Engineering, and the Institute of Medicine. The members of the committee responsible for the report were chosen for their special competences and with regard for appropriate balance.

This report has been reviewed by a group other than the authors according to procedures approved by a Report Review Committee consisting of members of the National Academy of Sciences, the National Academy of Engineering, and the Institute of Medicine.

The National Research Council was established by the National Academy of Sciences in 1916 to associate the broad community of science and technology with the Academy's purposes of furthering knowledge and of advising the federal government. The Council operates in accordance with general policies determined by the Academy under the authority of its congressional charter of 1863, which establishes the Academy as a private, nonprofit, self-governing membership corporation. The Council has become the principal operating agency of both the National Academy of Sciences and the National Academy of Engineering in the conduct of their services to the government, the public, and the scientific and engineering communities. It is administered jointly by both Academies and the Institute of Medicine. The National Academy of Engineering and the Institute of Medicine were established in 1964 and 1970, respectively, under the charter of the National Academy of Sciences.

Library of Congress Catalog Card Number 81-86661
International Standard Book Number 0-309-03239-3

Available from:

NATIONAL ACADEMY PRESS
2101 Constitution Ave., N.W.
Washington, D.C. 20418

Printed in the United States of America

PANEL ON TURKEY

NUSRET H. FIŞEK, Institute of Community Medicine, Hacettepe University, Ankara, Turkey
SEVİNÇ KAVADARLI, Institute of Population Studies, Hacettepe University, Ankara, Turkey
MIROSLAV MACURA, Economic Institute, Belgrade, Yugoslavia
FERHUNDE ÖZBAY, Research Institute of Social Sciences, Ankara Academy of Economics and Commerce, Ankara, Turkey
FREDERIC C. SHORTER. The Population Council, Cairo, Egypt
SAMİRA YENER, State Planning Organization, Ankara, Turkey

ROBERT J. LAPHAM, *Study Director*

COMMITTEE ON POPULATION AND DEMOGRAPHY

NOTE: Members of the Committee and its panels and working groups participated in this project in their individual capacities; the listing of their organizational affiliation is for identification purposes only, and the views and designations used in this report are not necessarily those of the organizations mentioned.

Contents

List of Tables

List of Figures

Preface

The Committee on Population and Demography was established in April 1977 by the National Research Council in response to a request by the Agency for International Development (AID) of the U.S. Department of State. It was widely felt by those concerned that the time was ripe for a detailed review of levels and trends of fertility and mortality in the developing world. Although most people in the demographic community agree that mortality has declined in almost all developing countries during the last 30 years, there is uncertainty about more recent changes in mortality in some countries, about current levels of fertility, and about the existence and extent of recent changes in fertility.

In 1963, a Panel on Population Problems of the Committee on Science and Public Policy of the National Academy of Sciences published a report entitled *The Growth of World Population*. The appointment of that panel and the publication of its report were expressions of the concern then felt by scientists, as well as by other informed persons in many countries, about the implications of population trends. At that time, the most consequential trend was the pronounced and long-continued acceleration in the rate of increase of the population of the world, and especially of the population of the poorer countries. It was estimated in 1963 that the annual rate of increase of the global population had reached 2 percent, a rate that, if continued, would cause the total to double every 35 years. The disproportionate contribution of low-income areas to that acceleration was caused by rapid declines in mortality combined with high fertility that remained almost unchanged: the birth rate was nearly fixed or declined more modestly than the death rate.

Since the earlier report, however, the peak rate of growth in the world's population has apparently been passed. A dramatic decline in the birth rate in almost all the more developed countries has lowered their aggregate annual rate of increase to well below 1 percent, and the peak rate of increase has also apparently been passed in the less-developed parts of the world as a whole. A sharp decline in fertility in many low-income areas has more than offset the generally continued reduction in the death rate, although the rate of population increase remains high in almost all less-developed countries.

The causes of the reductions in fertility--whether they are the effect primarily of such general changes as lowered infant mortality, increasing education, urban rather than rural residence, and improving status of women or of such particular changes as spreading knowledge of and access to efficient methods of contraception or abortion--are strongly debated. There are also divergent views of the appropriate national and international policies on population in the face of these changing trends. The differences in opinion extend to different beliefs and assertions about what the population trends really are in many of the less-developed countries. Because births and deaths are recorded very incompletely in much of Africa, Asia, and Latin America, levels and trends of fertility and mortality must be estimated, and disagreement has arisen in some instances about the most reliable estimates of those levels and trends.

It was to examine these questions that the Committee on Population and Demography was established within the Assembly of Behavioral and Social Sciences of the National Research Council. It was funded initially for a period of three years by AID under Contract No. AID/pha-C-1161. The Committee has undertaken three major tasks:

1. To evaluate available evidence and prepare estimates of levels and trends of fertility and mortality in selected developing nations;
2. To improve the technologies for estimating fertility and mortality when only incomplete or inadequate data exist (including techniques of data collection);
3. To evaluate the factors determining the changes in birth rates in less-developed nations.

Given the magnitude of these tasks, the Committee decided to concentrate its initial efforts on the first two tasks; it initiated work on the third task in 1979.

The Committee approaches the first task through careful assessment, by internal and external comparison, and through analysis, by application of the most reliable methods known, of all the data sources available. Each of the country studies therefore consists of the application of a range of methods to a number of data sets. Best estimates of levels and recent trends are then developed on the grounds of their consistency and plausibility and the robustness of the individual methods from which they were derived.

The Committee's second task, refinement of methodology, is seen as a by-product of achieving the first. The application of particular methods to many different data sets from different countries and referring to different time periods will inevitably provide valuable information about the practical functioning of the methods themselves. Particular data sets might also require the development of new methodology or the refinement of existing techniques.

The Committee set three criteria for identifying countries to study in detail: that the country have a population large enough to be important in a world view; that there be some uncertainty about levels and recent trends of fertility or mortality; and that sufficient demographic data be available to warrant a detailed study. After a country has been selected for detailed study, the usual procedure is to set up a panel or working group of experts, both nationals of the country and others knowledgeable about the demography and demographic statistics of the country. The role of these panels and working groups, which generally include at least one Committee member, is to carry out the comparisons and analyses required. A small staff assists the Committee, panels, and working groups in their work.

As of late 1981, 168 population specialists, including 94 from developing countries, have been involved in the work of the Committee as members of panels or working groups. The Committee, the Assembly, and the National Research Council are grateful for the unpaid time and effort these experts have been willing to give.

Each country being studied has a different mix of data sources and different problems with data errors. Therefore, there is no standard pattern for all the reports. However, each report includes a summary of the main findings regarding estimates of fertility and mortality, a description of the data sources available, and a presentation of the analyses that were carried out, classified by type of data analyzed; detailed methodological descriptions are included where necessary in appendixes.

In some of the reports the estimates of fertility and mortality are presented as ranges. The use of a range is deliberate. It indicates that the panel and the Committee are confident that the range includes the true value, but have concluded that the evidence does not warrant selecting a single figure as best. The range conveys an important aspect (uncertainty) of the estimation. Ideally, in constructing an average for several populations in each of which estimation is presented as a range, an aggregate range would be calculated (as the population-weighted average of the constituents). The user who selects a single figure from the middle of the range does so at the risk of misleading simplification.

This report is number 8 in a series produced by the Committee. The report analyzes available data and provides estimates of the levels and recent trends of fertility and mortality in Turkey. It has been prepared by Frederic C. Shorter and Miroslav Macura with advice, consultation, and technical review provided by the other members of the Panel.

The Panel on Turkey was formed in 1978, with assistance from the Institute of Population Studies and the Institute of Community Medicine at Hacettepe University in Ankara, Turkey. The Institute of Population Studies arranged meeting space and provided other assistance to the Panel during the two Panel meetings held in 1978 and in 1980. Appreciation is extended to both Institutes and especially to Mithat Coruh, director of the Institute of Population Studies at that time.

The Panel has functioned primarily in the planning and development of the project and in providing technical advice and critical review of the report. Review of draft tabulations and of the draft manuscript was carried out periodically between 1978 and 1980, both during and between Panel meetings. The Panel reviewed and approved the final manuscript.

The Turkey report is somewhat more detailed than other reports of the Committee because the Panel felt that a more detailed exposition would be useful for demographers and other persons concerned about population measurement in Turkey.

Special thanks and appreciation are due to Nusret H. Fişek, professor of community medicine and director of the Institute of Community Medicine, Hacettepe University. Dr. Fişek has been associated with population research and service delivery programs in Turkey for two decades, and he has provided an extensive background and insightful knowledge of population data and population phenomena in Turkey. Dr. Fişek was the first director of the Institute of Population Studies, a post he held for five years. In 1967 he organized the still-functioning Etimesgut Rural Health District, where integrated health services, including family planning, are provided to 80,000 people. The area is also used for epidemiologic, demographic, and health services research. Dr. Fişek was also instrumental in the establishment by the Institute of Community Medicine in 1975 of a field training and research program in the Cubuk Rural Health District (population 55,000). The Institute of Community Medicine is a collaborating center of the World Health Organization (WHO) in research and training on service delivery in the field of human reproduction.

This report takes into account and extends much prior analysis of population statistics for Turkey by the present authors and by other scholars whose work is referenced throughout this report. Most of this work has been done under the auspices of the Institute of Population Studies, the State Institute of Statistics, and the State Planning Organization of Turkey. Appreciation is expressed to the Institute of Population Studies for providing pregnancy history tabulations from the 1968 and 1973 fertility surveys.

The assistance of several individuals is acknowledged with warm thanks. Mahir Ulusoy and Osman Saracbasi of Hacettepe University produced the 1968 and 1973 pregnancy history tabulations. Robert Sendek of the Center for Policy Studies, Population Council, made useful tabulations from the 1963 Survey. Kadir Sumbuloglu, associate professor of biostatistics, Institute of Community Medicine, Hacettepe University, analyzed Turkey death registration data from province and district centers. Denise Batani, a graduate student in the Department of Statistics, University of Cairo, assisted with computations.

The Committee extends its sincere thanks for this study to all members of the Panel on Turkey, who managed amid busy schedules to assist with this project. Thanks are also extended to the staff of the Committee for their support, assistance, and advice. Katherine Miller edited the report and provided many ideas and suggestions for clarity and presentation. Eugenia Grohman, associate director for reports of the Assembly of Behavioral and Social Sciences, provided technical advice, and Elaine McGarraugh, editorial assistant, coordinated its production with the National Academy Press. Special thanks are due to Brenda Buchbinder, administrative assistant, for assisting with travel arrangements and other administrative tasks, and to Solveig Padilla, Benita Anderson, and Isis Bassili for typing the text and many tables. Carol Bradford Ward helped organize and proofread the tabulations and figures.

The Committee is also grateful to the individuals who have assisted in the review of early drafts of this report and to the members of the Assembly of Behavioral and Social Sciences and outside reviewers who reviewed the final draft. Their comments and suggestions have been most useful.

The Committee extends sincere appreciation to all of the individuals and institutions for their time and for the materials they provided for the preparation of this report.

ANSLEY J. COALE, *Chair*
Committee on Population and Demography

Summary

The data for this evaluation of fertility and mortality trends in Turkey cover a period of 40 years, from 1935 to 1975. The information is strongest and most detailed between 1945 and 1970, which includes the period when fertility commenced a sustained decline. This assessment examines both national trends and trends among divisions of the country. Since redistribution of the population by urbanization has been a major factor in the demography of the country, some information on these trends is also presented.

The Turkish transition from high birth and death rates was well advanced by the mid-1970s, but it was still far from reaching the low levels of European countries. During 1970-75, the most recent period for which reliable measures are available, the expectation of life at birth averaged 59 years, the infant mortality rate was approximately 126 deaths per thousand births, the crude birth rate was 34.9 per thousand population, and the total fertility rate was 5.05 children per woman.

After the work on the present report was completed, preliminary results of a national fertility survey conducted in 1978 became available. While these data may be subject to certain types of error, which would require adjustment when full details become available, they indicate a total fertility rate of 4.3 children per woman in 1977-78. An extrapolation of the accelerating downward trend from five years earlier yields a total fertility rate of 4.5 at the same date.

This summary presents an overview of the findings of the report, but reference must be made to the body of the report to obtain a more complete picture, including evaluation of the quality of estimates.

FERTILITY

The national fertility trend is measured by three major indexes: an index of fertility within marriage, the total fertility rate, and the crude birth rate. These three fertility indexes are related to each other through two intermediate indexes: an index of the proportions of women in the married state, and an index of age and sex structure for the population (see Figure 1).

Fertility within marriage is measured by the sum of age-specific marital fertility rates over the reproductive ages of women. The sum, which is denoted total marital fertility, began declining from a high plateau during the late 1940s or early 1950s, the exact year being impossible to specify with available data. The development of fertility control in some social groups within marriage probably predated the national decline of fertility because there were pre-existing differentials affecting at least small urbanized sections of the population. The sustained decline of marital fertility is accompanied by changes in the age pattern of marital fertility rates that clearly indicate increases in voluntary limitation of births. Indirect confirmation of the rise in birth planning is provided by data on contraceptive use by the married population over a limited segment of the trend period, from 1963 to 1973.

The total fertility rate, which measures the number of children women have on average given current age-specific rates, began its descent somewhat later than the decline of fertility within marriage. The reason for this delay was an increase in proportions of women exposed to childbearing up to the mid- or late 1950s. The marriage index, C_m, shows the proportions of women in a married state during the ages of potential childbearing increased. The upward trend in exposure was due to a downward trend in the age of marriage and to reductions in widowhood, the latter a consequence mainly of rising life expectancy for husbands. Only since the mid-1950s has the average age of first marriage for women begun to rise.

The overall decline of the total fertility rate is from a pre-decline level of 6.85 children to 5.05 children during 1970-75, amounting to 26 percent. Preliminary estimates from the 1978 national survey indicate that the decline is 37 percent when extended to a period of about 25 years. The rate of decline has been accelerating.

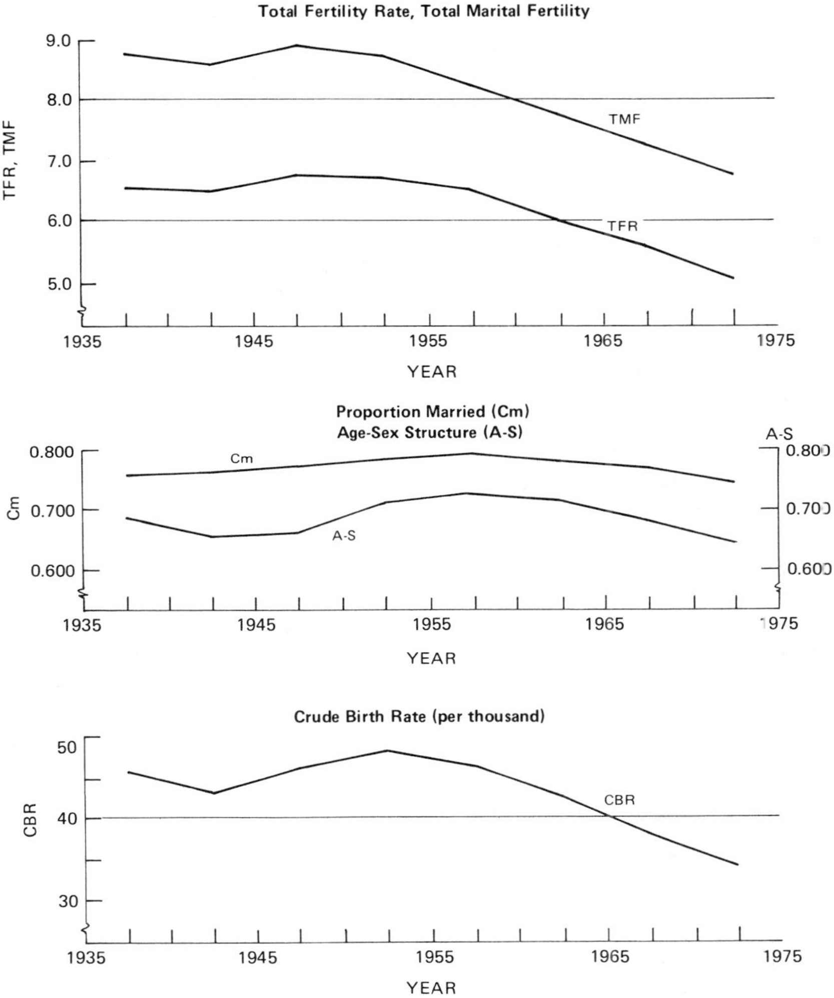

FIGURE 1 National Fertility Indexes, 1935–75: Turkey

The decline of total fertility up to 1970–75 can be factored into two elements: the decline of fertility within marriage and the reduction of marriage proportions. Eighty-one percent of the decline is due to reductions in marital fertility. Only 19 percent is due to marriage factors, specifically a rise in age of marriage, which came late, and some offsets due to declining widowhood.

The crude birth rate, which measures the growth of the population as a whole due to births, responded to the basic trend of total fertility, but it is affected in addition by slow changes in the age and sex structure of the population, denoted by A-S in Figure 1. Vacancies in the female age structure around the ages of highest childbearing during the late 1930s and 1940s are traceable to low numbers of births or low infant and childhood survival or some combination around the time that the Turkish Republic was established (1923). These vacancies meant fewer births and a depression in the crude birth rate during the period from roughly 1935 to 1950.

The exact trends of the different indexes of fertility prior to about 1950 are impossible to estimate with precision, due to certain weaknesses in the basic data. However, the general existence of a fertility plateau, with moderate fluctuations due to various causes before the decline, is confirmed.

The national trends of fertility from the end of the plateau period up to 1970 have been disaggregated by dividing the population into either three or six divisions. The three-part urban-rural division places the cities of Istanbul and Izmir at the most urban end of the scale. The rest of urban Turkey forms a second division. Ankara is included in the second division even though it is intermediate in size between Istanbul and Izmir. During the period of this study Ankara was a less urbanized city, demographically speaking, because its birth rates were higher and the proportion of the population having rural origins was higher than in Istanbul-Izmir. Rural communities, those with population less than 10,000, form a third division. Some of the analysis uses a six-part division involving three geographic regions of the rural and urban categories. Figure 2 shows fertility measures for the three major rural-urban divisions.

Based on the three-part urban-rural division, fertility in the mid-1940s was more than twice as high in rural Turkey as compared with Istanbul-Izmir, with the fertility of the "other urban" population intermediate between the two. Istanbul-Izmir was close to a replacement level of fertility in the late 1940s. Differentials of this type, which very likely had existed for some time, have narrowed somewhat since then. Rural fertility declined from the very beginning and there was a slight elevation of urban fertility, which then leveled off. However, the differential was still large in 1968, with

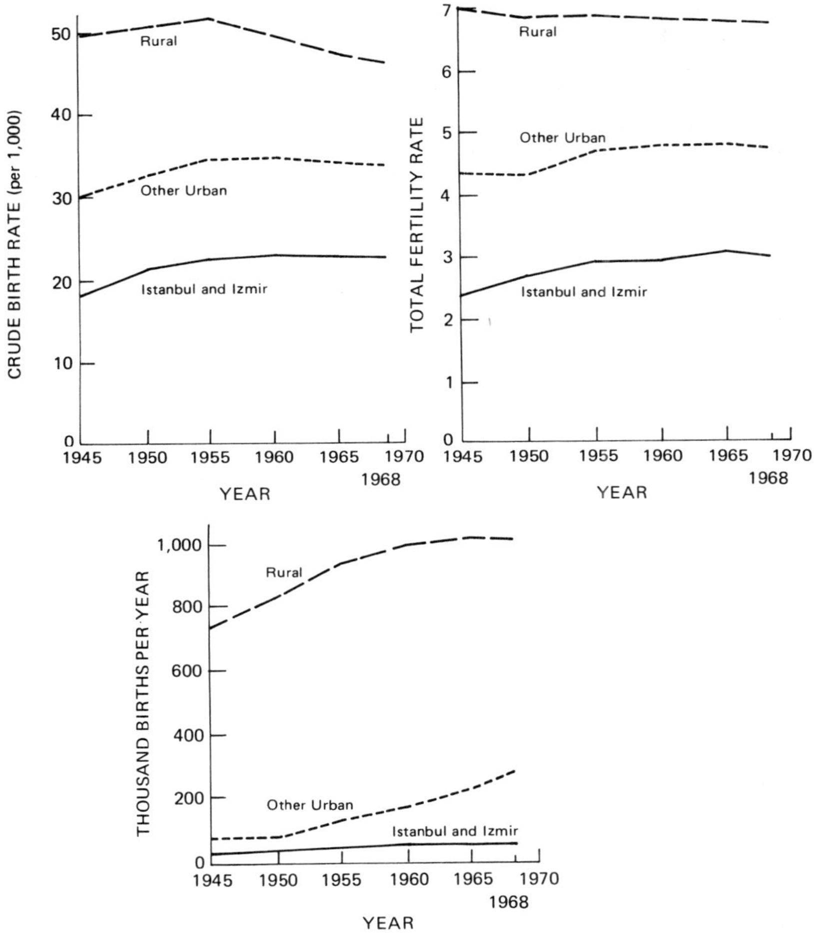

FIGURE 2 Crude Birth Rate, Total Fertility Rate, and Births by Rural-Urban Areas, 1945-68: Turkey

rural fertility at least double that of Istanbul-Izmir. Estimates by divisions for later dates are not possible with the available data.

The fertility of the national population could decline dramatically while the divisional levels changed little because the average fertility of families in the country as a whole is found by aggregating divisions of the population that changed in relative size. Prior to about

1950, the rate of growth of the urban population (due to all causes) was little different from that of the rural population, 2.5 percent per year compared with 2.1 percent, respectively. Thereafter, the urban growth rate jumped to a new and continuing level of around 6 percent per year, while the rural rate declined steadily, passing below 1 percent in the mid-1960s.

One of the connections between rural-urban migration and fertility is that the sons and daughters of rural parents move to the cities and have fewer children there than their parents' generation had in the villages. The cities have absorbed large numbers of people from rural areas without there being much change in average urban fertility, which was initially and still is much lower than rural fertility. Families of recent rural origin had more children than the original urban population, contributing to the slight elevation of overall urban fertility observed before the 1960s. However, downward fertility trends of various urban classes of population, including those of rural origin, are not ruled out by the observed overall elevation, because changes were taking place in the class composition of the urban population itself.

MORTALITY

The national decline in death rates probably reaches further back in time than can be captured by estimates for the 1935-75 period (see Figure 3). This at least is a good presumption, since the trend over those 40 years is downward, except for a rise in death rates during World War II. Although Turkey was not involved militarily, the material conditions of life deteriorated and there were a number of serious epidemics, both of which explain the reversal of trend.

For the late 1930s, various indices of mortality can be estimated only as orders of magnitude, due to the sparse nature of data for that period. The mortality indices can be estimated with greater confidence from the 1950s onward. On this understanding, life expectancy for both sexes combined appears to have risen from around 35 years in the 1950s to 59 years for the period 1970-75.

Infant and early childhood mortality is measured by the infant mortality index from the late 1940s up to the early 1970s. Estimates are reasonably strong from about 1960 onward and are acceptable indicators of national

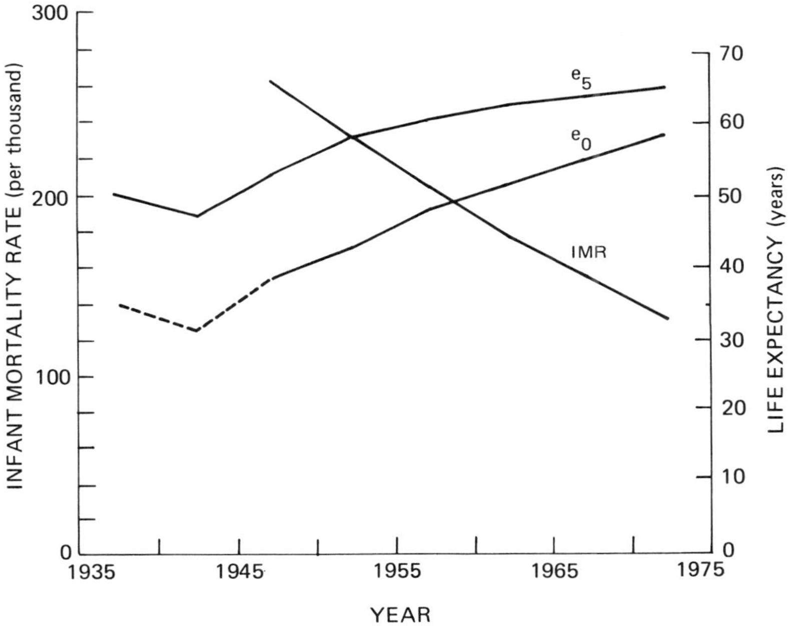

FIGURE 3 Mortality Measures for Both Sexes Combined, 1935-75: Turkey

Note: Dashed line shows that the estimate of e_0 was derived from e_5 by selecting split-model life tables to take the place of estimates for the IMR, which are unavailable for the earliest dates.

trends before that. Infant mortality declined from about 260 deaths per thousand births in the late 1940s to 126 per thousand in approximately 1973. The rate of decline does not seem to have changed much over the period, remaining near 3 percent per year.

In most populations that have as high an expectation of life after early childhood as in Turkey, the infant mortality rate would be around half the rate found in Turkey. The exact relationship varies considerably among countries, but there is no doubt that the infant mortality rate is exceptionally high in Turkey as compared historically and contemporaneously with other countries that have as low adult mortality as does Turkey. Whether the reduction of infant mortality has been held back by special disease factors, by unusual malnourishment, or by a general lag in infant and child care as compared with the health practices of adults, is an open question. The pattern of especially heavy infant mortality seems to apply to both sexes. Male infants have higher infant mortality than females by a margin similar to that found in many other populations.

The crude death rate is a less useful index of mortality than either life expectancy or the infant mortality rate, because it is affected markedly by age structure. Its level was on the order of 30 per thousand or a bit more in the late 1930s. It declined to a level of approximately 10 per thousand in the period 1970-75. As the proportion of population in the very lowest ages declines with falling birth rates, the persons subject to the highest age-specific death rates (infants) become less important as a source of deaths. Thus, part of the decline in the death rate is simply a reflection of declining fertility rather than declining mortality.

Infant mortality rates for divisions of the population were examined to estimate differentials and trends in those differentials (see Figure 4). Rural infant mortality was nearly twice that of Istanbul-Izmir in the late 1940s, with other urban places intermediate between the two. The differentials shrink over time, but infant mortality in rural areas was still almost two-thirds higher than in Istanbul-Izmir in the late 1960s. Estimates made separately by regions of the country suggest that there were sizeable differentials within the rural population in the late 1940s, but these regional differentials had largely disappeared by the late 1960s.

The decline of national infant mortality is connected with the divisional trends of infant mortality by the distribution of births among the divisions. As young adults migrate from rural to urban areas, the distribution of births shifts. Trends in the number of births by divisions show that urban births are increasing while rural births, though increasing at first, leveled off by the late 1960s. The rearing of proportionately more infants in urban family and community surroundings, which have lower risks of death than rural settings, contributes to the national decline.

POPULATION GROWTH

The trend of population growth in Turkey reflects births, deaths, and the international balance of migration (see

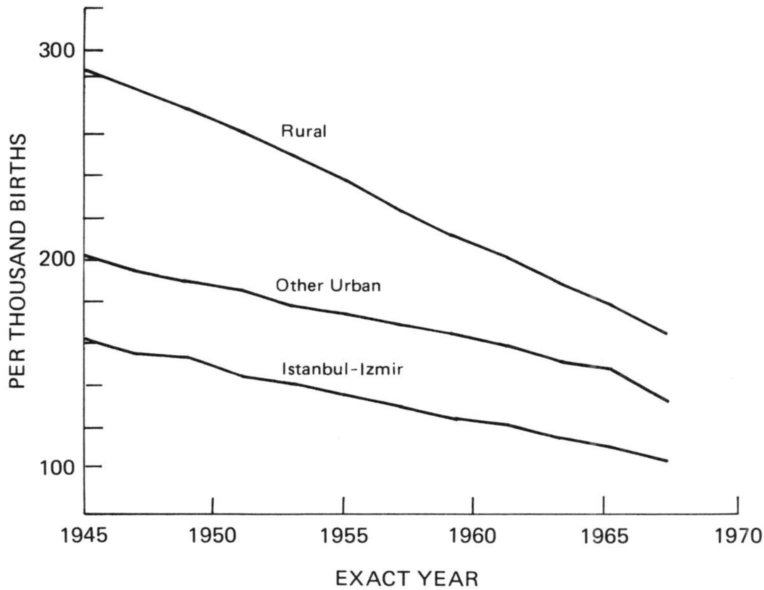

FIGURE 4 Infant Mortality Rates by Rural-Urban Areas, 1945-67: Turkey

Figure 5). The latter component was of little importance until the 1960s, when worker migration became a major economic factor with important demographic implications. Precise estimation of the volume of movements is impossible. There was a net loss of nearly one million persons from 1960 to 1975 (an estimate of 908 thousand is used in this report). The total number of Turks moving to other countries was some multiple of this figure, but many of these guest workers and their families returned to Turkey. In a population that was 40 million by 1975, the cumulative draw-down of the national population at home was not negligible. However, on an annual basis the effects on the total growth rate are rather moderate. The main components of population change over time are births and deaths.

The decline in mortality brought an increase in the growth rate, to a level averaging 2.8 percent per annum during the 1950s. Falling fertility and worker migration reduced the rate to approximately 2.4 percent per annum in the early 1970s. Declining fertility is a double-edged sword. Initially, it lowers the death rate through its

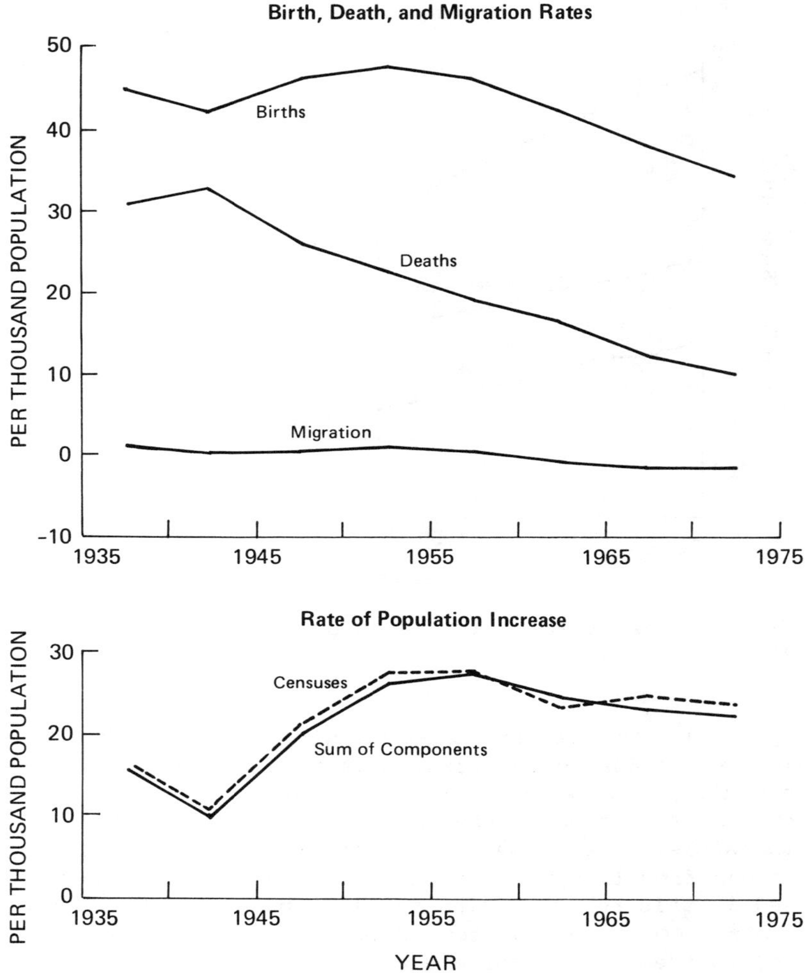

FIGURE 5 Overall Rate and Components of National Population Increase, 1935-75: Turkey

effects on the age structure at the same time as it lowers birth rates. The latter effect is, of course, the stronger one, and in time the effect on age structure disappears, due to aging of the reduced-size cohorts. Thus, the decline in fertility has not only brought a modest reduction in the growth rate, but has positioned the structure of the population for more decline in the future.

Combining estimates of the birth, death, and migration rates gives estimates of the total growth rate that are not much different from those estimated simply by comparing totals from one five-year census date to the next. This degree of consistency between the estimates of this report and the census-based growth rates is not altogether accidental, because the census data themselves play a major role in the estimation procedures. However, there are some important elements of independence between the two procedures for estimating the growth rate. Estimates for each component rest partially on independent data or on indirect techniques of measurement that are partially independent of changes in census coverage over time. Hence, general agreement of the sum of the components with the census growth rate is encouraging, but it is not conclusive assurance of accuracy.

1 Introduction

BACKGROUND

Turkey is the largest country in Western Asia, with a population of about 45 million in 1980. The country has extensive coastal areas on the Mediterranean, Aegean, and Black seas; extensive upland plains and hill areas including Central Anatolia; and rugged mountainous regions in the east and south. Turkey's political and territorial integrity date from 1923 when the Turkish Republic was founded. Fertility has declined in the past two and a half decades, but the extent of decline and the levels of recent fertility and mortality have not been estimated consistently by all observers.

Turkey has a variety of demographic data sources which have been used to estimate fertility and mortality levels and trends for the nation and for six divisions of the population. These data sources are reviewed in detail in this introductory chapter. Chapter 2 presents fertility estimates, Chapter 3 mortality estimates, and Chapter 4 discusses the cumulative effects of the various components of national population growth. Appropriate demographic techniques have been applied in constructing the estimates described below, among them a new technique called multiple reverse projection, which is described in detail in Appendix A. Appendix B describes a special technique used to estimate infant and early childhood mortality from birth-survival histories. Appendix C explains how census data were adjusted to correct for age misreporting, and Appendix D presents the available data on international migration from Turkey. Appendix E presents data on the population of six divisions of Turkey by age and sex as reported in the censuses from 1945 to 1970.

DATA SOURCES

Turkey conducted nine quinquennial censuses between 1935 and 1975. National-level data from the 1975 census are available only from a 1 percent sample of the census data, but more complete tabulations are available for the earlier censuses. Two national demographic surveys of the dual-record type have been conducted, the Turkish Demographic Survey of 1965-68 and a similar survey in 1974-75. Three national population surveys that included fertility histories and child-survival information were conducted in 1963, 1968, and 1973. A Turkey Fertility Survey was conducted in 1978 in collaboration with the World Fertility Survey, but those data were not available for use in this report.

Births in Turkey are registered for legal purposes, but the registration information is not cumulated for national statistical purposes and published. Death registration data for all district and province centers are available and these data sets have been examined. No death registration data are available for other cities or for villages. Also, fertility and mortality data are available from two special health training and research areas: the Etimesgut Rural Health District and the Yozgat (Province) Maternal, Child Health, and Family Planning Project.

Censuses

The first modern census was taken in 1927 but the series useful for demographic analysis begins with the report of the 1935 census. Turkey possesses an unbroken series of censuses from 1935 to 1975 at five-year intervals. The censuses were all taken at the same time of year and by essentially the same _de facto_ counting procedures. Reports for the nine censuses are available in comparable detail for most years. Additional detail comes from the separate provincial volumes produced in 1935 and 1970. A 1 percent sample of the 1975 census is available, but the planned provincial volumes are incomplete and the national report was not available for use in this report. Questions on age and sex are tabulated in comparable five-year age groups for all dates at the national level; the results are summarized in Table 1. Marital status was not tabulated in 1940 and lacks standard five-year age groups above age 25 in 1950.

TABLE 1 Population of Turkey by Age and Sex as Reported in the Censuses, 1935 to 1975[a] (in thousands)

Age	1935[b]	1940	1945	1950	1955	1960	1965	1970	1975[c]
Males									
0–4	1,454.8	1,387.0	1,288.4	1,585.1	1,985.5	2,184.7	2,359.3	2,661.7	2,765.2
5–9	1,230.2	1,419.0	1,350.1	1,338.5	1,677.0	2,076.9	2,418.8	2,611.0	2,795.7
10–14	862.7	1,190.0	1,286.5	1,275.6	1,295.8	1,691.2	2,061.1	2,363.4	2,728.7
15–19	567.8	829.7	1,050.0	1,271.3	1,248.3	1,249.9	1,548.6	1,924.7	2,314.2
20–24	761.4	524.5	790.0	990.9	1,210.2	1,178.2	1,213.1	1,496.6	1,833.1
25–29	632.1	684.6	484.9	727.0	959.5	1,157.5	1,056.7	1,108.2	1,452.3
30–34	594.0	618.6	732.1	524.3	749.0	1,028.3	1,140.4	1,019.2	1,092.6
35–39	494.4	590.5	608.1	688.4	519.5	749.7	999.1	1,117.4	1,034.3
40–44	328.9	466.4	543.0	552.0	666.8	506.0	705.8	921.5	1,095.2
45–49	246.9	303.3	401.8	499.8	525.0	610.4	446.2	644.7	903.6
50–54	229.5	248.2	283.2	389.6	505.4	548.5	613.1	457.1	654.5
55–59	164.8	175.2	171.3	214.3	327.2	424.7	450.2	497.1	388.8
60–64	178.2	190.2	200.1	197.1	243.1	369.0	453.5	476.5	517.5
65–69	101.9	100.1	98.8	114.5	126.4	166.5	258.3	321.6	353.4
70–74	92.5	83.1	80.1	77.3	98.5	113.9	145.9	220.9	261.9
75+	89.4	88.1	78.1	81.3	96.3	108.5	126.8	165.4	226.2
Sub-total	8,030	8,899	9,447	10,527	12,233	14,164	15,997	18,007	20,417

Females

0-4	1,318.2	1,258.0	1,186.5	1,509.3	1,879.4	2,078.9	2,264.8	2,594.8	2,652.5
5-9	1,146.3	1,266.0	1,244.1	1,238.3	1,562.0	1,927.7	2,252.3	2,484.0	2,665.9
10-14	758.0	991.2	1,075.6	1,082.2	1,090.6	1,488.5	1,812.3	2,167.3	2,495.7
15-19	493.7	698.9	932.7	1,119.7	1,088.1	1,059.2	1,365.8	1,770.7	2,160.2
20-24	650.5	518.6	692.6	974.2	1,111.1	1,127.9	1,134.5	1,355.5	1,713.9
25-29	732.9	705.9	620.0	752.6	1,021.7	1,177.3	1,162.6	1,154.0	1,394.4
30-34	652.4	715.9	700.6	591.3	731.3	985.8	1,135.9	1,165.7	1,098.9
35-39	517.8	568.7	579.2	600.7	525.8	693.8	935.8	1,097.3	1,141.3
40-44	481.6	530.7	558.8	595.9	621.5	548.4	677.7	900.0	1,065.8
45-49	319.9	348.4	379.0	445.8	473.1	500.0	430.1	564.1	826.0
50-54	390.6	416.5	434.7	472.0	528.2	581.3	591.6	516.3	645.3
55-59	198.4	217.3	219.7	260.5	308.8	369.4	415.6	440.6	392.3
60-64	302.2	327.4	349.7	359.2	387.3	461.4	502.1	529.9	551.8
65-69	106.6	114.1	124.8	154.4	172.8	213.8	271.5	319.4	370.4
70-74	128.1	131.2	133.2	138.2	171.2	195.7	221.0	265.5	298.0
75+	119.9	114.1	112.4	125.8	158.5	188.1	220.9	273.2	308.1
Sub-total	8,317	8,922	9,344	10,420	11,831	13,591	15,394	17,598	19,780
Total	16,347	17,821	18,790	20,947	24,065	27,755	31,391	35,605	40,198

Note: Numbers add correctly to totals; rounding of age groups and of totals independently gives the appearance of different totals.

[a]Persons with ages reported as unknown were redistributed in proportion to the number of persons in each age group at each census.

[b]Adjusted from 16,158 to 16,347 to correspond with national boundaries after the annexation of Hatay in 1939.

[c]Preliminary data from a one percent sample of the 1975 census.

This rich series of censuses implicitly contains the history of mortality and fertility for Turkey except for changes in population due to territorial change or international migration. The only territorial change between 1935 and 1975 was the annexation of Hatay province in 1939. International migration became an important influence on population size and age structure with the worker movements of the 1960s and 1970s. Information with which to assess recent migration is available from special surveys by the State Planning Organization and the censuses of the principal worker-receiving country, the Federal Republic of Germany. For earlier periods, special studies on population exchanges of minor demographic significance are available.

For subdividing the population into rural-urban and geographic divisions, data are available between 1945 and 1970 on age, sex, and marital status, classified by places with populations above and below 10,000. These data are available either from census reports (1970) or from the archives of the State Institute of Statistics. Demographers who have copied information from the archives and placed it in computer-readable form kindly made these materials available.

The 1965 boundaries of provinces were used as the standard for aggregating data by the six geographic rural and urban divisions. Adjustments for changes in boundaries prior to 1965 were made with information from Kemal Ozok's meticulous compilation (Turkey, Regional Planning Office, 1968). There were no further changes in province boundaries after 1965, so the six divisions for 1970 have the same boundaries as 1965 and the adjusted data for earlier dates. For some years, data on marital status by sex and five-year age groups are deficient below the national level. However, data are sufficient to compile age-sex distributions for 1945-70.

The 1970 and 1975 censuses asked about the cumulative fertility of ever-married women (total number of children born alive) and the survival status of their children (total number of children still living). These data are valuable for indirect estimation of infant and early childhood mortality when the tabulations include (1) numbers of children ever born and numbers surviving, cross-classified by five-year age groups of mothers from 15 to 34; and (2) distributions of all women by marital status by at least the same five-year age groups. Matching tabulations of (1) and (2) are available at the national level for 1970 and for the 1 percent sample of the 1975 census. The necessary coordination between tabulations of types (1) and (2) was not fully achieved for the rural-urban division of population in 1970 because province-level tabulations of type (1) refer to the administrative definitions of rural and urban, whereas those of type (2) refer to places with populations under and over 10,000. The second method of distinguishing rural and urban is preferable because it matches the dividing criterion used for age and sex distributions for Turkish censuses. Reports for provinces from the 1975 census are incomplete; some province reports show age and sex by the 10,000-population division of rural and urban, but they do not include any tabulations of types (1) and (2).

The 1970 and 1975 censuses also asked a question about the number of children born alive who died before reaching age 1. This question does not provide a reliable basis for infant mortality measurement, because misreporting of age at death is severe and the time in the past to which the mortality experience refers is unclear. In its place, the Panel suggests using a question on whether each ever-married woman had a live birth during the last year. The new question would provide a basis for estimating the current age pattern of fertility, provided it is tabulated by ages of mother in five-year age groups. In combination with other census data, this question would help to provide estimates of fertility levels in terms of crude birth rates and total fertility.

National Dual-Record Demographic Surveys

The Turkish Demographic Survey (TDS) was conducted between 1965 and 1968 by the School of Public Health in the Ministry of Health. A national area sample of 40,000 households was used to collect data on births, deaths, migrations, and population structure. The TDS used a monthly recording system and a semi-annual independent survey. Thirteen rural and urban subdivisions of the population were defined and brought into the national sample sequentially until all units were simultaneously under surveillance by June 1966. Complete national data are available for 1966-67 (Turkey, School of Public Health, 1970). The TDS estimates of birth and death rates are made by standard dual-record methods that include an estimate of omissions by both record systems.

In 1974, a second-generation TDS called the Turkish Population Survey (TPS) was started in the State Institute of Statistics. Its first report, for 1974-75, is available (Turkey, State Institute of Statistics, 1978), but the procedures for data collection and processing are not sufficiently well documented to permit an evaluation of the results. Consequently, these data were not used in this report.

National Population Surveys

The Ministry of Health held a national population survey in 1963, which included both a representative demographic sample of approximately 8,000 ever-married women and a subsample of 2,600 currently married women. Questions on contraceptive knowledge, attitudes, and practices were the main purpose of the subsample. Data concerning marital fertility and early childhood mortality from the 1963 demographic sample of 8,000 women are available.

In 1968, a representative national sample of 3,300 currently married women was interviewed in the Survey on Family Structure and Population Problems of the Institute of Population Studies of Hacettepe University. This included information on the fertility of currently married women, comparable to the 1963 survey. The same fertility questions were included in a third national survey of 4,600 currently married women conducted by the Hacettepe Institute in 1973.

Reports and tabulations from the 1968 and 1973 surveys are available for the country as a whole and for subdivisions that differ somewhat from the six population divisions used by the Panel. Special tabulations of birth histories and the survival of the children are available according to the Panel's six divisions from the 1968 and 1973 surveys. Of the two, only the 1968 tabulations are accompanied by sufficient information about the preparatory data processing to allow them to be evaluated. The 1968 data were therefore judged to be more useful and were used as one basis for estimating child mortality trends (see Chapter 3).

Birth and Death Registration

Birth registration is required in Turkey, and most persons have birth cards. However the system is not used to generate national statistics on birth events. Death registration is also required. Death statistics are gathered from the registration system by the Ministry of Interior for all cities and towns that are provincial or district headquarters. These data are published by the State Institute of Statistics. An evaluation by Kadir Sumbuloglu for 1960 to 1975 shows that underenumeration of deaths varies among cities and at different dates with no detectable systematic pattern that would permit adjustment. There is, in addition, differential omission of infant deaths (Sumbuloglu, 1978).

National Life Tables

A Turkish national life table is available based on data from the Turkish Demographic Survey. Life tables of apparently sound quality are also available for a nine-year period from the Etimesgut Rural Health District (population of 80,000 persons) and from the Yozgat provincial health project (population of 500,000 persons), which utilized a dual-record sample of 50,000 persons (Institute of Community Medicine, 1975; Tekce, 1979).

2 Fertility

NATIONAL CRUDE BIRTH RATES, 1935-75

A common technique for estimating fertility is reverse survival. In this report a more refined reverse survival alternative is applied. The following sections describe the general technique, the alternative used here and resulting estimates of crude birth rates. Estimates of crude birth rates by other means are also compared.

The General Technique of Reverse Projection

Measures of fertility for the years preceding a census can be estimated by projecting in reverse the number of persons at different ages at a given time before the census. Thus, the crude birth rate _t_ years before the census may be estimated by reverse projection to birth of the number of persons aged _t_ at the time of the census, combined with reverse projection of the whole population to determine the appropriate denominator for the birth rate _t_ years before the census.

The accuracy of an estimate of fertility for a particular time period derived by reverse projection depends on how well the projection allows for the actual change in the populations that form the numerator and denominator of the crude birth rate and on how accurately the census recorded the subgroups that were projected to form the numerator and denominator of the fertility measure. Since the birth rate is a ratio, however, equal proportionate errors in counting or projecting the two groups that form the numerator and denominator (for example, a 5 percent undercount of both populations or a 2 percent overstatement of the proportion surviving in each group) would still allow an accurate estimate of the birth rate. Therefore, changes in the extent of coverage from one census to the next, which has been a problem in Turkey, do not bias the fertility measure provided the under- or overenumeration is proportionate across the age groups used in calculating the numerators and denominators of the fertility measures.

Misreporting of age, which moves individuals from one age (or age group) to another, causes spurious intertemporal variation in fertility estimates derived by reverse projection. For example, systematic overstatement of age such that the true number of people under age 5 is understated and the number in the next age group (5-9) is overstated, creates the appearance of a decline in fertility from the period 5 to 10 years ago to the period 0 to 5 years ago. In Turkey, there is systematic age misreporting of the pattern just described. If the age distribution is distorted by age misreporting in the age groups that are projected, the trends of fertility that are estimated will be spuriously erratic.

The Turkish censuses extend backward in time from 1975 to 1935 at nearly exact five-year intervals. The data they provide are ideal for making estimates of fertility through reverse projection as long as appropriate assumptions about mortality can be made and the problems created by age misstatement can be overcome. Chapter 3 explains how mortality estimates were made to meet this first requirement. The solution to the other problem, that of age misstatement, may be approached in two different ways.

One approach is to adjust the censuses data for age misreporting. No attempt to correct for general coverage errors is necessary, because this type of error, as already explained, does not affect reverse-projection estimates of the crude birth rate. The method used to make these corrections for the Turkish censuses is explained in Appendix C. However, no known method is capable of eliminating all error due to age misstatement. The resulting reverse projections of fertility from a census adjusted for age misreporting are imperfect to the same extent.

Multiple Reverse Projection (MRP)

An alternative approach, suggested by Frederic Shorter, is called "multiple reverse projection" (MRP). Described in detail in Appendix A, this method has also been applied to the Turkish censuses. From each census, a time series of estimates of fertility is constructed by reverse projection. The series goes back in time from the date of the census as far as assumptions based on mortality estimation are warranted. This procedure gives fertility estimates for years t to t+5 years before the census, based on births whose survivors are in the age group t to t+5 of the census. For example, the births for the period 20 to 25 years before the census are calculated from the age group 20-25 in the census. The denominator of the crude birth rate is an estimate of the total population size during the same period 20 to 25 years before the census, which is also given by the reverse projection. When a sequence of censuses is available, an independent time series of fertility estimates can be calculated from each census.

In all reverse projections, there is a theoretical problem concerning how to "close" the population at the uppermost ages. In actual data the uppermost age group is an open-ended interval. For example, the Turkish data are divided into five-year age groups up to age 75 with an open-ended interval of "75 and over" as the last group. The population in this open age group consists of persons who were ages 70-74 and 75+ five years earlier. In order to use the survival rates of the life table to project backward in time, it is necessary to know how the population was divided between individuals less than 75 (those in the 70-74 age group) and those who were already 75 or over. Assumptions can be made and the errors in those assumptions will have little effect on a crude birth rate only five years earlier, because population size, the denominator of the crude birth rate, will be affected very little by the error. However, as the reverse projection extends further backward in time, errors in population size due to such assumptions are magnified and can create misleading results.

The multiple reverse projection method offers a simple solution that makes use of the data from prior censuses. While the total size of these prior censuses may not be correct, the relationship between the size of the open age interval and the next lower age interval can be accepted. That relationship is based on actual census data and reflects all the conditions of fertility, mortality, and migration in the past that have influenced the distribution by age at the uppermost ages. Multiple reverse projection uses this information from prior censuses to "close" the reverse-projected age distribution at the highest ages.

For Turkey, a series of crude birth rates from 1935 to 1975 was calculated from the 1975 census, a series from 1935 to 1970 from the 1970 census, and so on. Thus, eight independent estimates of the crude birth rate were made by reverse projection for the time period 1935-40, seven for 1940-45, and so on, creating multiple estimates for each five-year period. They vary among themselves for a given period to the extent that age misreporting has distorted the different age groups that are the basis of the single estimates. However, a shortage of persons in one age group due to age misstatement necessarily means an excess count of persons in another age group. When the age misreporting pattern is stable from one census to the next, the shortages and excesses occur in the same age groups in every census. Hence, birth rates for a given period that have been estimated from a series of censuses are based partly on overstated age groups and partly on understated age groups. Upward error due to age error in one census is matched by downward error in another census. Therefore, a strong estimate of the crude birth rate for a particular period is an arithmetic mean of the multiple estimates for the period.

Gains and losses in population due to migration in the past affect the number of survivors shown in the current age distribution. Therefore, migration must be included as one of the determining components of the reverse projection if migration is significant. During the 1960s and 1970s, worker migration to Europe became an important demographic influence in Turkey. Earlier there were smaller movements, principally as Turks in the Balkan countries relocated in Turkey. Estimates of migration were constructed independently from the reverse projection (as described in Appendix D), then introduced as component determinants of the reverse projection. The available distributions of migrants by age are only approximate, which causes distortions in the reverse-projected cohorts. These errors are similar to those of age misreporting and are mutually offsetting in the context of multiple reverse projection.

MRP Estimates of Crude Birth Rates

Multiple reverse projection was applied to the Turkish censuses first without any adjustment for age misreporting, and then with adjustment. The resulting estimates of the crude birth rate, shown in Table 2, were then averaged for each period of estimation. For every period of estimation from 1935 to 1975, the average estimates based on corrected and uncorrected age data are almost identical, except for the last, 1970-75. The reason for such excellent agreement is that the errors of estimation caused by age misreporting are offsetting errors. A valuable conclusion from this comparison is that the Turkish estimates of the crude birth rate do not depend upon the accuracy of adjustments for age misreporting. Indeed, robust estimates of the crude birth rate can be made without going through the prior step of correction for age misreporting.

The success of the method without adjustment being needed for age misreporting depends upon having more than one census from which to make estimates of the birth rate for a period. If data from only one census are used, the estimate of births for five years prior to that census typically lies below an estimate from multiple censuses (see Figure 6), because the 0-4 age group is understated by age misreporting. Single-census estimates of the

TABLE 2 National Crude Birth Rates, 1935-75, Estimated by Multiple Reverse Projection: Turkey

Period of Estimation	Census Year 1975	1970	1965	1960	1955	1950	1945	1940	Average of All Possible Censuses	Number of Reverse Projections
Part A. Estimates Based on Reported Age Distributions										
1935-40	46.5	45.1	44.2	44.5	45.4	46.2	50.0	44.7	45.8	8
1940-45	43.1	42.8	43.4	42.0	43.7	47.0	41.2	--	43.3	7
1945-50	45.0	44.3	44.9	48.5	49.4	43.9	--	--	46.0	6
1950-55	46.3	48.1	50.0	50.7	46.4	--	--	--	48.3	5
1955-60	47.9	48.5	49.2	42.4	--	--	--	--	47.0	4
1960-65	46.0	44.8	38.9	--	--	--	--	--	43.2	3
1965-70	40.0	37.6	--	--	--	--	--	--	38.8	2
1970-75	33.0	--	--	--	--	--	--	--	33.0	1
Part B. Estimates Based on Age Distributions Corrected for Age Misreporting										
1935-40	45.6	43.9	44.5	45.3	45.9	45.3	47.3	46.8	45.6	8
1940-45	41.9	43.0	44.2	42.1	42.6	44.6	43.0	--	43.1	7
1945-50	45.2	44.9	45.1	47.2	47.3	45.7	--	--	45.9	6
1950-55	46.9	48.1	48.7	49.0	48.4	--	--	--	48.2	5
1955-60	47.9	47.2	47.7	44.3	--	--	--	--	46.8	4
1960-65	44.7	43.4	40.7	--	--	--	--	--	42.9	3
1965-70	38.6	39.3	--	--	--	--	--	--	39.0	2
1970-75	34.5	--	--	--	--	--	--	--	34.5	1

Note: Rates are per thousand.

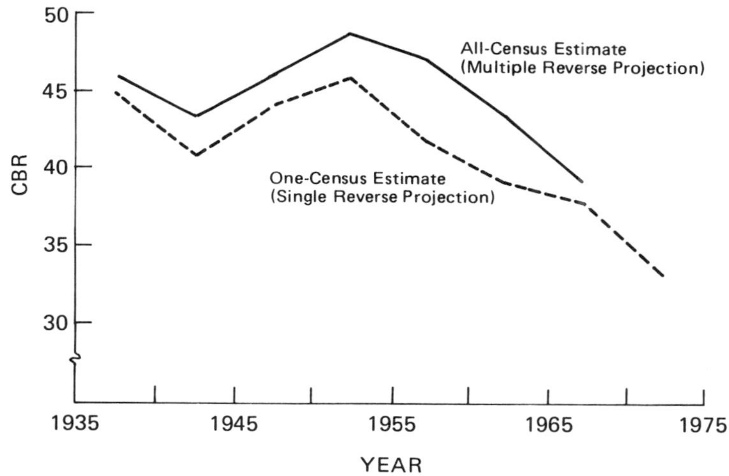

FIGURE 6 Estimates of Crude Birth Rate Based on Reported Age Distribution from One Census at End of Five-Year Period and Estimates Based on Distribution from all Available Censuses, 1935-75: Turkey

birth rate, therefore, are vulnerable and not acceptable. The extent of understatement by comparison with estimates from more than one census varies with age misstatement. Taking all multiple-census estimates (two or more), they average 5.9 percent higher than the single-census estimates, with a standard deviation of 3.5. If this degree of understatement is accepted as typical, an acceptable way to estimate the crude birth rate for 1970-75 is to raise the estimate based on one census of 33.0 per thousand by 5.9 percent to 34.9 per thousand. The result is then subject to a range of error of $\pm$ 1.2 per thousand population.

Other Estimates

Independent confirmation of the trend in crude birth rates can be sought in other estimates of the crude birth rate that are available for the periods 1955-60, 1966-67, and approximately 1970, each based on different types of data or methods. In the next section, total fertility rates are derived from the crude birth rate and also compared with independent estimates. This procedure provides further checking of the crude birth rate by confirming its implications.

The birth rate for 1955-60 was estimated by Demeny and Shorter (1968) using two different methods of indirect estimation:

Demeny-Shorter (1)

The first method calculated the natural intercensal rate of increase from the migration-adjusted census totals for 1955 and 1960. The death rate was then added to this to produce the birth rate. To determine the death rate, deaths above age 5 were calculated from model life tables; death rates from the table were multiplied by the mid-period census population in each age group. The model life table was selected using the intercensal forward-projection procedure (described in Chapter 3). Below age 5, the death rate was taken from a life table selected by the Brass child mortality method, using data from the 1963 national sample survey. (The Brass method is explained in Chapter 3.) There are two child mortality estimates (I and II) that describe the acceptable range. The crude birth rates for 1955-60 found by this approach were 46.6 (I) and 44.7 (II) per thousand.

Demeny-Shorter (2)

The second method used the reported population under age 10 from the 1960 census to make a single reverse projection. Since the errors in the two five-year age groups below age 10 proved to be offsetting (see Appendix C), the reported proportion of total population under age 10 is relatively accurate. For the reverse projection, the two child mortality estimates mentioned above (I and II) were used to obtain two alternative estimates. Alternative birth rates were calculated with the aid of tabulated stable populations (Coale and Demeny, 1966). A model life table was chosen on the basis of the $_2q_0$ value (proportion dying up to age 2); then the birth rate associated with a given proportion under age 10 was found from the tabulated stable population based on that model life table. This is an efficient and only trivially biased method for making reverse projections over short periods of time. Moreover, the method is not sensitive to the selection of a particular family of life tables so long as mortality is within the range of "normal" variation. Because Turkish mortality is strongly deviant (see Chapter 3), this characteristic imparts a slight downward bias to estimates of the birth rate derived by this method.

The common element of the two Demeny-Shorter methods is the estimate of mortality rates under age 5, which has two alternative values. The reliance on alternative child mortality rates (CMR) is noted below. As a result, two different measures of the crude birth rate (I and II) are produced for each indirect method of estimation. In other respects, methods (1) and (2) rely on different data and to that limited extent the estimates they produce are partially independent. The results for 1955-60 are crude birth rates as follows:

Method of Estimation	Estimate I (High CMR)	Estimate II (Low CMR)
1. Components of population change between two censuses	46.6	44.7
2. Reverse projection by tabulated models from a single census	46.3	44.5

A 1 percent sample of the 1975 census provides a basis for estimating the crude birth rate around 1970 using the second Demeny-Shorter method explained above (Özbay et al., 1977). The census included questions on number of children ever born and surviving; hence, an indirect estimate of child mortality could be calculated from the census itself, utilizing the Brass-Trussell method explained in Chapter 3. The proportion of the population under age 10 in the 1975 census was used for the single reverse projection. The resulting estimate of the crude birth rate is 35.8 per thousand. Since the mortality information on which this estimate is based refers to about 3.1 years before the census on average, and the information on survivors of births refers to a ten-year period prior to the census, there is an imperfect match of dates for the parameters. The birth rate estimate refers to a date circa 1970.

Turkish Demographic Survey Estimates

For 1966-67, the Turkish Demographic Survey (TDS) provides a preliminary estimate of 37.3 per thousand for the crude birth rate. The estimate is from a national household demographic survey conducted as part of a dual-record statistical system, in which births were found by both monthly visits and half-yearly surveys. When the dual-record methodology (see glossary) is applied, there is an upward adjustment for birth events missed by both systems; the final TDS estimate of the crude birth rate for 1966-67 is 39.6 thousand.

Estimates Based on National Fertility Surveys

The national surveys of the fertility of married women conducted in 1963, 1968, and 1973 do not provide a robust basis for the independent estimation of crude birth rates. The reasons are two: the sample size of the surveys is too small to allow the estimation of annual rates from only one year of events, and a number of design features place limits on how the data can be used.

Table 3 summarizes the CBR estimates derived from the various estimation procedures described above.

TABLE 3 Summary of National Crude Birth Rate Estimates, 1935-75: Turkey

	Period of Estimation							
Method of Estimation	1935-1940	1940-1945	1945-1950	1950-1955	1955-1960	1960-1965	1965-1970	1970-1975
Multiple Reverse Projection								
Reported age distribution	45.8	43.3	46.0	48.3	47.0	43.2	38.8	34.9[a]
Corrected for age misreporting	45.6	43.1	45.9	48.2	46.8	42.9	39.0	34.5
Demeny-Shorter (1)								
CMR I	--	--	--	--	46.6	--	--	--
CMR II	--	--	--	--	44.7	--	--	--
Demeny-Shorter (2)								
CMR I	--	--	--	--	46.3	--	--	--
CMR II	--	--	--	--	44.5	--	--	
1975 Census	--	--	--	--	--	--	--	35.8[b]
Turkish Demographic Survey	--	--	--	--	--	--	39.6[c]	

[a]Based on a single-census estimate that is adjusted as explained in the text.
[b]Circa 1970.
[c]1966-67.

NATIONAL TOTAL FERTILITY RATES, 1935-75

The trend of the crude birth rate (Table 3 and Figure 1) gives a less than complete description of the onset of fertility decline in Turkey. The age structure of the Turkish population was seriously scarred by excess infant and adult mortality during the Balkan wars and Turkey's own war of independence, which ended in 1922. Female birth cohorts affected by these events were passing through their childbearing years as late as the 1960s. These true irregularities of age and sex composition have themselves affected crude birth rates separately from the general trend of declining childbearing rates. It is useful, therefore, to evaluate the trend of fertility from the standpoint of the total fertility rate.

The total fertility rate describes the average total number of children born to a woman according to the current age-specific fertility rates (see glossary). Since the number of births in any year depends upon the number of women in each childbearing age group as well as on the age-specific fertility rates, there are two factors underlying the crude birth rate. The total fertility rate isolates and measures only the fertility component, leaving aside the effect of changes in age and sex distribution.

The following substitution procedure is used to calculate the total fertility rate (T) that implies the same number of births (B) as the crude birth rate:

$$T = 5 \cdot \sum_{i=1}^{7} \left[\frac{B}{B^*} \cdot F_i^* \right] \text{ where } B^* = 5 \cdot \sum_{i=1}^{7} \left[F_i^* \cdot \overline{W} \right]$$

W refers to the proportion of women in an age group i in the total population (both sexes), and F_i^* refers to a standard fertility distribution by age for the population in question. The age pattern, but not the level, of this fertility schedule determines T.

Standard Fertility Schedules

Any reasonable choice of fertility schedule provides a satisfactory basis for deriving the total fertility rates from crude birth rates. For Turkey, data are available to make this choice with some precision. A standard distribution of age-specific fertility is constructed from data on age-specific marital fertility and proportions married by age. Marital fertility schedules are available from national sample surveys (Table 4), and marriage proportions are available from the censuses (Table 5).

The marital fertility schedule for Turkey (shown in Figure 7) has a shape that characterizes populations practicing fertility control by contraception. When compared with a natural fertility schedule (one with no deliberate control), there is a noticeable clockwise rotation. This difference is due to birth limitation during the older ages of marriage. The rising trend of contraceptive control in Turkey is also confirmed by independent data on the prevalence of contraceptive use

TABLE 4 Percentage National Distribution by Age of Marital Fertility, 1963-73, Compared with a Schedule of Natural Fertility: Turkey

Age Group	Natural Fertility	National Sample Surveys 1963	1966-67	1968	1973
15-19	18.4	20.8	20.0	19.0	21.5
20-24	21.0	24.7	24.7	23.5	25.8
25-29	19.8	20.6	21.0	20.7	21.6
30-34	17.8	16.5	16.5	16.6	15.8
35-39	14.4	11.8	11.9	13.1	10.9
40-44	7.5	4.6	5.0	6.2	3.6
45-49	1.1	0.9	1.0	1.0	0.7
Total	100.0	100.0	100.0	100.0	100.0

Sources:

1963: Ministry of Health survey. Marital fertility is available from reports of births during the last year by mothers aged 15-44. Original data are extended by extrapolation to the 45-49 age group. An age adjustment is made to match age with births occurring an average of 6 months before the survey.

1966-67: Turkish Demographic Survey. Births are available by age of mother at time of birth. The numbers of married women are available for five-year age groups only up to age 24 and for ten-year age groups thereafter. Marital status information from the censuses of 1965 and 1970 was used to split the ten-year age groups. The fertility rate for ages 45-49 was extrapolated.

1968: Hacettepe survey; same type of data as in 1963.

1973: Hacettepe survey; same type of data as in 1963 and 1968. A direct estimate is available for the age group 45-49.

Natural Fertility Schedule: This is a standard schedule from Coale, Hill, and Trussell (1975).

TABLE 5 National Proportions of Females Married by Age, from 1935-75 Censuses: Turkey

Age Group	Census 1935	1940	1945	1950	1955	1960	1965	1970	1975[a]
15-19	.232	(.245)	.258	.313	.396	.333	.273	.247	.213
20-24	.802	(.796)	.790	.822	.848	.839	.827	.794	.749
25-29	.910	(.910)	.910	(.912)	.913	.941	.940	.931	.915
30-34	.911	(.914)	.916	(.915)	.914	.946	.954	.953	.942
35-39	.877	(.886)	.895	(.904)	.912	.933	.940	.948	.940
40-44	.768	(.799)	.830	(.851)	.872	.893	.904	.918	.913
45-49	.653	(.706)	.758	(.790)	.822	.855	.860	.879	.878

Note: Parentheses indicate that data are not available. Estimated values were inserted by linear interpolation between adjacent pairs of censuses.

[a]Based on a 1 percent sample of census data.

(Table 6). Studies of trends in the types of contraceptives that are used show, in addition, that progressively more effective methods are being used (Fisek, 1978).

It could be assumed that the marital fertility pattern in Turkey in the 1930s was not much different from a natural fertility pattern, and that it changed primarily after the post-war period (from 1945-50 onward), moving linearly to the 1963 and 1973 schedules. If these assumptions are accepted, Turkey would be described as having a changing pattern of marital fertility that follows the clockwise rotation noted above.

Total Fertility Rates

The multiple-reverse projections play a role in estimating total fertility rates (TFR) by providing estimates of the W values in Equation 1 (proportions of women in the populaton belonging to each age group), and by giving the numbers of births, B. A changing marital fertility pattern was assumed for the schedules of F_i^*, with results as follows:

Period	TFR
1935-40	6.66
1940-45	6.55
1945-50	6.85
1950-55	6.54
1055-60	6.54
1960-65	6.10
1965-70	5.63
1970-75	5.05

Alternatively, a single marital fertility standard, based on the 1963 pattern, could be assumed. The results of the two alternatives are shown in Figure 8. The assumption of a changing pattern is accepted as the most reasonable basis for calculating trends in the total fertility rate, but the range of possible overstatement of the total fertility level for the earlier years is

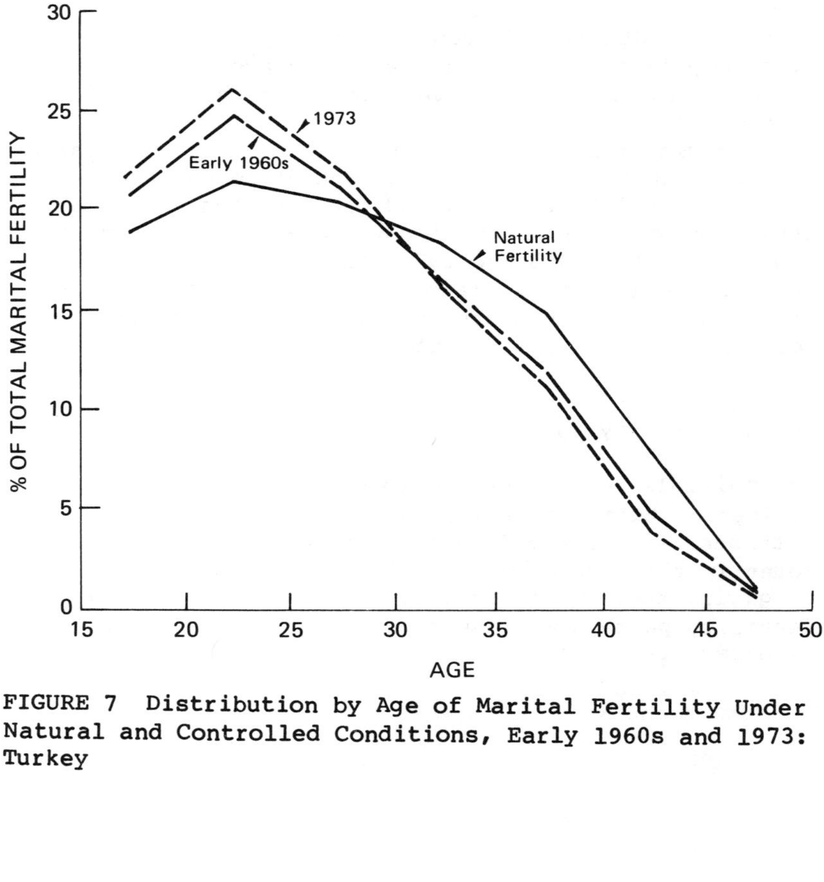

FIGURE 7 Distribution by Age of Marital Fertility Under Natural and Controlled Conditions, Early 1960s and 1973: Turkey

TABLE 6 National Proportions of Married Women Currently Using Some Method of Contraception by Age Group, Derived from National Sample Surveys in 1963, 1968, and 1973: Turkey

Part A. Number of Married Women Currently Using Some Method of Contraception (per thousand)

Birth Cohorts	Age at Interview <20	20-24	25-29	30-34	35-39	40-44
1919-23	--	--	--	--	--	175[a]
1924-28	--	--	--	--	241	320[b]
1929-33	--	--	--	279	369	314[c]
1934-38	--	--	259	416	442	--
1939-43	--	153	303	458	--	--
1944-48	89	247	435	--	--	--
1949-53	160	281	--	--	--	--
1954-58	160	--	--	--	--	--

Part B. Number of Respondents by Age Group

Sample Survey	Age Group <20	20-24	25-29	30-35	35-39	40-44
1963	143	435	577	598	452	350
1968	294	639	658	616	659	414
1973	342	819	774	709	839	649

[a]Diagonal shows estimates from 1963 survey.
[b]Diagonal shows estimates from 1968 survey.
[c]Diagonal shows estimates from 1973 survey.

Source: Özbay and Shorter (1970); Özbay (1979).

indicated by noting that use of the "early 1960s" pattern as a fixed standard would give somewhat lower estimates of the total fertility rate.

The point which is in doubt is the extent of deliberate fertility control in the 1930s. Differentials in marital fertility existed at that time between rural and urban, and between eastern and western Turkey. The size of the differentials apparently was substantial (Taeuber, 1958), but the proportionate weight of the lower fertility groups in the total population presumably was small, because the level of national fertility was high at that time. Since natural fertility itself can vary as to

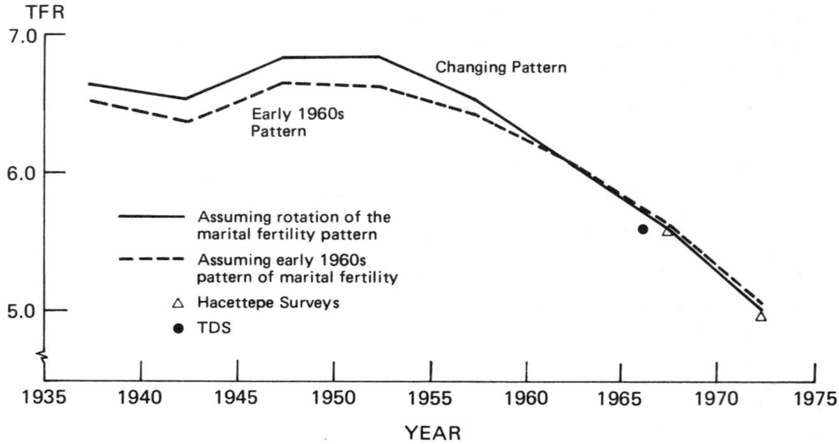

FIGURE 8 Estimates of Total Fertility Rate, 1935-75: Turkey

level, this could have been a contributory factor to the differentials of marital fertility in the 1930s, but the complete story remains obscure.

Other Estimates

The trend of total fertility rates may be checked for the more recent years by examining the results of fertility surveys that include information on both marital fertility and proportions married by age. The Hacettepe national surveys of 1968 and 1973 are of this type. The principal risk with this type of single-round survey data is a problem known as "reference-period error." When women (or other persons on their behalf) are asked to report births during the year preceding a survey, they easily become confused about the period being referred to or simply may not know whether recent births occurred exactly within the last year. When this happens, there is usually an accumulation of error which implies shortening or lengthening of the reference period, rather than offsetting errors.

The count of births in the 1973 survey illustrates how different results may emerge, the most probable cause of the differences being reference-period error. The 1973 survey contained two questions on the number of births in the last year. The first was included on the household questionnaire and was asked of the women, if they were available, but otherwise of an adult respondent, usually the head of household. The second was asked on a questionnaire administered only to the married women themselves. The second questionnaire collected a complete pregnancy history and great care was taken to date events as accurately as possible within the limitations of the respondents' knowledge and understanding. The first procedure yielded a total fertility rate of 4.66 children (Toros, 1978); the second, based on tables from the same survey, a rate of 5.00 children. Presumably the second is more nearly accurate than the first; however reference-period error remains as a distinct possibility.

Total fertility rates for the year preceding each of the Hacettepe surveys, which are subject to reservations about reference-period error, may be used as point-in-time estimates. These rates are also plotted in Figure 8 to be compared with the trend derived from crude birth rates.

Another estimate shown in Figure 8 comes from the Turkish Demographic Survey's dual-record system, which is less subject to reference-period error because of repeated interviewing of the same persons. Reported births, when raised by the standard dual-record adjustment for omissions, give a total fertility rate of 5.62 for 1966-67.

Finally, a preliminary TFR estimate for 1977-78 is given by the first report of the Haceteppe survey of 1978 (Hacettepe Institute of Population Studies, 1980), which was released after the Panel had completed its work. Based on births reported in the pregnancy histories, the estimated TFR is 4.3 children. Although this estimate is not shown in the figure, an extrapolation of the solid curve in that figure would give an estimate for 1977-78 that is very close to the survey estimate. However, no firm judgment can be reached about the level of fertility in 1977-78 because the types of data available so far are inadequate for that purpose.

Since total fertility rates derived from the trend of crude birth rates stand up well when compared with survey-based estimates, both the crude birth rates and derived total fertility rates may be considered as broadly confirmed for the decade from roughly 1965 to 1975.

NATIONAL TRENDS IN MARITAL FERTILITY, 1935-75

It can be assumed that virtually all births in Turkey are legitimate. That being so, all Turkish fertility is fertility within marriage, for which an appropriate measure of trends would be an index of marital fertility. The changing shape (age distribution) of marital fertility has been discussed in the preceding section. In addition, it is useful to measure the level of marital fertility and its trend.

Index of Marital Fertility

A suitable index of marital fertility is total marital fertility (TMF), defined as $\sum \underline{g}(\underline{a})$, where $\underline{g}(\underline{a})$ is the age-specific marital fertility rate for the ages, $\underline{a}$, of reproduction. TMF measures the average number of births women would have if they lived in a continuously married state from age 15 through 49. Since few women are married so early for an uninterrupted 35 years, total marital fertility is not actually achieved by the average woman. Nevertheless, it shows the level of fertility taking place within marriage. The index changes as the interplay of natural controls (e.g., breastfeeding) and voluntary controls (e.g., contraception) affect marital fertility.

The index is estimated below, but first it is necessary to estimate an index for marriage, which provides a convenient intermediate factor for the computation and is of interest in itself.

Index of Proportions Married

The difference between total marital fertility (TMF) and the total fertility rate (TFR), which is necessarily lower, is due to women spending part of their reproductive years unmarried. The greater the extent of non-marriage during these years, weighted by potential childbearing, the greater the difference between TMF and TFR. An index of proportions married, C_m, captures this factor (Bongaarts, 1978):

$$C_m = \frac{\sum m(a)g(a)}{\sum g(a)}$$

where m(a) is the schedule of proportions married by age a and the other terms are as above. When all women are married at all ages from 15 through 49, the value of the index is one; when none are married, it is zero. Since the schedule for marital fertility, g(a), is simply a weighting device, standard schedules of marital fertility are suitable. A changing age-pattern of marital fertility based on the rotation assumption (see above) was used to calculate the index, together with the information on proportions married given in Table 5.

Relationships Among the Indexes

So long as there are no births outside marriage, the marriage index is a direct link between TMF and TFR, that is: TFR = C_m (TMF). This relationship allows TMF to be estimated when the other two variables are already known, as in the present instance. The results for all three indexes are presented in Table 7. (See also Figure 12).

Factoring the total fertility rate into its two components, marriage and marital fertility, shows how the decline of total fertility came about. Although exact dating of turning points is impossible with the data at hand, the decline in marital fertility appears to have begun around 1950. Proportions married, however, were rising at that time and continued to rise for perhaps a half or full decade. By around 1960, though, the marriage index also began to decline. Because of later

TABLE 7 National Fertility Indexes, 1935-75: Turkey

Period	Total Fertility Rate (TFR)	Index of Marriage (C_m)	Total Marital Fertility (TMF)
1935-40	6.66	.747	8.92
1940-45	6.55	.753	8.70
1945-50	6.85	.766	8.94
1950-55	6.85	.784	8.74
1955-60	6.54	.793	8.25
1960-65	6.10	.782	7.81
1965-70	5.63	.764	7.37
1970-75	5.05	.740	6.82

timing in the marriage turnabout, the decline of total fertility did not get securely under way until about the mid-1950s.

The table below shows the approximate relative contribution of the two factors to the decline of total fertility.

	TFR	C_m	TMF
1950-55	6.85	.784	8.74
1970-75	5.05	.740	6.82
Annual percentage rate of decline	1.52	0.29	1.24
Relative contribution to the decline in TFR	100%	19%	81%

The stronger contribution of changes in marital fertility, accounting for 81 percent of the decline in total fertility, suggests that voluntary control of fertility within marriage has been more important than the reduction in the prevalence of a married state during the reproductive ages. Nevertheless, the marital status of the female population remains an important factor. It accounted for 19 percent of the decline up to 1970-75, and the currently high marriage proportions make it a potential factor for future change.

Marriage Trends

Sustained fertility decline is typically the outcome of changes in demographic behavior that occur earlier in time. This is true of the impact of marital status on fertility in Turkey. Whenever the age of first marriage changes, some years pass before the change in number of newly married women moves through the initial ages of childbearing and has its full impact. In Turkey, the time lag is not much more than the period to the next census (five years), because almost all Turkish women have married by their mid-20s in any event.

The mean age of first marriage for different cohorts, shown in Table 8, was calculated by the Hajnal method

TABLE 8 National Number of Women Ever Married, per 1,000 Women by Cohorts, and Mean Age of First Marriage (SMAM), 1930-35 to 1970-75: Turkey

Age Group	Cohorts Identified by Period When Age 15 Attained								
	1930-1935	1935-1940	1940-1945	1945-1950	1950-1955	1955-1960	1960-1965	1965-1970	1970-1975
15-19	237	a	265	318	403	339	277	251	216
20-24	a	812	836	862	851	838	804	738	--
25-29	941	945[b]	933	958	956	946	932	--	--
30-34	969[b]	951	976	978	976	966	--	--	--
35-39	973	980	982	984	979	--	--	--	--
40-44	985	984	985	979	--	--	--	--	--
45-49	984	985	983	--	--	--	--	--	--
SMAM	20.0	19.9	19.6	19.1	18.8	19.2	19.8	20.2	20.8[c]

Note: In instances in which data were not available for the cohort's entire history, SMAM was calculated by fitting a standard marriage schedule (Coale, 1971) to the available data.

[a]The 1940 census does not provide information on marital status.
[b]Data for a ten-year age group in the 1950 census were split.
[c]The SMAM for the 1970-75 cohort is a preliminary estimate based on the assumption that the past association between SMAM and the proportion of ever married among women aged 15-19 (as expressed by a fitted curve) continues to prevail.

(see Hajnal, 1953, and singulate mean age of marriage in glossary). Cohorts of women are identified by the periods during which they pass the age of 15. Thus, women aged 15-19 in a census all entered marriageable ages during the preceding five-year period.

The use of five-year age groups and the effect of age misreporting in the census (Yener, 1969) biases the estimates of SMAM upward; however, the error would be at most half a year. Because the error is a systematic one due to stable features of the underlying data, these SMAM estimates can be used as a satisfactory indicator of trends. Data from surveys of married women that ask the age at which the women were first married were not used to estimate average age of first marriage. Recall error is present in data of this type, and there is a selection factor (only women already married are interviewed) that seriously biases the estimate downward. Neither of these forms of error exists in the census-type data to which the Hajnal method was applied.

Figure 9 illustrates the lagged effect on proportions married of new cohorts coming along with higher or lower mean ages of first marriage. The inverse relationship holds for both downward and upward movements of the SMAM. It can safely be predicted, therefore, that the continuing increase in the SMAM for the cohort entering marriageable ages in 1970-75 will cause a further decrease in the index of marriage in 1975-80.

One consistent upward pressure on the marriage index during the entire period from 1935 to 1975 was a decline in widowhood. This force is now largely spent, because widowhood within the main reproductive years has fallen to near negligible levels. In 1935, 39 percent of women at the end of the reproductive period (age 50) had been widowed without remarrying; in 1975, this proportion was down to 12 percent. The main cause of this change has been the rising expectation of life of husbands.

A good way to measure the effect of changing widowhood on the index of proportions married, C_m, is to calculate an analagous index for widowhood, C_w by substituting values of $w(a)$ for $m(a)$ in the definition of C_m, where w is the proportion widowed. These calculations yield the following results:

Index	1935-40	1955-60	1970-75
C_m (proportions married)	.747	.793	.740
C_w (proportions widowed)	.047	.020	.012

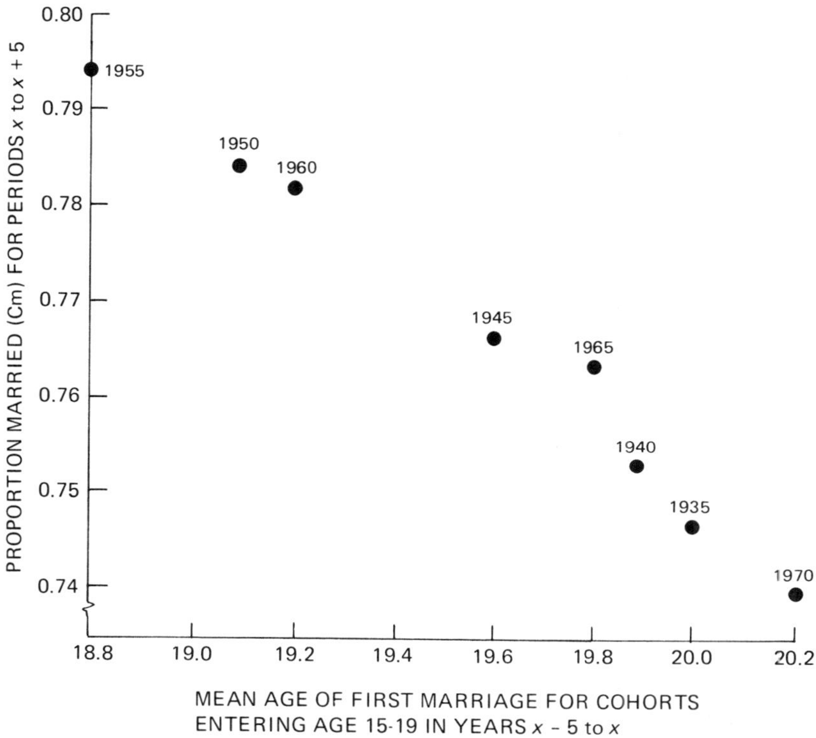

FIGURE 9 National Mean Age of First Marriage for Cohorts and Current Index of Proportion Married (C_m), 1935-75: Turkey

Note: For each point, the date x is shown. As an example, the point labeled 1955 plots the value of C_m for 1955-60 against the value of SMAM for the cohort entering marriageable ages 1950-1955.

When the index of proportions married was rising from 1935-40 to 1955-60, the main factor responsible was declining widowhood (which accounts for more than half the change), not a declining age of marriage although marriage was occuring earlier. During this period, irregularities of the age and sex structure were working themselves out, and economic conditions in agriculture improved, leading to earlier marriage. Nevertheless, the most important indirect influence on fertility was the reduction of death rates, because it reduced widowhood among women.

FERTILITY BY DIVISIONS OF THE POPULATION, 1945-68

The history of the fertility plateau and the subsequent decline of fertility in Turkey can be enriched by examining trends in subdivisions of the population. Data for this purpose are not as abundant nor as tractable by robust methods of estimation as the national data, so the same degree of precision cannot be claimed for divisional as for national estimates. Nevertheless, the broad outlines that can be documented are sufficiently unusual when compared with the demographic history of other countries to constitute a valuable addition to information about Turkey.

Divisions of the Population

The classic method of defining subpopulations in censuses is by the administrative divisions of the country. While subdivisions along socioeconomic dimensions would probably be more illuminating for the analysis of fertility differentials and changes, census and survey reports typically do not exploit this potential. However, a modest socioeconomic dimension can be introduced by making an urban-rural distinction. The number of divisions that can be defined is limited by the sample size of the surveys that are used at certain points in the estimation process. The six divisions finally demarcated, three urban and three rural, are shown in Figure 10.

The cities of Istanbul and Izmir were combined in a single division in order to create a sample size large enough for estimating the mortality parameters that are used for indirect estimation. Studies of fertility at the level of individual cities, conducted in 1966-67 by the Turkish Demographic Surveys, show that Ankara had substantially higher fertility than either Istanbul or Izmir, which were similar to each other (Turkey, School of Public Health, 1970). Because the robustness of divisional estimates is increased by aggregation, considerable use is made below of a three-division urban-rural grouping in which the rank order is (1) Istanbul and Izmir cities, (2) other urban (populations of 10,000 and over), and (3) rural (populations under 10,000).

For the divisional estimates of fertility, census information at a provincial rural-urban level was

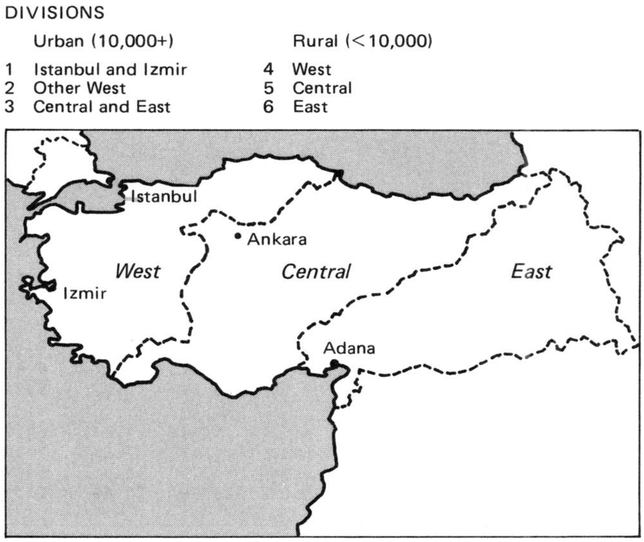

FIGURE 10 Urban-Rural and Regional Divisions of Turkey

aggregated into six divisions (combined for some purposes into three divisions) for the six censuses from 1945 to 1970. Table 9 presents a summary of population size and growth by divisions, which is based on these aggregations. The results of the aggregations are given in full detail in Appendix E (Table E-1). The other key element in the procedure for indirect estimation of fertility is information on infant and early childhood mortality by divisions, which is drawn from estimates described in Chapter 3.

Estimating Crude Birth Rates

The crude birth rate has been estimated using a method that depends upon an age distribution from a single census and child mortality for the period immediately preceding the census (U.N., 1967). The first step in the method is to choose a model life table on the basis of the child mortality information. Tabulated stable populations based on the selected life table are then used to look up the birth rate associated with a population proportion under age 10. This is an efficient

TABLE 9 Population Size and Growth by Six Divisions, 1945-70: Turkey

Population Unit	Census 1945	1950	1955	1960	1965	1970
Part A. Population Size (in millions)						
National	18.8	20.9	24.1	27.8	31.4	35.6
Urban						
Istanbul-Izmir	1.06	1.21	1.57	1.83	2.15	2.77
Other West	.93	1.08	1.45	2.16	2.78	3.74
Central and East	1.45	1.61	2.37	3.28	4.41	6.21
Subtotal	3.44	3.90	5.39	7.27	9.34	12.72
Rural						
West	6.22	6.68	7.24	7.76	8.17	8.28
Central	5.47	6.12	6.67	7.39	7.99	8.26
East	3.66	4.25	4.77	5.34	5.89	6.33
Subtotal	15.35	17.05	18.68	20.49	22.05	22.87
Part B. Percentage of Total Population						
Urban						
Istanbul-Izmir	5.6	5.8	6.5	6.6	6.9	7.8
Other West	5.0	5.1	6.0	7.8	8.9	10.5
Central and East	7.7	7.7	9.9	11.8	14.0	17.4
Subtotal	18.3	18.6	22.4	26.2	29.8	35.7
Rural						
West	33.1	31.9	30.1	28.0	26.0	23.3
Central	29.1	29.2	27.7	26.6	25.5	23.2
East	19.5	20.3	19.8	19.2	18.8	17.8
Subtotal	81.7	81.4	77.6	73.8	70.2	64.3
Total	100.0	100.0	100.0	100.0	100.0	100.0

and only trivially biased method for making reverse projections over a short period of time. Turkish mortality has a strongly deviant age pattern (see Chapter 3) which imparts a slight downward bias to the birth rate estimated by this method.

The proportion of the population under age 10 is used, rather than some other index of the age distribution, because age misreporting under age 10 causes over- and understatements at different ages, which are largely offsetting. Using age 5 as the upper limit would give proportions that were too low. Data on porportions under age 10 are taken from Appendix E, Table E-1. Infant mortality estimates for approximately three years before each census are the estimates made below in the chapter on mortality (see Table 20 for rural and 23 for urban). A small amount of extrapolation of the mortality series before 1945 and after 1967 was necessary to provide appropriately dated mortality assumptions for the earliest and latest censuses (1945 and 1970, respectively).

The crude birth rate was then estimated for periods centered at five-year intervals, approximately 1943, 1948, . . . 1968. To emphasize that these are estimates of the birth rate for a period of time before the census date, which cannot be dated precisely, and to avoid having to make any assumptions about the special circumstances of the 1940-45 World War period, the initial series of estimates of the birth rate were treated as preliminary. Pairs of estimates for successive periods were then averaged. For example, the estimates for about 1940-45 (centered on 1943) and for 1945-50 (centered on 1948) were averaged to obtain an estimate corresponding approximately with the census of 1945, which is exact year 1945.8. Thus, a series of crude birth rates by divisions was produced for the census years 1945, 1950, . . . 1965, followed by an estimate for 1968 that is dependent on the single census of 1970.

Table 10 presents, as an example, the computations for Istanbul and Izmir. A summary of the results for all divisions is shown in Table 11, together with a population-weighted mean for the nation. The national means are not expected to agree exactly with crude birth rates estimated earlier by multiple reverse projection (Table 2), because a different procedure is involved.

A possible source of error in making the divisional estimates of births is the effect of migration on the divisional age structures. The critical index of age structure used for indirect estimation is the proportion under age 10, denoted as C(10). If the proportions migrating above and below age 10 are similar, the amount of error is limited. Although migration is age-selective in favor of young adults in the working ages, it also includes children under age 10 as part of family migration, which tends to limit changes in the index C(10) due to migration. A study of the net balance of urbanward migration in Turkey shows that 30 percent of the total population of migrants from 1955 to 1965 was under age 10 (Tekce, 1974). This is somewhat below the C(10) value for the rural population (32 percent), and above that for the urban population (24 percent).

TABLE 10 Estimation of Crude Birth Rate for Istanbul and Izmir, 1945-68: Turkey

Census Information[a]			Infant Mortality		Preliminary CBR	Final CBR	
Exact Date of Census[b]	C(10) Female	C(10) Male	Exact Date of Estimate[b]	$_1q_0$ (Both Sexes)	(Per 1000)	Date of Estimate	(Per 1000)
1945.8	.1464	.1363	1943.0[c]	.166	17.42	1945	18.7
1950.8	.1657	.1576	1948.0	.152	19.92	1950	21.0
1955.8	.1896	.1698	1953.0	.138	22.14	1955	22.5
1960.8	.1977	.1772	1958.0	.123	22.79	1960	22.9
1965.8	.2005	.1837	1963.0	.110	23.06	1965	22.8
1970.8	.2014	.1824	1968.0[c]	.096	22.62	1968	22.6[d]

[a]From Appendix E, Table E-1.
[b]Decimals indicate the exact date of the census or estimate to the nearest one-tenth year. For example, the 1965 and 1970 censuses in Turkey were conducted on 24 October and 25 October, respectively. The dates 1943.0, 1948.0, etc. refer to the beginning of each indicated year.
[c]Extrapolated from nearest date.
[d]For all dates except 1968, estimates are based on information from two censuses. The estimate for 1968 depends on the census of 1970 only.

Migration has little effect on estimates of the crude birth rate for the rural population, because the amount of migration is small relative to the total base population. However, migration does produce some upward bias in estimates of the urban crude birth rate.

Another possible source of error is variations in age misreporting from census to census which could upset the choice of C(10) as a good measure of population structure. Because of these sources of error, one must be wary in drawing conclusions beyond noting the main differentials and trends.

TABLE 11 Estimated Crude Birth Rates by Six Divisions, 1945-68: (per thousand population): Turkey

Approximate Date of Estimate	Urban: Istanbul and Izmir	Urban: Other West	Urban: Central and East	Rural: West	Rural: Central	Rural: East	National[a]
1945	18.7	26.0	32.8	39.2	56.5	56.0	45.2
1950	21.0	28.5	35.0	40.6	55.5	57.4	46.2
1955	22.5	29.8	36.8	42.2	55.0	59.8	46.7
1960	22.9	29.7	37.5	41.0	51.4	58.2	44.6
1965	22.8	28.9	37.0	38.5	48.9	56.2	42.3
1968	22.6	28.7	36.4	37.1	47.8	55.3	40.7

[a]Population-weighted mean of the separate divisional estimates.

The Turkish Demographic Survey provides some independent estimates of urban and rural birth rates for 1966-67. When the TDS estimates for Istanbul and Izmir in that year are combined, they give an estimated CBR of 24.3 births per thousand (Turkey, School of Public Health, 1970). This is slightly higher than the estimate of 22.7 per thousand for approximately the same date, interpolated from Table 11. The TDS estimate of the rural birth rate is 43.9 per thousand for a slightly different definition of rural, lower than the combined rural estimate of 46.5 interpolated for the same date from Table 11. Thus, the spread of birth rates between the divisions of the country is somewhat larger when estimated by the procedures used here than by those of the Turkish Demographic Survey. These differences, while not very great, underline the importance of accepting only the broad outlines of results rather than their specific details, especially where errors of this magnitude could upset conclusions.

Various Fertility and Marriage Indexes

Once crude birth rates are known by divisions, the same procedures used to derive the various national fertility and marriage indexes may be applied to divisional data. The principal additional data requirements for these calculations are proportions of women married by age and standard distributions for marital fertility, both shown in Table 12. The marital fertility schedules in Figure 11 show the characteristic differences between a rural population using relatively little fertility control and urban populations exercising greater control.

The additional measures of fertility and marriage shown in Figure 12 and Table 13 reveal that urban-rural differentials have persisted in Turkey for some time, probably going further back in history than can be measured with available data. There appears to have been some narrowing over the period covered here, due to both a slight rise in urban fertility and a decline in rural fertility. This rise in urban fertility since 1945 is a genuine finding; it is not a statistical artifact connected with the definitions of rural and urban. During this period the urban population's age of first marriage and the prevalence of widowhood fell. In addition, strong streams of migration to the cities of more people with rural origins probably tended to raise the average level of urban fertility (see Table 14).

TABLE 12 Proportions Married Females by Divisions of the Population, 1945-68 and Standard Marital Fertility Schedule: Turkey

Age Group	Proportions Married						Marital Fertility[c] (percent)
	1940[a]	1950[a]	1955	1960	1965	1968[b]	
Istanbul and Izmir							
15-19	.143	.186	.232	.201	.192	.201	17.1
20-24	.503	.570	.647	.661	.653	.660	30.5
25-29	.680	.740	.785	.819	.843	.840	25.4
30-34	.778	.794	.830	.857	.881	.892	15.8
35-39	.780	.803	.814	.850	.869	.879	8.4
40-44	.733	.779	.797	.816	.834	.848	2.2
45-49	.662	.642	.730	.771	.775	.780	.5
Other Urban							
15-19	.199	.241	.305	.276	.238	.232	21.6
20-24	.728	.757	.781	.791	.776	.763	29.3
25-29	.884	.886	.887	.910	.916	.913	22.1
30-34	.913	.914	.915	.928	.939	.940	12.8
35-39	.886	.895	.903	.918	.926	.932	9.6
40-44	.820	.840	.861	.876	.891	.897	3.9
45-49	.738	.769	.800	.829	.837	.846	.7
Rural							
15-19	.277	.336	.425	.360	.294	.279	19.6
20-24	.816	.849	.876	.867	.864	.848	23.6
25-29	.926	.928	.929	.959	.958	.953	20.4
30-34	.920	.921	.922	.959	.966	.964	17.7
35-39	.906	.916	.924	.947	.953	.954	13.2
40-44	.839	.860	.881	.904	.917	.922	4.6
45-49	.773	.805	.838	.873	.879	.886	1.0

[a]With the exception of Istanbul and Izmir, for which separate census data are available, estimates for 1945 and 1950 are based on the assumption that proportions married changed in each age group in each division from 1945 to 1955 in the same proportions as they changed in the national population.
[b]Based on interpolation between 1965 and 1970.
[c]From 1963 National Population Survey.

A by-product of the fertility estimates by divisions of the population is information on the number of annual births. In 1945, 90 percent of births in Turkey were rural; by 1968, the proportion was 75 percent. The quantity of rural births is no longer increasing and will almost certainly decline, while that of urban births is on the increase. Further increases in urban births are firmly indicated by the underlying demographic structure and trends.

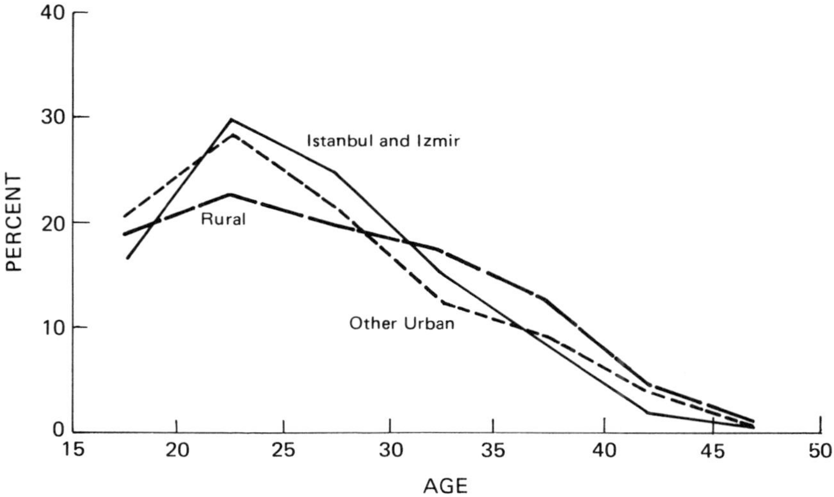

FIGURE 11 Distribution of Marital Fertility by Age, from 1963 National Population Survey: Turkey

Fertility by Province

A striking characteristic of social and economic data for Turkey is the large size of the differentials by province. There are 67 administrative provinces, and a great deal of information is compiled on this basis. The spatial distribution of characteristics blurs the possibly more important rural-urban differences but is nevertheless valuable when used in conjunction with other data.

By utilizing special tabulations of the 1965 census, it is possible to estimate fertility by province for a reference date around 1960. Information on place of birth for the population under age 10 was used to assemble the data by province of birth, thus controlling for the effect of migration on indirect estimates of births. The crude birth rate can then be estimated by province according to the following equation:

$$\text{CBR} = \frac{\text{Yearly Births}}{\text{Mid-period Population}} = \frac{P(0\text{-}9)/{}_{10}L_0}{P(\text{Tot})}$$

where P(0-9) refers to the population under age 10 born in the province and surviving at the time of the 1965

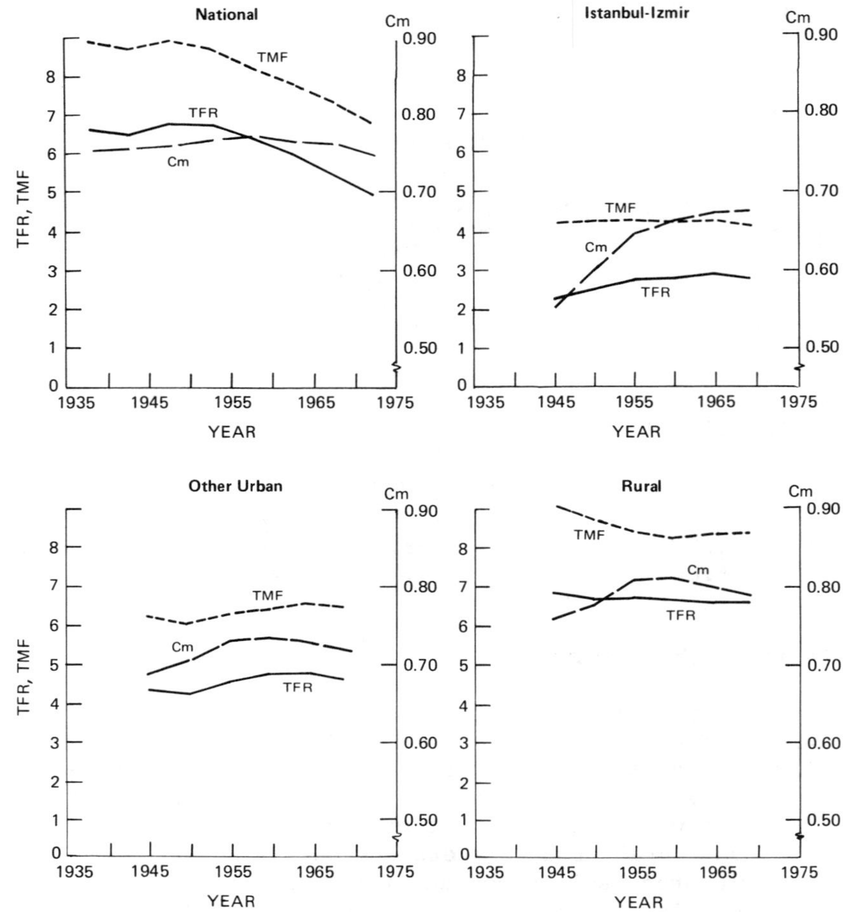

FIGURE 12 Fertility Measures and Marriage Indexes, 1935-75: Turkey

census enumeration. This population of survivors is divided by the person-years lived in a suitable life-table between birth and age 10 using a radix of 1.0. The resulting numerator is an estimate of average annual births for the province over the preceding 10 years. The denominator is the total population enumerated in the province five years earlier, in 1960.

Total fertility rates can also be calculated by choosing standard age-specific fertility distributions

TABLE 13 Fertility and Marriage Indexes by Divisions, 1945-68: Turkey

	Fertility and Mortality Indexes					First Marriage Indexes	
Date	CBR	Births (000s)	TFR	C_m	TMF	Proportion Single (15-19)	SMAM[a]
Istanbul-Izmir							
1945	18.7	20	2.41	.558	4.32	.851	22.4
1950	21.0	25	2.65	.607	4.37	.808	21.5
1955	22.5	35	2.91	.657	4.43	.761	20.8
1960	22.9	42	2.96	.673	4.40	.792	21.1
1965	22.8	49	3.04	.681	4.46	.804	21.0
1968	22.6	55	2.99	.686	4.36	.785	21.1
Other Urban							
1945	30.1	72	4.36	.691	6.31	.796	20.6
1950	32.4	87	4.31	.711	6.06	.754	20.1
1955	34.2	131	4.60	.734	6.27	.690	19.6
1960	34.4	187	4.72	.759	6.39	.719	19.9
1965	33.9	243	4.78	.731	6.54	.759	20.2
1968	33.5	281	4.70	.726	6.47	.772	20.5
Rural							
1945	49.4	758	6.99	.765	9.14	.718	19.5
1950	50.1	855	6.84	.787	8.69	.659	18.9
1955	51.3	957	6.86	.814	8.43	.568	18.5
1960	49.2	1009	6.82	.816	8.36	.635	18.9
1965	47.0	1036	6.78	.805	8.42	.703	19.5
1968	45.9	1028	6.73	.797	8.44	.736	19.8

[a]SMAM refers to the cohort passing age 15 during the five years preceding the date shown. Estimates of SMAM have an upward bias of up to one-half year (see text for further discussion).

based on TDS data and following the procedures described above for estimating divisional and national total fertility. The results are shown in Figure 13.

For the production of these estimates mortality assumptions in terms of ${}_{10}L_0$ from the Turkish Demographic Survey for 1966-67 were accepted. They refer to five regions and separately to Istanbul, Izmir, and Ankara cities. They were scaled so that the computed national birth rate would equal an estimate of the 1960 national birth rate of 45 births per thousand population. These mortality assumptions by TDS regions do not capture the finer detail of province-by-province differences in child mortality. The sensitivity of estimates of births to error in the mortality assumptions can be judged by making the extreme assumption of western Turkish mortality for the east of the country. In that event, the estimate of the total fertility rate for Hakkari province in the southeast corner of Turkey would be reduced from 10.6 to 9.5 children per woman indicating rather limited sensitivity.

TABLE 14 Components of Urban Population Growth, 1945-70: Turkey

Component	1945-1950	1950-1955	1955-1960	1960-1965	1965-1970	Total (millions)
	(Thousands)					
Total Increase	459	1,491	1,882	2,072	3,381	9.3
Births	510	695	988	1,303	1,680	5.2
Deaths	-329	-374	-454	-527	-600	-2.3
Natural increase	181	321	534	776	1,080	2.9
Reclassification	50	210	330	390	650	1.6
Migration	228	960	1,018	906	1,651	4.8
International	14	56	54	-121	-201	-0.2
Internal	214	904	964	1,027	1,852	5.0
Annual Percentage Growth Rate	2.5	6.5	6.0	5.0	6.2	

Note: This table is based on Tekce's (1974) chapter on the components of urban population growth from 1935 to 1970. The most problematic estimates are the allocations of international migration to the urban or rural populations. For 1945-60, Tekce divided international migration into urban and rural destinations on the basis of information about resettlement locations in Turkey for immigrant Turks; for 1960-75, she used reports of the worker recruitment services to divide into urban and rural origins.

Tekce's estimates of the components of urban growth are revised here by using birth rates from the present report. Her death rate is the TDS estimate for 1966-67 (11 per thousand) extended backward in time by linear interpolation to an assumed value of 18 per thousand during 1945-50. The assumed decline in the death rate was less steep in urban than rural Turkey, consistent with the estimates in Figure 4. The net balance of internal rural-to-urban migration is an unknown in the overall balance equation for each period and is therefore estimated as a residual. Errors in other components affect the internal migration estimate.

Variations in age misreporting, child mortality within regions of the TDS, and census coverage between 1960 and 1965 are all possible sources of error in provincial estimates. Nevertheless, the broad tendencies of the results by province are probably valid and are a valuable complement to other social data at the provincial level, such as infant mortality (see Table 24).

Fertility by Social Class

Although a classification of the whole population by socioeconomic groups is not feasible, some information is available about differences along this dimension. Using

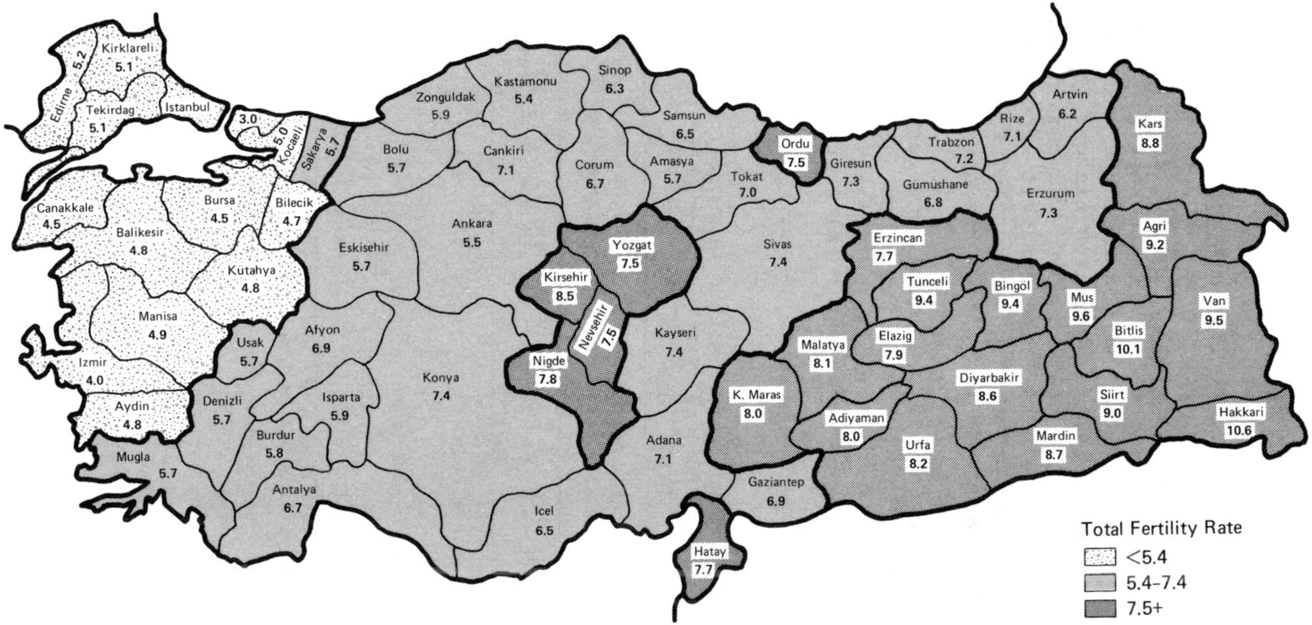

FIGURE 13 Total Fertility Rates by Province, 1960: Turkey

mother's education as an approximate index of social class, Timur (1974) estimated fertility differentials from the 1968 Hacettepe Survey (Table 15). These data suggest, although they do not prove conclusively, that relative expansion of the size of the lower socioeconomic groups in the cities does tend to raise fertility overall. Such a simple interpretation of the increase in urban fertility, however, would miss complex factors that lie outside the scope of the present work. It remains to be explained, for example, how urban fertility could cease to increase when the proportions of rural-origin, lower-class population in the cities has apparently continued to increase.

For the rural areas, Timur's data show very little differential in fertility by social class when class is measured by education of mothers. While this rules out a simple numeric connection between rural fertility trends

TABLE 15 Births by Education of Mother, Standardized by Duration of Marriage, from the 1968 Hacettepe Survey: Turkey

Educational Attainment	Three Largest Cities	Other Cities	Town	Village
Part A. Number of Children Ever Born per Married Women Under Age 45				
Illiterate	4.1	3.8	4.3	4.3
Some schooling	2.5	3.1	3.1	3.8
Primary (5 years)	2.6	2.7	2.6	3.2
Secondary (8 years)	1.9	2.9	a	a
Total	2.7	3.2	3.8	4.2
Part B. Proportionate Distribution (percentages)				
Illiterate	20	51	61	83
Some schooling	23	18	15	8
Primary (5 years)	33	26	21	9
Secondary (8 years)	24	5	a	a
Total	100	100	100	100

[a]Too few cases to make an estimate.

Source: Timur (1974).

and rural class structure at different dates, investigation of fertility differentials and trends by different rural social groups may nevertheless be a profitable line of inquiry (Özbay, 1978). This subject, however, lies, beyond the scope of the present work.

3 Mortality

NATIONAL INFANT AND EARLY CHILDHOOD MORTALITY, 1945-75

When trends of infant and early childhood mortality cannot be estimated accurately from vital registration data, which is the situation in Turkey, a common approach is indirect estimation. Numbers of births in the past and the survival status of those children logically imply measures of past infant and early childhood mortality levels. An indirect estimation procedure is developed to handle the Turkish data and used to estimate past trends. The results are then checked for segments of the entire period 1945-75 by comparison with other types of estimates. Life table information on the age pattern of mortality below age 5 is also presented.

Strategy of Estimation

Infant and early childhood mortality are estimated in Turkey by indirect methods because death registration data are incomplete and defective (see Chapter 1). Miroslav Macura (1975a and b) has developed an indirect method of estimating trends that uses the birth-survival histories contained in the pregnancy history material of national sample surveys. This method, described in detail in Appendix B, was applied to the birth-survival histories collected by the 1968 Hacettepe Survey, which is the only national survey that provides tabulations of the type required.

The trend revealed by the birth-survival history method was then checked at various dates by a second method of indirect estimation originally developed by William Brass (1968). The Brass method, as modified by

James Trussell (1975), uses information from a survey or census about the proportions of children born alive who have died up to the time of the survey or census. The information on births and deaths is cross-classified by the ages of the women bearing these children. A second variant of the method cross-classifies the information by the duration of marriage of the women. In both instances, the information about parity and child survival is sufficient to make robust estimates of child mortality that refer to dates several years before the survey or census. For Turkey, two surveys and two censuses contain the type of data needed to make these national point-in-time estimates of child mortality.

Finally, the Turkish Demographic Survey provides an estimate of infant and early childhood mortality for one year, 1966-67, based on direct enumeration of the death events. This estimate is useful as another check point for the national trend of childhood mortality.

Both the Macura and Brass methods of indirect estimation utilize model life tables in their procedures. Although general measures of child mortality, such as those expressed by the proportion dying by age 2 (${}_2q_0$), are not highly sensitive to the choice of a standard family of models for the estimation procedure, precision is increased when this choice is based on direct information about the age pattern of childhood mortality. The life-table index most often referenced in the analysis of child mortality is the infant mortality rate, ${}_1q_0$. Estimation of this particular index, as contrasted with ${}_2q_0$, is more sensitive to the choice of the model family. It is useful, therefore, to begin by presenting information that justifies the selection of the "East" family of model life tables for the Turkish case. Once satisfied on this point, it is permissible to refer to infant mortality rates as a shorthand description of the general level of infant and early childhood mortality.

Age Pattern of Mortality

Data of adequate quality on deaths by age and sex are available from two dual-record systems in Turkey: the nationwide Turkish Demographic Survey (TDS) of 1966-67 and a 1976 rural health project in Yozgat province. Additional data based on health service records are available from two rural areas: Etimesgut and Cubuk.

The TDS data were used to construct a national life table for 1966-67. This involved a preliminary adjustment of the data to take account of the dual-record omission rate. The TDS data make it possible to estimate omissions separately for births, deaths under age 1, and deaths at higher ages. The life table, shown in Table 16, was constructed from the original TDS data after including this adjustment for omissions.

Another national life table for 1966-67, apparently based on the same data, is available from the State Institute of Statistics (S.I.S.) (Turkey, State Institute of Statistics, 1971). However, since the methods used to adjust the data are not explained, it is not possible to evaluate this table fully. The S.I.S. statistics on infant mortality are the same as those in Table 16, but the mortality rates at higher ages are all lower. Apparently S.I.S. did not use the TDS omission rate to adjust deaths above age 1, with the result that the S.I.S. tables give slightly higher estimates of the expectation of life at birth: 1.0 years higher for males and 1.4 years higher for females.

The age pattern of mortality in Turkey up to age 5, as shown in Table 16, was compared with the four Coale-Demeny (1966) regional families of models (see glossary). This was done by selecting a model level from each family that exactly matches the infant mortality rate of the Turkish table. Figure 14 shows the four model levels that match the Turkish data on proportion of births surviving to age 1 (ℓ_1). Each of the four models predicts a proportion surviving to age 5 (ℓ_5), which is then compared with the Turkish life-table value. As shown, the "East" family gives the best representation of the Turkish childhood age pattern, with "West" being second best.

Further tests were carried out by making the same comparisons by sex, by rural-urban subdivision of the national population, and using the data from the three area studies mentioned above. The results are shown in Table 17. Up to age 5 the national life tables agree most closely with the "East" models. The Yozgat life table is also based on a dual-record system with a sample size similar to that of the TDS (50,000 persons). The Etimesgut and Cubuk life tables are least similar to the "East" models, but even for them the "East" models are the best available representation. The choice of "East" implicitly accepts the "East" pattern of heavy mortality under age 1 as compared with the next higher ages of early childhood. More information concerning the national age pattern of deaths below age 1 and between age 1 and 5 is not available.

Estimates Derived from Birth-Survival Histories

The Macura method for estimating trends in child mortality from birth-survival histories uses information on the date of each birth, survival status of each live-born child at the time of the survey, and the date of death of each child who died before the survey. Implicit in this information is a history of the child survival trends. The mothers alive at the time of the survey are accepted as a representative sample of mothers having children and experiencing child mortality in the past. The procedure is to select model life tables that could account for the levels of survivorship found at the time of the survey in the different birth cohorts of children reported by the mothers. (See Appendix B for a more detailed explanation of the procedure.)

To inspect the consistency of results going back in time from the 1968 survey to 1945, the procedures were applied separately to six subdivisions of the population and then aggregated to obtain the national results shown in Table 18. (The divisional estimates, which are useful for other purposes, are presented later.) When the data are disaggregated to the divisional level, there is sufficient consistency among them to justify accepting the national trend estimates as a valid independent series for childhood mortality. Their origin in a single set of data (the 1968 survey) that gives estimates for different dates all by the same method increases their credibility for trend analysis. Nevertheless, data errors and biases due to unfulfilled assumptions are possibilities, and these are elaborated in Appendix B. It is useful, therefore, to have additional evidence against which to check the results given by this method.

Estimates Derived by the Brass-Trussell Method

The estimation of child mortality from information collected in a census or survey on children ever born (CEB) and children surviving (CS) was first developed by Brass (1968), who calculated a table of multipliers for converting statistics on the proportion dead among CEB

TABLE 16 National Life Table, Based on One Year of Data Centered on February 1967: Turkey

Age(x)	q(x) (1,000)	d(x)	m(x) (1,000)	l(x)	L(x)	P(x)	T(x)	e(x)	Age(x)
Females									
0	143.8	14,380	159.6	100,000	90,077.8	.83914[a]	5,482,588.2	54.826	0
1	56.7	4,853	14.7	85,620	329,493.9	.95746[b]	5,392,510.4	62.982	1
5	10.5	846	2.1	80,767	401,722.1	.99083	5,063,016.4	62.687	5
10	7.9	628	1.6	79,922	398,037.5	.99084	4,661,294.3	58.323	10
15	10.5	830	2.1	79,293	394,391.4	.98798	4,263,256.8	53.766	15
20	13.6	1,066	2.7	78,463	389,650.2	.98538	3,868,865.5	49.318	20
25	15.7	1,212	3.2	77,397	383,953.1	.98356	3,479,215.3	44.953	25
30	17.2	1,312	3.5	76,184	377,642.1	.98099	3,095,262.2	40.629	30
35	20.8	1,560	4.2	74,872	370,462.0	.97712	2,717,620.1	36.297	35
40	25.0	1,830	5.1	73,312	361,987.5	.96874	2,347,158.1	32.016	40
45	37.7	2,697	7.7	71,483	350,671.3	.95707	1,985,170.7	27.771	45
50	48.3	3,325	9.9	68,786	335,617.4	.93670	1,634,499.4	23.762	50
55	79.0	5,173	16.5	65,461	314,372.5	.91034	1,298,882.0	19.842	55
60	101.2	6,102	21.3	60,288	286,185.3	.87462	984,509.5	16.330	60
65	152.3	8,251	33.0	54,186	251,304.4	.79480	698,324.2	12.887	65
70	267.7	12,295	61.8	45,935	198,940.8	.69610	448,019.8	9.753	70
75	353.4	11,889	85.9	33,641	138,481.8	.44402[c]	249,078.9	7.404	75
80	1,000.0	21,752	196.7	21,752	110,597.2	.0	110,597.2	5.084	80

Males									
0	162.0	16,200	183.1	100,000	88,498.0	.81978[a]	5,148,866.6	51.489	0
1	61.3	5,139	16.0	83,800	321,391.0	.95327[b]	5,060,368.6	60.386	1
5	13.1	1,028	2.6	78,661	390,733.8	.98926	4,738,977.5	60.246	5
10	8.4	651	1.7	77,633	386,536.3	.99110	4,348,243.8	56.010	10
15	9.4	726	1.9	76,982	383,095.0	.98669	3,961,707.5	51.463	15
20	17.2	1,313	3.5	76,256	377,997.9	.98329	3,578,612.5	46.929	20
25	16.2	1,213	3.3	74,943	371,682.8	.98253	3,200,614.7	42.707	25
30	18.9	1,384	3.8	73,730	365,190.4	.97944	2,828,931.9	38.369	30
35	22.4	1,619	4.5	72,346	357,681.8	.97330	2,463,741.4	34.055	35
40	31.1	2,200	6.3	70,727	348,133.2	.95819	2,106,059.7	29.777	40
45	52.8	3,621	10.9	68,527	333,579.5	.94472	1,757,926.4	25.653	45
50	57.8	3,754	11.9	64,905	315,140.7	.92600	1,424,346.9	21.945	50
55	91.1	5,574	19.1	61,151	291,821.6	.88191	1,109,206.2	18.139	55
60	147.7	8,211	31.9	55,578	257,360.5	.83849	817,384.6	14.707	60
65	177.7	8,415	39.0	47,367	215,795.3	.76674	560,024.2	11.823	65
70	300.9	11,720	70.8	38,951	165,458.4	.64415	244,228.8	8.837	70
75	434.5	11,831	111.0	27,232	106,580.7	.40381[c]	178,770.4	6.565	75
80	1,000.0	15,400	213.3	15,400	72,189.7	.0	72,189.7	4.688	80

[a]P(Birth).
[b]P(0-4).
[c]T(80)/T(75).

Source: Based on data from the 1966-67 Turkish Demographic Survey.

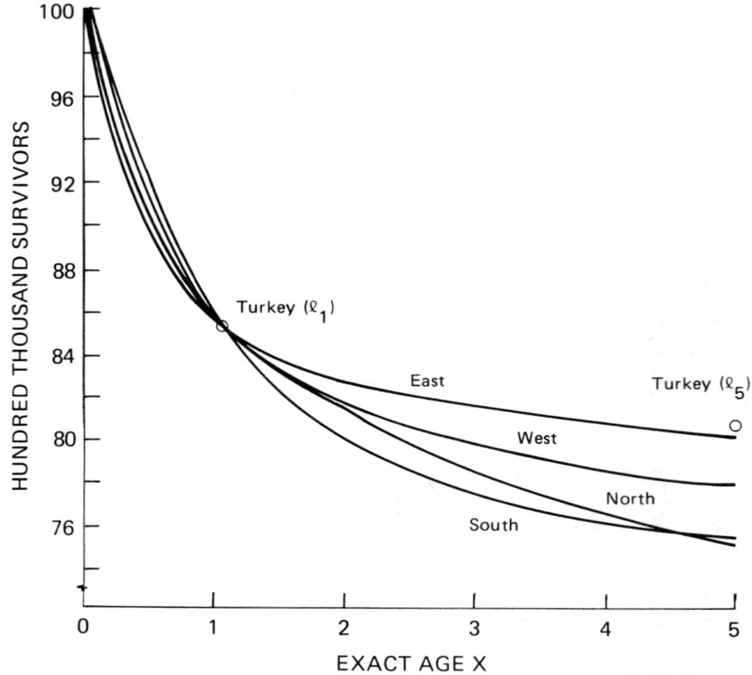

FIGURE 14 Survivors from a Cohort of 100,000 Female Births (ℓ_x). Four Regional Models with same Values for ℓ_1 for Demographic Survey Estimates, 1966-67: Turkey

reported by women in age groups 15-19, 20-24, 25-29, etc., into estimates of the probability of dying before reaching certain exact childhood ages. In conventional terminology D(i) denotes the proportion dead of CEB in successive five-year age groups, with i=1 indicating the age group 15-19, i=2 the age group 20-24, etc. In effect, the Brass multipliers convert D(i) values into estimates of q(x), where q(x) = 1 - l(x), the probability of dying between birth and exact age x.

Brass found that the relationship between corresponding pairs of D(i) and q(x) is primarily influenced by fertility patterns and, in particular, by the age at onset of childbearing. Therefore, the appropriate value of a conversion multiplier depends on the value of P(1)/P(2)--a good indicator of early fertility conditions--where P(i) is the average parity observed among women belonging to age group i. Brass evaluated

TABLE 17 Age Patterns of Early Childhood Mortality in Turkish Life Tables and in the "East" and "West" Families of Model Life Tables: Turkey

Data Source and Population	Observed Proportion Surviving Up to		Proportion Surviving Up to Age 5 Predicted by	
	Age 1	Age 5	"East" Models	"West" Models
TDS (1966-67)				
National females	.856	.808	.801	.777
National males	.838	.787	.788	.764
Rural, both sexes	.832	.773	.773	.749
Urban, both sexes	.887	.858	.852	.835
Yozgat (1976)				
Females	.862	.818	.810	.787
Males	.860	.831	.818	.799
Etimesgut				
Both sexes, 1967-68	.865	.840	.821	.799
Both sexes, 1971-77	.904	.889	.876	.863
Cubuk (1977)				
Both sexes	.868	.844	.825	.804

Note: Data are presented for both sexes combined whenever the number of cases is too small to support separate estimates for each sex.

the appropriate multipliers by modeling fertility schedules as third-degree polynomials. Later, Sullivan (1972) computed another set of multipliers by using regression techniques applied to data obtained from observed fertility schedules. More recently, Trussell (1975) created a third set by the same means but using data generated from the model fertility schedules developed by Coale and Trussell (1974). Of the three sets, the Sullivan and Trussell multipliers are easier to apply. The Trussell multipliers were used in this report.

National data for Brass-type estimates are available from four sources: the 1963 survey of the Ministry of Health, the initial interviews in 1965 and 1966 of the Turkish Demographic Survey, and the censuses of 1970 and 1975. Although appropriate data were collected in the 1968 and 1973 Hacettepe surveys, they are not available. The age model was used for all four sources, because only one (the 1963 survey) contains data suitable for the marriage-duration method of estimation. Since the 1963 survey does not include information on the total number of women but only the number of married women in each age group, data on marital status from the censuses of 1960

TABLE 18 National Infant Mortality Rate, 1945-70: Turkey

Exact Reference Date[a]	Infant Mortality Rate ($_1q_0$) (Both Sexes)	Regrouped by Intercensal Periods	Infant Mortality Rate ($_1q_0$)
1945	274	1945-50	260
1947	270	1950-55	233
1949	255	1955-60	203
1951	245	1960-65	176
1953	235	1965-70	151[b]
1955	224		
1957	212		
1959	199		
1961	189		
1963	178		
1965	169		
1967	156		

[a]Exact reference dates are used for point-in-time dating of estimates. They refer to the exact beginning of the year if no decimal digits are shown.
[b]Extrapolated for second half of period.

Source: The single-date estimates are the result of applying the Macura birth-survival method to the 1968 Hacettepe survey data. The five-year estimates are averages for intercensal periods, from October of each census year to the next, matched to the dates of the multiple reverse projections shown in Table 2.

and 1965 were used to fill this gap in the basic data. Because the age model was used for data from all four sources, comparability of the estimation method is assured.

The Brass method provides an estimate of the child mortality experience of women of successively higher ages. Reliable estimates are usually obtained from women aged 20-24, 25-29, and 30-34. The results are expressed in terms of the infant mortality rate for each age group, using "East" models. When the infant mortality rate is falling, the estimates from women 25-29 should be higher than those from the younger women aged 20-24. The Turkish estimates, presented in Table 19, do not have this pattern; instead, data from women 25-29 yield lower estimates of child mortality than those from women 20-24. This pattern holds true in all four sources. Estimates from women aged 30-34 fall into no regular pattern.

Finding lower estimates of infant mortality associated with women of higher ages is logically acceptable only if the trend of infant mortality is upward. However, the

TABLE 19 Estimates of the National Infant Mortality Rate Based on Reports of Mothers at Different Ages, Four Sources: Turkey (Infant Deaths per Thousand Births)

Source of Data	Age of Mothers Giving Reports 20-24	25-29	30-34	Mean for Ages 20-29[a]	Reference Year
1963 survey	211	206	174	208	1960
1965-66 TDS	189	170	164	180	1963
1970 census	154	144	159	149	1967
1975 census	130	128	139	129	1972

[a]Rounding of the numbers that are averaged makes the means appear to contain small errors when they do not.

overall level of the Turkish estimates from each source declines with time. Hence, some form of systematic data error is present. There are various possible explanations.

One theory starts with the observation that women who have had none of their children die have more living children than other women of their same age and fertility. A tendency toward female age exaggeration in precisely the age ranges used for Brass-type estimates is noted elsewhere (see Appendix C on age misreporting). Thus, it is likely that the women with fewer (or no) child deaths, and hence more surviving children will be perceived as being older and will be misreported accordingly. Such selective transfer of women to higher age groups raises the infant mortality rate estimated from the 20-24 age group relative to that estimated from the 25-29 age group.

Another possible explanation is based on the fact that women of low socioeconomic status not only experience higher child mortality than women of higher status but they also marry earlier. Therefore, the women associated with high mortality are a greater proportion of the mothers in the 20-24 age group than in the next higher age group. Most Turkish women have married by their early 20s, so this type of selectivity cannot be very strong in the age group 20-24, but to the extent that it does exist it contributes to the puzzling reversal in the estimates.

Because of these systematic errors in the data, an average of the estimates for the 20-24 and 25-29 age groups is a stronger estimate of the level of childhood mortality than any one of the three available estimates taken alone. Mortality information provided by the women aged 30-34 was not included because the data errors appear to be less systematic from one source to the next.

The Brass-type estimates refer to an average of experience for a number of years preceding the survey date. The date on which this experience centers is calculated and comes to 3.1 or 3.2 years before the survey for the estimates made here (averaged over two age groups of women). For example, the last Turkish census was taken in October 1975; the child mortality estimate based on this census refers to a period centered on mid-1972.

The estimates of childhood mortality (based on the age

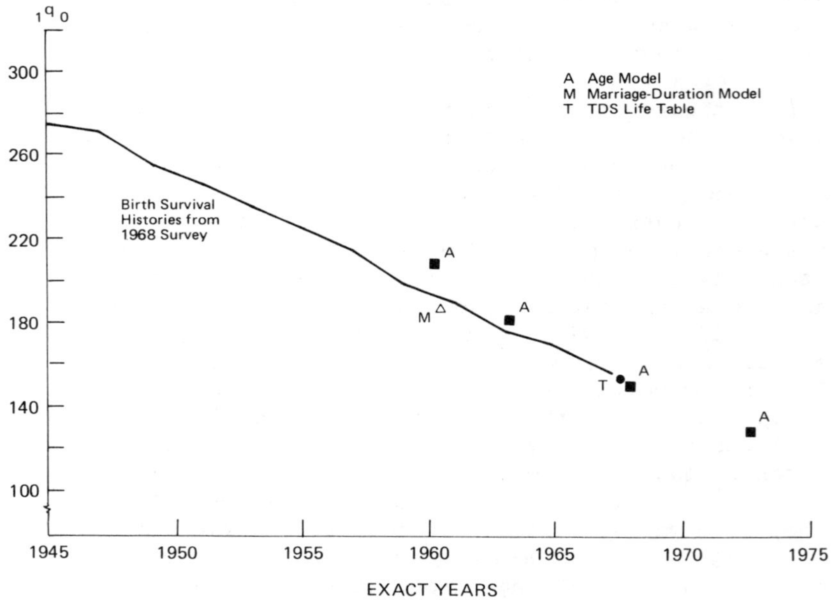

FIGURE 15 Early Childhood Mortality Expressed in Terms of Infant Mortality Rate, 1945-75 (per thousand): Turkey

Source: Tables 18 and 19.

model) are shown in Table 19 and plotted in Figure 15 together with the trend estimates derived from the birth-survival histories. Two points are plotted from the 1963 survey, both dated early 1960; the higher estimate is based on the Brass-Trussell age model and is comparable in terms of method of estimation with the other points shown as A. However, the basic data for the 1960 estimate were incomplete as explained earlier in this section. Fortunately, the 1963 national population survey contains data with which to bypass the problem. Tabulations were made of CEB and children who have died (CD) by the duration of marriage of women in the national sample. A variant of the Brass-Sullivan-Trussell method applies a marriage duration model to the data to reach an estimate of the infant mortality rate. The result is shown by the point M plotted in Figure 15. While this estimate is not comparable in method to the other points A, it is soundly based on a single sample of women (not mixed with census data), and may be interpreted as a lower-limit estimate for 1960.

Finally, the figure shows a single life-table estimate T of infant mortality from the TDS. Since this chart refers to mortality for both sexes combined, the infant mortality rates for each sex (${}_1q_0$ in Table 16) are combined according to a sex ratio at birth of 105 males per 100 females. The resulting infant mortality rate of 153 per thousand is dated 1967.2 (the midpoint of the enumeration period).

Juxtaposing all these single-date estimates with the trend estimates strongly confirms the results of the Macura method of birth-survival histories for the period from 1960 to 1968. These favorable results create a presumption, although not complete assurance, that trend estimates for earlier dates derived by the same birth-survival method are also reliable. Going back as far as 1945 from 1968, the number of women old enough in 1968 to give reports diminishes, because the upper age limit for the survey was 45 years of age. Since these older women were having their first children at the early dates around 1945, and first-order children have higher risks of death than second and higher order children, the infant mortality experience reported by them is probably higher than for all children born during that early period. This could exert an upward bias on estimates at very early dates. No attempt was made to carry the trend back further than 1945.

Use of the Estimates in Multiple Reverse Projections

The child mortality trend estimates are important assumptions underlying the multiple reverse projection method described in Chapter 2. Since the projections are made by intercensal five-year periods, the necessary estimates are centered on exact between-census dates: 1938.3, 1943.3,...1973.3. For the period 1945-70 the centered estimates were computed from the trend shown in Table 18. For 1973.3, an estimate of 126 was obtained by extrapolation of less than one year from the Brass-Trussell estimate for 1972.7, which was based on the census of 1975. For years earlier than 1945, the assumptions for child mortality were derived from estimates of adult mortality by a procedure explained below in the section on general mortality.

INFANT AND EARLY CHILDHOOD MORTALITY BY DIVISIONS, 1945-67

The data and methods for examining differentials and trends in infant mortality by divisions are the same as those used for the national estimates. Since the data are mainly from surveys, although checked for some dates by census data, the material is less satisfactory for any single division than for the national estimates, due to the small numbers involved. In addition some special problems of interpretation that do not affect national estimates arise in the case of divisional estimates. The strategy of deriving divisional estimates, therefore, was to begin with preliminary estimates based on the birth-survival history method. These results were then checked against trends estimated from independent data by the Brass-Trussell method. Finally, a number of adjustments were made to handle the special problems that affect only the divisional estimates.

Preliminary Estimates

The estimates obtained by application of the birth-survival history method are shown without adjustment in Table 20. These estimates were compared with estimates derived by the Brass-Trussell method for the dates 1960, 1963, and 1967 by using values of the birth-survival estimates interpolated for the same dates.

TABLE 20 Estimates of Infant Mortality by Divisions, 1945-70: Turkey

Exact Reference Date[a]	Urban (preliminary) Istanbul and Izmir	Other West	Central and East	Rural West	Central	East
1945	190	216	252	227	344	280
1947	181	208	241	221	330	277
1949	175	200	231	218	315	266
1951	164	194	221	209	297	261
1953	158	187	209	205	278	254
1955	149	180	201	200	258	245
1957	140	172	191	194	230	236
1959	130	163	180	190	208	228
1961	124	157	169	186	191	222
1963	114	146	159	178	173	206
1965	108	142	149	172	164	187
1967	100	135	140	166	155	166

Note: The urban estimates are preliminary, because they require adjustment as explained in the text and in Table 23. The rural estimates are accepted as explained in the text.

[a]See footnote a, Table 18.

Source: Based on birth-survival histories of 1968 Hacettepe survey.

The comparison is made after grouping the birth-survival history estimates into the three urban-rural divisions shown in Table 21 and plotted in Figure 16. Without exception, the independent sources confirm the existence of substantial rural-urban differentials. The downward trends are confirmed over all segments of time except one, the 1960-63 period for Istanbul-Izmir. There is no explanation for this anomaly in the data other than the ever-present possibility of error affecting one of the two data sources. The downward trend for Istanbul-Izmir is firmly supported, however, by comparing either of the first two paired estimates (1960 or 1963) with the paired estimates for 1967, which are clearly lower. The slope of the downward trend for Istanbul-Izmir is left in some doubt.

The independent estimates of 1963 for "other urban" and rural reflect a division between urban and rural at a population size of 2,000 instead of the 10,000 used in all the other data sources. This classification of rural, small-town populations as urban probably raises

TABLE 21 Infant Mortality Rates by Divisions from Birth-Survival Histories (BSH) Compared with Brass-Trussell Estimates from Various Sources, 1960, 1963, 1967: Turkey

	1960			1963			1967		
Division	BSH	Survey of 1963	Date of Estimate	BSH	TDS	Date of Estimate	BSH[a]	Census of 1970	Date of Estimate
Istanbul and Izmir	126	122	1960.4	114	128	1963.1	98	104	1967.6
Other Urban	168	179	1960.3	154	175[b]	1963.3	135	141	1967.7
Rural	202	217	1960.2	185	184[b]	1963.0	158	157	1967.7
National[c]	194	208	1960.1	178	180	1963.1	151	149	1967.7

[a]Extrapolated for fraction of year.

[b]The TDS division between rural and urban is 2,000 persons, whereas 10,000 applies to all other sources above.

[c]Note that the dating of estimates by divisions varies. The national estimates differ slightly from theoretical averages, which are birth-weighted means. Estimates were made separately for divisions and for the national total.

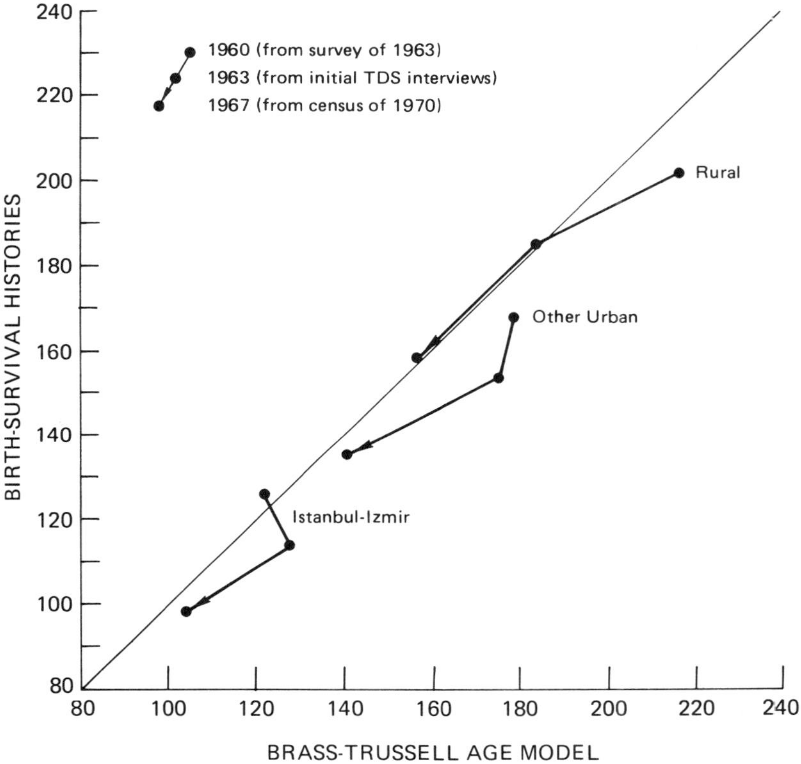

FIGURE 16 Comparison of Infant Mortality Estimates from Birth-Survival Histories with Independent Brass-Trussell Estimates by Rural-Urban Divisions (rates per thousand): Turkey

both the rural estimate of infant mortality and the "other urban" estimate. This could account for the leftward kink in the rural curve, but not the rightward kink in the "other urban" curve. Some error is evidently present in the data blurring the broad confirmation of trends.

Additional estimates for all six divisions were tested by the same procedure, and the results are shown in Figure 17. The effect of sampling error and other types of data error on estimates is bound to increase as smaller divisions are demarcated. For example, the independent estimates for "other urban west" show an

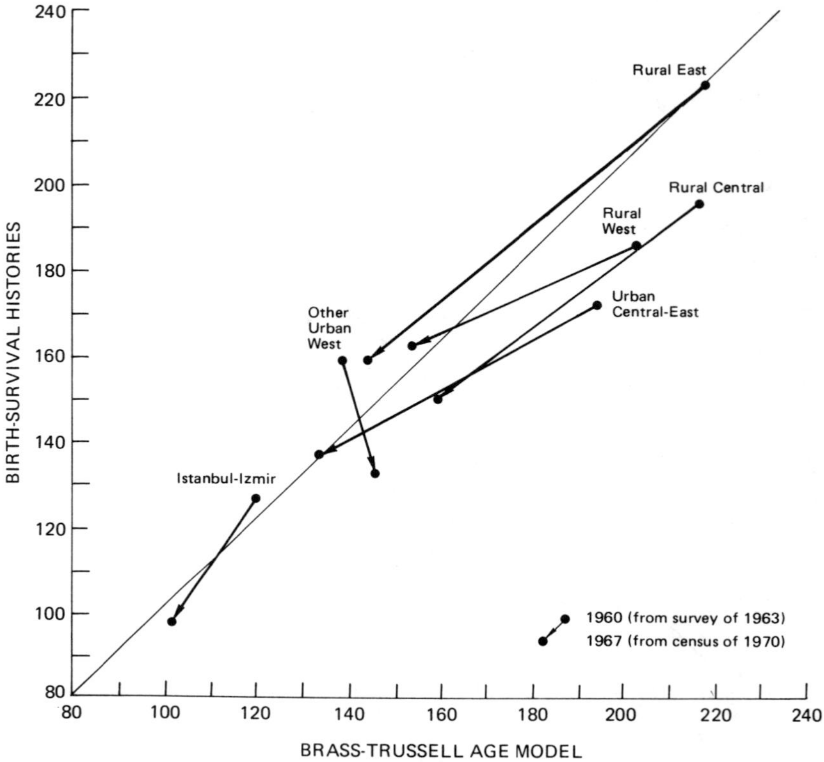

FIGURE 17 Comparison of Infant Mortality Estimates from Birth-Survival Histories with Independent Brass-Trussell Estimates by Regions within Rural and Urban Divisions (rates per thousand): Turkey

increase rather than a decline from 1960 to 1967. This raises a question about the direction of the trend; however, the consistent confirmation of downward trends in the other divisions argues for accepting the downward trend for "other urban west" as well. In all other respects, there is reasonable agreement among the estimates from the birth-survival histories and independent sources.

Data with which to make independent tests of the trends earlier than 1960 are not available. However, some value can be attached to the earlier estimates keeping in mind that divisional estimates are inherently less robust than national ones (sample size) and there remain some issues of interpretation to be discussed below. Furthermore, if the birth-survival histories are a reasonable basis for sketching the main outlines of mortality trends during the period for which they can be checked, they are likely to be valid for the earlier dates as well.

Adjusting for Rural Births and Deaths Reported by Urban Mothers

Measurement methods that look back in time from a survey carry with them the problem of allocating the births and deaths reported by mothers to the different divisions of the country. The mothers interviewed in 1968 are representative of mothers living in the divisions at that time; however some births and deaths of their children occur in different divisions if the mothers migrate after childbearing starts. In addition, some of the towns where the survey is conducted are urban at the time of the survey but were part of the rural division at an earlier date. These two circumstances create possibilities for measurement error that are discussed below. Neither type of error affects national estimates, because both involve allocating information about infant mortality between divisions, not its relevance to the country as a whole.

The Hacettepe tabulations of 1968 assign births and survival histories to the rural and urban divisions according to the mothers' place of residence in 1968. Tabulations for the independent Brass-Trussell estimates are also made in the same way in all sources. Thus, for example, the Ministry of Health's survey in 1963 (providing Brass-Trussell estimates for 1960) is tabulated according to residence in the rural and urban divisions of 1963.

Errors Due to Migration of Mothers

The first problem to take up, which applies equally to the birth-survival history method and the Brass-Trussell method, is the effect of rural-to-urban migration of mothers. Since the rural setting has higher infant mortality rates than the urban setting, the inclusion of rural birth-survival experience in the data for urban estimates causes an upward error for the urban division.

It is not clear whether omission of this rural mortality experience from the rural estimation procedure causes error in the rural division estimates as well. If the misallocated information refers to average rural experience, there will be no error in the rural estimate. If there is a difference, the practical effect is likely to be trivial, because the number of misallocated rural births is so small relative to total rural births in Turkey.

The likelihood of upward error in the urban estimates of infant mortality rests on three conditions that must all be present: higher rural than urban mortality rates, rural-to-urban migration by mothers, and pre-migration childbearing. All of these conditions are fulfilled in Turkey. It is necessary, therefore, to evaluate their importance in the Turkish setting during the period of estimation.

Some information on this point comes from a 1966 survey of women in Ankara city carried out by the Sociology Department of Middle East Technical University under the direction of David Goldberg. A well-designed representative sample of 803 women was interviewed. The survey occurred only two years prior to the 1968 survey that is the source of the birth-survival histories. The Ankara survey follows a decade of high rural-to-urban migration, about which more is said below. Adlakha (1970) makes use of migration information in the survey to divide the births by rural and urban settings. It is assumed that in most instances the mother did not bring the newborn child to the city immediately, so its survival experience during infancy and early childhood is assumed to belong to the setting of its birth.

Infant mortality rates are calculated in various ways, making it possible to isolate clearly the error that occurs when rural births are included in the urban data. For six years immediately preceding the Ankara survey, 8.5 percent of births were rural, leading to an infant mortality rate 5.0 percent higher than the "true" urban rate of 109 per thousand births. For an earlier period, 7 to 16 years preceding the survey (1950-59), the error is greater. Rural births were 27.3 percent of births reported for this period, and the infant mortality rate was 18.6 percent higher than the "true" urban rate of 133 per thousand births. In the Ankara study, "urban" was defined as the entire urban sector, not limited to Ankara city alone.

The higher degree of error for earlier dates is not intrinsic to the estimation procedure but is due to a different pattern of premigration childbearing at that time. As rural-to-urban migration picked up speed in Turkey, starting from modest levels in the 1940s (see Table 14) some women who had already started their childbearing migrated to the cities. During this period, women typically followed or joined their husbands in the city. In the 1960s, a new pattern was established wherein migrant women had all, or nearly all, of their children in the city after migration. This change was supported by a rising age of marriage for rural women and by the existence of more possibilities to marry "upward" to men who became established in ever increasing numbers in the cities. In addition, a second generation of "village" men became available as boys migrated in their teens to the homes of relatives in the cities and grew up there.

The Ankara study provides a standard by which to evaluate the error in mortality rates due to the rural-urban migration of mothers. Since migration is the cause of the error, migration rates for women aged 15-39 are a good indicator of the relative importance of the estimation error in different parts of the urban population. Detailed migration estimates by age and sex for Turkish cities are available for the decade 1955-65, a period that closely precedes the 1968 Hacettepe survey (Tekce, 1975). The female migration rate for ages 15-39 for Ankara was 61.5 per thousand annually, one of the highest city rates in Turkey, showing that the Ankara standard represents estimation error due to migration at its extreme. The general rate, for all cities over 10,000 population, was 25.9 per thousand. For Istanbul-Izmir and "other urban," the migration rates were 24.2 and 26.4, respectively. No further subdivision by urban regions was made.

Undoubtedly the relationship between a migration rate preceding a survey and the proportions and dating of rural births that are misallocated to the urban division is complex. Nevertheless, the assumption of a reasonably direct linkage is justified since the source and size of error are clearly tied to the proportion of women in the childbearing ages who are migrants. On this basis, the Ankara standard of error was assumed to be applicable as an adjustment factor, when multiplied by the ratio of the divisional migration rates to the Ankara migration rate. These ratios are shown below:

Istanbul-Izmir: $\underline{r}$ = 24.2/61.5 = .393
Other urban : $\underline{r}$ = 26.4/61.5 = .429

The standard (Ankara) migration errors in the mortality estimates, dated according to the period of birth and stated as proportions of the "true" infant mortality rate, are as follows:

Period of Birth	Standard (Ankara) Error
1950-59	.186
1960-65	.050

Since information on the extent of pre-migration childbearing is not available prior to the 1950s, it was assumed that the proportionate error is the same for 1945-50 as immediately thereafter. In order to indicate gradual changes in the extent of pre-migration childbearing over all the years for which adjustments are needed (1945-67), the standard was interpolated and extended a short distance at each end, as follows:

1945 to 1955	.186 (as estimated)
linear decrease to:	
1963	.050 (as estimated)
linear decrease to:	
1967	.025 (by assumption)

An adjustment multiplier, $\underline{m}$, for application to the preliminary urban mortality rates was then calculated as follows:

$$\underline{m} = 1/[1+(\underline{r})(\underline{s})]$$

For example, the multiplier for Istanbul-Izmir in 1945 is 1/[1 + (.393)(.186)] = .932. The preliminary infant mortality rate of 190 per thousand is then adjusted by this multiplier to 177 per thousand. The adjustments for the urban divisions were carried out for all dates in the same way, after considering a second type of birth misallocation.

Errors Due to Transfer of Communities from Rural to Urban Status

Part of the urban sector in 1968 was still rural at earlier dates. Therefore, women residing in 1968 in places that had transferred from rural to urban status reported some births that were pre-transfer births. The proportion of urban births that are misclassified as rural births due to this change in status increases as estimates are made for dates further back in time. The Ankara study does not identify error of this type because all the interviews were held in Ankara city, which had been an urban place at all the earlier dates.

The rural places in 1945 that transferred to the urban sector by 1968 were listed and found to have a population of approximately .50 million in 1945 as compared with an urban population of 3.44 million at that time. The relationship between these two population sizes immediately suggests that the allocation of rural births to the urban sector in 1945 by reports of women in 1968 is not small. Table 22 presents an approximation of the error in 1945 made on the basis of some simple and plausible assumptions. The column on the rural sector is included not out of necessity for the computations but to draw attention to the large size of the rural sector in terms of births and deaths relative to the size of the urban sector at that time.

The effects of community transfers are evaluated for the urban sector as a whole, because records for Istanbul and Izmir to trace the transfer of rural communities into the urban sector and from there to annexation by expansion of the municipal boundaries are not available. The Istanbul-Izmir division is defined by its municipal boundaries at the different dates of the study. The results of the computation at 1945 show that the migration-adjusted mortality rate for all urban areas must be adjusted additionally for community transfers by a multiplier as follows (Table 22):

$$(\text{line } 8) \;/\; (\text{line } 5) = 193 \;/\; 213 = .906.$$

Since this cause of error approaches zero as the date of the estimate approaches the survey date, a linear interpolation from .906 to 1.000 from 1945 to 1967, respectively, was used to provide a multiplier for each date. These multipliers are shown in column t, Table 23.

Final Estimates

The final adjustment of the urban trends of infant mortality, consisting of an adjustment for both migration of mothers and transfers of communities, is shown in

TABLE 22 Adjustment of Urban Infant Mortality Rate for Transfer of Rural Communities to Urban Sector, 1945: Turkey

Situation in 1945	Rural	Urban
Actual situation in 1945		
1. Population (millions)	15.35	3.44
2. Crude birth rate (per thousand)	49.4	26.6
3. Births (thousands)	758.3	91.5
As seen from 1968		
4. Births (thousands)	733.6	116.2
5. Migration-adjusted infant mortality rate (per thousand)	287	213
6. Deaths up to age 1 (thousands)	210.5	24.8
Actual mortality in 1945		
7. Deaths up to age 1 (thousands)	217.6	17.7
8. Infant mortality rate (per thousand)	287	193

Notes

Line 1: From Table 9.

Line 2: The birth rates are population-weighted means calculated for rural and urban from Table 11. The birth rates themselves are estimated utilizing infant mortality as a parameter. A trial value for urban infant mortality was computed in the format of the present table, followed by revision of the crude birth rate and a second trial. This process of successive approximation was repeated until mutually consistent adjusted mortality rates (Table 23) and crude birth rates (Table 11) were reached. The convergence was rapid because the crude birth rate is estimated with a second independent parameter, C(10), which has a strong effect on the final estimate of the crude birth rate.

Line 3: (1) x (2).

Line 4: Reflects transfer of rural births from rural to urban, .5 x 49.4 = 24.7.

Line 5: The rural mortality rate does not require adjustment. The urban mortality rate comes from the original unadjusted mortality rates adjusted for migration as explained in the text. The migration-adjusted urban mortality rate used here is the birth-weighted mean of the urban divisional mortality rates.

Line 6: (4) x (5).

Line 7: Reflects transfer of misallocated rural deaths from urban to rural, 24.7 x .287 = 7.1.

Line 8: (7)/(3).

Table 23. As explained above, the rural estimates do not require adjustment, so they are the same as those in the rural columns of Table 20.

The general pattern of differentials and trends across divisions, shown in Figure 18, may be accepted as valid, but there should be skepticism about specific values at particular dates. The picture is one of much higher rural than urban infant mortality at the earliest dates.

TABLE 23 Urban Infant Mortality Rates Adjusted for Reporting Error Due to Migration of Mothers and Transfers of Communities from Rural to Urban, 1945-67: Turkey

Exact Reference Date[a]	Adjustments s	Adjustments t	Istanbul and Izmir	Other Urban West	Urban Central and East
1945	.186	.906	160	181	211
1947	.186	.915	154	176	204
1949	.186	.923	151	171	197
1951	.186	.932	142	167	191
1953	.186	.940	138	163	182
1955	.186	.949	132	158	177
1957	.152	.957	126	155	172
1959	.118	.966	120	150	166
1961	.084	.974	117	148	159
1963	.050	.983	110	141	153
1965	.038	.991	105	138	145
1967	.025	1.000	99	134	139
			r = .393	r = .429	r = .429

Note: The multiplier is: M = [1/(1 + rs)] x t, where s is the standard, r is the ratio for the division to the standard, and t is the adjustment for community transfers from rural to urban. See text for details and an example of the calculations.

[a]See note a, Table 18.

The rural mortality rates are spread across a large range with especially high mortality rates in the central part of Turkey. Estimates for the eastern rural area, which includes the southeast, are not the highest even though social indicators consistently rank this rural region lowest in Turkey during the period evaluated here. The rate of decline of mortality rates, however, is most rapid in the central region. By the 1960s, rural differentials essentially disappear across all three regions. This equalization, however, is not accomplished by reaching what would be considered "low" levels of infant mortality in all divisions, because even levels on the order of 160 per thousand (the combined rural estimate in 1967) certainly must be regarded as still high. Small differences among the rural regions and rearrangements of rank order at the end of the period are not significant, because the strength of the data cannot support precise measurement. The general rural pattern, and the convergence of rural trends by the mid-1960s, are acceptable findings.

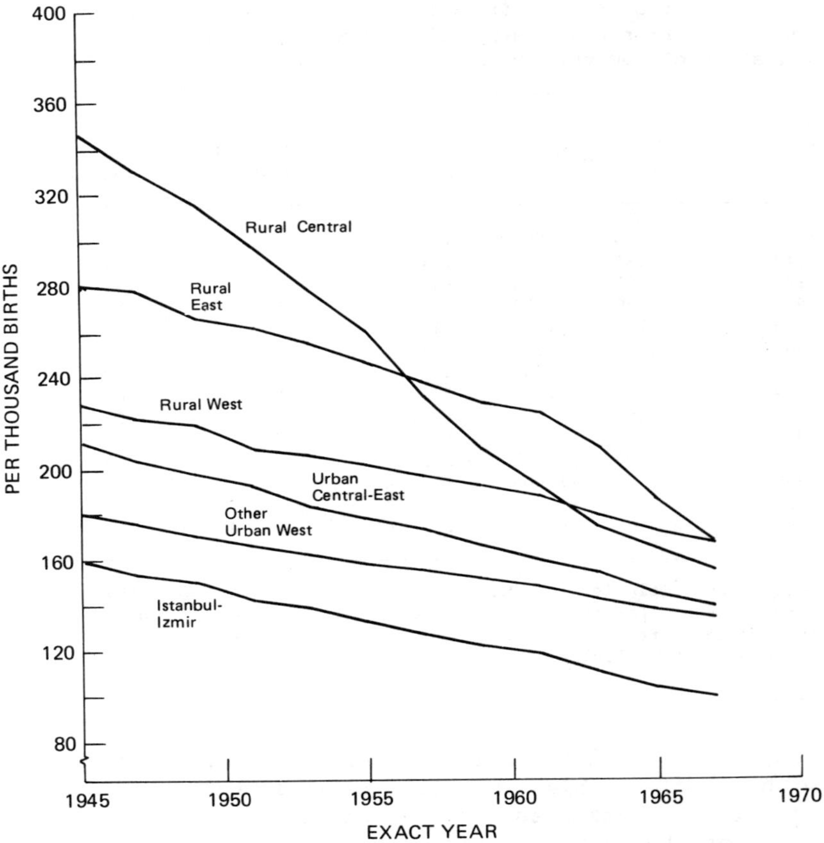

FIGURE 18 Infant Mortality Rates by Divisions, 1945-67: Turkey

Urban mortality rates declined more slowly than the rural ones and there was little change in the urban differentials across regions. Infants and young children continued to survive in 1967 more successfully if born and reared in a metropolitan city than in rural or less urban communities, just as was true two decades earlier.

Infant Mortality by Province

The 1970 census was tabulated and published by province. It included the "Brass questions," which are used to estimate infant mortality by the Brass-Trussell method. Since the census volumes also present the data separately for the rural and urban populations, a rather finely drawn picture can be produced of infant mortality at the provincial level. Variation in age misstatement and completeness of reporting for children born who died following birth are sources of error. A map of the results (Figure 19) and the more detailed presentation for rural and urban separately (Table 24) provide unusual and valuable material for use in conjunction with other social data at the provincial level.

Infant Mortality by Social Class

Some information is available regarding infant mortality differences by social class, but it is limited in coverage and time. The Ankara study (Adlakha, 1970) makes a distinction between upper and lower status women. In 1950-59, the two status groups accounted, respectively, for 35 percent and 65 percent of total births. The urban infant mortality rates were 93 and 149 per thousand, respectively. For the next period, 1960-65, the infant mortality rates by social status were 47 and 123 per thousand, respectively. (Some farmers were left out of the tabulations by social status, so these data are not fully comparable with the urban mortality estimates cited above from the Ankara survey.) When differences of infant mortality by social status are this large by comparison with the divisional differences, it is apparent that more information classified by social status would be useful to detect mortality differentials in Turkey.

NATIONAL MORTALITY ABOVE AGE 5, 1935-75

The method most suitable for estimating mortality above age 5 in Turkey is forward projection, utilizing a cumulation procedure that minimizes the effects of age misreporting. In a closed population an intercensal life table from childhood onwards may be estimated "directly" by tracing birth cohorts from one census to the next.

FIGURE 19 Infant Mortality Rates by Provinces, 1967 (per thousand population): Turkey

These estimates will be correct only if the population is truly closed, the two censuses have the same level of completeness, and there is no age misreporting. In actual populations these assumptions rarely hold simultaneously. Yet, by combining these ideas with their model life-table system, Coale and Demeny (United Nations, 1967) devised a technique that attempts to identify the mortality level to which a population is subject on the basis of intercensal comparisons. This technique assumes that the age pattern of mortality in the observed population conforms to a selected mortality pattern from a family of model life tables such as those of Coale and Demeny (1966).

Once a pattern has been selected, the population enumerated at the first census is projected to the time of the second census (forward projection) by using survival rates derived from a range of mortality levels from the chosen family of model life tables. For each age x, a model life table is selected that reproduces by forward projection exactly the observed population over age x+t at the second census (t being the length of the intercensal interval). A representative mortality level is then chosen, generally by taking the median of the life tables selected to match the populations projected above the ages 5, 10, ... 40, 45. Because the population is cumulated in each projection for ages x and over, rather than handled separately by five or ten-year cohorts to estimate mortality levels, the effects of age reporting errors are minimized though not necessarily eliminated. The estimates yielded by this technique are generally acceptable, but they are sensitive to differential completeness of enumeration between the censuses used.

The method is at its best when the intercensal interval is 5 rather than 10 years, and it can provide estimates when satisfactory death registration data are not available. Both of those conditions prevail in Turkey and have made the method particularly suitable (Demeny and Shorter, 1968). The data requirements are a series of censuses and information on international migration. The latter is used to adjust the initial (or terminal) census in each five-year pair of censuses so that the two censuses represent a population closed to migration. After this adjustment, the only remaining source of population change above age t is mortality, which is estimated by the forward projection technique.

TABLE 24 Infant Mortality and Fertility Indexes by Province, Circa 1967 and 1960: Turkey

Province	Infant Mortality, Around 1967 (per thousand births)			Fertility, Around 1960	
	Rural	Urban	Total	CBR (per thousand)	TFR (per woman)
(1)	(2)	(3)	(4)	(5)	(6)
1 Adana	128	123	125	46.7	7.10
2 Adiyaman	136	148	139	58.4	7.97
3 Afyon	189	149	180	49.2	6.91
4 Agri	149	146	148	59.9	9.19
5 Amasya	218	174	206	41.1	5.67
6 Ankara	177	134	147	40.5	5.52
7 Antalya	110	118	112	46.5	6.68
8 Artvin	165	136	161	44.8	6.15
9 Aydin	137	117	131	35.5	4.75
10 Balikesir	160	121	148	35.5	4.83
11 Bilecik	173	162	169	35.8	4.72
12 Bingol	146	170	150	63.5	9.40
13 Bitlis	134	140	136	65.0	10.10
14 Bolu	157	130	152	40.9	5.65
15 Burdur	144	123	138	41.0	5.83
16 Bursa	173	138	158	33.9	4.45
17 Canakkale	142	116	136	32.4	4.52
18 Cankiri	192	149	184	52.6	7.10
19 Corum	215	181	208	50.5	6.74
20 Denizli	148	118	140	42.1	5.68
21 Diyarbakir	136	144	139	56.4	8.59
22 Edirne	190	149	177	37.4	5.19
23 Elazig	164	167	166	55.5	7.86
24 Erzincan	173	157	169	53.8	7.74
25 Erzurum	214	210	213	51.4	7.32
26 Eskisehir	195	146	171	40.7	5.71
27 Gaziantep	133	132	133	48.0	6.86
28 Giresun	115	104	113	53.7	7.27
29 Gumushane	182	159	179	53.8	6.78
30 Hakkari	140	136	139	67.7	10.56
31 Hatay	120	105	114	50.7	7.68
32 Isparta	158	116	144	40.0	5.86
33 Icel	141	122	132	43.8	6.54
34 Istanbul	135	126	131	23.1	3.04
35 Izmir	130	121	126	29.8	3.99
36 Kars	197	170	192	58.0	8.84
37 Kastamonu	168	122	161	40.3	5.43
38 Kayseri	175	146	164	52.3	7.35
39 Kirklareli	196	140	178	35.1	5.13
40 Kirsehir	156	128	150	59.3	8.51
41 Kocaeli	143	131	137	35.1	4.96
42 Konya	167	142	159	51.3	7.37
43 Kutahya	183	159	178	37.2	4.84
44 Malatya	139	129	135	56.7	8.14
45 Manisa	145	132	141	36.1	4.93

TABLE 24 (continued)

Province	Infant Mortality, Around 1967 (per thousand births)			Fertility, Around 1960	
	Rural	Urban	Total	CBR (per thousand)	TFR (per woman)
(1)	(2)	(3)	(4)	(5)	(6)
46 Maras	131	131	131	55.1	8.01
47 Mardin	125	129	126	60.1	8.65
48 Mugla	112	92	109	40.1	5.71
49 Mus	158	143	155	64.5	9.61
50 Nevsehir	151	142	149	54.1	7.54
51 Nigde	179	157	174	54.7	7.76
52 Ordu	137	121	134	58.8	7.49
53 Rize	101	101	101	52.1	7.05
54 Sakarya	139	127	136	40.3	5.72
55 Samsun	160	147	157	46.7	6.51
56 Siirt	142	134	139	61.9	8.98
57 Sinop	165	124	159	45.3	6.34
58 Sivas	198	170	191	54.6	7.44
59 Tekirdag	175	142	164	35.1	5.05
60 Tokat	207	174	199	51.1	6.96
61 Trabzon	91	96	92	53.1	7.20
62 Tunceli	135	123	132	63.2	9.41
63 Urfa	109	118	113	56.8	8.15
64 Usak	198	164	187	42.4	5.66
65 Van	155	127	147	63.5	9.52
66 Yozgat	169	149	166	54.0	7.54
67 Zonguldak	167	124	155	41.8	5.90
Total	157	134	149	45.1	6.30

Effects of International Migration

Between 1935 and 1960, the balance of international migration was positive, due to the relocation in Turkey of small Turkish populations from the Balkan countries. After 1960, Turkish workers were attracted in great numbers to West European labor markets, primarily West Germany, and the balance of migration became negative. Statistics on these movements, presented in Appendix D, are adequate to describe general orders of magnitude but are not of high quality. Statistics on total migration by sex are more reliable than those that describe the distributions by age. Fortunately, the forward projection method is not affected seriously by errors in the age distributions, because this form of error is similar to age misstatement. The forward projection method uses a cumulation procedure that minimizes estimation error caused by age mistatement.

Age Pattern of Mortality Above Age 5

Model life tables that represent the age pattern of Turkish mortality above age 5 are needed in the forward projection method of mortality estimation. Once again, the life table of the Turkish Demographic Survey was used to choose among the Coale-Demeny regional families, which are indexed by level numbers. The choice is made by examining the levels within a family that exactly match the expectations of life at each age from age 5 upward. The relevant range for matching is from age 5 to 45, because the forward projection method cumulates the projections of deaths and survivors from ages within this range to the end of life. Some differences from actual age patterns of the selected model family above age 45 are tolerable so long as the cumulative measure, e_x, within the range x=5 to 45, matches well.

The goodness of fit of each family is shown by the chart in Figure 20. A precise horizontal line indicates a perfect fit of the family to the Turkish life table. The chart is constructed by calculating an index of fit, R_x:

$$R_x = (\text{Level at } e_x) \div (\text{Level at } e_5)$$

The Coale-Demeny families of models are indexed continuously from 1 to 24 within a family, the level number rising with increased expectation of life. At each value of e_x in the Turkish life table there is a unique model level in the family of models in question that has the same value of e_x. These unique matches are found for each value of e_x and divided in the expression above by the model level at e_5. Thus, the index of fit R_x takes a value of 1.0 at age 5 by definition. At higher ages R_x varies for each family and sex.

"East" fits marginally better than "West," particularly for females, but there is little overall difference in goodness of fit between the two. The other two families are clearly less good matches. The choice of the "East" family above age 5 is independent of the choice made earlier to use "East" for infant and early childhood mortality. The model levels, as well as the

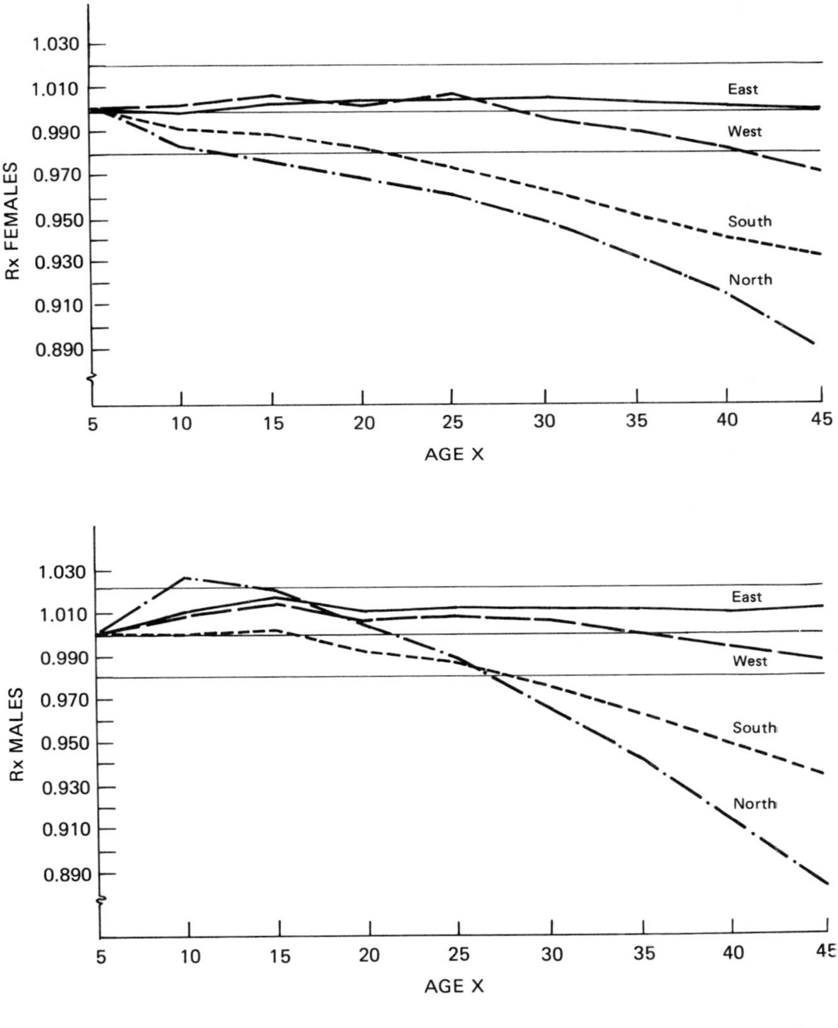

FIGURE 20 Comparison of Mortality Above Age 5 in Turkish Life Tables with Four Families of Model Life Tables: Turkey

families, were finally selected independently for adult and child mortality and then joined to form unique "split-level" models, as explained in the next section. Here, for adult mortality estimates, only the choice of a family above age 5 is needed.

Mortality Estimates Above Age 5

The results of applying the forward projection method are shown in Table 25, columns 2 and 3, and plotted in Figure 21. Estimates for a single intercensal period are sensitive to changes in census coverage, because increases in coverage cause survivorship to appear higher than it is and decreases in coverage have the opposite effect. Over a number of periods the total increase or decrease in census coverage can be assumed to be small even though estimates for particular five-year periods are elevated or depressed in irregular sequences. It is justified, therefore, to arrive at measures of a trend by smoothing with a graphing procedure, which is shown by the dashed line in Figure 21 and in columns 4 and 5 of Table 25.

Estimates through 1950 were allowed to stand without smoothing, because it is very likely that death rates were indeed higher in the 1940-1945 period than in earlier and later periods. From 1939 to 1946, Turkey faced several epidemics and severe shortages of food, especially in the cities, and a scarcity of drugs (Turkey, Ministry of Health and Social Welfare, 1973). Although estimates of mortality levels cannot be made from such information, the decrease in the expectation of life could be explained by such factors instead of by changes in census coverage.

For periods after 1950, a smooth trend can be graphed without difficulty except for the last five-year period, 1970-1975. The forward projection estimate for males appears to be unusually high relative to the previous period and relative to the gain in life expectancy measured for females. Several types of data error could be responsible, including migration error and an increase in census coverage as compared with 1970. For example, if the balance of male migration were assumed to be zero instead of -248,000 (Appendix Table D-1), the estimate of expectation of life at age 5 would drop from 69.7 years to 65.3 years.

At the time of the 1975 census (October), many Turkish males had not returned to their jobs in West Germany following the summer holidays. The economic recession in West Germany at that time caused restrictions and reduced incentives for workers to move there for jobs. The West German data on workers (see Appendix D) are not altogether adequate to date the worker flows. To the extent that Turkish workers are counted as outmigrants (part of the stock in Germany) and are enumerated at the same time in

TABLE 25 Estimates of Mortality Above Age 5 by Forward Projection, 1935-75: Turkey

	Expectation of Life in Years at Age 5, "East" Models			
	Preliminary Estimates by Forward Projection		Final Estimates by Graphing	
Dating of the Estimate	Males	Females	Males	Females
(1)	(2)	(3)	(4)	(5)
1935-40	51.4	50.2	51.4	50.2
1940-45	47.6	47.9	47.6	47.9
1945-50	56.9[a]	57.1[b]	53.1	54.0
1950-55	56.9[a]	57.1[b]	57.8	59.1
1955-60	63.4	64.8	60.4	61.9
1960-65	60.4	61.2	62.3	63.8
1965-70	61.5	64.3	63.5	65.5
1970-75	69.7[b]	67.1[b]	64.3	66.6

[a]A ten-year estimate was made in order to avoid using the 1950 census, which appears to have lower coverage of males and higher coverage of females than the previous or following censuses, causing disturbances in the orderly trend of estimates. The five-year points were then interpolated before making the final estimates by graphing.
[b]See discussion in text.

the *de facto* Turkish census, an upward bias is given to the estimated expectation of life at age 5 for 1970-75.

Another piece of evidence that weighs in the judgment about recent levels of mortality above age 5 is the life table being used, one based on TDS data for 1966-67 (Table 16). The life table shows an expectation of life at age 5 of 62.7 years for females and 60.2 years for males. The reference period is a year centered on 1967.2. For that same date the graphed estimates (after smoothing) in Figure 21 are 65.0 for females and 63.2 for males. The TDS evidence weighs against accepting higher estimates for life expectancy than the graphed trend. Since the life table provides estimates for one date only, rather than successive estimates over time by a comparable method, some difference between the level of the TDS estimates and the level of the trends graphed in Figure 21 is acceptable.

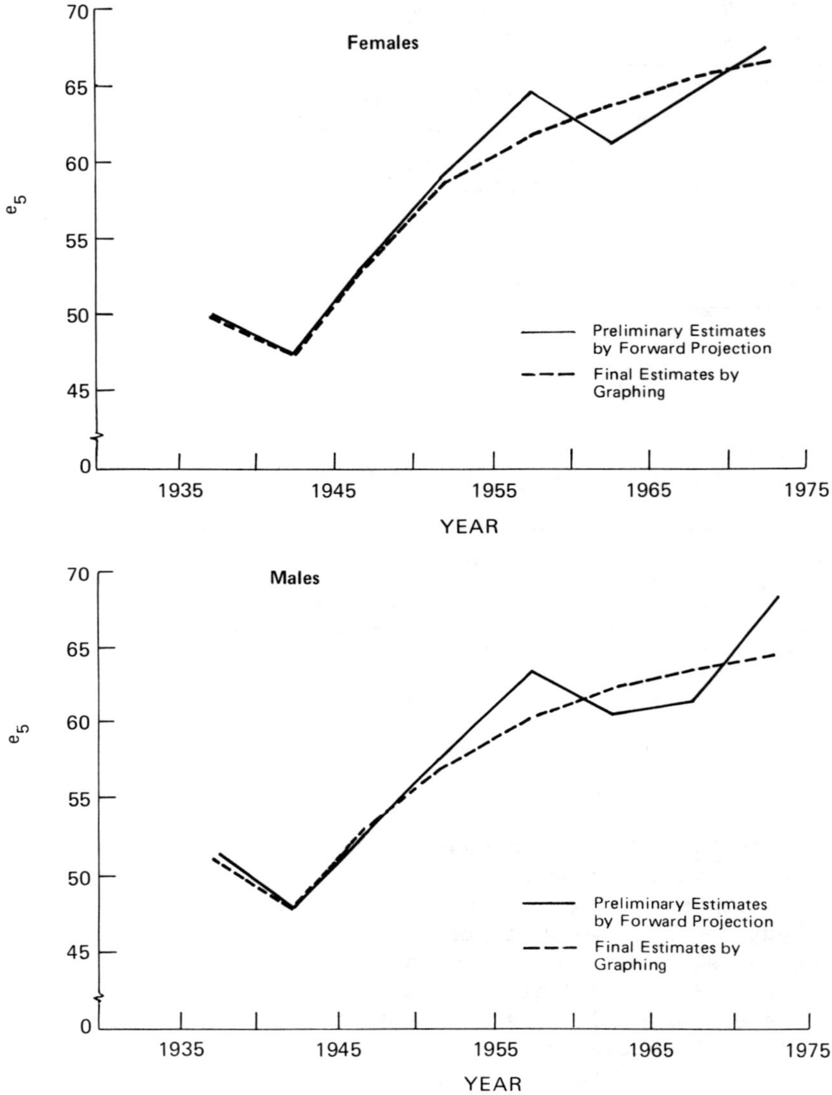

FIGURE 21 Estimates of Mortality Above Age 5 by Forward Projection, 1935-75: Turkey

NATIONAL GENERAL MORTALITY, 1935-75

While estimates of infant mortality and mortality rates above age 5 are valuable in themselves, the purpose of the following sections is to derive combined measures that express the general mortality of the population as a whole. This is done by constructing complete life tables for various dates that may be accepted as representative for the population as a whole.

Expectation of Life at Birth

The most general index of mortality is the expectation of life at birth, e_o, which summarizes the average survival experience of persons born into the population up to the end of life. Estimates of infant and early childhood mortality are joined with estimates of mortality above age 5 to form this general index. In effect, two life-table segments, one representing child mortality and one representing adult mortality, are joined to form a single life table that describes mortality in its entirety.

Numerically, the procedure is to utilize the following definition from the life table (radix = 1.):

$$e_o = {}_5L_o + T_5 = {}_5L_o + l_5 \times e_5$$

where ${}_5L_o$ and l_5 are from the life table representing mortality below age 5 and e_5 corresponds with a life table above age 5. As an example, the calculations for 1970-75 are shown below.

The index for child mortality is an infant mortality rate (${}_1q_o$) for both sexes combined of .126. This rate corresponds with a particular "East" model life table from which the corresponding indexes for ${}_5L_o$ and l_5 are derived for each sex separately (radix = 1.). The "East" model relationship of the sexes is assumed.

Index	Females	Males
${}_5L_o$	4.357	4.244
l_5	.8456	.8219

The measures of e_5 by sex for 1970-75 are from Table 25: 66.6 years for females and 64.3 years for males.

(1) e_o (females) $= 4.357 + (.8456)(66.6) = 60.7$
(2) e_o (males) $= 4.244 + (.8219)(64.3) = 57.1$
(3) e_o (both sexes) $= [60.7 + (1.05)(57.1)] \div 2.05 = 58.9$

The final equation for both sexes (3) recombines child mortality and exactly eliminates the "East" model assumption about sex differentials. The estimate resting most firmly on Turkish data, therefore, is the expectation of life at birth for both sexes combined.

Inspection of the actual sex differential in child mortality at the national level shows a difference from "East." In Table 26 the proportions of each sex dying up to ages 1 and 5 are taken from the 1966-67 life table. As in most populations, male mortality rates are higher in Turkey than female rates. However, they are not quite as much higher as the "East" model relationship predicts. Compared with the "East" populations (historical life tables of central and eastern Europe; north and central Italy), Turkish female infants and young children have lower survival rates. Consequently, there is a slight upward bias in estimates of e_o for females, and a corresponding downward bias for males. The bias calculated for 1966-67 is +0.2 years for females; for males it is -0.2 multiplied by the reciprocal of the sex ratio at birth. The bias at other dates is not known. For both sexes combined, however, no such bias exists (Table 27).

TABLE 26 Sex Differentials in Infant and Early Childhood Mortality Compared with Differentials Predicted by the "East" Models: Turkey

	Proportions Dying Up to Age x ($_xq_o$)		
	TDS Life Table		
Age x	Females	Males	Males Predicted by "East" from Females
1	.144	.162	.172
5	.192	.213	.219

TABLE 27 Expectation of Life at Birth, 1945-75: Turkey

Period	Females	Males	Both Sexes
1945-50	39.6	36.7	38.1
1950-55	45.2	42.0	43.6
1955-60	49.7	46.5	48.1
1960-65	53.7	50.5	52.1
1965-70	57.4	53.9	55.6
1970-75	60.7	57.1	58.9

Deviant Child-Adult Age Pattern

Although the age pattern of Turkish mortality is well represented by the model life tables within the age ranges below and above age 5, the overall Turkish relationship of child to adult mortality deviates markedly from the "East" pattern. This can be seen by noting the infant mortality rate that is predicted by the model life table from the known expectation of life at age 5, or by making the prediction starting from infant mortality as the known value. These two ways of viewing the deviant character of Turkish mortality are shown in Figure 22.

None of the four families of model life tables closes the gap displayed in the figure. The "South" models are somewhat closer to the Turkish child-adult relationship, but still far removed (Demeny and Shorter, 1968). It must be concluded, therefore, that high Turkish death rates in infancy and early childhood, as compared with mortality at higher ages, exceed the "normal" bounds observed in the history of Europe and other now-developed countries that are the basis for the Coale-Demeny models. This in no way damages the estimates made above of child, adult, and general mortality, because the models are used independently above and below age 5.

The deviation from "normal," taking "East" as a standard of normal, increases from the date of the first available measurement (1945-50) until around 1960. It peaks in 1960-65 by one index and in 1955-60 by the other. Thereafter the gap diminishes. Thus, it is evident that the decline of child mortality lags behind

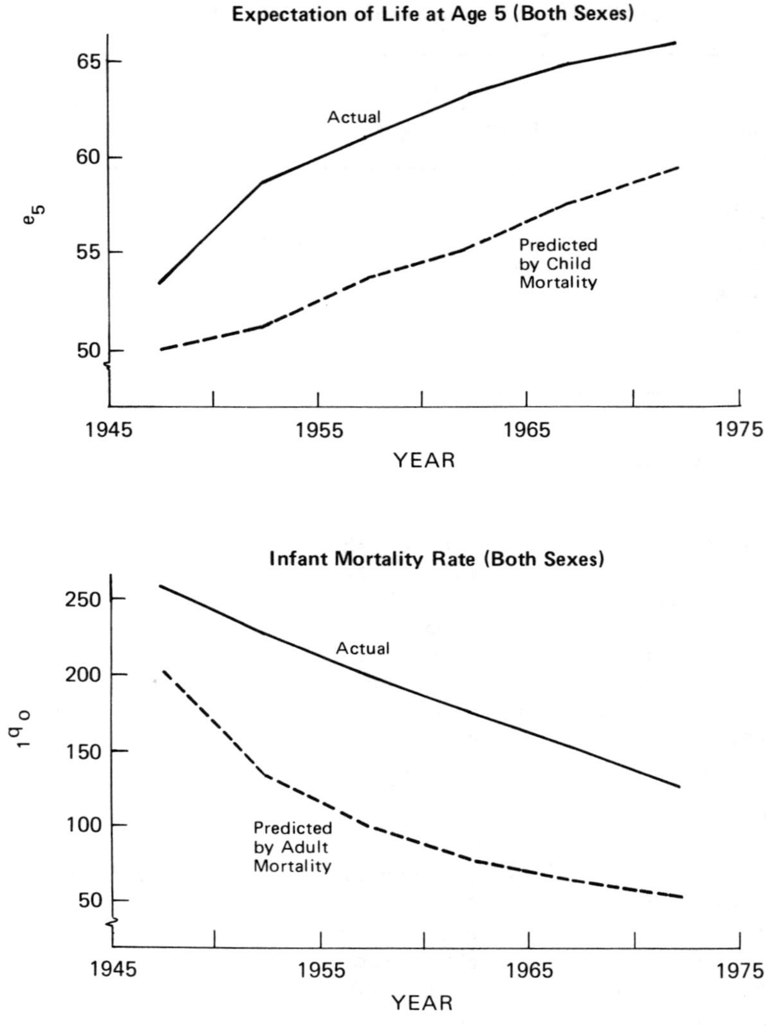

FIGURE 22 Changes in the Deviant Child-Adult Pattern of Turkish Mortality, 1945-75: Turkey

that of adult. The size of the gap may be interpreted as a measure of the inequality in health status between children and older persons, relative to an "East" historical standard.

Assumptions for Multiple Reverse Projections

The mortality assumptions needed for multiple reverse projections are now in hand for 1935 to 1975, excepting only infant and early childhood mortality for the earliest ten years, 1935 to 1945. The relationship of adult to child mortality just noted provides a basis for carrying the infant mortality assumptions back to this early period. The measured gap, in terms of the index $_1q_0$ in Figure 22 expands from .054 in 1945-50 to .103 in 1955-60, doubling in ten years. A simple reverse extrapolation to about one-half the initial value for ten years earlier in 1935-40 justifies an assumed gap at that time of .025. During the war years, 1940-45, very high adult mortality presumably caused the child-adult gap to disappear temporarily, so no gap is assumed. Based on these plausible assumptions the levels of infant mortality implied by adult mortality in 1935-40 and 1940-45 respectively were 273 and 306 per thousand assuming the relations of the "East" family of life tables. These assumed values for infant mortality complete the estimates needed as assumptions for the multiple reverse projections and are shown in Table 28.

TABLE 28 National Mortality Assumptions of the Multiple Reverse Projections, 1935-75: Turkey

Reverse Projection Period	Infant Mortality Rate, Both Sexes (per 1000 births)	Expectation of Life at Age 5 (years)		Both Sexes e_0
		Males	Females	
1970-75	126	64.3	66.6	58.9
1965-70	151	63.5	65.5	55.6
1960-65	176	62.3	63.8	52.1
1955-60	203	60.4	61.9	48.1
1950-55	233	57.8	59.1	43.6
1945-50	260	53.1	54.0	38.1
1940-45	306	47.6	47.9	31.4
1935-40	273	51.4	50.2	35.4

Source: Tables 18 and 25; see related text.

4 National Population Growth, 1935-75

Estimates from the preceding chapters are now brought together to describe the general process of population increase at a national level.

COMPONENTS OF POPULATION INCREASE

Changes in population size (p) are determined by the net effect of three components of change: births (b), migration (m), and deaths (d). Each of these components can be expressed as an annual rate of change in population size. The rates are additive when defined as geometric rates of increase: $p = b + m - d$. This equation provides a convenient basis for discussing the components of population increase.

Births and Migration

The rate of increase in population due to births, b, is the same as the crude birth rate. The rate of population change due to migration, m, is calculated from estimates of international migration (Appendix Table D-2) divided by the geometric midperiod means of population size according to the censuses (Table 1). These results are shown in the first two columns of Table 29.

Deaths

The third component, deaths, is measured by two alternative approaches. The first approach is to calculate the intercensal rate of population increase

TABLE 29 Rates of Population Change and Two Alternative Estimates of the Death Rate, 1935-75: Turkey

Period of Estimate	Rates of Population Change				Based on p from Reverse Projections	
	Births b	Migrations m	Increase p	Deaths d Est. I	p[a]	d Est. II
	(1)	(2)	(3)	(4)	(5)	(6)
1935-40	45.8	1.5	17.3	30.0	15.9	31.4
1940-45	43.3	.3	10.6	33.0	9.7	33.9
1945-50	46.0	.3	21.7	24.6	19.3	27.0
1950-55	48.3	1.3	27.8	21.8	26.1	23.5
1955-60	47.0	1.0	28.5	19.5	28.2	19.8
1960-65	43.2	-1.3	24.6	17.3	25.5	16.4
1965-70	38.8	-2.1	25.2	11.5	23.2	13.5
1970-75	34.9	-2.0	24.3	8.6	21.3	11.6

[a]The reverse projections are made from reported age distributions, except 1970-75, which is from an adjusted age distribution of a 1 percent sample of the 1975 census.

(from the population totals of Table 1), which gives p, shown in column 3 of Table 29, and then to utilize the equation, d = b + m - p. This first procedure yields Estimate I, shown in column 4 of Table 29.

The second approach is to utilize the rates of population increase implied by the multiple reverse projections (column 5 of Table 29) in the estimating equation. The result is Estimate II (shown in column 6). The two series of estimates are compared in Figure 23.

Each series of estimates has strengths and weaknesses. Estimate I errs in a downward direction whenever there is a relative increase in census coverage from one census to the next, because that raises p (column 3) erroneously. The upward kink in the curve of Estimate I at 1960-65 could be due to a decrease in census coverage in 1965 or to an increase in census coverage in 1970 (and 1975) relative to 1960. The reverse-projection estimates do not have this particular problem because, as explained in Chapter 2, each projection is made from a single census and therefore produces estimates that are independent of changes in census coverage.

In the reverse projections, the selected model life tables and age structures determine the number of persons

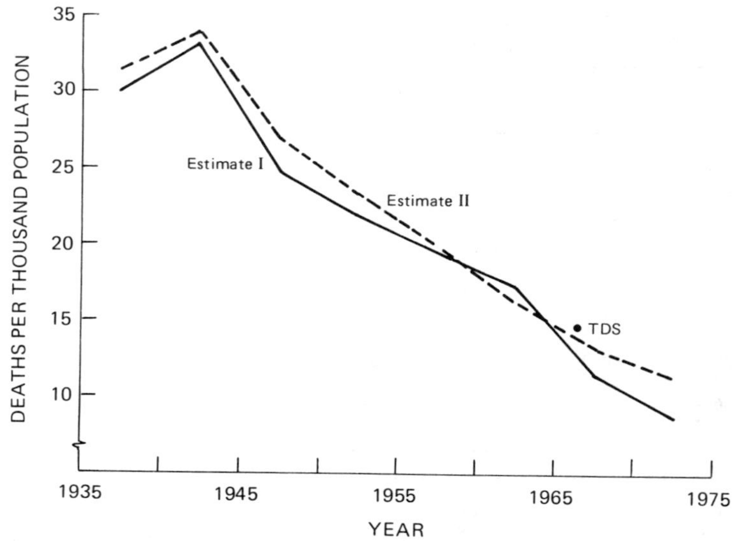

FIGURE 23 Alternative Estimates of the Crude Death Rate, 1935-75: Turkey

Source: Table 29.

removed from the population by death and hence are a factor in determining the rate of population increase, p (column 5). The age pattern of mortality involves most deaths at the very youngest and oldest ages, which are the locations in the age distribution most subject to errors of estimation. In addition, some error in the representation of Turkish conditions by the pattern of death rates in model life tables is to be expected at the extremities of age. This is not such a serious problem at young ages because reasonably strong estimates of infant and early childhood mortality are available (see Chapter 3), but adult mortality is not measured as accurately.

The level of Estimate II relative to Estimate I suggests that the errors in either or both series are systematic over time, because there is a more or less constant differential between the two. Whatever the source of the differences between Estimate I and II, the slope of the trend is very similar in both series. Thus, either estimate of trend would tell practically the same story. It is also reassuring to note that a wholly independent estimate of the death rate in 1966-67 by the Turkish Demographic Survey tends to confirm the level of Estimate II.

SUM OF COMPONENTS

Figure 5 in the Summary presents a convenient overall picture of the different components of population change and their sum, p, which is the rate of population increase. The two estimates of the death rate are averaged at each date for presentation in the upper panel. However, in order to show the official census estimates of the rate of population increase, an additional dashed curve of p is included in the lower panel. The general agreement of the two curves strengthens confidence in the estimated crude birth and death rates. Some error no doubt remains, particularly because estimates of international migration, which play a role in the indirect estimation procedures, are less strong than the other data.

Appendix A
Estimation of Fertility by Multiple Reverse Projection

Frederic C. Shorter

Reverse projection is known chiefly for its use in estimating past trends of fertility. Age structure is the crucial element of the census data from which inferences are drawn. Errors in the reporting of age are common in many countries, so use of census data for reverse projection requires methods that insulate the results from these age errors. Multiple reverse projection is such a method. It relies on reverse projections from a series of censuses arranged so that the effects of age reporting errors on estimates are systematically offset.

The method, and its application to the estimation of crude birth rates in Turkey, is explained in general terms in Chapter 2. The purpose of this appendix is to explain the data requirements of the method, its mathematical statement, and the results. One of the multiple reverse projections for Turkey is reproduced in detail below. This example illustrates how all components of population change--including fertility, mortality, and migration--are evaluated in a consistent manner over time.

DATA REQUIREMENTS

The minimum set of information needed for a reverse projection includes (1) a distribution of the population by age and sex and (2) assumptions about mortality over the period of the reverse projection. In a reverse projection, the number of births is reconstructed from information on the number of survivors in the current population distribution and the mortality to which they were subject in the past. Therefore, no fertility assumptions are necessary. Nevertheless, the results include numbers of births, crude birth rates, and general fertility rates.

The reverse projection is made by five-year age groups in steps of five years, going back in time as far as necessary. The minimum data may take the form of the following:

1. An age distribution for each sex in five-year age groups from age 0 to an open-ended interval 75+.
2. A set of life table survival rates for each sex for each five-year reverse projection period. These are normally selected from model life tables.

Optional data are the following:

3. For each sex separately, the proportion of the population aged 70+ that is aged 75+, based on data from actual censuses dated in multiples of five years prior to the starting date of the reverse projection. This information allows the distribution of population by age in the open interval, 75+, to be calculated using assumptions from the actual population rather than from the stationary population of the life table.
4. Net migration by five-year age groups for each sex for each five-year reverse-projection period. This information allows the effect of migration on the indirect estimates to be removed.
5. Age-specific and total fertility rates may also be calculated, if a standard age-specific fertility schedule is provided.

MATHEMATICAL STATEMENT

The basic element of a population projection is a group of persons whose common identification is their sex and period of birth. They form a birth cohort, which for convenience in calculations is defined as a five-year cohort. A reverse projection is made by "reverse surviving" each cohort separately back through time, in cycles of five years. Each cycle is a separate reverse projection providing the starting point for the next five years. The projection keeps track of each cohort separately as it is increased by reverse survival (deaths are restored to the population), by reversing in- and out-migrations, and removing cohorts from the population as the cohorts are carried back to birth. Cohorts are designated as follows for each five-year cycle:

Cohort index (c)	Age at Year -5	Age at year 0
0	Born	0-4
1	0-4	5-9
2	5-9	10-14
3	10-14	15-19
4	15-19	20-24
5	20-24	25-29
6	25-29	30-34
7	30-34	35-39
8	35-39	40-44
9	40-44	45-49
10	45-49	50-54
11	50-54	55-59
12	55-59	60-64
13	60-64	65-69
14	65-69	70-74
15	70-74	75-79
16	75+	80+

The reverse-survival equation, omitting migration for the moment, is as follows:

$$C^{-5}_{s,c} = C^{0}_{s,c}/S_{s,c} \quad (c = 0,16;\ \text{migration} = 0) \qquad (1)$$

where C is the five-year birth cohort, s stands for sex (male or female), c stands for the cohort index number, and S is the five-year survival rate. The superscript, 0 or -5, refers to the date in years.

When the reverse-survival equation is applied to the youngest birth cohort, c=0, the result is a quantity of births, B, during the five-year period:

$$B_s = C^{-5}_{s,o} \qquad (2)$$

At the upper end of the age distribution the two age groups 75-79 and 80+ are combined into 75+ in the initial data for year 0. In order to reverse-project this uppermost age group, the two cohorts that it contains (15 and 16) must be split out separately. The reverse-survival equation cannot be applied to cohorts 15 and 16 until this splitting has been performed.

In the absence of other information, the proportion of the life table population aged 75+ that is aged 75-79 is used as the basis for splitting:

$$C_{s,15} = [{}_5L_{75}/({}_5L_{75} + T_{80})] \cdot A \tag{3}$$

$$C^{o}_{s,16} = A - C^{o}_{s,15} \tag{4}$$

where ${}_5L_{75}$ and T_{80} are life table notation that refer respectively to person-years lived in the age interval 75-80 and from 80 years of age to the end of life. The notation A refers to the size of the given population that is aged 75+ at the base year of the projection (year 0).

The assumption of a stationary life table age distribution at the uppermost ages is usually incorrect in applied work, because mortality and fertility were neither equal nor constant in the past. Migration causes additional deviations from the stationary pattern. Nevertheless, for short reverse projections, such as five or ten years, an incorrect assumption about age structure at the highest ages will have a negligible effect on estimates of recent demographic rates (e.g., CBR and CDR). For longer reverse projections, however, the cumulative effect of error over a number of five-year cycles is a matter of concern.

A second approach to splitting the uppermost age group is to utilize independent information from a census at date -5 years concerning the actual distribution of population above age 70. Let p be the proportion of the population aged 70+ that is aged 75+ at date -5. The following four equations are solved for four unknowns to split out the two cohorts:

$$C^{-5}_{s,16} = p\,[C^{-5}_{s,15} + C^{-5}_{s,16}] \qquad \text{p is given} \tag{5}$$

$$A = C^{o}_{s,15} + C^{o}_{s,16} \qquad \text{A is given} \tag{6}$$

$$C^{-5}_{s,16} = C^{o}_{s,16}/S_{s,16} \qquad S_{s,16}\text{ is given} \tag{7}$$

$$C^{-5}_{s,15} = C^{o}_{s,15}/S_{s,15} \qquad S_{s,15}\text{ is given} \tag{8}$$

Four unknowns: $C^{-5}_{s,15}$; $C^{-5}_{s,16}$; $C^{o}_{s,15}$; $C^{o}_{s,16}$

An additional complexity is migration, which is included in the general formulation of the reverse projection. When migrations are distributed equally over the five-year period, a good approximation for the survival rate applicable to migrants is the following:

$$\frac{1+S_{s,c}}{2} \qquad \text{(for } c = 1,16\text{)}$$

For migrants in the youngest cohort, those who were born and who migrated during the interval, an approximation for the survival rate is the following (Shorter and Pasta, 1974:120-121):

$$.67 + .33\ S_{s,c}$$

To take migration into account equation (1) is replaced by two equations: one for the youngest cohorts (those born during the period) and a second for the remaining cohorts:

Youngest cohort:

$$C^{-5}_{s,o} = \frac{C^{o}_{s,o} - M_{s,o}[.67 + .33S_{s,o}]}{S_{s,o}} \tag{9}$$

Remaining cohorts:

$$C^{-5}_{s,c} = \frac{C^{o}_{s,c} - M_{s,c}\ (1+S_{s,c})/2}{S_{s,c}} \qquad [c = 1,16] \tag{10}$$

where $M_{s,c}$ refers to the migration information by sex and cohort. If the age group 75+ is split according to the procedures of equations (5) through (8), the effect of migration is included by substituting equation (10) for equations (7) and (8).

Births are produced separately by sex in the reverse projection. The sex ratio of births is a consequence of the relative sizes of the 0-4 age groups and the assumed mortality rates by sex. The proportion of births that are girls, g, where f and m refer to females and males respectively, is

$$g = C^{-5}_{f,c}/(C_{f,o} = C^{-5}_{m,o}) \tag{11}$$

Various fertility indices are calculated from the resulting projection. Total births are the sum of births by sex given by equation (2). The crude birth rate is total births divided by the geometric mean of the total population at dates 0 and -5. The general fertility rate is total births divided by the geometric mean of female population aged 15 to 44 at dates 0 and -5.

Age-specific fertility rates are calculated by introducing independent information about the distribution of childbearing by age of woman. These data are a model age-specific fertility schedule or a representative schedule from the population itself, expressed as rates or as a percentage distribution across the age range of 15-49. The schedule is denoted by F^*_i where the index, i, refers to the 7 five-year age groups from 15 to 49. The shape of the schedule, not its level, is used to distribute births by age of woman and thus to estimate the age-specific fertility rates.

A preliminary step is to calculate the geometric mean of women in each age group from 15 to 49, $\overline{W}_i$. A trial number of births, B*, is then calculated as follows:

$$B^* = 5 \cdot \sum_{i=1}^{7} (F^*_i \cdot \overline{W}_i) \tag{12}$$

Since the age-specific fertility rates, F^*_i, are not the actual ones, they must be revised by a multiplier, k, which brings B* into agreement with B.

$$k = B/B^* \tag{13}$$

$$F_i = kF^*_i \quad [i = 1,7] \tag{14}$$

The total fertility rate, T, is the sum of the age-specific rates:

$$T = 5 \cdot \sum_{i=1}^{7} F_i$$

MULTIPLE REVERSE PROJECTIONS FOR TURKEY

For the period from 1935 to 1975, there are nine censuses of which the last eight (1940 to 1975) provide the initial age data by sex for each reverse projection. The survival rates for 8 five-year periods (1935 to 1975) were taken from split-level "East" model life tables (Table 28). All the options for finer calculation and for the production of total fertility rates were used. The proportion of the population aged 70+ that was aged 75+ in each prior census (1935 to 1970) was obtained from the census age distributions (Table 1). Migration estimates provide assumptions for each five-year period from 1935 to 1975 (Appendix Table D-2). Standard schedules of age-specific fertility are also used (see section on standard fertility schedules).

The actual computations were made with a computer package available from the Population Council (Shorter and Pasta, 1974; Shorter, 1980). An example of the results for one reverse projection is shown in Table A-1.

The present study utilized multiple reverse projections based first upon age distributions as reported (Table 1) and then as adjusted for age misreporting (Appendix Table C-3). Standard fertility schedules were used reflecting both the "early 1960s" and the changing pattern assumptions.

The method works best when censuses are available at five-year intervals, but it can also be used with censuses spaced ten years apart. Using only the ten-year censuses for Turkey from 1945 to 1975, another series of estimates was produced. Both series are shown in Figure A-1. Since the reverse projections were made in steps of five years, estimates of the birth rate were obtained every five years and should be averaged over ten-year periods to reflect the lower degree of precision in the basic data.

TABLE A-1 Sample Reverse Projection (in thousands) from 1975 (1935-40 not shown): Turkey

FEMALES AGE	1940	1945	1950	1955	1960	1965	1970	1975
0	1450.9	1318.9	1593.3	1885.7	2324.8	2640.3	2767.7	2652.5
5	1239.2	1275.6	1197.4	1475.9	1771.7	2198.7	2518.3	2665.9
10	970.4	1195.9	1247.8	1188.5	1469.7	1757.8	2177.8	2495.7
15	779.7	942.0	1173.5	1238.2	1183.6	1457.6	1742.3	2160.2
20	493.0	749.3	918.3	1159.5	1227.6	1164.0	1433.3	1713.9
25	750.2	469.3	725.7	904.7	1146.5	1203.0	1132.1	1394.4
30	563.9	708.5	452.6	712.8	893.1	1124.3	1172.4	1098.9
35	557.3	529.6	679.6	443.4	701.5	875.3	1095.7	1141.3
40	490.9	520.6	506.0	661.1	435.2	685.9	850.1	1065.8
45	445.6	455.9	494.6	490.1	643.2	423.4	665.3	826.0
50	409.0	407.2	427.4	473.2	472.4	619.9	409.5	645.3
55	369.9	360.4	371.4	400.0	447.3	447.9	591.2	392.3
60	320.9	306.0	313.5	334.7	365.9	411.6	415.8	551.8
65	268.8	239.8	246.3	264.9	289.0	319.4	363.8	370.4
70	184.2	172.6	170.9	187.1	207.4	230.2	258.8	298.0
75+	160.2	145.6	155.6	173.2	199.4	230.1	266.3	308.1
TOT	9454.1	9797.3	10673.9	11992.8	13778.2	15789.3	17860.5	19780.5

MALES AGE	1940	1945	1950	1955	1960	1965	1970	1975
0	1460.9	1391.4	1665.8	2007.1	2492.2	2885.5	2905.3	2765.2
5	1371.7	1280.5	1258.8	1538.6	1882.5	2352.0	2749.1	2795.7
10	1115.3	1328.7	1255.9	1252.0	1534.8	1870.7	2331.3	2728.7
15	826.3	1087.1	1306.5	1248.2	1247.8	1524.1	1854.4	2314.2

20	512.5	794.8	1059.2	1289.6	1236.5	1217.7	1503.5	1833.1
25	751.0	488.9	770.1	1042.2	1273.7	1174.5	1166.6	1452.3
30	601.5	713.5	472.8	757.1	1029.0	1211.1	1097.1	1092.6
35	577.2	566.4	685.3	463.6	745.6	990.7	1143.6	1034.3
40	500.8	535.6	538.6	665.0	454.1	720.6	942.1	1095.2
45	358.4	456.3	502.0	517.1	642.9	436.8	685.5	903.6
50	288.9	318.9	419.0	472.8	492.0	611.9	414.4	654.5
55	252.1	248.2	283.9	383.5	437.7	457.3	571.8	388.8
60	216.2	204.9	210.7	249.1	341.2	391.7	412.1	517.5
65	196.5	160.7	161.4	173.0	208.5	288.2	333.8	353.4
70	143.3	126.8	112.3	119.0	131.0	160.2	224.2	261.9
75+	151.9	123.6	118.1	116.4	124.8	139.3	167.9	226.2
TOT	9324.6	9826.3	10820.3	12294.3	14274.2	16432.3	18502.7	20417.2
GRAND TOTAL	18778.7	19623.7	21494.2	24287.1	28052.4	32221.5	36363.2	40197.7

MIDPERIOD INDICES FOR FIVE-YEAR TIME PERIODS

POPULATION SIZE	19196.5	20537.6	22848.0	26101.9	30064.8	34229.8	38232.4
YEARLY BIRTHS	827.4	924.3	1057.2	1250.6	1382.2	1368.8	1263.0
YEARLY DEATHS	663.1	557.1	526.7	524.4	511.0	471.3	421.1
NET YEARLY MIGRANTS	4.7	6.9	28.1	26.9	-37.4	-69.2	-75.0

YEARLY RATES PER THOUSAND POPULATION

GFR=BIRTHS/FEM(15-44)	221.3	223.0	222.9	235.3	229.8	197.1	158.5
BIRTH RATE	43.1	45.0	46.3	47.9	46.0	40.0	33.0
DEATH RATE	34.5	27.1	23.1	20.1	17.0	13.8	11.0
NATURAL INCREASE	8.6	17.9	23.2	27.8	29.0	26.2	22.0
NET MIGRATION	0.2	0.3	1.2	1.0	-1.2	-2.0	-2.0
POP INCREASE	8.8	18.2	24.4	28.9	27.7	24.2	20.1

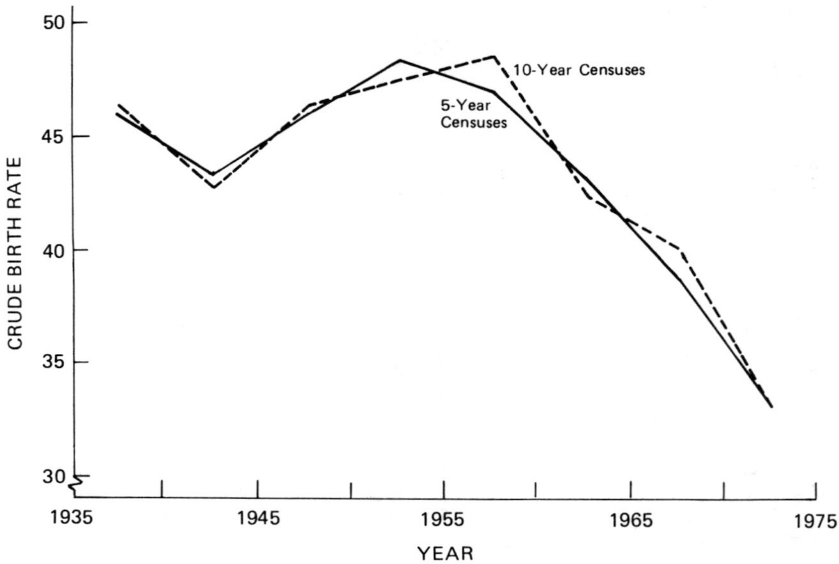

FIGURE A-1 Comparison of Estimates of CBR from Censuses Spaced Five and Ten Years Apart: Turkey (National, Reported Age Distributions)

Appendix B
Estimation of Trends in Infant and Early Childhood Mortality from Birth-Survival Histories

Miroslav Macura

This appendix describes a method for estimating time trends of infant and early childhood mortality for both sexes from birth-survival histories collected in a single sample survey. The method was developed expressly to estimate trends in Turkey from the birth-survival histories recorded in the 1968 Hacettepe survey. It was first employed in 1975 to obtain estimates for Turkey and her regional and urban-rural subpopulations (Macura, 1975a and 1975b). In the present study, the method was used to produce trend estimates for the six divisions of the country (Table 20).

DATA REQUIREMENTS

Application of the method entails the use of data routinely collected in birth-survival histories. The data refer to each live-born child and include: year of birth, the child's survival status at the time of survey, and the year of death if the child died before the survey year. The information is used to tabulate separately live-born and deceased children of both sexes by calendar year of birth. Among the former, only children born before the survey year are included. Among the latter, only those born and deceased before the year are covered. The tabulations are used to divide the numbers of deceased children by the corresponding numbers of live-born children by year of birth. The results are reported proportions dead prior to the survey year in single-year birth cohorts of children. The cohort proportions dead are used to estimate the trend of infant and early childhood mortality by the present method.

When estimates are sought for divisions of the country, as in the present study, women are classified by residence at the time of survey. The proportions dead obtained then pertain to selected divisions, subject to a number of reservations about the allocation of women's births to divisions different from present residence. Those are discussed in detail in Chapter 3.

APPLICATION OF THE METHOD

The method is described in two sections. The first explains a version of the method applicable to error-free data. In the second section, the version is extended to cope with certain imprecisions in data that normally arise in applying the method.

Estimation from Accurate Data

Let the year immediately prior to the survey year be denoted as t=0 and let time be measured in terms of calendar years, taking t=0 as the origin. Let d_a stand for the proportion dead at the end of the year t=0 in a cohort aged a years last birthday at this date. Let L_x be the life table number of person-years lived between exact years of age x and x+1. Now, there is an equation showing the relationship that exists between a cohort proportion dead and the cohort's probabilities of surviving through consecutive calendar years between birth and the end of t=0. If the life table radix, ℓ_0, is set equal to 1 and if an equation is written for each cohort, starting with the cohort aged 0 last birthday at the end of the year t=0, the following system of equations is obtained:

$$1 - (L_0)_0 = d_0$$

$$1 - (L_0)_{-1} \cdot (L_1/L_0)_0 = d_1$$

$$1 - (L_0)_{-2} \cdot (L_1/L_0)_{-1} \cdot (L_2/L_1)_0 = d_2$$

where subscripts of the survival ratios denote calendar years.

When information on d_a (for a=0, 1, 2, ...) is available from the birth-survival histories, the above equations make it possible to estimate the infant mortality rate, q(1), for each t (t=0, -1, -2,...) by utilizing Coale-Demeny model life tables (Coale and Demeny, 1966). The estimation procedure reduces to finding a model life table for each t, as follows.

First, a table for t=0 is located. It is the one that embodies the L_0 that satisfies the first equation. The table is found by interpolating linearly between both-sexes model life tables at integer levels of mortality of the selected Coale-Demeny family. It is then used to compute the survival ratios to which cohorts born before t=0 are exposed to in t=0: $(L_1/L_0)_0$, $(L_2/L_1)_0$,...

Next, a table for t=-1 is located. Given $(L_1/L_0)_0$, it embodies the L_0 for t=-1 that satisfies the second equation. The table is used to compute survival ratios to which cohorts born prior to t=-1 are exposed to in t=-1: $(L_1/L_0)_{-1}$, $(L_2/L_1)_{-1}$,...

Then, given $(L_1/L_0)_{-1}$ and $(L_2/L_1)_0$, the table for t=-2 which embodies the L_0 that satisfies the third equation is located. Further computations proceed in the same fashion.

Once the model tables for individual calendar years are located, the trend estimate is reached simply by associating the q(1)'s embodied in the tables with respective calendar years.

Estimation from Defective Data

Unless mortality rises strongly over time, the cohort proportions dead should increase as the cohort year of birth moves backward from t=0. When there are short-run fluctuations in mortality, the time schedule of proportions zigzags accordingly. Whenever the information used is defective, however, the schedules zigzag much more than could be possibly explained by the short-run fluctuations. Under most circumstances these excessive variations could plausibly be attributed to a more or less random misreporting of the year of birth and probably to sampling variance too. Both the misreporting and the sampling variance appear to affect the proportions of the cohorts born at earlier dates (say 20 to 30 years prior to t=0) more than those of cohorts born closer to the survey.

If the method is applied to proportions that are defective due to sampling variance and random misreporting, estimates of infant mortality rates referring to most of the years are biased; some are biased upward, the others downward. As a rule, estimates referring to years in which cohorts with unduly high proportions dead were born are upwardly biased and vice versa. Fortunately, it is largely possible to remove the bias arising from the data errors by utilizing smoothing, which is described next.

The proportions dead are first plotted against time (year of birth) and then approximated by a smooth, free-hand-drawn time schedule of proportions dead. Then, values of the proportions are read from the smooth schedule and converted into a trend estimate, as if the data utilized were error-free. Next, the time period spanned by the schedule is split into two intervals of approximately equal length and a ratio is calculated for each interval. The denominator of the ratio for the given time interval is the reported number of deaths that occurred before the survey year in cohorts born within the interval. The numerator is the number of deaths that would have occurred before the survey year if the cohorts born within the interval had been exposed to mortality conditions consistent with the smooth proportions.

To show how a ratio for a particular interval is computed, let S_a and D_a be, respectively, reported numbers of surviving and dying children before the end of t=0 in a cohort age a. Let d'_a be a "smooth" proportion dead of the same cohort and D'_a be the number of deaths consistent with d'_a, where D'_a is calculated as $(d'_a)(S_a)/(1-d'_a)$. The formula for calculating D'_a is derived from the definition of the smooth proportion dead: $d'_a = D'_a/(D'_a+S_a)$. Now the ratio of the time interval $-a_1$ to $-a_2$, a_2 a_1, is computed as:

$$\sum_{a=a_1}^{a_2} D'_a \div \sum_{a=a_1}^{a_2} D_a$$

where a is an age variable and a_1 and a_2 are years of age at the end of t=0 of cohorts born in the latest and the earliest years of the interval, respectively.

When the smooth schedule is a poor approximation of the observed proportions, the segment of the trend that refers to a few years immediately prior to t=0 is sawtoothed or kinked and/or one or both ratios differ markedly from unity. The ratio for a particular interval that exceeds (or falls short of) unity results from smooth proportions which on the average exceed (or fall short of) the corresponding observed proportions. Normally, it is necessary to draw a few smooth schedules before the one that approximates observed proportions closely is reached. The ratios implied by this schedule are close to unity and the trend obtained is smooth throughout. The trend is an estimate of the past time path of infant and early childhood mortality.

Use of Aggregated Cohorts

It is possible to save the time and effort entailed in estimating the trends if proportions of aggregated--say, two-year--rather than single-year birth cohorts are used. The use of three- or five-year cohort proportions is possible too. However, in order to control for imprecisions arising from the aggregation itself, estimation for Turkey was based on the proportions of the two-year cohorts.

BIASES ARISING FROM ERRORS IN DATA AND ASSUMPTIONS

The estimates of trends in infant and early childhood mortality based on birth-survival histories may suffer from several errors in data and assumptions. Concerning data inaccuracies, the trend estimates could be biased due to sampling variance and random misreporting of the year of birth, the two causes of data errors discussed earlier. They could also be defective as a result of selective omission of deceased children and misreporting that exaggerates time elapsed since birth.

To offset adverse effects of the sampling variance and the random misreporting, smoothing was incorporated into the estimation. It is fairly likely that under most circumstances smoothing keeps biases associated with these data problems under control. Under special conditions, however, smoothing is not equally useful; for example, when the number of children included in birth-survival histories is very limited and/or when year-of-birth misreporting, although largely random, is particularly pronounced. Under such circumstances, the trend obtained may depend to a considerable degree on the choice of the intervals for which ratios are computed.

Errors in data associated with selective omission of deceased children and year-of-birth misreporting that exaggerates time elapsed since birth affect the trend estimates fully. To the extent these two problems exist, they probably affect more strongly information pertaining to children born longer ago. Hence, it is quite likely that these two causes of data errors, when present, result in proportions dead that rise less steeply than in reality with the cohort year of birth, as it moves backward from the survey year. When the proportions dead are defective in the way just described, infant mortality rates referring to earlier years are downwardly biased and consequently the overall rate of mortality decline is underestimated.

The trend estimation is based on a few implicit assumptions. Whenever the method is applied, two assumptions are used. The first maintains that the age pattern of mortality between ages 0 and 25 to 30 embodied in the Coale-Demeny model family used closely approximates the pattern prevailing in the population for which the estimate is sought. The second assumption postulates no association between the survival of mothers and the mortality of their children.

When the estimation is performed for regional and urban-rural divisions of the national population, two additional assumptions are made. According to the first, effects on the trend estimates arising from transfers of infant and childhood mortality experience across divisional boundaries are minor; the transfers are assumed to be the consequence of pre-survey migration of women. According to the second, transfers of the mortality experience across urban-rural boundaries, which arise from reclassification of communities as their size changes, have negligible effects on trend estimates.

Nonfulfillment of the assumptions leads to biases in the estimates. Thus, when the model and real age patterns of mortality differ, the trend estimate is erroneous. Likewise, when the assumptions on approximate neutrality of transfers of infant and childhood mortality experience are violated, the divisional estimates are bound to be biased. These qualifications of the estimates are discussed in greater detail in Chapter 3 and adjustments are introduced to take the more important biases into account.

Appendix C
Adjustment of the National Censuses for Age Misreporting

Age misreporting is a common defect of censuses, and a variety of methods have been developed to deal with the problem. A procedure suitable for the Turkish censuses was developed by Demeny and Shorter (1968). In recent years, refinements of the method have appeared in the literature, and they are useful for interpreting the age misreporting pattern.

Misreporting consists of raising or lowering one's age, which affects the standard census age distribution by transferring some persons across the boundaries of standard five-year age groups. Das Gupta (1975) applied a model of these transfers to Turkish females in the 1955 and 1960 censuses, and showed that misreporting for females typically consists of upward transfer (Table C-1). Above age 40, age heaping (see glossary) dominates, but it does not stop the persistent upward "slide" that starts from the very youngest age group. The overall pattern is the so-called Asia-Africa one described in Manual IV (United Nations, 1967); it was identified in Turkey by Demeny and Shorter and confirmed by Das Gupta (1975) and Ntozi (1978), each using somewhat different methods.

A fine example of Turkish age exaggeration comes from the 1935 census, which tabulated persons aged 100 years old and over by province. In that census, 2,256 males and 3,985 females claimed to be centenarians. The centenarian rates were approximately 1,000 per million inhabitants in Eastern Turkey and 200 in Western Turkey. An old but reasonably accurate Japanese life table with a life expectation of 42 years for males (similar to that of Turkey in 1935) shows only 2 centenarians per million inhabitants.

TABLE C-1 Proportions of "True" Population of Females in 1955 Transferred Upward or Downward from Five-Year Age Groups by Misreporting: Turkey

Age Group	Population[a] (thousands) Enumerated	"True"	Direction of Transfer	Population Transfers Up	Down	Proportions of "True" Population Transferred Up	Down
0-4	1,889	1,970.7	up	81.7	--	.041	--
5-9	1,570	1,531.7	up	43.4	--	.028	--
10-14	1,097	1,113.4	up	59.8	--	.054	--
15-19	1,094	1,167.0	up	32.8	--	.114	--
20-24	1,117	1,131.2	up	47.0	--	.130	--
25-29	1,027	954.1	up	74.1	--	.078	--
30-34	735.1	689.1	up	28.1	--	.041	--
35-39	528.5	515.5	up	15.1	--	.029	--
40-44	624.7	587.3	neither	--	--	--	--
45-49	475.6	544.6	both	46.7	22.3	.086	.041
50-54	531.0	479.4	neither	--	--	--	--
55-59	310.4	383.5	both	68.2	4.9	.178	.013
60-64	389.3	301.1	neither	--	--	--	--
65-69	173.7	216.2	both	22.5	20.0	.104	.093
70-74	172.1	155.2	up	5.6	--	.036	--
75 +	159.3	153.0	neither	--	--	--	--
Total	11,893	11,893					

[a]The population of 1955 is adjusted relative to 1960 for the effect of international migration as required by the correction procedure.

Source: Computed from Das Gupta (1975).

The elegant representation of misreporting achieved by the Das Gupta refinement of the Demeny-Shorter procedure requires elaborate computer work; a different program is required for each sex and every pair of censuses. Comparing Das Gupta's results with those of Demeny-Shorter's original, rather simple method shows that there is little practical difference (Table C-2). Therefore, the simpler approach is preferable for practical applications.

PATTERNS OF AGE ERROR BY SEX

The pattern of age error for Turkish females and males differs markedly, though not in the youngest two age groups. The amount of excess or deficient reporting due to age transfers is shown in Figure C-1 for each age

TABLE C-2 Comparison of Demeny-Shorter (D-S) and P. Das Gupta (PDG) "Corrections" of Age Distributions for Misstatement of Age, Females, 1955 and 1960: Turkey

1960 Census (in thousands)				Size of "Correction" (percents)			
		"Corrected"		1960		1955[a]	
Age Group	Census as Enumerated	D-S	PDG	D-S	PDG	D-S	PDG
0-4	2,079.0	2,159.0	2,169.0	4	4	4	4
5-9	1,928.0	1,892.0	1,892.0	-2	-2	-2	-2
10-14	1,489.0	1,512.0	1,517.0	2	2	1	2
15-19	1,059.0	1,100.0	1,103.0	4	4	7	5
20-24	1,128.0	1,128.0	1,152.0	0	2	1	0
25-29	1,177.0	1,108.0	1,114.0	-6	-5	-7	-6
30-34	985.8	955.7	937.9	-3	-5	-6	-4
35-39	693.8	694.8	676.2	0	-3	-2	0
40-44	548.4	518.9	504.3	-5	-8	-6	-6
45-49	500.0	570.8	572.1	14	14	15	15
50-54	581.2	530.9	526.1	-9	-9	-10	-9
55-59	369.4	450.9	456.5	22	24	24	24
60-64	461.4	359.9	355.6	-22	-23	-23	-23
65-69	213.8	258.5	265.9	21	24	24	24
70-74	195.7	175.7	174.8	-10	-11	-10	-11
75+	182.1	177.3	175.2	-3	-4	-4	-5
Total	13,591	13,591	13,591	0	0	0	0

Note: These "corrections" were in both instances based on the use of "South" model life tables. Subsequent research has shown that split-level "East" models are the best fit to Turkish mortality. Adjustments of age distributions by the panel are based on the "East" models.

[a]Enumerated and corrected data not shown in this table.

Sources: Demeny and Shorter (1968:33, 53-54); Das Gupta (1975:311).

group by selecting a reasonably representative pair of censuses (1955 and 1960) to show the differences by sex. Females are underreported in the range of 10 to 25 years of age and overreported from 25 to 35. This particular vacating of one age range and overreporting of another is probably due to claims of a higher-than-true age immediately after marriage or childbearing. Note that the quantitative amounts of error do not necessarily imply that very large numbers of people misreport age.

Males on the other hand, are attributed ages on a different social basis than females, with the result that they are overreported in the 10-20 age range and underreported from 20 to 30. Some persons apparently claim, or are judged by enumerators, to be below the age

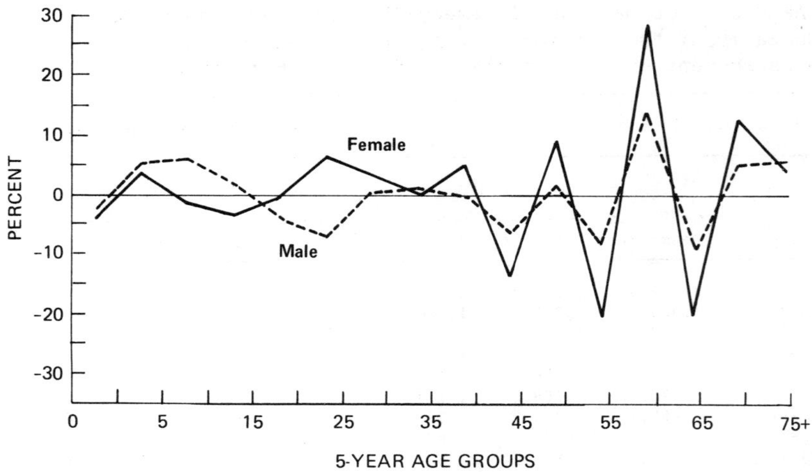

FIGURE C-1 Age Errors by Sex: Difference Between Enumerated and Corrected Population by Five-Year Age Groups: Turkey (excess as percent of corrected)

Source: For 1955-60 pair of census, see Tables 1 and C-3.

of military service (about age 20), or marriage (mid-20s) until these events actually occur. This causes many males to be reported at a lower age when they are actually in the 20-30 range, thus depleting the number reported in the upper range. At the upper end of the 20-30 range, some men may well be reported at ages above 30 if they are married. Males typically marry in their mid- and late 20s and thereafter become known as 30 or above even if they are not in fact that old.

Age heaping on tens above age 40 is stronger for females than males, suggesting that female age reporting is generally less accurate than male reporting.

AGE CORRECTIONS FOR 1935-75

The Demeny-Shorter method was applied to all pairs of censuses from 1935-40 to 1970-75. The method works well for the period from 1935 to 1960. Thereafter, out-migration was substantial and age errors in the migration data cause errors in the estimated correction factors themselves. The pattern of age errors detected for each sex is stable over the 1935-60 period, with a slight trend toward reduced magnitude in general. The corrections for 1935 to 1960 were carried out, therefore, by fitting a linear trend to the age correction factors for each age group between 1935-40 and 1955-60. The factors were then held constant after 1960. The corrected national age distributions are shown in Table C-3 and Figure C-2.

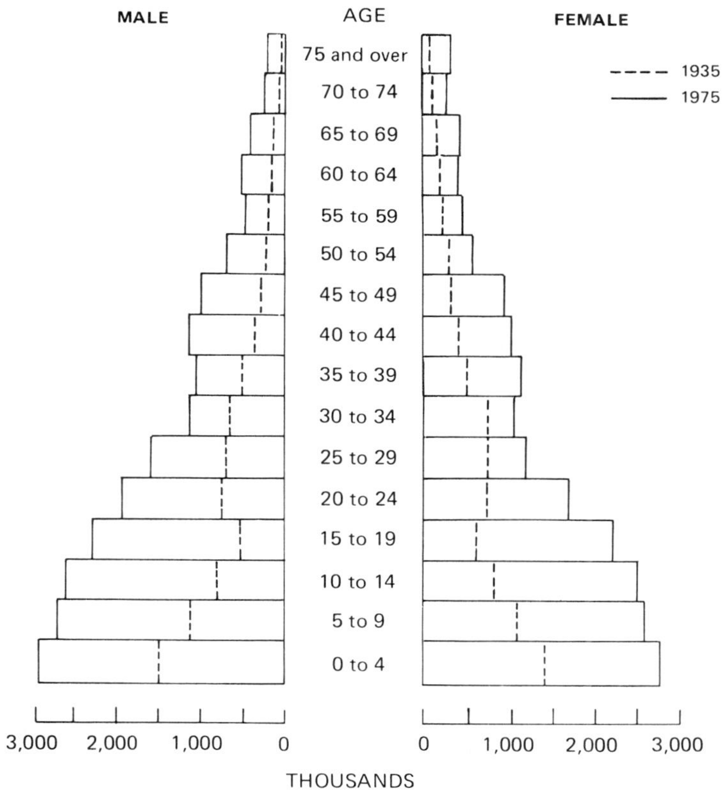

FIGURE C-2 Population by Age and Sex Corrected for Age Misreporting, 1935 and 1975: Turkey

Source: Table C-3.

TABLE C-3 Population (in thousands) by Age and Sex, Corrected for Age Misreporting, 1935-75: Turkey

Age	1935[a]	1940	1945	1950	1955	1960	1965	1970	1975[b]
Males									
0-4	1,486.0	1,427.0	1,331.0	1,638.0	2,053.0	2,270.5	2,462.5	2,775.4	2,882.0
5-9	1,122.0	1,312.0	1,261.0	1,258.0	1,587.0	1,987.0	2,323.0	2,505.0	2,681.1
10-14	802.1	1,115.0	1,210.0	1,201.0	1,221.0	1,601.1	1,958.7	2,243.8	2,589.5
15-19	541.5	798.9	1,018.0	1,235.0	1,217.0	1,228.3	1,527.6	1,896.9	2,279.6
20-24	767.2	533.4	809.1	1,017.0	1,245.0	1,221.6	1,262.5	1,556.0	1,905.1
25-29	691.3	748.3	528.2	785.9	1,030.0	1,238.3	1,134.8	1,188.9	1,557.4
30-34	647.4	663.6	770.6	538.5	751.7	1,011.6	1,126.1	1,005.5	1,077.4
35-39	519.4	614.1	624.2	694.1	514.9	733.0	980.6	1,095.6	1,013.7
40-44	348.0	489.0	562.6	562.3	668.5	501.3	701.9	915.6	1,087.6
45-49	263.2	324.6	430.5	533.2	558.5	650.6	477.4	689.1	965.3
50-54	222.7	242.3	277.4	381.1	494.2	538.5	604.2	450.0	644.1
55-59	186.7	197.7	192.1	237.5	358.9	463.3	492.9	543.7	425.1
60-64	146.0	158.9	169.9	169.3	211.4	326.1	402.2	422.2	458.4
65-69	117.3	114.5	111.9	127.8	139.1	181.6	282.8	351.8	386.4
70-74	89.7	80.5	77.3	74.0	93.6	107.8	138.6	209.7	248.6
75+	79.5	79.7	71.7	75.4	90.3	103.3	121.2	157.9	215.8
Subtotal	8,030	8,899	9,447	10,527	12,233	14,164	15,997	18,007	20,417

Females									
0-4	1,399.0	1,328.0	1,245.0	1,574.0	1,962.0	2,163.4	2,356.4	2,693.2	2,752.0
5-9	1,074.0	1,192.0	1,176.0	1,174.0	1,498.0	1,867.2	2,181.1	2,399.7	2,574.5
10-14	809.3	1,044.0	1,117.0	1,106.0	1,106.0	1,496.9	1,822.2	2,173.7	2,502.2
15-19	563.1	780.2	1,018.0	1,194.0	1,141.0	1,091.7	1,407.4	1,820.1	2,219.7
20-24	683.7	538.3	709.3	983.7	1,115.0	1,123.0	1,129.3	1,346.0	1,701.2
25-29	680.1	655.7	575.9	698.9	956.2	1,107.4	1,093.3	1,082.6	1,307.6
30-34	590.0	656.0	649.9	554.7	699.2	959.8	1,105.7	1,131.9	1,066.7
35-39	515.2	566.4	577.0	598.0	527.6	700.5	944.6	1,105.0	1,148.9
40-44	442.3	490.5	519.4	557.0	588.0	525.2	648.9	859.6	1,017.6
45-49	386.4	416.4	448.0	520.8	550.4	578.4	497.4	650.8	952.6
50-54	332.2	359.9	381.2	419.8	479.8	538.3	548.0	472.1	596.1
55-59	278.6	297.4	292.8	337.5	391.8	458.0	515.1	544.8	484.5
60-64	213.3	236.0	257.3	269.4	298.2	363.8	395.9	416.8	433.3
65-69	159.3	164.0	172.1	203.8	219.7	261.2	331.6	389.2	451.2
70-74	101.8	106.8	111.0	117.8	150.2	176.4	199.2	238.7	267.9
75+	89.3	90.3	94.2	111.1	148.3	179.7	217.9	268.9	303.1
Subtotal	8,317	8,922	9,344	10,420	11,831	13,591	15,394	17,598	19,780
Total	16,347	17,821	18,790	20,947	24,065	27,755	31,391	35,605	40,198

[a]Includes province of Hatay, annexed in 1939.
[b]Preliminary: estimated from a one percent sample of the 1975 census.

Appendix D
International Migration

Data on international migration are required for several of the procedures used in this report: estimating crude birth rates by multiple reverse projections (Chapter 2), estimating mortality above age 5 by forward projection (Chapter 3); and adjusting the censuses for age misreporting (Appendix C). Available data were used, therefore, to establish estimates of the net balance of migration and its distribution by sex and age.

MIGRATION VOLUME

The censuses of West Germany enumerate population by national origin. These censuses, reports by the Labor Bureau in Turkey, and special studies of the State Planning Organization based on Turkish consular surveys and other sources, were used to formulate the migration estimates from 1960 to 1975. For 1935 to 1960, volume estimates by Turkish scholars are available (Geray, 1962; Turkay, 1962).

Censuses of destination countries such as West Germany are particularly useful in making migration estimates, because they keep track of the stock of Turks living abroad. Two-way circulation with the home country shows up as changes in this stock after allowance for natural increase. To illustrate how this estimation procedure works, the use of the West German censuses to estimate the net flow during 1970-75 is explained below.

The Turkish population in West Germany increased from 429.4 thousand in May 1970 to 1,079.3 thousand at the end of September 1976. (Data for the exact five-year period, 1970-75, are not available.) This change amounts to an annual rate of increase of 14.5 percent. Births to

Turkish parents living in Germany (both parents Turks) were 161.4 thousand, implying a crude birth rate among the migrants of 43 per thousand. Since the death rate presumably is low (perhaps about 8), natural increase may be assumed to be 3.5 percent. A population increase of 11 percent (14.5 percent less 3.5 percent) due to migration implies the volume of Turkish migration to Germany during the five years from October 1970 to October 1975. To calculate the growth of the migrant population over the five-year period, the following equation is used:

$$P_1 = P_o(e^{rt})$$

where P_1 is the population to be estimated, P_o is the original population, r is the yearly rate of growth, and t is time elapsed (years) between the dates of P_o and P_1.

Size of Migrant Stock	Thousands
Oct. 1970: 429.4 $e^{(.145)(.5)}$	461.7
Oct. 1975: 429.4 $e^{(.145)(5.5)}$	953.3
Change in size over five years	+491.6
Allocate 11.0/14.5 to migration	372.9
Balance due to natural increase	118.7

A second source of information is annual data from West Germany on migrant movements themselves. These data, shown below, justify a five-year net migration estimate of 300 to 400 thousand:

Year	Net Migrants (thousands)
1971	+126.4
1972	not available
1973	+162.8
1974	+ 50.0
1975	- 49.9

An upward bias may exist in these particular data because they are described as including "short-term" in-migrants. The out-migrant data, on the other hand, are deletions from local population registers where Turks have registered their residence.

Allowing a margin for net migration to other countries, and for demographic growth of the net migrant flow after arrival abroad, the demographic effect on the Turkish population in Turkey for 1970-75 is estimated at a loss of 400 thousand persons. This estimate, taken together with estimates from other sources for other dates, provides the series shown in the last column of Table D-1.

The distribution of migrants by sex and age for the years since 1960 is found in a sample survey by Abadan (1964), the censuses of the Federal Republic of Germany, and Turkish consular reports collected and analyzed by

TABLE D-1 Demographic Effect of International Migration on National Population Size, 1935-75: Turkey

Intercensal Period of Migration	Change in National Population (thousands)		
	Males	Females	Total
1935-40	67.3	67.5	134.8
1940-45	12.6	12.4	25.0
1945-50	18.6	18.4	37.0
1950-55	77.8	75.2	153.0
1955-60	73.5	70.5	144.0
1960-65	-161.8	-37.8	-199.6
1965-70	-256.0	-114.6	-370.6
1970-75	-248.0	-152.0	-400.0

Note: The demographic effect of migration at the end of a five-year period of migration differs from the actual number who migrate during the period, because the migrant population continues to change with natural increase between the dates of migration and the second census date of the period.

Sources: Estimates for 1935-60 are based on Geray (1962) and Turkay (1962). For 1960-70, estimates are from the State Planning Organization. The 1970-75 estimate is from an analysis of the census and vital statistics of the Federal Republic of Germany and from information on the pattern of destinations in prior years.

the State Planning Organization. For periods prior to 1960, international migration was chiefly whole families, because it was relocation of population. A reasonable assumption is that migration up to 1960 had the same sex and age distribution as the Turkish population.

The estimates that provide the assumptions for the multiple reverse projections of Chapter 2 are shown in Tables D-2 and D-3. Adjustments for age misreporting and the estimation of mortality above age 5 make use of the material in Table D-1.

The migration data are useful as intermediate estimates for other calculations, even though they are subject to considerable possibilities for error. The methods used to estimate fertility and mortality were handled with an awareness of the extent of error introduced by migration error. Judgment based on general knowledge of the Turkish situation has been used to accept some implications and not others.

TABLE D-2 Average Yearly International Migration for Intercensal Periods, 1935-75: Turkey

	Net Migration (thousands)		
Period	Males	Females	Total
1935-40	12.8	12.9	25.7
1940-45	2.4	2.3	4.7
1945-50	3.5	3.4	6.9
1950-55	14.3	13.8	28.1
1955-60	13.7	13.2	26.9
1960-65	-30.3	- 7.1	-37.4
1965-70	-47.8	-21.4	-69.2
1970-75	-46.5	-28.5	-75.0

TABLE D-3 Distribution of Net International Migration by Age, for Each Sex, 1960-75: Turkey

Age Group	1960-65 Males	1960-65 Females	1965-75 Males	1965-75 Females
0-4	5.2	21.4	4.4	9.5
5-9	2.2	9.0	4.6	9.4
10-14	-1.2	-4.5	3.9	7.6
15-19	1.1	13.0	0.5	3.3
20-24	20.5	30.2	4.8	20.6
25-29	40.2	21.4	26.8	17.7
30-34	19.4	9.0	26.8	13.7
35-39	9.1	4.2	16.0	10.6
40-44	2.9	1.1	9.7	8.4
45-49	1.6	0.8	3.5	1.2
50-54	-0.4	-1.3	-0.3	-0.5
55-59	-0.2	-1.1	-0.2	-0.4
60-64	-0.2	-1.3	-0.2	-0.4
65-69	-0.1	-0.8	-0.1	-0.3
70-74	-0.0	-0.5	-0.1	-0.2
75+	-0.0	-0.5	-0.0	-0.2
Total	100.0	100.0	100.0	100.0

Appendix E
Population by Six Divisions by Age and Sex, 1945-70

TABLE E-1 Population of Six Divisions by Age and Sex as Reported in the Censuses, 1945-70: Turkey[a]

	Urban			Rural			
	Istanbul Izmir	Other West	Central East	West	Central	East	National
Part A	1945						
Males							
0-4	36,917	41,900	78,949	395,816	416,395	318,378	1,288,355
5-9	38,388	44,888	85,383	424,906	437,495	319,078	1,350,138
10-14	45,774	51,471	89,755	424,415	413,602	261,523	1,286,540
15-19	64,117	57,064	94,640	341,004	305,360	187,794	1,049,979
20-24	78,613	88,732	124,208	252,073	124,759	121,620	790,005
25-29	39,791	31,612	47,815	154,439	120,546	90,695	484,898
30-34	53,597	43,629	63,731	254,561	203,634	112,995	732,147
35-39	42,011	34,702	49,134	216,404	170,736	95,098	608,085
40-44	35,045	30,278	43,236	193,174	153,045	88,175	542,953
45-49	32,821	24,943	34,015	140,803	102,784	66,475	401,841
50-54	24,583	16,988	23,606	86,851	68,229	62,934	283,191
55-59	18,313	12,640	13,979	59,729	36,602	30,086	171,349
60-64	17,768	11,334	15,777	58,182	46,181	50,896	200,138
65+	24,578	15,893	18,079	85,493	58,304	54,620	256,967
Total	552,316	506,074	782,307	3,087,849	2,657,675	1,860,363	9,446,584
Females							
0-4	36,546	40,351	72,585	375,792	383,100	278,173	1,186,547
5-9	37,609	43,820	80,811	403,697	402,375	275,768	1,244,080
10-14	42,466	46,751	78,339	370,285	337,495	200,263	1,075,599
15-19	52,722	46,974	73,702	321,772	275,483	162,094	932,747
20-24	47,537	35,363	55,711	221,194	194,233	138,608	692,646
25-29	33,767	25,602	43,532	195,388	193,413	128,257	619,959
30-34	42,428	31,697	50,784	229,827	213,470	132,442	700,648
35-39	39,783	29,720	46,941	199,696	169,498	93,556	579,194
40-44	35,229	27,049	41,626	182,625	163,731	108,518	558,778
45-49	32,207	22,507	28,822	138,723	103,347	53,399	379,005
50-54	28,806	20,479	29,464	140,420	129,665	85,873	434,707
55-59	22,412	14,823	15,514	87,750	53,582	25,602	219,683
60-64	22,375	16,756	23,316	119,748	104,391	63,092	349,678
65+	32,751	23,861	24,737	141,059	92,259	55,662	370,329
Total	506,638	425,753	665,884	3,127,970	2,816,039	1,801,309	9,343,593

TABLE E-1 (continued)

	Urban			Rural			
	Istanbul Izmir	Other West	Central East	West	Central	East	National
Part B 1950							
Males							
0-4	51,123	57,768	102,165	479,374	504,149	390,542	1,585,121
5-9	47,999	53,142	92,025	404,788	417,761	322,823	1,338,538
10-14	46,063	51,591	88,788	400,441	405,436	283,253	1,275,572
15-19	73,033	60,490	98,020	400,668	385,181	253,943	1,271,335
20-24	85,009	76,805	131,902	291,041	228,648	177,478	990,883
25-29	54,547	26,828	53,682	251,731	190,636	149,606	727,030
30-34	50,047	49,724	57,592	140,459	124,257	102,236	524,315
35-39	44,964	42,810	52,735	244,674	192,124	111,113	688,420
40-44	47,367	31,989	50,390	187,206	150,145	84,878	551,975
45-49	36,174	31,057	39,901	176,251	134,652	81,765	499,800
50-54	27,625	22,586	29,839	139,588	106,826	63,142	389,606
55-59	19,710	12,142	15,059	69,763	49,749	47,877	214,300
60-64	17,978	15,627	16,678	59,849	44,316	42,637	197,085
65+	27,360	19,215	19,840	85,159	60,644	60,883	273,101
Total	628,999	551,774	848,616	3,331,000	2,994,523	2,172,177	10,527,089
Females							
0-4	49,872	57,730	97,766	461,487	483,081	359,327	1,509,263
5-9	46,488	52,998	88,608	381,115	388,523	280,598	1,238,330
10-14	44,099	50,170	80,713	350,108	339,463	217,598	1,082,151
15-19	53,871	55,178	82,013	369,687	346,503	212,423	1,119,675
20-24	58,974	51,116	75,552	307,322	286,422	194,772	974,158
25-29	44,082	29,013	52,420	236,532	226,637	163,898	752,582
30-34	41,326	38,895	50,993	163,055	171,474	125,573	591,316
35-39	42,350	36,501	47,255	196,536	175,302	102,793	600,737
40-44	43,642	31,069	47,191	198,486	174,704	100,854	595,946
45-49	34,907	27,186	32,610	148,641	126,240	76,216	445,800
50-54	34,075	26,192	34,999	162,872	134,917	78,990	472,045
55-59	21,541	15,252	16,351	91,029	71,489	44,838	260,500
60-64	27,997	22,953	26,424	125,309	97,797	58,731	359,211
65+	38,396	30,635	29,045	153,631	104,606	62,067	418,380
Total	581,620	524,888	761,940	3,345,815	3,127,159	2,078,682	10,420,104

TABLE E-1 (continued)

	Urban			Rural			
	Istanbul Izmir	Other West	Central East	West	Central	East	National
Part C 1955							
Males							
0-4	77,909	85,441	164,721	558,347	610,046	489,040	1,985,504
5-9	67,679	79,421	148,881	485,189	503,988	391,878	1,677,036
10-14	62,405	68,055	122,250	383,616	382,733	276,749	1,295,808
15-19	97,437	75,322	138,168	356,702	333,466	247,160	1,248,255
20-24	117,603	135,143	227,681	295,676	224,347	209,753	1,210,203
25-29	97,519	69,301	117,198	288,674	230,292	156,500	959,484
30-34	72,323	57,518	85,221	223,471	171,091	139,413	749,037
35-39	45,525	36,411	56,518	148,826	132,841	99,331	519,452
40-44	57,160	47,787	69,572	215,298	176,704	100,254	666,775
45-49	44,183	37,626	50,224	184,462	135,671	72,843	525,009
50-54	35,939	32,431	45,045	173,405	138,896	79,650	505,366
55-59	29,372	23,896	30,550	113,048	81,641	48,717	327,224
60-64	20,125	15,767	21,102	69,872	57,772	58,415	243,053
65+	32,256	23,586	27,291	97,629	68,305	72,138	321,205
Total	857,435	787,705	1,304,422	3,594,215	3,247,801	2,441,841	12,233,419
Females							
0-4	69,795	80,694	151,808	540,869	588,189	448,010	1,879,365
5-9	64,412	76,304	140,675	459,561	473,412	347,622	1,561,986
10-14	54,084	61,212	101,603	344,163	320,223	209,301	1,090,586
15-19	59,249	61,979	102,166	341,221	319,146	204,346	1,088,107
20-24	66,601	64,197	104,925	334,571	318,692	222,113	1,111,099
25-29	68,063	59,063	95,831	303,483	296,589	198,621	1,021,650
30-34	53,007	44,458	69,385	210,911	200,563	152,963	731,287
35-39	39,803	32,835	52,764	157,142	145,743	97,553	525,840
40-44	46,788	37,467	56,715	194,363	176,153	110,059	621,545
45-49	41,482	32,472	44,433	164,177	126,302	64,261	473,127
50-54	38,407	30,804	44,839	169,519	150,464	94,174	528,207
55-59	31,264	24,378	27,627	114,837	75,430	35,237	308,773
60-64	27,311	22,835	30,951	124,673	109,832	71,684	387,286
65+	47,629	38,118	41,107	181,979	121,598	72,056	502,487
Total	707,895	666,816	1,064,829	3,641,471	3,422,333	2,327,999	11,831,343

TABLE E-1 (continued)

	Urban			Rural			
	Istanbul Izmir	Other West	Central East	West	Central	East	National
Part D 1960							
Males							
0-4	87,964	124,784	225,878	578,497	651,961	515,622	2,184,706
5-9	86,656	126,238	223,957	553,824	604,831	481,354	2,076,854
10-14	82,458	116,801	198,568	453,532	475,720	364,111	1,691,190
15-19	107,246	112,258	184,880	320,203	296,749	228,606	1,249,942
20-24	108,123	182,638	258,351	249,481	200,786	178,851	1,178,230
25-29	108,414	107,167	159,001	319,563	273,856	189,521	1,157,522
30-34	94,291	94,845	139,312	287,012	247,523	165,325	1,028,308
35-39	69,746	71,998	96,030	214,840	168,756	128,338	749,708
40-44	43,963	43,687	62,004	134,165	125,445	96,721	505,985
45-49	54,822	56,515	71,303	196,253	153,667	77,877	610,437
50-54	43,668	45,053	55,196	179,073	142,304	83,178	548,472
55-59	32,611	35,623	43,142	149,752	110,794	52,800	424,722
60-64	27,262	27,481	35,075	112,332	94,162	72,647	368,959
65+	38,014	35,191	38,394	112,685	83,371	81,202	388,357
Total	985,238	1,180,279	1,791,085	3,861,201	3,629,928	2,716,158	14,163,389
Females							
0-4	84,227	120,827	214,287	557,045	625,511	477,026	2,078,923
5-9	82,240	120,398	209,603	525,216	561,931	428,285	1,927,673
10-14	73,160	102,663	164,507	425,792	423,845	298,547	1,488,514
15-19	68,128	84,127	126,921	307,004	282,724	190,334	1,059,230
20-24	73,957	84,551	134,576	313,377	300,953	220,440	1,127,854
25-29	75,666	85,614	133,055	330,330	331,804	220,846	1,177,315
30-34	71,336	76,943	113,237	274,183	266,901	183,190	985,790
35-39	57,915	60,780	83,098	200,790	173,908	117,273	693,764
40-44	39,283	38,608	59,040	147,147	152,608	111,745	548,431
45-49	46,222	43,328	55,396	161,938	128,675	64,423	499,982
50-54	43,634	41,551	57,362	177,159	159,238	102,376	581,320
55-59	36,062	34,093	39,080	128,645	89,690	41,860	369,430
60-64	33,008	33,207	43,601	142,949	125,047	83,558	461,367
65+	57,288	55,395	56,058	205,013	136,215	81,373	591,342
Total	842,126	982,085	1,489,821	3,896,578	3,759,048	2,621,274	13,590,932

TABLE E-1 (continued)

	Urban			Rural			
	Istanbul Izmir	Other West	Central East	West	Central	East	National
Part E	1965						
Males							
0-4	100,684	150,141	304,989	566,996	685,907	550,623	2,359,340
5-9	110,463	168,269	315,207	593,197	682,567	549,137	2,418,840
10-14	105,638	165,479	290,501	517,076	550,899	431,493	2,061,086
15-19	142,907	162,003	273,437	364,024	340,388	265,850	1,548,609
20-24	112,222	207,775	287,033	240,384	185,395	180,272	1,213,081
25-29	103,584	113,934	175,547	271,641	222,934	169,081	1,056,721
30-34	103,677	118,016	179,634	297,011	259,556	182,513	1,140,407
35-39	91,308	105,601	154,597	265,542	226,994	155,106	999,148
40-44	67,458	76,257	101,607	190,792	149,277	120,409	705,800
45-49	43,145	46,131	62,094	120,089	101,401	73,355	446,215
50-54	54,082	59,563	76,034	186,793	151,222	85,430	613,124
55-59	39,070	44,085	51,841	152,431	110,491	52,291	450,209
60-64	29,199	35,712	47,080	140,905	121,088	79,495	453,479
65+	46,073	49,952	57,960	156,303	121,987	98,628	530,903
Total	1,149,510	1,502,918	2,377,561	4,063,184	3,910,110	2,993,681	15,996,964
Females							
0-4	95,815	144,857	289,204	550,152	664,517	520,287	2,264,832
5-9	105,701	161,090	294,223	564,567	640,069	486,617	2,252,267
10-14	95,525	145,026	242,742	483,551	494,419	351,033	1,812,296
15-19	95,208	124,630	198,813	366,054	346,223	234,837	1,365,765
20-24	84,506	100,807	164,427	286,934	281,261	216,586	1,134,521
25-29	80,676	100,981	162,749	294,523	305,365	218,260	1,162,554
30-34	79,000	99,631	151,795	297,836	300,208	207,464	1,135,934
35-39	77,149	90,495	133,234	256,489	230,730	147,712	935,809
40-44	57,294	62,364	86,930	181,310	164,985	124,780	677,663
45-49	39,490	40,658	55,619	122,487	105,736	66,131	430,121
50-54	48,711	49,707	68,435	173,920	154,557	96,315	591,645
55-59	41,137	41,960	49,708	138,416	99,065	45,331	415,617
60-64	36,503	40,637	55,618	151,860	133,284	84,184	502,086
65+	68,379	73,569	78,014	236,567	164,051	92,758	713,338
Total	1,005,094	1,276,412	2,031,511	4,014,677	4,084,472	2,892,291	15,394,457

TABLE E-1 (continued)

	Urban			Rural			
	Istanbul Izmir	Other West	Central East	West	Central	East	National
Part F 1970							
Males							
0-4	134,208	233,596	432,755	559,660	692,281	609,221	2,661,721
5-9	134,688	213,996	443,357	553,484	680,894	584,572	2,610,991
10-14	151,154	234,356	435,943	522,212	568,046	451,730	2,363,441
15-19	189,172	241,424	411,060	397,130	375,049	310,851	1,924,686
20-24	163,945	254,663	388,990	267,685	219,179	202,173	1,496,635
25-29	134,295	148,803	227,458	238,936	201,176	157,531	1,108,199
30-34	105,270	133,219	197,970	233,491	194,369	154,856	1,019,175
35-39	107,746	136,433	204,674	272,292	233,238	162,993	1,117,376
40-44	93,088	116,626	165,111	230,735	184,819	131,102	921,481
45-49	69,551	80,785	107,290	172,115	123,852	91,152	644,745
50-54	45,068	50,381	72,120	114,589	98,630	76,302	457,090
55-59	50,284	55,351	72,190	153,784	114,212	51,230	497,051
60-64	37,749	45,402	60,368	141,793	116,172	74,971	476,455
65+	57,754	70,890	91,760	209,621	166,828	111,087	707,940
Total	1,473,972	2,015,925	3,311,046	4,067,527	3,968,745	3,169,771	18,006,986
Females							
0-4	129,763	203,102	404,356	553,412	699,839	604,299	2,594,771
5-9	130,890	190,269	410,243	546,750	662,433	543,390	2,483,975
10-14	131,816	209,807	366,971	516,283	552,171	390,207	2,167,255
15-19	131,666	187,609	312,455	425,722	418,782	294,485	1,770,719
20-24	123,771	149,271	251,801	307,093	296,636	226,958	1,355,530
25-29	100,552	123,324	208,378	260,745	264,127	196,827	1,153,953
30-34	91,238	133,009	200,247	263,112	276,986	201,117	1,165,709
35-39	93,105	121,622	187,426	277,336	253,631	164,136	1,097,256
40-44	83,244	100,198	146,586	228,122	203,352	138,452	899,954
45-49	60,964	64,242	88,454	154,742	118,519	77,214	564,135
50-54	43,746	50,477	75,652	130,138	125,045	91,267	516,325
55-59	47,421	48,107	62,661	135,221	99,862	47,304	440,576
60-64	43,836	49,731	72,858	151,162	130,523	81,825	529,935
65+	82,332	95,697	113,782	267,021	193,277	105,988	858,097
Total	1,294,344	1,726,465	2,901,870	4,216,859	4,295,183	3,163,469	17,598,190

[a]Persons with ages reported unknown are redistributed in proportion to the number of persons in each age group.

Glossary

AGE HEAPING A tendency for enumerators or respondents to report certain ages instead of others; also called age preference or digit preference. Preference for ages ending in 0 or 5 is widespread.

AGE PATTERN OF FERTILITY The relative distribution of a set of age-specific fertility rates. It expresses the relative contribution of each age group to total fertility.

AGE RATIO The ratio of the population in a given age group to the average of the populations in the two neighboring age groups, times 100.

AGE-SPECIFIC FERTILITY RATE The number of births occurring during a specified period to women of a specified age or age group, divided by the number of person-years-lived during that period by women of that age or age group. When an age-specific fertility rate is calculated for a calendar year, the number of births to women of the specified age is usually divided by the midyear population of women of that age.

AGE-SPECIFIC MORTALITY RATE The number of deaths occurring during a specified period to persons (usually specified by sex) of a specified age or age group, divided by the number of person-years-lived during that period by the persons of that age or age group. When an age-specific mortality rate is calculated for a calendar year, the number of deaths to persons of the specified age is usually divided by the midyear population of persons of that age. Age-specific mortality rates are generally denoted by ${}_nM_x$, the annual death rate to persons aged x to x + n.

AGE STANDARDIZATION A procedure of adjustment of crude rates (birth, death, or other rates) designed to reduce the effect of differences in age structure when comparing rates for different populations.

BIRTH HISTORY A report of the number and dates of all live births experienced by a particular woman; see also pregnancy history. The sex of each child, the survival of each child to the date of the interview, and, where pertinent, the date of death are also generally recorded.

BIRTH ORDER The ordinal number of a given live birth in relation to all previous live births of the same woman (e.g., 5 is the birth order of the fifth live birth occurring to the same woman).

BIRTH RATE See crude birth rate.

CHANDRASEKARAN-DEMING TECHNIQUE A procedure to estimate the coverage of two independent systems collecting information about demographic or other events, based on the assumption that the probability of an event being recorded by one system is the same whether or not the event is recorded by the other system. The events from both systems are matched to establish M, the number of events recorded by both systems; U_1, the number recorded only by system 1; and U_2, the number recorded only by system 2. The Chandrasekaran-Deming formula then estimates total events, N, as

$$\hat{N} = M + U_1 + U_2 + \frac{U_1 U_2}{M}.$$

CHILDBEARING AGES The span within which women are capable of bearing children, generally taken to be from age 15 to age 49 or, sometimes, to age 44.

CHILDREN EVER BORN(E) The number of children ever borne alive by a particular woman; synonymous with parity. In demographic usage, stillbirths are specifically excluded.

COHORT A group of individuals who experienced the same class of events in the same period. Thus an age cohort is a group of people born during a particular period, and a marriage cohort is a group of people who married during a particular period. The effects of a given set of mortality or fertility rates are often illustrated by applying them to hypothetical cohorts.

COHORT FERTILITY The fertility experienced over time by a group of women or men who form a birth or a marriage cohort. The analysis of cohort fertility is contrasted with that of period fertility.

CRUDE BIRTH RATE The number of births in a population during a specified period divided by the number of person-years-lived by the population during the same period. It is frequently expressed as births per 1,000 population. The crude birth rate for a single year is usually calculated as the number of births during the year divided by the midyear population.

CRUDE DEATH RATE The number of deaths in a population during a specified period divided by the number of person-years-lived by the population during the same period. It is frequently expressed as deaths per 1,000 population. The crude death rate for a single year is usually calculated as the number of deaths during the year divided by the midyear population.

CUMULATED FERTILITY An estimate of the average number of children ever borne by women of some age x, obtained by cumulating age-specific fertility rates up to age x; also often calculated for age groups.

DEATH RATE See crude death rate.

DE FACTO POPULATION A population enumerated on the basis of those present at a particular time, including temporary visitors and excluding residents temporarily absent. See de jure population.

DE JURE POPULATION A population enumerated on the basis of normal residence, excluding temporary visitors and including residents temporarily absent. See de facto population.

DIGITAL PREFERENCE See age heaping.

DUAL RECORD SYSTEM See Chandrasekaran-Deming Technique

EXPECTATION OF LIFE AT BIRTH The average number of years that a member of a cohort of births would be expected to live if the cohort were subject to the mortality conditions expressed by a particular set of age-specific mortality rates. Denoted by the symbol e(o) in life table notation.

FERTILITY HISTORY Either a birth history or a pregnancy history.

FORWARD SURVIVAL A procedure for estimating the age distribution at some later date by projecting forward an observed age distribution. The procedure uses survival ratios, often obtained from model life tables. The procedure is basically a form of population projection without the introduction of new entrants (births) to the population.

GENERAL FERTILITY RATE The ratio of the number of live births in a period to the number of person-years-lived by women of childbearing ages during the period. The general fertility rate for a year is usually calculated as the number of births divided by the number of women of childbearing ages at midyear.

GROSS REPRODUCTION RATE The average number of female children a woman would have if she survived to the end of her childbearing years and if, throughout, she were subject to a given set of age-specific fertility rates and a given sex ratio at birth. This number provides a measure of replacement fertility in the absence of mortality.

GROWTH RATE The increase or decrease of a population in a period divided by the number of person-years-lived by the population during the same period. The increase in a population is the result of a surplus (or deficit) of births over deaths and a surplus (or deficit) of immigrants over emigrants. (The annual increase is often expressed as a fraction of the total population at the beginning of the year, but this convention has the inconvenient characteristic of not being readily defined for a five-year interval and of being unequal to the difference between the birth rate and the death rate even in the absence of migration.) See also rate of natural increase.

INFANT MORTALITY RATE The number of deaths of children under 1 year of age occurring in the same year; also used in a more rigorous sense to mean the number of deaths that would occur under 1 year of age in a life table with a radix of 1,000, in which sense it is denoted by the symbol $_1q_0$.

LIFE TABLE A listing of the number of survivors at different ages (up to the highest age attained) in a hypothetical cohort subject from birth to a particular set of age-specific mortality rates. The rates are usually those observed in a given population during a particular period of time. The survivors of the radix to age x are generally denoted by l(x). The tabulations commonly accompanying a life table include other features of the cohort's experience: its expectation of life at each age x, denoted by e(x); the probability of surviving from each age x to age x + n, denoted by $_nq_x$; the person-years-lived by the hypothetical cohort as it ages from age x to age x + n, denoted by $_nL_x$ (also equivalent to the population aged x, x + n in a stationary population experiencing a number of births each year equal to the radix of the life table); and the person-years-lived by the hypothetical cohort from age x onward, denoted by T(x).

LOGIT The logit of a proportion p is 1/2 ln[p/(1 - p)]. As a linearizing transformation, the logit has been proposed as the basis of a model life table system in which the logit of a probability of dying by age x (${}_xq_o$) is related linearly to the logit of a standard probability of dying by age x (${}_xq_o^s$) so that

$$\text{logit}\ ({}_xq_o) = \alpha + \beta\ [\text{logit}\ ({}_xq_o^s)],$$

where α is a measure of mortality level relative to the standard and β is a parameter that alters the shape of the standard mortality function.

MARITAL FERTILITY Any measure of fertility in which the births (in the numerator) are births to married women and in which the number of person-years-lived (in the denominator) also pertains to married women. In some instances, the designation "married" includes persons in consensual unions.

MEDIAN The value associated with the central member of a set that is ordered by size or some other characteristic expressed in numbers.

MEAN AGE OF CHILDBEARING The average age at which a mortality-free cohort of women bear their children according to a set of age-specific fertility rates.

MEAN AGE OF CHILDBEARING IN THE POPULATION The average age of the mothers of the children born in a population during a year. This measure incorporates the effects of both mortality and the age distribution.

MIGRATION RATE Number of migrants during a specified period divided by the person-years-lived of the population exposed to migration. Also see population change due to migration.

MODEL LIFE TABLE An expression of typical mortality experience derived from a group of observed life tables.

MOVING AVERAGES The successive averaging of two or more adjacent values of a series in order to remove sharp fluctuations.

MYERS INDEX An index of digit preference that essentially sums in turn the population ending in each digit over some age range, often 10-89, expressing the total as a percentage of the total population, and which avoids the bias introduced by the fact that the population is not evenly distributed among all ages by repeating the calculations 10 times, once for each starting digit, and averaging the results. The difference between the average percentage for each digit and the expected value of 10 percent provides a measure of the preference for or avoidance of the digit over the age range considered.

NATURAL FERTILITY The age pattern of marital fertility observed in non-contraceptive populations where reproductive behavior is not affected by the number of children already born.

NET MIGRATION The difference between gross immigration and gross emigration.

NET REPRODUCTION RATE The average number of female children born per woman in a cohort subject to a given set of age-specific fertility rates, a given set of age-specific mortality rates, and a given sex ratio at birth. This rate measures replacement fertility under given conditions of fertility and mortality: it is the ratio of daughters to mothers assuming continuation of the specified conditions of fertility and mortality.

OWN-CHILDREN METHOD A refinement of the reverse-survival procedure for fertility estimation, whereby estimates of age-specific fertility rates for the recent past are obtained by relating mothers to their own children, using information on relationship and other characteristics available from a census or survey.

PARITY See children ever born.

PARTIAL BIRTH RATE The proportion of the population that enters (that is, is "born" into) a given age category in a year. The age categories used are normally open-ended, thus the partial birth rate x+ designates the proportion of the population becoming x years and older.

PARTIAL DEATH RATE The proportion of the population that leaves (that is, "dies" out of) a given age category in a year. See partial birth rate.

PERIOD FERTILITY The fertility experienced during a particular period of time by women from all relevant birth or marriage cohorts; see also cohort fertility.

P/F RATIO METHOD A consistency check for survey information on fertility. Information on recent fertility is cumulated to obtain measures that are equivalent to average parities. Lifetime fertility in the form of reported average parities by age group (P) can then be compared for consistency with the parity-equivalents (F) by calculating the ratio P/F for successive age groups. If certain assumptions about error patterns are met, an improved estimate of fertility can sometimes be obtained by correcting the age pattern of current fertility to agree with the level of lifetime fertility reported by younger women.

POPULATION CHANGE DUE TO MIGRATION The sum of in-migrants minus out-migrants during a specified period of time. The change may also be expressed as a rate by dividing the change by person-years-lived in the population during the same period.

PREGNANCY HISTORY A report of the number and the dates of occurrence of all the pregnancies experienced by a particular woman. The outcome of the pregnancy--live birth, stillbirth, fetal death--is also recorded.

RADIX The hypothetical birth cohort of a life table. Common values are 1, 1,000, and 100,000.

RATE OF NATURAL INCREASE The difference between the births and deaths occurring during a given period divided by the number of person-years-lived by the population during the same period. This rate, which specifically excludes changes resulting from migration, is the difference between the crude birth rate and the crude death rate.

RETROSPECTIVE SURVEY A survey that obtains information about demographic events that occurred in a given past period, generally terminating at the time of the survey.

REVERSE PROJECTION See reverse survival.

REVERSE SURVIVAL A technique to estimate an earlier population from an observed population, allowing for those members of the population who would have died according to observed or assumed mortality conditions. It is used as a method of estimating fertility by calculating from the observed number of survivors of a given age x the expected number of births that occurred x years earlier. (In situations for which both fertility and mortality are known or can be reliably estimated, reverse survival can be used to estimate migration.)

ROBUSTNESS A characteristic of estimates that are not greatly affected by deviations from the assumptions on which the estimation procedure is based.

SEX RATIO AT BIRTH The number of male births for each female birth, or male births per 100 female births.

SINGULATE MEAN AGE AT MARRIAGE (SMAM) A measure of the mean age at first marriage, derived from a set of proportions of people single at different ages or in different age groups, usually calculated separately for males and females.

STABLE POPULATION A population exposed for a long time to constant fertility and mortality rates, and closed to migration, establishes a fixed age distribution and constant growth rate characteristic of the vital rates. Such a population, with a constant age structure and constant rate of growth, is called a stable population.

STATIONARY POPULATION A stable population that has a zero growth rate, with constant numbers of births and deaths per year. Its age structure is determined by the mortality rates and is equivalent to the person-years-lived (${}_nL_x$) column of a conventional life table.

SURVIVAL RATIO The probability of surviving between one age and another; often computed for age groups, in which case the ratios correspond to those of the person-years-lived function, ${}_nL_x$, of a life table. Also called survivorship probabilities.

SURVIVORSHIP PROBABILITIES See survival ratio.

SYNTHETIC PARITY The average parity calculated for a hypothetical cohort exposed indefinitely to a set of period age-specific fertility rates.

TOTAL FERTILITY RATE (TFR) The average number of children that would be born per woman if all women lived to the end of their childbearing years and bore children according to a given set of age-specific fertility rates; also referred to as total fertility. It is frequently used to compute the consequence of childbearing at the rates currently observed.

UNITED NATIONS AGE-SEX ACCURACY INDEX An index of age reporting accuracy that is based on deviations from the expected regularity of population size and sex ratio, age group by age group. The index is calculated as the sum of (1) the mean absolute deviation from 100 of the age ratios for males, (2) the mean absolute deviation from 100 of the age ratios for females, and (3) three times the mean of the absolute difference in reported sex ratios from one age group to the next. The United Nations defines age-sex data as "accurate," "inaccurate," or "highly inaccurate" depending on whether the index is less than 20, 20 to 40, or greater than 40.

WHIPPLE'S INDEX A measure of the quality of age reporting based on the extent of preference for a particular target digit or digits. The index essentially compares the reported population at ages ending in the target digit or digits with the population expected on the assumption that population is a linear function of age. For a particular age range, often 23 to 62, the population with ages ending in the target digits is divided by one-tenth of the total population, the result then being multiplied by 100 and divided by the number of different target digits. A value of 100 indicates no preference for those digits, whereas values over 100 indicate positive preference for them.

References

Abadan, Nermin (1964) Batı Almanya'daki Türk Iscileri ve Sorunları (Turkish Workers in West Germany and Their Problems). Ankara: State Planning Organization.

Adlakha, Arjun L. (1970) A Study of Infant Mortality in Turkey. Sociology dissertation. University of Michigan, University Microfilms 71-4553.

Bongaarts, John (1978) A framework for analyzing the proximate determinants of fertility. Population and Development Review 4(1):105-132.

Brass, William (1968) Methods of analysis and estimation. Pp. 88-150 in W. Brass et al., ed., The Demography of Tropical Africa. Princeton, N.J.: Princeton University Press.

Coale, Ansley J. (1971) Age patterns of marriage. Population Studies 25(2):193-214.

Coale, Ansley J., and P. Demeny (1966) Regional Model Life Tables and Stable Populations. Princeton, N.J.: Princeton University Press.

Coale, Ansley J., Allan G. Hill, and T. James Trussell (1975) A new method of estimating standard fertility measures from incomplete data. Population Index 41:182-210.

Coale, Ansley J., and T. James Trussell (1974) Model fertility schedules: variations in the structure of childbearing in human populations. Population Index 40(2):185-258.

Das Gupta, Prithwis (1975) A general method of correction for age misreporting in census populations. Demography 12(2):303-312.

Demeny, Paul, and Frederic C. Shorter (1968) Estimating Turkish Mortality, Fertility, and Age Structure: Application of Some New Techniques. Faculty of Economics, Istanbul University, Pat. No. 1306.

Fisek, Nusret H. (1978) Türkiye'de Asırı Dogurganlık ve Kullanilan Gebeligi Önleyici Yöntemler (Excess Fertility and Contraceptive Methods in Turkey). In S. Uner, et al. Türkeiyede Nüfus Yapısı ve Nüfus Sorunlar: 1973 Arastırması (Population Structure and Population Problems in Turkey: 1973 Survey). Hacettepe University, Publication No. D-25.

Geray, Cevat (1962) Türkiye'den ve Türkiye'ye Göcler ve Göcmelerin Iskanı 1923-1961 (Migration from and to Turkey and the Settlement of Immigrants). Turk Iktisadi Gelismesi Arastirma Projesi, No. 9, Ankara.

Hacettepe Institute of Population Studies (1980) Turkish Fertility Survey, 1978. First Report, Vol. II: Statistical Tables. Hacettepe University.

Hajnal, John (1953) Age at marriage and proportions marrying. Population Studies 7:111-132.

Institute of Community Medicine (1975) An Account of the Activities of the Etimesgut Rural Health Disrict, 1970-1974. Hacettepe University, School of Medicine.

Macura, Miroslav (1975a) Estimates of Infant Mortality Trends in Turkey, 1944-67. Paper presented to the Second Conference on Turkish Demography, Hacettepe Institute of Population Studies, Cesme, Turkey.

Macura, Miroslav (1975b) Estimating Trends of Infant Mortality from Pregnancy Histories. Seminar on Infant Mortality in Relation to the Level of Fertility. (Bangkok, May 6-12, 1975.) Paris: Committee for International Coordination of National Research in Demography.

Ntozi, James Patrick Manyenye (1978) The Demeny-Shorter and three-census methods for correcting age data. Demography 15(4):509-521.

Özbay, Ferhunde (1979) Türkiye'de 1963, 1968 ve 1973 Yıllarında Aile Planlamasi Uygulamalarında ve Dogurganlıktakı Degismeler (Changes in Contraceptive Use and Fertility in Turkey 1963, 1968 and 1973). Istatistik 1(2):31-47. Istatiskciler Dernegi, Ankara.

Özbay, Ferhunde (1978) Education and fertility in rural Turkey. Studies in Development 22/23. Journal of Middle East Technical University, Ankara.

Özbay, Ferhunde, and Frederic C. Shorter (1970) Turkey: changes in birth control practices, 1963 to 1968. Studies in Family Planning 51:1-7.

Özbay, Ferhunde, Frederic C. Shorter, and S. Yener (1977) Accounting for the Trend of Fertility in Turkey. Paper presented to UN/UNFPA Expert Group Meeting on Demographic Transition and Socioeconomic Development, Istanbul.

Shorter, Frederic C. (1980) Computational Methods for Regional Population Projections and Reverse Projections. Regional Papers. Population Council, Cairo.

Shorter, Frederic C., and David Pasta (1974) Computational Methods for Population Projections with Particular Reference to Development Planning. The Population Council, New York.

Sullivan, Jeremiah (1972) Models for the estimation of the probability of dying between birth and exact ages of early childhood. Population Studies 26(1):79-97.

Sümbüloglu, Kadir (1978) Il ve Ilce Merkezlerinden Devlet Istatistik Enstitüsüne Bildirilen Ölümler Sayisal Yönden Yeterli: Midir?" (Are the Numbers of Deaths Reported From Province and District Centers to the State Institute of Statistics Numerically Complete?). Faculty of Medicine, Hacettepe University.

Taeuber, Irene (1958) Population and modernization in Turkey. Population Index 24(2):101-122.

Tekce, Belgin (1974) Urbanization and Migration in Turkey. Sociology dissertation. Princeton University, University Microfilms 76-269.

Tekce, Belgin (1975) Migration to Cities in Turkey: Estimates for 1955-60 and 1960-65. Ankara: State Institute of Statistics.

Tekce, Belgin (1979) The Yozgat (Turkey) Maternal and Child Health and Family Planning Project: Baseline Information on Socioeconomic and Demographic Conditions. Regional Papers. Population Council, Cairo.

Timur, Serim, et al. (1971) Türkiyede Aile Yapısı ve Nüfus Sorunları Arastırmasının Veri Toplam Teknikleri (1968) (Methodology of Survey on Family Structure and Population Problems in Turkey). Hacettepe University, Publication No. D-9.

Timur, Serim (1974) Fertility. In Figen Karadayi, et al., The Population of Turkey. World Population Year Series. Hacettepe University and CICRED: Institute of Population Studies.

Toros, Aykut (1978) 1973 Arastırmasında Dogurganlık (Fertility in the 1973 Survey). In S. Uner et al. Türkeiyede Nüfus Yapısı ve Nüfus Sorunlar: 1973 Arastırması (Population Strucutre and Population Problems in Turkey: 1973 Survey). Hacettepe University, Publication No. D-25.

Trussell, T. James (1975) A re-estimation of the multiplying factors for the Brass technique for determining childhood survivorship rates. Population Studies 29(1):97-108.

Turkay, Orhan (1962) Türkiye'de Nüfus Artısı ve Iktısadı Gelisme (Population Growth and Economic Development in Turkey). Ankara.

Turkey, Ministry of Health and Social Welfare (1973) Saglik Hizmetlerinde 50 Yil (50 Years in Health Services). Ankara: Ministry of Health and Welfare Publications.

Turkey, Regional Planning Office (1968) Il ve Ilcelerin Nüfus Düzeltmeleri: 1935-1965 (Adjustments of Province and District Population: 1935-1965). Ankara: Ministry of Housing and Resettlement.

Turkey, School of Public Health (1970) Vital Statistics from the Turkish Demographic Survey: 1966-67. Ankara: Ministry of Health and Social Welfare.

Turkey, State Institute of Statistics (1971) Türkiye Hayat Tablolari, 1966-67 (Life Tables of Turkey, 1966-67). Publication No. 623, Ankara.

Turkey, State Institute of Statistics (1978) Türkiye Nüfus Arastırması: 1974-75 (Turkish Population Survey: 1974-75). Publication No. 841, Ankara.

U. N. (1967) Manual IV: Methods of Estimating Basic Demographic Measures from Incomplete Data. Department of Economic and Social Affairs, Population Studies, No. 42.

Yener, Samira (Berksan) (1969) Marriage patterns and their effect on fertility in Turkey. In Turkish Demography: Proceedings of a Conference. Hacettepe University: Institute of Population Studies.